Integration Patterns

patterns & practices

David Trowbridge, Microsoft Platform Architecture Guidance

Ulrich Roxburgh, Microsoft Consulting Services (Australia)

Gregor Hohpe, ThoughtWorks, Inc.

Dragos Manolescu, ThoughtWorks, Inc.

E.G. Nadhan, EDS

ISBN 0-7356-1850-X

Contents

Preface   **xi**

Who Should Read This Book xi
How This Book Is Organized. xii
Documentation Conventions xiv
Community xiv
Feedback and Support xv
Contributors xv
About the Principal Authors xvi

Chapter 1

Integration and Patterns   **1**

The Problem of Integration. 2
    Integration Architecture 2
    Applications 3
The Global Bank Scenario 4
    Context. 4
    Requirements 4
    Next Steps 6
Patterns 7
    Patterns in Sports 7
    Patterns in Music 9
    Pattern Structure 9
    Pattern-Based Design 10
Patterns at Global Bank. 11
Next Chapter. 17

Chapter 2

Using Patterns to Design the Baseline Architecture   **19**

Meeting the Requirements of Global Bank 19
    Using Patterns to Communicate Design Decisions 20
    The Role of a Baseline Architecture 21
Designing the Global Bank Baseline Architecture 21
    View Scheduled Payments Use Case 22
    Adding a Message Broker for the Loan Systems 29
    Execute Scheduled Payment Use Case. 33
    Designing for Execute Scheduled Payment and Receive Payment Response. 35
    Accessing Account Services on the Mainframe. 44
    The Portal Web Application 46
    Global Bank Portal Application 49
    Implementing the Global Bank Scenario 50
Next Chapter. 53

Chapter 3

Integrating Layer   55

Level of Automation 55
Level of Abstraction. 56
Maintaining State 56
Coupling 57
Semantic Dissonance 57
Choosing an Integration Layer Type 57
   Portal Integration 58
   Entity Aggregation 59
   Process Integration 59
Integrating Layer Patterns 60
Entity Aggregation 61
   Context. 61
   Problem 61
   Forces 61
   Solution 62
   Example 72
   Resulting Context 73
   Testing Considerations 74
   Security Considerations. 74
   Operational Considerations 74
   Known Uses 75
   Related Patterns 75
Process Integration 76
   Context. 76
   Problem 76
   Forces 76
   Solution 77
   Implementation Details 80
   Example 82
   Resulting Context 82
   Testing Considerations 84
   Related Patterns 85
   Acknowledgments 85
Implementing Process Integration with BizTalk Server 2004 86
   Context. 86
   Background 86
   Implementation Strategy 86
   Example 91
   Resulting Context 103
   Testing Considerations 104
   Security Considerations. 104
   Operational Considerations 105
   Related Patterns 105
   Acknowledgments 105

Portal Integration 106
    Context. 106
    Problem 106
    Forces 106
    Solution 107
    Example 109
    Resulting Context 109

Chapter 4

System Connections   111

Connecting to Layered Applications 111
Data Integration 114
Presentation Integration 117
Functional Integration 118
    Credit Scoring Example 119
    Kinds of Functional Integration 119
System Connection Patterns 120
Data Integration 124
    Context. 124
    Problem 124
    Forces 124
    Solution 125
    Example 127
    Resulting Context 127
    Acknowledgments 134
Functional Integration 135
    Context. 135
    Problem 135
    Forces 135
    Solution 136
    Resulting Context 138
    Testing Considerations 144
    Security Considerations. 144
    Acknowledgments 145
Service-Oriented Integration. 146
    Context. 146
    Problem 146
    Forces 146
    Solution 148
    Example 153
    Resulting Context 153
    Security Considerations. 155
    Related Patterns 155
    Acknowledgments 155

Implementing Service-Oriented Integration with ASP.NET 157
   Context. 157
   Background 157
   Implementation Strategy 158
   Example: Building an ASP.NET Web Service to Access the Mainframe Gateway 164
   Resulting Context 179
   Testing Considerations 179
   Security Considerations. 181
   Acknowledgments 181
Implementing Service-Oriented Integration with BizTalk
   Server 2004 182
   Context. 182
   Background 182
   Implementation Strategy 183
   Example 186
   Resulting Context 203
   Testing Considerations 204
   Security Considerations. 204
   Operational Considerations 205
   Acknowledgments 205
Presentation Integration 206
   Aliases 206
   Context. 206
   Problem 206
   Forces 206
   Solution 207
   Example 209
   Resulting Context 210
   Testing Considerations 211
   Security Considerations. 212
   Acknowledgments 212

Chapter 5

Integration Topologies   213

Point-to-Point Connection 214
Broker 215
   Broker Examples 218
Message Bus 221
Publish/Subscribe. 223
   List-Based Publish/Subscribe 223
   Broadcast-Based Publish/Subscribe 224
   Content-Based Publish/Subscribe 224
A More Detailed Look at Topologies 225
   Topology Levels. 225

Using Topologies Together 229
    Point-to-Point Connection 230
    Broker 231
    Message Bus and Publish/Subscribe 231
Integration Topology Level Patterns 236
Message Broker 237
    Aliases 237
    Context 237
    Problem 237
    Forces 237
    Solution 238
    Example 239
    Resulting Context 240
    Testing Considerations 242
    Security Considerations 242
    Operational Considerations 243
    Known Uses 243
    Variants 243
    Related Patterns 243
    Acknowledgments 244
Implementing Message Broker with BizTalk Server 2004 245
    Context 245
    Background 245
    Implementation Strategy 246
    Example 249
    Resulting Context 255
    Testing Considerations 256
    Security Considerations 256
    Operational Considerations 257
    Variants 257
    Business Rule Engine 257
    Related Patterns 258
    Acknowledgments 259
Message Bus 260
    Context 260
    Problem 260
    Forces 260
    Solution 261
    Example 266
    Resulting Context 269
    Security Considerations 270
    Operational Considerations 270
    Related Patterns 271
    Acknowledgments 271

Publish/Subscribe. 272
   Aliases 272
   Context. 272
   Problem 272
   Forces 272
   Solution 273
   Example 280
   Resulting Context 280
   Testing Considerations 281
   Security Considerations. 281
   Operational Considerations 281
   Related Patterns 282
   Acknowledgments 282

Chapter 6

Additional Integration Patterns   283

Pipes and Filters. 283
Gateway 284
Integration Layers Patterns 285
Pipes and Filters. 286
   Aliases 286
   Context. 286
   Problem 286
   Forces 286
   Solution 287
   Example 290
   Resulting Context 292
   Testing Considerations 293
   Known Uses 293
   Related Patterns 295
   Acknowledgments 295
Implementing Pipes and Filters with BizTalk Server 2004 296
   Context. 296
   Background 296
   Implementation Strategy 297
   Example 299
   Resulting Context 305
   Testing Considerations 305
   Security Considerations. 306
   Operational Considerations 306
   Acknowledgments 307

Gateway 308
    Context. 308
    Problem 308
    Forces 308
    Solution 309
    Example 312
    Resulting Context 314
    Testing Considerations 315
    Security Considerations. 316
    Operational Considerations 317
    Related Patterns 317
    Acknowledgments 318
Implementing Gateway with Host Integration Server 2004. 319
    Context. 319
    Background 319
    Implementation Strategy 320
    Example 331
    Resulting Context 339
    Tests 339

Chapter 7

Project Notebook   341

Interpreting the Artifacts 342
Global Bank Business Context 342
    Convergence in the Banking Industry 342
Stakeholder Viewpoints 344
    Board of Directors Viewpoint 344
    Chief Executive Officer 346
    General Manager of Banking 351
    Director of Electronic Bill Presentment and Payment 354
    Electronic Bill Presentment and Payment Supervisor. 355
From Business Scenario to Technical Solution 355
    Viewpoints Within the Enterprise Architecture. 357
    Business Architecture Views 358
    Integration Architecture Views 365
    Integration Patterns 369
Going Forward 378

Appendix   379

List of Patterns and Pattlets 379

Bibliography   385

Index   389

Preface

Welcome to *Integration Patterns,* the third patterns release in the pattern & practices series from Microsoft. Building on the application patterns presented in *Enterprise Solution Patterns Using Microsoft .NET*, this guide applies patterns to solve integration problems within the enterprise.

Integration Patterns explains how the authors of this guide used patterns to design and build an integration architecture in the context of a representative customer scenario. The guide contains a catalog of 18 integration patterns, including implementations that use BizTalk Server 2004, Host Integration Server 2004, ASP.NET, Visual Studio .NET, Visio 2003, and the .NET Framework.

Why does this guide include a scenario? Although reader feedback on previous patterns releases was positive, they also gave us suggestions for improvement. Readers said that they liked the pattern catalog, but they wanted help understanding how to apply patterns to a real scenario. In response to this feedback, the authors used a pattern-based approach to build and test a baseline architecture that meets the needs of an integration scenario. We incorporated the essence of our actual design discussions into the scenario to show how we used patterns to communicate and make design decisions. .Because a well-designed architecture must be traceable to the needs of the business, we included a set of artifacts that trace from high-level business processes down to code.

The chosen scenario is an online bill payment application in the banking industry. Although we don't presume to be experts in banking, we did want to use a scenario with sufficient complexity to illustrate our approach to solving significant technical challenges. We expect that you will use your own skills and experience to tailor your systems to your enterprise. We hope you find this guide to be a practical and helpful resource during this effort.

Who Should Read This Book

If you are new to patterns, we suggest that you read *Enterprise Solution Patterns Using Microsoft .NET* before you read this guide. This prerequisite reading will introduce you to patterns that you can apply during the design and implementation of applications.

Integration Patterns is for readers in one or more of the following categories:

- Chief technology officers, architects, designers, and developers who understand application patterns but are new to integration patterns

- Chief technology officers, architects, designers and developers who are already experienced in using integration patterns to integrate enterprise solutions
- Chief information officers, chief technology officers, technology directors, and IT managers who are responsible for aligning business with technology and integrating multiple systems

For those in the first group, the first two chapters are very important to understanding the context of integration and the use of patterns during the design process. These chapters will help you understand the next four chapters, which collectively form a pattern catalog. You are likely to discover that you have implemented some of these patterns before without knowing that they were patterns.

Readers in the second group can go directly to chapters three through six and use them as a pattern catalog. After you find a particular pattern you are interested in, it is helpful to review the introductory material at the beginning of the chapter to better understand the relationship of this pattern to other adjacent patterns. As you consider design alternatives for your enterprise, you are likely to find chapter seven helpful. This chapter contains examples of business and technology alignment artifacts and more information on the pattern-based design approach.

Readers in the last group should read chapter one, then go directly to chapter seven. This chapter explains how Global Bank approached the issue of business and technology alignment. This chapter contains example artifacts and more information on the role of patterns in the design process. If you would like more information about a specific pattern, use chapters three through six as a pattern catalog and find the appropriate pattern.

How This Book Is Organized

Chapter 1, "Integration and Patterns" introduces the Global Bank scenario that is used throughout this guide and briefly discusses how patterns can help development teams find workable answers to integration challenges.

Chapter 2, "Using Patterns to Design the Integration Baseline Architecture" uses the language of patterns to explore the decisions and tradeoffs that the members of the Global Bank architecture team made while designing and implementing their bill payment system.

Chapters 3 through 5 present a catalog of 18 patterns, which are grouped into clusters. Each chapter starts by describing how the patterns in a particular cluster are related and then gives direction on when to use the patterns. The implementation patterns include step-by-step instructions and code examples where applicable. Code examples are written in C# and are for example purposes only. The example code is not meant to be used in production.

Chapter 3, "Integrating Layer" describes the different strategies for designing an integration layer and the tradeoffs involved in choosing an alternative. An integration layer can automate complex business processes or provide unified access to information that is scattered across many systems.

This chapter includes the following patterns:

- *Entity Aggregation*
- *Process Integration*
- *Implementing Process Integration with BizTalk Server 2004*
- *Portal Integration*

Chapter 4, "System Connections" builds on Chapter 3 by describing how to connect individual systems. Each system allows certain types of access and restricts others. This chapter presents a series of related patterns that will help you analyze the alternative methods and the tradeoffs to consider when you choose your system connections.

This chapter includes the following patterns:

- *Data Integration*
- *Functional Integration*
- *Service-Oriented Integration*
- *Implementing Service-Oriented Integration with ASP.NET*
- *Implementing Service-Oriented Integration with BizTalk Server 2004*
- *Presentation Integration*

Chapter 5, "Integration Topologies" builds on previous chapters by describing overall integration topologies. This chapter presents a series of related patterns that help you analyze the alternative methods and the tradeoffs to consider when you choose between integration topology alternatives.

This chapter includes the following patterns:

- *Message Broker*
- *Implementing Message Broker with BizTalk Server 2004*
- *Message Bus*
- *Publish/Subscribe*

Chapter 6, "Additional Integration Patterns" presents two important patterns: *Pipes and Filters* and *Gateway*. Many integration architectures are based on pipes and filters and on gateways. Gateways are useful design elements that encapsulate access to enterprise resources such as mainframes. This chapter explains both patterns and then traces them to implementations that use the Microsoft platform.

This chapter includes the following patterns:

- *Pipes and Filters*
- *Implementing Pipes and Filters with BizTalk Server 2004*
- *Gateway*
- *Implementing Gateway with Host Integration Server 2004*

Chapter 7, "Project Notebook" takes a broader view of the Global Bank scenario by showing the link between business and technology viewpoints. It starts with an overview of the Global Bank business environment, and then describes the viewpoints of five key business stakeholders. The chapter then presents a series of models that the Global Bank team produced as they designed the baseline architecture based on business requirements. These models trace a path from the Chief Executive Officer to the technical solution and show how the team used patterns during the design process. The chapter also includes additional details about the pattern based approach used in this guide.

Appendix, "List of Patterns and Pattlets," presents a list of patterns and *pattlets* that this guide mentions, but that it does not discuss in detail. *Pattlets* are actual patterns that this book refers to; however, the book does not discuss them in detail.

Documentation Conventions

This guide uses the following style conventions and terminology.

Table 1: Style Conventions Table

Element	Meaning
Bold font	Objects, classes, methods, predefined functions, and events.
Italic font	Names of patterns and pattlets referenced in this guide. New terminology also appears in italic on first use.
Monospace font	Code examples.
Note	Alerts you to supplementary information.

Community

The patterns in this guide are part of a new Patterns community on GotDotNet. GotDotNet is a Microsoft .NET Framework Community Web site that uses workspaces in an online collaborative development environment where .NET Framework developers can create, host, and manage projects throughout the project life cycle. You can also use this Patterns community to post questions, provide feedback, or connect with other users for sharing ideas.

Access to the Patterns community is available from the following Web site:

http://gotdotnet.com/team/architecture/patterns

Feedback and Support

Questions? Comments? Suggestions? For feedback on this guide, please send e-mail to pnppatfb@microsoft.com.

The patterns documented here are designed to jump-start the architecture and design of systems integration. Patterns are simple mechanisms that are meant to be applied to the problem at hand and are usually combined with other patterns. They are not meant to be plugged into an application. Example code is provided "as is" and is not intended for production use. It is only intended to illustrate the pattern, and therefore does not include extra code such as exception handling, logging, security, and validation. Although this deliverable has undergone testing and review by industry luminaries it is not supported like a traditional Microsoft product.

Contributors

Thanks to the following contributing authors: Ward Cunningham, Microsoft Platform Architecture Guidance; Ramkumar Kothandaraman, Microsoft Developer and Platform Evangelism Architecture Strategy Team; Bill Mc Donald, Robert Miles, Ascentium Corporation; Javier Mariscal, Two Connect, Inc.; Raymond Laghaeian, Implement.Com.

Many thanks to the following reviewers who provided invaluable assistance and feedback: John Sullivan, Thoughtworks; Ralph Johnson, University of Illinois at Urbana-Champaign; Eddie Hulme, EDS; Dave Swift, Chief Architect, Zurich Financial Services; Rupert D.E. Brown, CTO Team Reuters; United Kingdom Architect Council – Patterns Working Group; Richard Sears, Sears and Associates; Michael Platt, Scott Woodgate, Satish Thatte, Phil Teale, Alex Weinert, Marc Levy, Ulrich Homann, Dave Green, Paul Larsen, Jack Greenfield, Keith Short, David Lavigne, Chris Houser, Anil Balakrishnan, Shawn Henretty, Doug Carrell, Joe Sharp, Miles Ulrich, Steve Smaller, Shanku Niyogi, Wojtek Kozaczynski, Jonathan Wanagel, Jason Hogg, Jim Newkirk, Ed Lafferty, Sandy Khaund, Ken Perilman, Mauro Regio, Microsoft Corporation.

Thanks also to the many contributors who assisted us in the production of this book, in particular: Matt Evans, Larry Brader, Microsoft Platform Architecture Guidance; Abhijit Somalwar, Jude Yuvaraj, Anuradha Sathyanarayana, Infosys Technologies Ltd; Tyson Nevil, Susan Filkins, Entirenet; Claudette Iebbiano, CI Design Studio; Sanjeev Garg, Satyam Computer Services; Blaine Wastell, Ascentium Corporation

About the Principal Authors

David Trowbridge is an Architect with the Platform Architecture Group at Microsoft. He is one of the driving forces behind Microsoft's pattern initiative. David was also the lead author of *Enterprise Solution Patterns Using Microsoft.NET*. Prior to joining Microsoft, David designed and delivered numerous enterprise transactional systems, commercial shrink-wrapped software products, and custom integration solutions.

Ulrich Roxburgh has over 20 years academic and IT experience. He has worked for Microsoft for the last seven years as a consultant specializing in e-business systems, both in New Zealand and Australia. He is currently an architect with Microsoft Consulting Services, based in Sydney. He has worked closely with the BizTalk Server team since early 2000. In the process, he wrote some of the first training material for BizTalk Server 2000, and he has published several whitepapers on BizTalk Server, application integration, and business process automation.

Gregor Hohpe leads the Enterprise Integration practice at ThoughtWorks, Inc., a specialized provider of application development and integration services. Gregor is a widely recognized thought leader on asynchronous messaging architectures and co-author of the seminal book *Enterprise Integration Patterns* (Addison-Wesley, 2004). Gregor speaks regularly at technical conferences around the world and maintains the Web site www.eaipatterns.com.

Dragos A. Manolescu is a software architect with ThoughtWorks. He has been an active member of the patterns community since 1996. He has published patterns on data flow, information retrieval, multimedia, workflow engines and e-business, and chaired the 6th Conference on Pattern Languages of Programs (PLoP). He holds a Ph.D. in Computer Science from the University of Illinois at Urbana-Champaign.

E. G. Nadhan is a Principal in EDS with over 21 years of experience in software development and engineering in distributed environments. Nadhan has successfully led the implementation and deployment of several integration solutions for EDS clients in multiple industries including the financial, chemical, healthcare, and manufacturing industries. He has always encouraged the adoption of a pattern-based approach to the architecture of these solutions.

1

Integration and Patterns

"The significant problems we face cannot be solved at the same level of thinking we were at when we created them." — Albert Einstein

Few enterprise applications exist in isolation. Most are connected to other applications and services by data feeds and common reference data. Others are connected through elaborate integration networks. If you look above the level of single applications and focus on an enterprise's whole software portfolio, you often see a complex collection of silo applications, heterogeneous platforms, and islands of sometimes duplicated data and services that are interconnected by messages, objects, file transfers, batch feeds, and human interactions.

At the same time, businesses consider information technology (IT) to be a key element of both operational efficiency and competitive advantage. There are high expectations of technical investments despite rapidly changing business conditions and operating environments. Compounding this problem is the rate of change in technology, as innovations such as Web services emerge. Although adopting this new technology promises a new level of interoperability between systems and enterprises, it also demands that practitioners devise an integrated, enterprise-level approach to building applications and services.

Given today's complex technical and business environment, how do you create an integrated portfolio of applications and services for your enterprise?

This guide discusses known good ways to integrate systems, and it uses patterns to describe them. To ground the discussion in something tangible, the guide:

- Describes a representative scenario in detail
- Builds out a performance-tested, baseline architecture to validate the approach
- Uses the vocabulary of patterns to describe important design tradeoffs
- Traces the patterns to an implementation that uses the Microsoft® platform

The guide does not:

- Describe a feature-complete or fully secure implementation
- Assert that there is only one right answer when it comes to design
- Promote patterns as a silver bullet for solving all design problems

The Problem of Integration

Many enterprises create overly complex integration architectures in very predictable ways. Business units within the enterprise often have a strong business case for an IT capability. They fund and staff projects to provide this capability, while tracking primarily the delivered functionality. However, they often have little regard for the technical architecture underneath. Assuming the business case is sound, this is often in the best interest of the business—at least in the short run.

In the long run, however, building business capabilities without careful consideration of an enterprise-wide technical architecture can lead to a high cost for IT operations, an inflexible portfolio of applications and services, and a high cost for new application development. Even worse, the enterprise will be at a distinct disadvantage with respect to other competitors that have built well-factored, agile, and well-integrated applications and services. This is especially true in industries where information has a high economic value and new business models emerge quickly, posing real economic threats.

The balance between these business and technology forces is delicate. Moving too fast to enable business capabilities can result in a glut of architecturally incompatible applications, which likely will need to be rationalized and integrated later at a high cost to the enterprise. On the other hand, unchecked indulgence of the natural engineering tendency to study the problem deeply before acting can lead to long and costly enterprise architecture engagements. Not only do these efforts take significant time to execute (at a high opportunity cost), but, if not carefully managed, they risk producing little more than a set of binders that sit unused on a shelf.

Integration Architecture

An enterprise's integration architecture balances the requirements of the business and the requirements of individual applications. Inside this integration architecture, you often find an overwhelming maze of systems, connections, and channels. If you study enough of these, you see common combinations of integrated systems such as portals, networks of connections such as message brokers, buses, and point-to-point connections, and numerous individual connections and channels. To understand the maze, it is helpful to understand how many of these integration architectures evolve—one application at a time.

Many developers and architects start by designing and building stand-alone applications. They then progress to more complex enterprise applications. As applications require connections to shared enterprise resources, it is natural to create abstractions and wrappers that encapsulate these resources *from an application-centric point of view.* After all, it is just one more connection to the enterprise resource. Further enterprise-level work is often out of scope for the application project.

Although this approach works well from the perspective of a single application, connecting all applications in this way is unlikely to produce a well-ordered set of applications. Instead, you need a logical design at the integration level, just like you need a logical design at the application level. To think clearly about an integrated portfolio of applications and services at the enterprise level, you must invert your viewpoint. You must first consider the needs of the enterprise as an integrated whole and then consider how to expose shared functionality through networked applications. This kind of thinking is quite different from traditional monolithic application development or *n*-tier development. It begs the question: what is an application anyway?

Applications

Most software-related definitions describe applications as "any part of a software system used to deliver end-user functionality" [Firesmith95] or "a computer program designed to help people perform a certain type of work" [Microsoft02-3]. If you think of design from a traditional application-centric point of view, you usually expect to encapsulate functionality into one or more executable files and then deploy them to necessary servers. You do not expect to use existing services to any large degree. However, if you approach this same problem from an integration architecture perspective, the ideal application is a thin layer of presentation that consumes shared functionality or data at the enterprise level. Ideally, much of this functionality already exists and is accessible at a level of granularity that is meaningful to the business. And if new functionality must be built, it is designed not to stand alone, but to be shared with other enterprise applications and services.

To show how this kind of thinking might be practically applied, the remainder of this guide uses some of these concepts in an interesting, yet challenging, online bill payment scenario called Global Bank. This scenario introduces enough complexity to illustrate the design tradeoffs without introducing too many details.

The Global Bank Scenario

Although talking about architecture and design at a conceptual level helps to set guiding principles, there is nothing like building out an actual system against requirements to gain common understanding at a more technical level. That is why the authors of this guide have developed an executable baseline architecture against a concrete scenario: Global Bank. Later chapters of this guide describe the design and implementation details of the solution, but first, let's look at some of the context and requirements of this scenario.

Context

Global Bank is a midsize, traditional bank that has acquired a complete range of financial services capabilities through a series of acquisitions. It has a limited online banking presence that is fragmented across its various divisions. As part of its strategy to expand with the limited cash it has available, Global Bank has decided to innovate in the online banking market by providing a host of value-added services in addition to a fully integrated financial management capability.

Note: This chapter contains an intentionally brief overview of Global Bank's business context and approach to building integration architecture. For more detailed information, see Chapter 7, "Project Notebook."

The chief executive officer (CEO) decided the first step was to immediately add an electronic bill payment capability to the current online banking system. This would allow customers to schedule electronic payments online from their checking accounts—a high demand feature providing greater customer convenience. The CEO believed this added convenience would have an immediate impact upon customer satisfaction and loyalty, while demonstrating tangible progress to his board of directors. To initiate this effort, the CEO brought in his chief technical officer (CTO) and the vice president for consumer banking and asked them to deliver this capability before the end of the fiscal year. He expected rough-order-of-magnitude (ROM) cost and schedule estimates within six weeks.

Requirements

The CTO immediately involved a senior program manager to create a project around this initiative. The program manager formed a team to build a high-level project plan and to start gathering requirements. Unlike many projects, the CTO expected to not only gather requirements from the consumer banking division, but to also negotiate requirements with the consumer banking division based on the overall needs of the business.

As he reflected on the overall initiative, the CTO felt confident that the business would continue to invest in additional financial services for its customer base and that additional acquisitions were likely to follow. This was clearly not an isolated initiative; rather, it reflected a longer-term strategy for the company. He realized it was important to have a well-conceived technical architecture at the enterprise level that would smoothly support these corporate goals.

Beyond the functional requirements that would emerge, he wanted a solid technical foundation that would allow him to meet operational requirements as well. He pulled together an architecture team and asked them to create a baseline architecture that would support this initiative and future initiatives. As a first approximation, he started with the following high-level requirements and constraints:

- Build a baseline architecture for a Web-based online banking portal that allows customers to pay bills online from their checking accounts.

- All account-related transactions will use the current system, which resides on an IBM mainframe (OS390) using Customer Information Control System (CICS) based transactions.

- The online bank system will reside in the corporate data center in Seattle, Washington. It will be connected to an acquired bank's data center in Los Angeles, California though a private leased line.

- Loan information will be pulled from the acquired bank's loan systems, which reside on systems that are based on IBM WebSphere J2EE.

- All customer profile information will use the current Customer Relationship Management (CRM) system.

- Domestic electronic payments will use the current payment system, and international electronic payments will use SWIFT-based transactions through an external payment gateway. Payees that cannot receive electronic payments will be paid using electronic transactions to a manual fulfillment center, which will then make the payments manually through the U.S. mail.

- Except for the systems previously identified, the system will be based on the Microsoft platform.

- The system's overall transaction rates, concurrent users, and response time must meet the first year's projected usage plus an engineering safety factor of 3x (or three times the first year's projected usage) to handle burst load.

- The system must meet or exceed the service level agreement (SLA) for our current online system.

Next Steps

If you were part of this architecture team, how would you proceed? If you were fortunate, someone on this team would have built a system like this before and would apply those experiences and lessons learned to this effort. This would be optimal, but is not probable. It is more likely that members of your team are very proficient with a set of technologies that might solve part of this problem. For example, they might be proficient with object-oriented design, message-oriented middleware, integration servers, or distributed object systems. Naturally, team members want to apply the tools they have used before to solve future problems, but how do you know which technology is appropriate for which area of the design and when? When the problem and the technology align, you can move quickly and effectively to build the solution. However, we have all seen familiar technology applied in unfamiliar areas for which it is suboptimal.

Wouldn't it be great to be able to break this problem down into relatively atomic decision points and understand the design alternatives available to you at each point? For each alternative, wouldn't you want to know how others have implemented similar choices and what the resulting advantages and disadvantages were? Although you may not have the luxury of an experienced person to discuss this with, the next best alternative is a catalog of best practices that are documented as patterns. Before continuing with the Global Bank scenario, let's discuss the concept of patterns at a very high level and how they might apply to software development.

Note: Rather than repeat the introductory material from *Enterprise Solution Patterns Using Microsoft .NET* or from a formal pattern description found in an introductory patterns book, this chapter relaxes the formal pattern description and provides some examples from everyday life. This is an effort to make the pattern idea more approachable. The chapter then shows the results of applying pattern-based thinking to an integration scenario. Later chapters explain specific patterns in more detail.

Patterns

People think in patterns. It is the way we naturally communicate ideas related to complex subject areas such as music, science, medicine, chess, and software design. Patterns are not new. We all use them intuitively as part of the learning process without really thinking about it. And because our minds naturally use patterns to perform complex tasks, you can find patterns nearly everywhere.

Patterns in Sports

Consider what happens during a soccer game or an American football game.

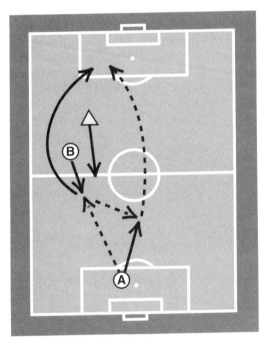

Figure 1.1
Patterns in soccer

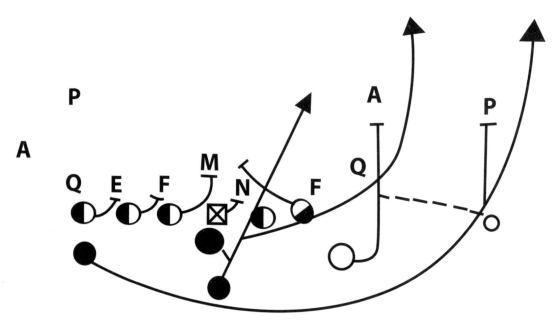

Figure 1.2
Patterns in American football

Individuals who are acting according to predetermined patterns move quickly and decisively against targeted opponents. Each individual's pattern of movement is also part of a larger pattern of orchestration where each player has clear responsibilities and scope. In addition, the entire team is in a binary state—either offense or defense. Without patterns in sports, the games would not be as rich and interesting. Can you image how long the huddle would be in an American football game without the language of plays (patterns)?

Note: Software patterns are significantly more complex than these simple examples. The examples are intended to make the notion of software patterns more approachable at the expense of being less technically rigorous. For more rigorous introductions to patterns, see the bibliography section.

If you look closer at patterns, you will find relationships between them. In sports, for example, teams have certain plays for offense and certain plays for defense; the patterns that describe two players' actions must fit into a larger pattern that the team is following. In this sense, patterns can be described in terms of hierarchies.

Patterns in Music

Another example of how people think in patterns is the patterns found in music, such as rock and roll. In rock and roll, a rhythm guitar player usually repeats a pattern of chords in a specific key. Against this backdrop, a lead guitarist plays a freeform series of notes from a candidate pattern of notes that correspond to the chord progression being played. Figure 1.3 shows a pattern chart that lead guitarists use to learn the correct finger positions on a guitar neck.

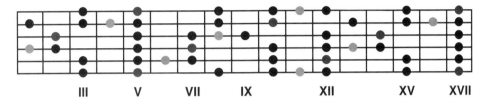

III   V   VII   IX   XII   XV   XVII

● minor pentatonic scale note   ● blue note

● root note

Figure 1.3
Pentatonic scale patterns in the key of A

The root note in Figure 3 indicates the key that the song is in. Within the song's key, the lead guitar player is free to improvise, although most of the notes he or she plays will correspond to the pattern chart in Figure 3. The order and sequence of the notes may vary according to artist, style, and song, but the pattern of actual notes played remains. If the key changes, the scale pattern moves to a different place on the guitar neck that corresponds to the song's new key. Interestingly enough, this notion of one layer of patterns constraining another is exactly what happens when you apply pattern-based design methods. This is just as true in software design as it is in other design disciplines.

Pattern Structure

Patterns have a natural relationship with each other. Perhaps the most often used example is the interplay between patterns for designing towns, which in turn, contain patterns for designing clusters of buildings and roads. The building cluster and road patterns, in turn, contain patterns for designing buildings. Figure 1.4 shows these relationships.

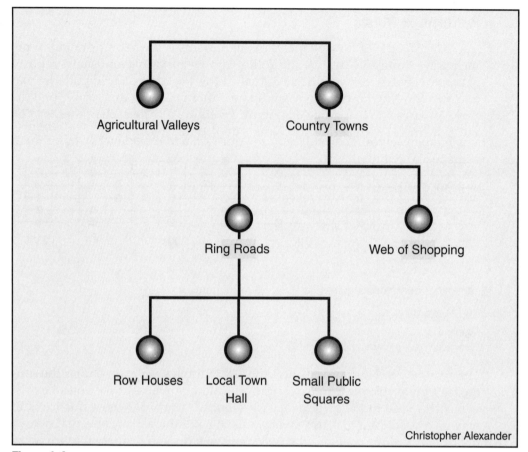

Figure 1.4
Hierarchy of patterns

Pattern-Based Design

While pattern-based design is relatively new in the field of software development, industrial technology has used pattern-based design for decades, perhaps even centuries. Catalogs of mechanisms and standard configurations provide design elements that are used to engineer automobiles, aircraft, machine tools, and robots. Applying pattern-based design to software development promises the same benefits to software as it does to industrial technology: predictability, risk mitigation, and increased productivity.

Experience is Key

Of course, pattern-based design alone is no guarantee of success in either software design or industrial technology. Known good mechanisms can be used to build planes that do not fly, cars that do not handle well, and applications that do not scale. There is simply no substitute for the skill and experience of designers and engineers in any subject area, and software is no exception. Although patterns help by offering manageable portions of design knowledge, they are not complete solutions by themselves. They still require your skill and experience to tailor them to your specific requirements.

Applying Patterns

Applying patterns to a specific scenario usually involves an iterative design process. As a guiding principle, you want to keep your design as "simple as possible and no simpler," as Albert Einstein once said. Although you can use patterns to solve design problems, make sure that you have a legitimate problem first before applying a pattern. Do not use patterns just for the sake of using them.

Although design guidelines and process are related topics (and worthy of dedicated works), this book focuses on the tangible outputs of the design process. It focuses in particular on the role of patterns as they are applied to problems. To examine the concrete artifacts produced by a pattern-based design process, let's go back to Global Bank and see what came out of the design sessions as the team worked on the baseline architecture.

Patterns at Global Bank

The architecture team analyzed the high-level requirements and constraints provided by the CTO and reviewed existing technical architecture models of the enterprise. The architecture team also designated several members of the team to do a build-versus-buy analysis of related commercial off-the-shelf software (COTS) packages that might meet the requirements.

Based on the build-versus-buy analysis, the team decided to build a custom extensible portal by using commercial platform infrastructure components such as Web servers and database servers, but not to use packaged portal applications. Figure 1.5 shows their initial approximation of the server types in a network diagram.

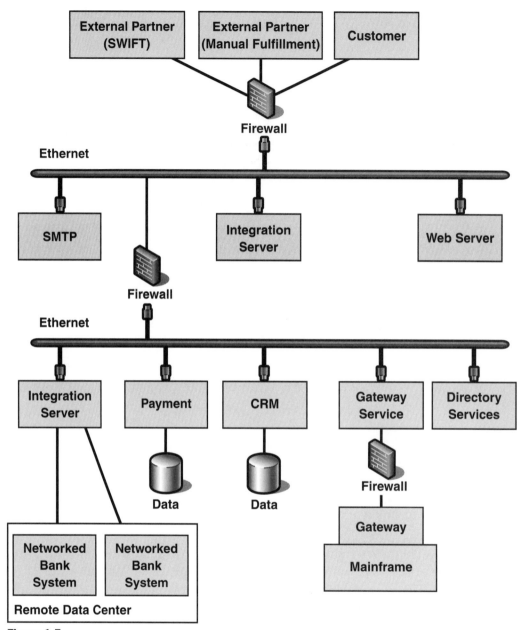

Figure 1.5
Initial network diagram with server types

For each key use case, the team determined the sequence of system interactions that must occur to fulfill the stated requirements. They described these interactions in terms of server types and message sequences. Figure 1.6 shows the View Scheduled Payments use case realization in the form of a collaboration diagram.

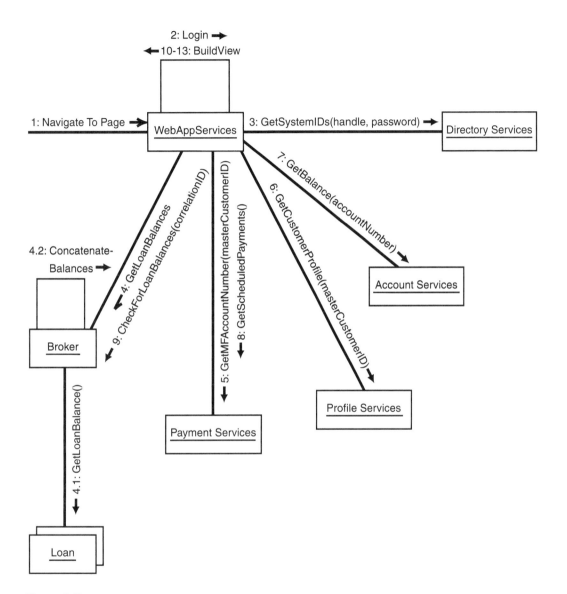

Figure 1.6

View Scheduled Payments collaboration diagram

The flow of the use case in Figure 1.6 is:

1. A customer navigates to the online bill payment application.
2. The Web server prompts the customer for a user name and password.
3. The Web server authenticates the customer by using information retrieved from the directory server.
4. The Web server sends an asynchronous request to the integration server asking for related loans.
5. The Web server retrieves the customer's mainframe account number from the payment server.
6. The Web server retrieves customer profile information from the CRM server.
7. The Web server retrieves account balance information from the mainframe.
8. The Web server retrieves a list of scheduled payments from the payment server.
9. The Web server checks the integration server to see whether any loan information has been retrieved.
10. The Web server builds the presentation, which displays account balance, scheduled payments, and customer profile information.
11. If loan information is available, it appends this optional information onto the presentation.
12. The Web server returns the presentation code back to the browser.
13. The browser renders the view.

This use case realization is a representative sample of the bill payment application's significant use cases. The team took a similar approach to analyze other use cases, identify server types, and design message interactions. To create these use case realizations, the team conducted a series of iterations, each beginning with a design session using class-responsibility-collaboration (CRC) style techniques. Although similar in nature to CRC sessions, these sessions were not limited to class-level abstractions. Often these sessions involved subsystems, server types, processes, and channels as well.

The team's goal, as they considered the necessary collaborations between elements, was to design the simplest system that would satisfy all current requirements and account for system constraints. While working through the alternatives, they relied on the language of patterns to provide a common vocabulary for the team. Patterns were also useful as a concise way to communicate the context, forces, and tradeoffs involved in each design decision. At times, they realized that certain patterns only added complexity to the design, so they eliminated those patterns.

As they completed each iteration, they created a pattern model of the system to record their decisions. The model from the last iteration is shown in Figure 1.7. This pattern model represented the simplest system that realized the target use cases and constraints. To keep their models simple, they represented patterns as circles and added other high-level design elements to the model to communicate the overall design.

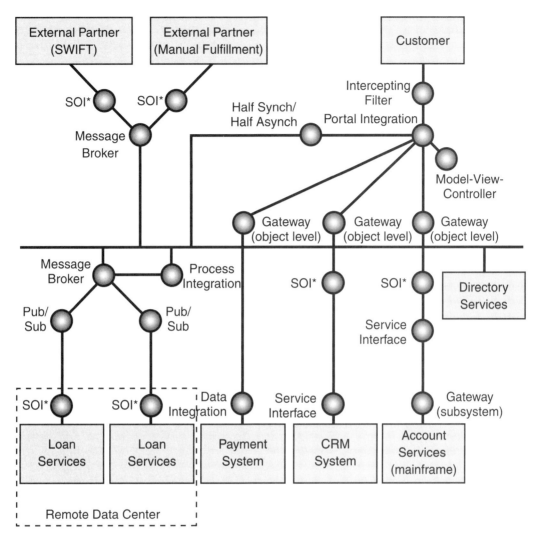

Figure 1.7
Patterns and design element model

The next chapter captures some of the pattern-based discussion that occurred during the design process. For now, just notice how the patterns connect key design elements such as the customer and the mainframe system.

Note: Because architects and developers are the primary audience for this guide, this discussion moved quickly into applying patterns to a specific scenario. For a more detailed discussion of pattern-based design, see Chapter 7, "Project Notebook."

The next step was to map these patterns to an implementation technology and to iterate again. In this case, many of the platform decisions were already made, and these platform decisions constrained the design choices. Sometimes, the implementation constraints forced the team to reconsider their design, and they adjusted accordingly. When they finished, they produced the platform-level implementation diagram shown in Figure 1.8.

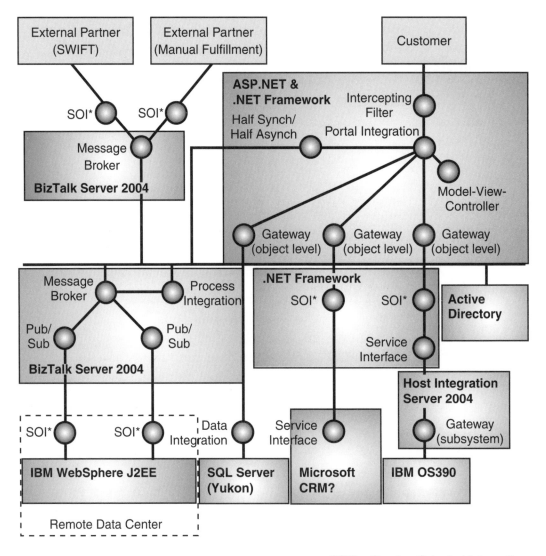

SOI* = Service-Oriented Integration

Figure 1.8
Pattern diagram mapped to implementation technology

Figure 1.8 shows that the Global Bank integration architecture is composed of numerous pattern-based design elements implemented on the Microsoft platform. To trace the implementation of these elements down to running bits, refer to the appropriate implementation pattern later in this guide. For example, to understand how to implement the gateway to the mainframe, refer to *Implementing Gateway with Host Integration Server 2004*. This pattern includes the details associated with connecting Global Bank's .NET Framework portal application with their existing COBOL-based CICS transactions.

Next Chapter

This chapter introduced the Global Bank scenario that is used throughout this guide and briefly discussed how patterns can help development teams find workable answers to integration challenges. The next chapter uses the language of patterns to explore the decisions and tradeoffs that the Global Bank architecture team made while designing and implementing their bill payment system.

2

Using Patterns to Design the Baseline Architecture

"It's all talk until the code runs." — Ward Cunningham

The last chapter introduced a banking scenario that posed many technical integration challenges. It also presented patterns as an effective means of communicating design decisions. This chapter walks though the application of integration patterns in the context of the Global Bank scenario.

Although the scenario is a fictitious story for conveying design decisions, it is important to note that the authors actually built and performance tested this design in the *patterns & practices* lab at Microsoft. The design team consisted of field-experienced practitioners with access to the latest product builds. The decision points in the story correspond to real decision points in the lab, although this description shapes them into a more readable story than the actual effort. Also, the actual development process was more iterative than the story might suggest; some portions of the system evolved incrementally. Later in this guide, you will find that the implementation patterns contain extracts of the code used to run the Global Bank baseline architecture. You will also find more detailed explanations of the patterns mentioned in this chapter.

Meeting the Requirements of Global Bank

At the end of the last chapter, the Global Bank architecture team applied a pattern-based design approach to its bill payment system's requirements and arrived at an initial technical architecture blueprint. At this point, the team felt fairly satisfied about the initial design, at least on paper. The members of the team knew the value of creating these design models, but they also knew that they would learn other things only from the running code. They were anxious to validate their models with executable bits.

To validate their thinking, the members of the Global Bank team built a baseline architecture in the test lab and implemented five of the most architecturally significant use cases. They chose these particular use cases to help define and validate the most important mechanisms in the design. They did not intend the use cases to be functionally complete—that would come later when the functional requirements firmed up. At this point, they wanted to refine the riskiest parts of their design down to the level of executable code, the most concrete form of design.

As they implemented this baseline architecture, members of the team also performance tested many parts of the system to validate their design assumptions and tradeoffs. This helped them to further understand the overall scalability of their solution as they considered the impact of additional users over time. All of this implementation and testing contributed to their overall confidence in the patterns they had selected.

The bulk of this chapter explores the decisions and tradeoffs that the Global Bank architecture team made during the design and implementation process, and it takes a closer look at the implemented system. The discussion uses the language of patterns to convey these decisions and tradeoffs, as well as the intentions behind them, as discrete and comprehensible decision points. Throughout the discussion, pattern names appear in title capitalization and italic (for example, *Portal Integration*). This treatment of pattern names emphasizes the building of a pattern vocabulary and signals that the concepts are explained as patterns later in this guide.

Using Patterns to Communicate Design Decisions

Each pattern clearly limits the scope of its problem and solution to a discrete and comprehensible, or "mind-sized," decision point. By considering relatively small atomic design decisions one at a time, you are better prepared to manage the overall complexity of the system. As you build a complex system, you aggregate these small design decisions together to eventually form a larger hierarchy, or frame, of decisions.

Of course, changes at the top of the hierarchy may affect the elements below, and it is unrealistic to expect your first design to be just right. Most likely, you will need to iterate. However, having a set of discrete decision points makes it easier to iterate when you need to.

Remember, in complex environments, there is often no single right answer for a given problem. For any set of requirements, each group of designers may arrive at different, yet equally valid, designs. Usually, the difference reflects a different set of tradeoffs and priorities. What is most important to understand about the design process is that:

- A series of technical decisions must be made.
- Each design decision involves tradeoffs—both advantages and disadvantages.
- Tradeoffs made at one level constrain the decisions at other levels.
- The sum of these design decisions must result in an architecture that meets both the functional and nonfunctional requirements of the system.

With these guidelines in mind, the architecture team set out to build a baseline architecture.

The Role of a Baseline Architecture

A baseline architecture is a thin executable slice through the overall system that is designed to implement the most architecturally significant use cases. As you implement these key use cases, you want to define the key mechanisms and components in the system and retire the most serious technical risks early. If you do this well, the baseline architecture does not become a prototype to be thrown away. Instead, it becomes the skeletal structure of the system. The baseline provides sufficient stability so that subsequent iterations can smoothly evolve the running system into one that meets all of the functional and nonfunctional requirements. The baseline architecture is intentionally incomplete.

How do you actually design a baseline architecture? To answer this question, let's trace the architecture team's steps during the design sessions.

Designing the Global Bank Baseline Architecture

As the team dissected the high-level requirements of the chief technology officer (CTO), the members of the team arrived at the following use cases:

- Schedule Payments
- View Scheduled Payments
- Execute Scheduled Payment
- Receive Payment Response
- Add Payee

The first use case they discussed was the View Scheduled Payments use case. This use case involved a portal that allowed users to see their account information, including their current account balance and a list of scheduled payments. To build this portal, the team would need to connect to multiple back-end systems and to aggregate the results in a single view. Implementing this use case would require the team to resolve several key technical issues. Let's look now at the use case in more detail and understand the team's thinking as they approached the problem.

View Scheduled Payments Use Case

To implement View Scheduled Payments, the portal would have to display the following information:

- Account information from the mainframe
- Profile information such as name and address from the Customer Relationship Management (CRM) system
- Scheduled payment information from a payment system

Optionally, the portal would have to display any other loans the customer might have with newly acquired banks so that the customer could submit electronic payments toward these loans.

Initially, members of the team had slightly different opinions of what a portal was. However, they eventually agreed that a portal is a single view into many back-end systems that are integrated "at the glass," or, in other words, at the user presentation level. Thus, *Portal Integration* is a type of integration that looks like Figure 2.1.

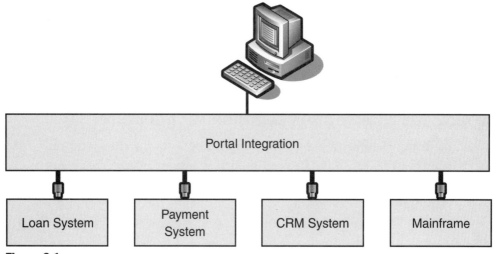

Figure 2.1
Portal integration to multiple back-end systems

The members of the Global Bank team needed to make individual connections to many different kinds of systems to make *Portal Integration* work. They considered each connection individually to determine exactly how they were going to connect to the system.

Note: At this point in the story, the payment system does not exist. It is, however, included in Figure 2.1 as a placeholder to use for planning purposes.

System Connections

As the members of the team thought more about this problem, they debated the kinds of connections they could make. The discussion was full of overloaded terms and individual biases toward the methods that each member was most familiar with. To make matters worse, the team did not share a common design vocabulary because some members of the team had never worked together before.

Finally, the members of the team realized they had to narrow the discussion to a few practical choices for each system. To do so, they would have to tighten their frame of reference when they compared their connection options. They finally agreed to approach the problem from the perspective of integrating by using a *Three-Layered Services Application* [Trowbridge03]. As shown in Figure 2.2, a *Three-Layered Services Application* defines three distinct logical layers: *data*, *business logic* (functional), and *presentation*.

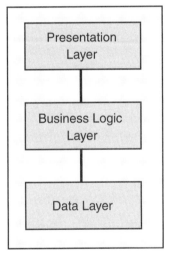

Figure 2.2
Three-Layered Services Application

They also agreed that although not every system was designed as a *Three-Layered Services Application*, using these three logical layers would give them a common way to reason about other systems. Using these layers to shape their discussion, they began to discuss the relative tradeoffs between each connection alternative.

Note: To present an overview of the design, this chapter discusses tradeoffs between design alternatives at a high level only. For more detailed information regarding these tradeoffs, see the pattern chapters (Chapters 3 through 6). If you want to see a visual model of all of these patterns and their relationships, see Chapter 7, "Project Notebook"

First, they could use *Data Integration* to connect at the logical level of data, making the same data available to more than one application. This approach worked well when there was very little business logic to reuse across applications. For other applications, they knew that raw data was not enough; they wanted to reuse the functionality of a given application. This functionality often contained business logic, process, or calculated values. In this case, they would need to use *Functional Integration* to connect at the business logic layer. And although they preferred to connect to systems directly to share either function or data, they acknowledged that sometimes the only practical way to integrate with a system was through *Presentation Integration*, also known as *screen scraping*. Moving away from a pure systems perspective, they also discussed human integration as a means to integrate with a system. However, because they were focused on building a baseline architecture, they considered human integration to be out of scope—at least for the moment.

Now that they agreed on an approach to the alternatives before them, the members of the team returned to the set of individual connection decisions they had to make. The first system to connect to was the payment system.

Connecting to the Payment System

The members of the team knew they would need a system to hold all the scheduled payments along with related information. They decided the simplest thing to do was to build a payment system that persisted this information in a database with Web-based administrator screens to manage the data. They decided to use *Data Integration* to connect the portal to the payment system because no additional system functionality or behavior seemed important to share.

Connecting to the CRM System

The next system to connect to was the existing CRM system. The members of the team analyzed the system architecture and realized there was only one practical choice: *Functional Integration*. That is because the software vendor used a highly abstracted schema within a relational database to store information and recommended against *Data Integration*. Instead, the vendor provided a functional Web services interface to encapsulate access to the data. This was the same kind of encapsulation at a system level that good object-oriented designers perform at a class level when they create private instance variables and public accessor methods.

Although encapsulation is generally a good thing, in this case the members of the team marked it as a technical risk. They marked it as a risk because the vendor's implementation was effectively "black box," or unknown to the Global Bank team. The members of the team also knew from experience how difficult it is to build high performance abstract interfaces. Furthermore, because profile information from the CRM was required with each View Scheduled Payments request, performance was critical. They decided to mark this interface as a key test point and to stress test it early to discover the point where additional load would compromise system performance. They needed this information soon so they could consider compensating design alternatives, if necessary.

Connecting to the Mainframe

Integrating with the mainframe was critical because it was the system of record for all account information. Over the years, the organization had invested significantly to develop solid Customer Information Control System (CICS) transactions. Any integration with the account system would need to use this functionality; therefore, the team chose *Functional Integration* but deferred the connection details until later.

The team created the diagram in Figure 2.3 to record the design decisions made so far. The team used squares to represent design elements, circles to represent patterns, and lines to indicate relationships between the patterns and other design elements.

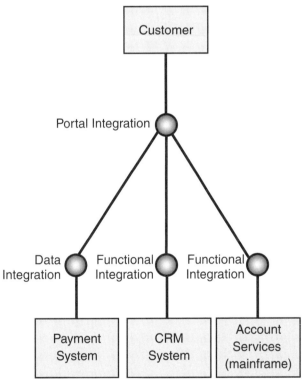

Figure 2.3
Connecting the payment, CRM, and mainframe systems to a portal

Connecting to Loan Systems

The final connections to consider were the connections to the acquired bank systems that were located in a remote data center. This optional part of the use case involved finding all loans a customer might have with these banks so that the customer could schedule payments toward them. This requirement presented many challenges. First, *Data Integration* would be complex because of the many different data formats. The many different data formats would require multiple transformations. Next, because more acquisitions were likely, the team wanted to minimize the cost of integrating additional systems into this consolidated loan information request. The team decided to use *Functional Integration* in the form of request and response messages and to expect each system involved in this collaboration to provide the appropriate response. This decentralized approach would make it easier to integrate new systems in the future.

As the members of the team thought more about the connections to the remote data center, they realized there was another complication with these connections. All of the links between previous connections were reliable connections within the same enterprise (*near links*). The connection to the remote data center spanned multiple enterprises and was not considered reliably connected (a *far link*). Based on previous experience, they preferred to use a message queue or message-oriented middleware, to buffer connections between far links to improve reliability. They also knew that there were more issues than the reliability of the far link connections. With this in mind, they decided to consider their growing network of connection points more carefully.

Integration Topology

Although the team was making progress toward determining the best way to connect to each system, choosing the right topology to link these connection points seemed less clear. As the members of the team discussed alternatives, they arrived at three possible ways to connect three or more systems together: *Point-to-Point Connection*, *Message Broker*, and *Message Bus*.

The easiest way to connect the systems was to use the *Point-to-Point Connection* pattern, as shown in Figure 2.4.

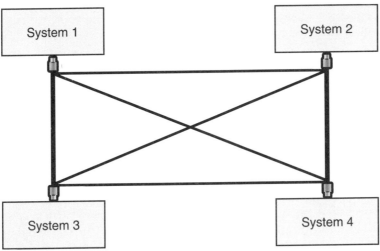

Figure 2.4
Connecting four systems through point-to-point connections

Point-to-Point Connection is effective and simple for a small number of systems. A liability of this approach, however, is that each system must have information about each endpoint that it connects to. The members of the team knew that as they added more systems to their integration architecture, it would become more and more complex to add each additional system, making it expensive to extend and manage.

The team considered inserting a *Message Broker* to act as an intermediary between senders and receivers, as shown in Figure 2.5.

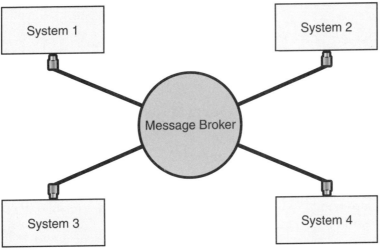

Figure 2.5
Connecting four systems by using a message broker

The advantage of using a *Message Broker* is that it decouples the receiver from the sender. Instead of sending the message to a specific endpoint, the sender can send messages to the broker. The broker then routes the message to the proper recipients. In addition, the broker often transforms the messages from one format to another to resolve the incompatible message formats between endpoints.

Finally, the team considered connecting multiple systems by using a *Message Bus*. A *Message Bus* (see Figure 2.6) requires each system on the bus to share a common data format, a common set of command messages, and a common infrastructure. A system sends a message to the *Message Bus*, and the *Message Bus* then transports the message to the other systems by way of the common infrastructure.

The members of the team liked the fact that after a *Message Bus* is built, the cost of adding another system to the message bus is negligible to the existing systems. As they thought further about implementation, they discussed different ways the common infrastructure might be built and soon found themselves in a heated debate over such issues as broadcast and *Publish/Subscribe* (*Pub/Sub*). They agreed to postpone further discussion of these issues until or unless they decided to incorporate a *Message Bus* into the actual design.

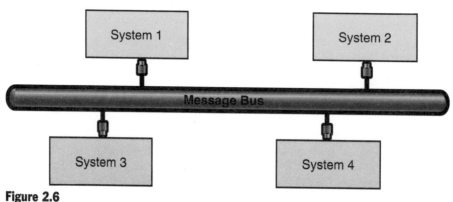

Figure 2.6
Four systems connected with a message bus

Now that the members of the team had brainstormed alternative integration topologies, they brought their attention back to the View Scheduled Payments use case. They knew there were many kinds of systems providing loan information to this use case. They also knew it was likely that the bank would acquire even more financial services companies in the future. These potential acquisitions represented even more sources of loan information to be integrated. They wanted the system to be flexible in its ability to handle these kinds of changes.

Adding a Message Broker for the Loan Systems

They decided to employ a *Message Broker* between Global Bank's data center and the remote data center housing the other loan systems. They intended to send a loan information request message to the broker, and the broker would then forward it to other systems interested in this type of message. As these systems responded with loan information, the broker would pull the information together and make it available as a consolidated whole.

By using a message queue to implement *Message Broker*, they would also create the kind of buffer they wanted between their data center and the far link that connected it to the remote data center.

Figure 2.7 shows how the members of the team modified their original diagram to include the message broker connecting the portal to the remote data center.

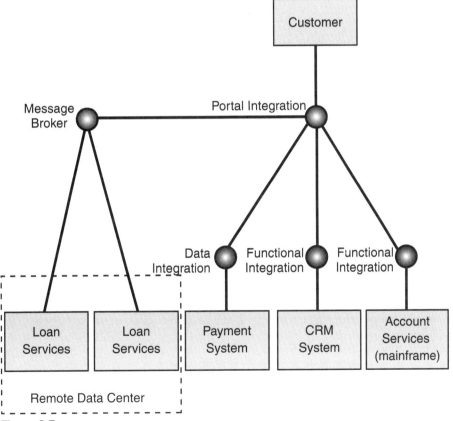

Figure 2.7
Connecting the portal to the remote data center

To show the dynamic nature of the system and to document how the system would realize the View Scheduled Payments use case, the team drew the collaboration diagram that is shown in Figure 2.8.

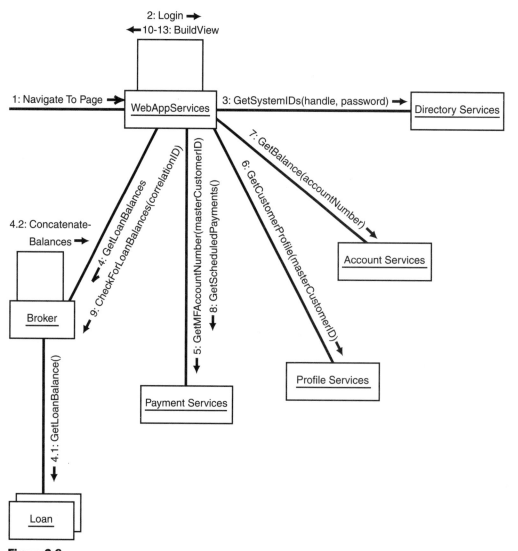

Figure 2.8
View Scheduled Payments collaboration diagram

The following is the flow of the use case that is shown in Figure 2.8:

1. A customer browses to the online bill payment application.
2. The Web server prompts the customer for a user name and password.
3. The Web server authenticates the customer by using information retrieved from the directory server.
4. The Web server sends an asynchronous request to the integration server asking for related loans.
5. The Web server retrieves customer profile information from the CRM server.
6. The Web server retrieves the customer's mainframe account number from the payment server.
7. The Web server retrieves account balance information from the mainframe.
8. The Web server retrieves a list of scheduled payments from the payment server.
9. The Web server checks the integration server to see whether any loan information has been retrieved.
10. The Web server builds the presentation, which displays account balance, scheduled payments, and customer profile information.
11. If loan information is available, it appends this optional information to the presentation.
12. The Web server returns the presentation code back to the browser.
13. The browser renders the view.

So far, the members of the team had a pattern-based design model and a collaboration diagram that showed how the system would realize the View Scheduled Payment use case. They wanted one more model that showed the static nature of their system with well-defined high-level boundaries. To portray this view, they used a *port-and-wire* model as shown in Figure 2.9. The outgoing ports are depicted as black squares, and the incoming ports are depicted as white squares.

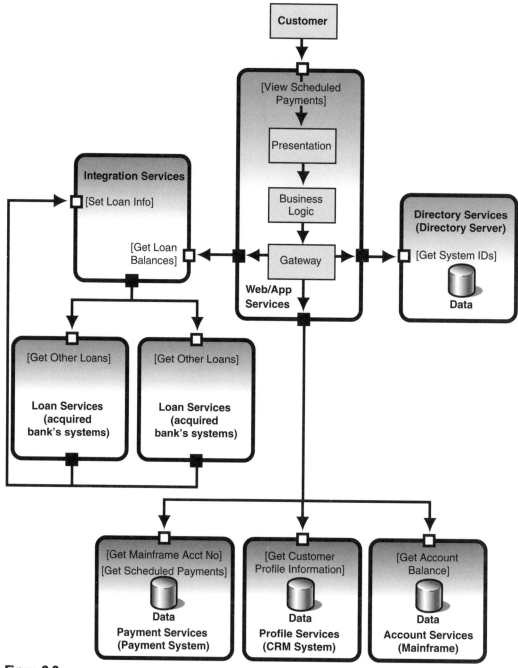

Figure 2.9
View Scheduled Payments message flow

Although all the details were certainly not worked out for this use case, the members of the team felt that the use case was at a sufficient level of detail to proceed to the next use case. They would return to refine the design later, after exploring whether parts of this design would realize other use cases as well.

Execute Scheduled Payment Use Case

The next use case they considered was the Execute Scheduled Payment use case. To implement this use case, the system would:

- Start up at a system-defined interval.
- Retrieve the set of payments to be made on or before the current date.
- For each payment, the system would verify that there were sufficient funds in the payment account and then debit the account for the payment amount.
- Send the payment to an appropriate payment channel.

There were four kinds of payment channels currently in scope: domestic payments through a clearing house, electronic payment gateways using Society for Worldwide Interbank Financial Telecommunication (SWIFT) transactions, electronic payments to a manual fulfillment house, and account-to-account transfers within the bank's internal system.

Focusing on the Baseline Architecture

As the members of the team talked though this use case, they tried to avoid discussing domain-specific details that had more to do with business logic than technical architecture. Although they knew these details were important, they also realized that the purpose of the baseline architecture was to mitigate technical risk, not to fully refine the business requirements. They knew the requirements team was on track to do exactly that job, so they focused on the items that worried them the most from a technical perspective. They also deemphasized some of the use case areas that did not represent top technical challenges.

Payment Channels

One area of concern was the SWIFT payment *Gateway*.

Note: The *Gateway* pattern abstracts access to an external resource by presenting a single interface to the integrated applications while hiding the external resource interface. For more information, see "Gateway" later in this chapter.

The members of the team knew the requirements would include making international transactions to support their wealthiest clients, and for this they would use SWIFT transactions. They also knew there would be requirements for domestic payments, and for those payments they would use the existing system. It would be too expensive to pay a SWIFT transaction fee for domestic payments, especially when they already had an existing payment system.

The existing payment system was technically straightforward. It used a leased secure line for *Point-to-Point Connection* with a clearing house and secure file transfer. The bank and the clearing house exchanged files that contained both outgoing and incoming data records. This was a simple form of *Data Integration* that the bank had used for years. The team would use this system for domestic transfers. Because they understood it well, there was little reason to build and test this system early, so these details were omitted from the initial use case.

However, the SWIFT payment *Gateway* was a very different story. They would need to package the transaction securely in an XML message and use Web services to send it to the payment *Gateway* over the Internet. Because this part of the use case was new to the team and presented many technical risks, it was one of the top priorities for the baseline architecture. They wanted to build it early and test it.

Using Domain Knowledge to Guide Design Decisions

Because many members of the team had been in banking for years, they naturally brought their business knowledge into the design sessions. Although this business knowledge was invaluable, the team had to sort out what was relevant for the baseline architecture and what was not. This sorting was, of course, a judgment call, but it was necessary for the team to stay focused on mitigating the most important technical risks first.

For example, the members of the team knew that any time the bank would initiate a payment through an external party such as a clearing house or a payment *Gateway*, the confirmation would be delayed. The rules of double entry accounting would not allow funds to be in limbo during this period. Therefore, a holding account would have to be credited at payment initiation and debited upon payment confirmation. This would keep the system in balance at all times.

Although implementing a holding account was critical to the final use case, it was not critical for the early baseline architecture. The team was proficient at enlisting debits and credits in the same transactions across most of the systems in the bank. They did not consider this to be a technical risk. Therefore, the team decided to defer the implementation of this logic until after the requirements team defined the specific holding accounts to use.

Using SWIFT Gateway for the Baseline Architecture

The rules to determine the right payment channel were straightforward. When a customer scheduled a payment, the customer could select either a domestic or an international payment. If the payment were domestic, the customer would provide an American Bankers Association (ABA) routing number for the intended payee. If this field were left blank, the system would send an electronic payment to a company that specialized in paper check writing and mailing services (a manual fulfillment house). If the field were not blank, the system would check the routing number against a list of internal banks. If the numbers matched, the system would make a payment by transferring money internally from one account to another. If the routing number were valid but did not match the internal banks, the standard domestic payments system would make the payment by secure file transfer. Finally, payments marked as international would use the SWIFT payment *Gateway*. Because the system would send the payment to an appropriate channel, there would be a system-based acknowledgment that the message was received.

To simplify the initial use case, the members of the team omitted any routing to their domestic payment system and instead routed these payments through the SWIFT *Gateway* for test purposes. This exercised the SWIFT *Gateway* by using the test data. The test data was based on domestic accounts instead of international accounts. It would be easy to add international routing and test data later, but they wanted to pressure test the *Gateway* payment mechanisms early.

As they continued to walk though the use case flow, the members of the team realized that a key element was missing. Currently, the system would receive an acknowledgment that the payment message was sent, but how would the system know if the payment was received by the intended payee? What would happen if the payment *Gateway* or manual fulfillment house could not pay the payee? These questions led them to the Receive Payment Response use case.

Designing for Execute Scheduled Payment and Receive Payment Response

The Receive Payment Response use case described the behavior of the payment *Gateway* and the manual fulfillment house after they processed the payment request. In this use case, these payment channels returned the result of their processing to Global Bank's system. If the payment was successful, the payment status and transaction ID were updated in the payment system. If the payment failed, a compensating transaction to credit the account was first issued to the mainframe and then status and ID fields were updated accordingly in the payment system.

Because of the close relationship between Execute Scheduled Payments and Receive Payment Response, the team decided to evaluate *Process Integration* for both use cases.

Process Integration

Process Integration adds a layer of software on top of other applications and services to coordinate the execution of a long-running business function, as shown in Figure 2.10.

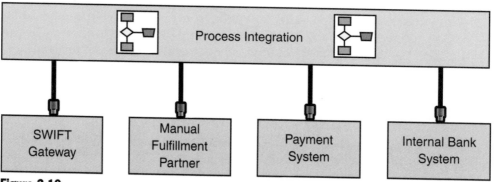

Figure 2.10

Process Integration, a coordinating layer above other applications and services

The members of the team knew they would need a layer like this to coordinate the two use cases, and they discussed the best way to design it. Some members of the team suggested an integration server. Integration servers often include orchestration tools for this purpose. Other members of the team wanted to build a custom coordinating layer by encapsulating process and activity components. They thought the integration server was excessive. After some debate, they decided to choose the integration server approach. They reasoned it was likely that the bank would continue to add more financial services and external partners in the future, and that these services and partners would need *Process Integration* capabilities also. And although the use of an integration server might initially cost them some time for installation and training, the cost would be more than repaid through the reduced development time and overall flexibility of the system.

The members of the team updated their design model to incorporate *Process Integration*, as shown in Figure 2.11. Notice that process integration needs to communicate with the message broker and the payment systems, but it does not need to connect directly to the portal.

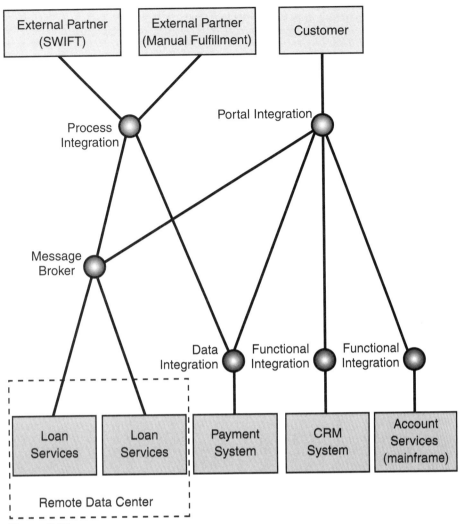

Figure 2.11
Incorporating Process Integration into the baseline architecture

Message Broker for Payment Channels

Although *Process Integration* would handle the orchestration needs of long-running transactions, the members of the team knew that each payment channel was likely to need a different message format, thus requiring transformation code. They would need a SWIFT-compliant XML schema in the case of the payment *Gateway* and a more generic XML schema in the case of the manual fulfillment house. Worse, they anticipated that the bank would add more external partners who would use more message formats in the future. To avoid duplicating this transformation logic across the system and to take advantage of transformation tools, they decided to use a

Message Broker as an intermediary between Global Bank's system and their trading partners' systems.

Like the other *Message Broker* in this design, the queue-based message broker implementation would buffer the somewhat unreliable connections between systems.

Message Broker Using Functional Integration with SOI

Even though they decided to use a message broker to communicate with trading partners, they still had to decide how to connect the *Message Broker* to the target system. *Message Brokers* can use *Data Integration* to connect at the logical data layer. For example, *Message Brokers* can connect at the logical data level by sending files by using File Transfer Protocol (FTP). Or, *Message Brokers* can use *Functional Integration* to connect at the business logic layer. For example, they can connect by using Web services.

The members of the team knew there were many ways to share functionality. The three most common methods are distributed objects (.NET Framework remoting, COM+, Common Object Request Broker Architecture (CORBA)), Remote Method Invocation (RMI); proprietary message-oriented middleware, and Web services. Some of the team members came from large enterprises where they had built logical services on top of proprietary message-oriented middleware. This approach had had worked well for them in the past. However, all the members of the team were intrigued by the possibility of using Web services because of the potential interoperability between platforms and the support of major platform vendors. Not surprisingly, they decided to connect with partners by using a kind of *Functional Integration* based on Web services: *Service-Oriented Integration (SOI)*.

To record their design decisions, the members team modified their design model to include an additional message broker and the use of *Service-Oriented Integration*, as shown in Figure 2.12. They also rationalized the communication lines with a common bus to make the model more readable.

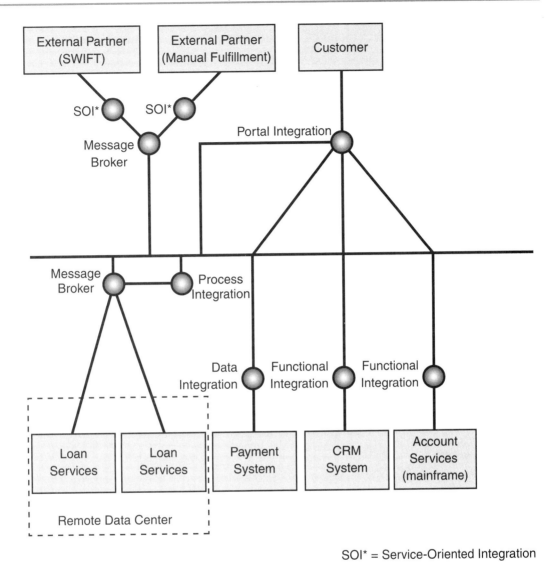

SOI* = Service-Oriented Integration

Figure 2.12
Incorporating Message Broker and Service-Oriented Integration for connections with trading partners

Models for Execute Scheduled Payment and Receive Payment Response

In addition to the pattern-based design model, the team decided to create a collaboration diagram for the Execute Scheduled Payment use case, as shown in Figure 2.13.

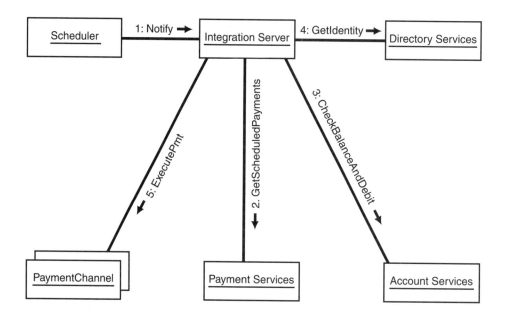

Figure 2.13
Execute Scheduled Payment collaboration diagram

The following is the flow of the use case that is shown in Figure 2.13:

1. A system scheduler in the integration server initiates this use case and begins to execute the payment.

2. The integration server requests the list of payments to make from the payment system.

3. For each payment, the integration server checks the account balance in the mainframe. The integration server debits the account if sufficient funds exist.

4. The integration server retrieves the appropriate security credentials for the message exchange.

5. The integration server sets the routing information, transforms the message to the format understood by the recipient, and then sends the message.

To show a static view of the system with boundaries, they created a port-and-wire drawing, as shown in Figure 2.14.

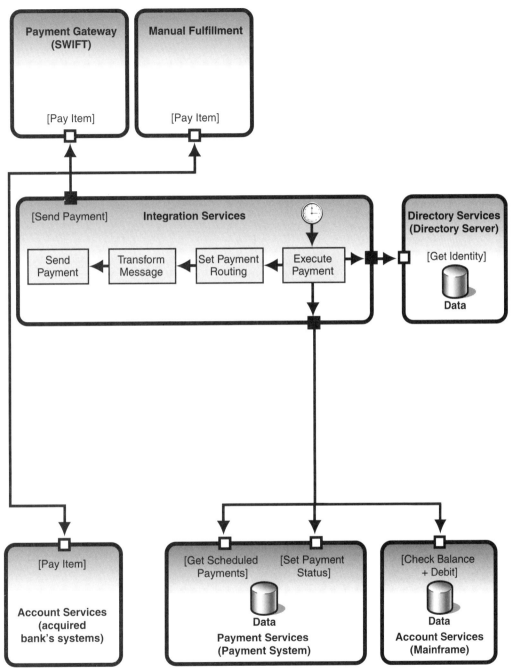

Figure 2.14
Execute Scheduled Payment use case realization

Because the Receive Payment Response use case was related to the View Scheduled Payments use case, the team created a collaboration diagram for this use case, as shown in Figure 2.15.

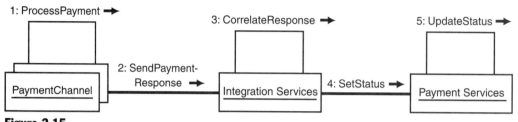

Figure 2.15
Receive Payment Response collaboration diagram

The following is the flow of the use case that is shown in Figure 2.15:

1. The precondition for this use case is that a payment message has been sent to one of the payment recipients: the SWIFT payment gateway, the manual fulfillment partner, or an acquired bank.

2. After processing the payment request, the payment recipient sends a payment response to the integration server.

3. The integration server correlates the response to the originating request.

4. If the payment failed, the integration server credits the customer account on the mainframe.

5. The integration server updates the payment record in the payment system with status and transaction ID.

Just as they did for the previous use case, the members of the team also produced a port-and-wire diagram for Receive Payment Response, as shown in Figure 2.16.

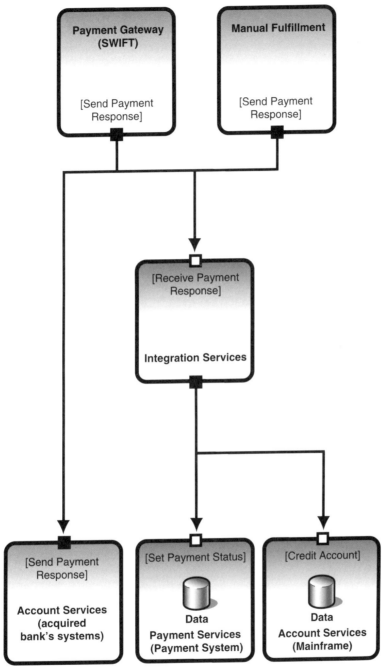

Figure 2.16
Receive Payment Response use case realization

Accessing Account Services on the Mainframe

As the members of the team reviewed the Receive Payment Response use case, they realized there was still a key issue to resolve. Both this use case and the View Scheduled Payments use case needed to access the mainframe by using *Functional Integration*, although exactly how that was going to be done was still unclear. There were clear differences in application programming and potential differences in network protocols that had to be resolved, not to mention security and transactions. How would the team manage this complexity and not let it overcomplicate the design? One team member suggested a *Gateway*.

Gateway

A *Gateway* is a design element that encapsulates outbound access to an external system. There are *Gateways* at the application level that are usually implemented as classes. For more information, see *Enterprise Solution Patterns Using Microsoft .NET* [Trowbridge03] or Martin Fowler's *Patterns of Enterprise Application Architecture* [Fowler03]. There are also *Gateways* at the integration level that are usually implemented as processes or subsystems. Based on the CTO's constraints, the members of the team knew that the system platform would be based on Microsoft technology, while the mainframe was based on an IBM CICS system. They decided to employ a *Gateway* to bridge the communication and programming model between these different technologies.

Although the team decided to use a *Gateway* to bridge technologies, the team needed to decide how to connect the application to the *Gateway*. One method was to connect the Web server directly to the mainframe *Gateway*, resulting in the least number of network hops, while placing a mainframe connection in the *perimeter network* (also known as DMZ, demilitarized zone, and screened subnet). Although this direct connection was likely to be fast, it would require deploying the connection to every Web server used for this purpose. It also made the team nervous that a hacked Web server could be used to gain mainframe access.

Another choice was to wrap the mainframe *Gateway* with a *Service Interface* [Trowbridge03] by using Web services and to then have the ASP.NET page from the Web servers make the call to the *Service Interface*. The *Service Interface* would then access the mainframe through the *Gateway*. The additional network hops and serialization would have performance implications, but this approach would also have the advantage of exposing the mainframe functionality (*Functional Integration*) to other applications in the enterprise by using a platform-independent connection (*Service-Oriented Integration*). To secure this connection, the members of the team considered a Web Services Security (WS-Security) implementation, but they realized there would be a performance tradeoff for the necessary encryption and decryption routines.

Capturing the design decisions made so far, the members of the team modified their design model to reflect the *Gateway* and *Service Interface* patterns shown in Figure 2.17.

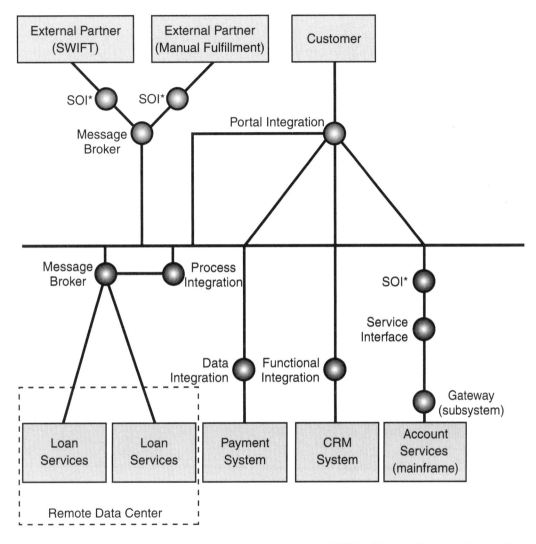

SOI* = Service-Oriented Integration

Figure 2.17
Incorporating the Gateway and Service Interface to communicate with the mainframe

Performance vs. Extensibility Tradeoff

The team knew that the account system on the mainframe was a key system to the enterprise and that many other systems and services would need to use it. Because so many systems depended on it, they also knew that performance was important.

Based on these considerations, the members of the team created test request and response messages with realistic payloads, and they created three test points that were designed to measure relevant performance.

The first test point ran from the Web server directly to the *Gateway* system. The second test point ran from the Web server to a Web services–based *Service Interface*. The *Service Interface* then used a *Gateway* system to call the mainframe. Finally, the last test point ran the same Web services–based *Service Interface* but implemented WS-Security. They stressed the system to find out where the transaction rates, concurrent users, and response times flattened. They would need to know this information to compare it to the operational requirements being captured by the project team. Using the actual performance against the requirements would help them determine how to best meet the requirement for the system to handle up to three times the anticipated load. Ultimately, it would help them make the tradeoffs in performance and flexibility that they needed to make.

At this point, the team felt they had worked out most of the necessary resource connections and communication mechanisms to meet the current use cases. They now turned their attention to the portal Web application itself.

The Portal Web Application

To refine the portal application, the team needed to decide the identification, authentication, and authorization mechanisms the Web application would use to identify a customer and authorize access. They decided to use *Intercepting Filter* and the Active Directory® directory service.

Following the steps of the View Scheduled Payments use case, a customer uses a Web browser to go to the Global Bank Web site where an *Intercepting Filter* intercepts the Web request and prompts the user for a user name and password. The Web server requests the user's credentials from the directory server, authenticates the user, associates the user with a role, and then returns a set of credentials to the Web server.

Figure 2.18 shows how the members of the team modified their pattern-based design model to document these decisions.

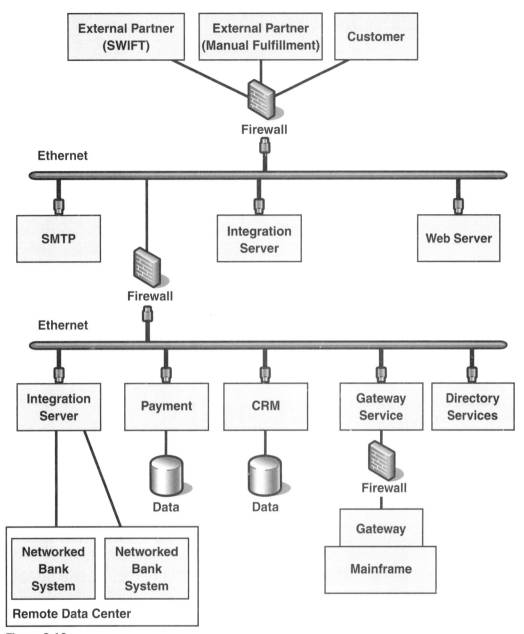

Figure 2.18

Adding Intercepting Filter and Directory Services to the design model

Refining the portal application required the use of other related patterns that solve other problems beyond integration. These problems appear almost any time you want to build a Web-based application.

Application vs. Integration Patterns

The *Intercepting Filter* pattern just introduced into the Global Bank design is not part of this *Integration Patterns* guide. Neither are the *Service Interface* or class-level gateways, such as *Service Gateway*, that also become part of the design later in this chapter. These other patterns are from *Enterprise Solution Patterns Using Microsoft .NET*, which is a recommended prerequisite to this guide. Additionally, the *Data Integration* pattern later in this guide refers to *Data Patterns*, which is another previous patterns guide. Figure 2.19 shows the relationship between these three guides.

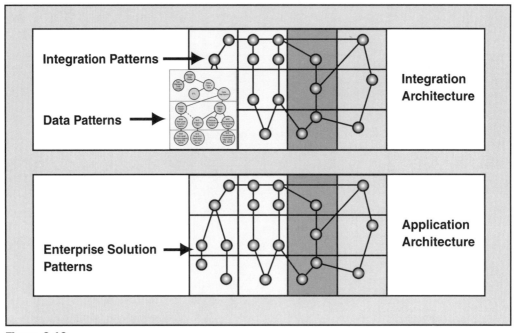

Figure 2.19
Relationship between Integration Patterns and other Microsoft patterns guides

For more information about previously released patterns, refer to the guides and their references. Now let's return to the Global Bank scenario.

Global Bank Portal Application

In the View Scheduled Payments use case, after the Web server obtains and validates security credentials, the Web server uses these credentials to issue an asynchronous request for loan information from within a synchronous method. This approach is the *Half Synch/Half Asynch* pattern [Schmidt00]. Next, the Web server uses a *Gateway* object to access the mainframe's *Gateway* subsystem and retrieve an account balance.

Note: The *Gateway* in this case is a class-level or object-level *Gateway*, whereas the *Gateway* that translates network and programming model calls to the mainframe is a subsystem-level *Gateway*. For information about class-level *Gateways*, see *Service Gateway* in *Enterprise Solution Patterns for Microsoft .NET* and *Data Table Gateway* in Martin Fowler's *Enterprise Application Architecture*. Information about subsystem-level gateways is contained later in this guide.

The Web server then uses a *Gateway* object to call the CRM system. The CRM system has encapsulated its functionality with a Web services–based *Service Interface*. Finally, the Web server checks to see whether the asynchronous request has returned a loan information response. After all this data is retrieved, the Web server then builds a presentation that displays all the requested information. If the loan system request returned any entries, the presentation appends this information to the display as optional information.

Figure 2.20 shows how the members of the team updated the pattern-based design model to document these decisions.

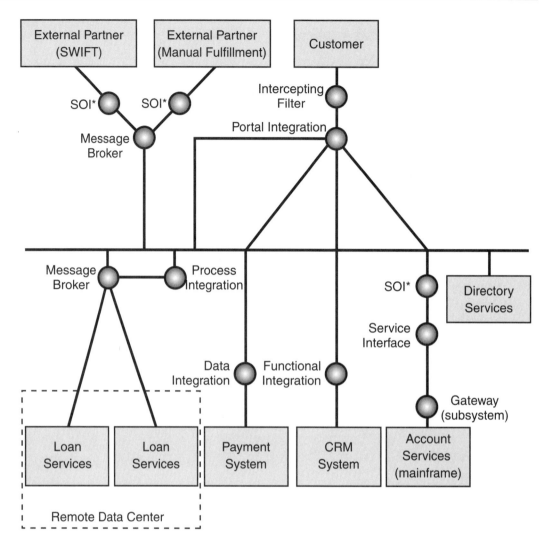

SOI* = Service-Oriented Integration

Figure 2.20
Adding Gateways to the design model

Implementing the Global Bank Scenario

If you consider all of the patterns in Figure 2.20 as high-level design elements (un-bound) and walk thorough the use cases presented so far, you can see how these elements collaborate at an abstract level to realize these use cases. To refine this design further, you must map these patterns to an implementation platform. Doing so usually requires additional iterations across the design because the chosen implementation may constrain or enable certain pattern-based design decisions.

For example, some of the implementation decisions will be constrained by decisions that the enterprise has already made. To understand these constraints, you need to understand the current technical architecture within your enterprise and make an intelligent initial allocation of functionality to server types. The members of the Global Bank team did this for their scenario and arrived at the model of their technical architecture that is shown in Figure 2.21.

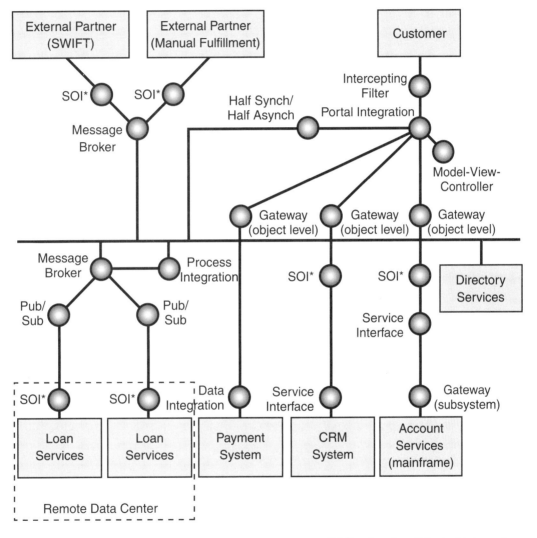

SOI* = Service-Oriented Integration

Figure 2.21

Initial Global Bank network diagram with server types

To refine this model more, the members of the team needed to decide the platform or platforms to build their system on. Given the CTO's constraints, some of the platform infrastructure decisions were easy. For example, the account information of record would reside on the mainframe. The mainframe is based on an IBM OS/390 operating system. The acquired banks ran on systems based on WebSphere Java 2 Enterprise Edition (J2EE). The rest of the systems would be based on the Microsoft platform, as shown in Figure 2.22.

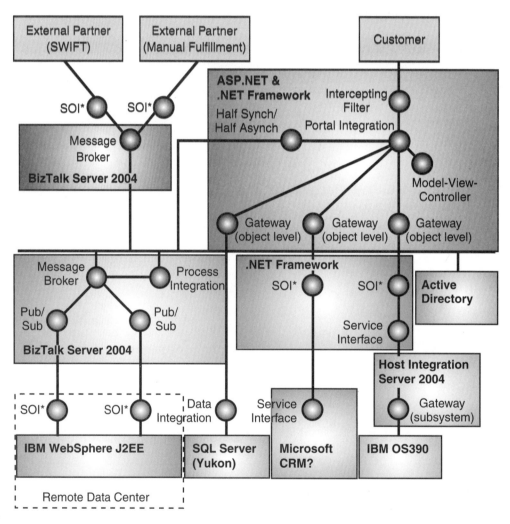

SOI* = Service-Oriented Integration

Figure 2.22
Mapping the baseline architecture and patterns to technologies

Notice the mix of Microsoft and third-party technologies, as well as the question mark associated with the Microsoft CRM system. The question mark indicates that the Global Bank team is still testing whether this system meets its requirements. The team will compare the performance test results with the actual operational requirements obtained from the project team to see if this implementation meets its performance needs.

Later in this book, you will find these patterns described in detail, with matching implementation patterns to Microsoft technologies.

Note: The preview release of this guide does not document all the patterns that appear in Figure 2.22. For example, only some architecture and design patterns have matching implementation patterns. However, some patterns have multiple implementation patterns, such as *Implementing Service-Oriented Integration with ASP.NET* and *Implementing Service-Oriented Integration with BizTalk Server 2004*.

Next Chapter

This chapter showed how the Global Bank team applied patterns to design their baseline architecture. The description moved quickly over a wide range of patterns and technical challenges. The next chapter is the first of three pattern cluster chapters that describe these patterns in greater detail. Chapter 7, "A Language of Patterns," uses a visual model to tie these patterns and their relationships together and to explain how the Global Bank team used this visual model to guide them through their design choices.

3

Integrating Layer

"Any problem in computer science can be solved with another layer of indirection." —
David Wheeler (chief programmer for the EDSAC project in the early 1950s)

As described in Chapter 1, connecting multiple systems requires an infrastructure
that moves data between the systems. However, you often want the solution to do
more than just pass data around. You want to add an additional layer of functionality on top of the functional assets that reside inside the existing applications. This
layer can automate complex business processes or provide unified access to information that is currently scattered across many systems.

How should such an integrating layer be designed, and what choices do you have?
Unfortunately, there is no single right answer for all enterprise architectures. This
chapter discusses some of the key considerations to help you to understand the
tradeoffs associated with the various alternatives and to find the most suitable
approach.

Level of Automation

A fully integrated enterprise seems to be any CIO's idea of perfection. Complex
interactions between systems are orchestrated through precisely modeled business
process definitions. Any data format inconsistencies are resolved through the integration layer. Relevant summary data is presented to executive dashboards with up-
to-the-minute accuracy. Such visions are surely enticing, but should every enterprise
set out to build such a comprehensive and inherently complicated solution?

It is not likely that anyone would build such a solution because of the time and
money it takes to build a complex enterprise integration solution. Therefore, deciding how far to go is an important step when planning an integration solution.
Automation brings efficiency and can help eliminate inconsistencies in current

business practices. However, complete automation can require an enormous upfront effort that delays the tangible benefits to the business. A simpler solution might only achieve a portion of the business benefit, but it achieves that benefit much sooner and with much less risk. For example, displaying information from multiple systems in a single screen that is divided into individual panels can increase productivity, and it does not require the system to resolve all the differences between existing systems.

Level of Abstraction

Object-oriented design principles teach the benefits of abstraction. Abstracting one system's internals from other systems allows you to change one system without affecting the other systems. This ability to limit the propagation of changes is a key consideration for integration solutions where connections can be plentiful and making changes to applications can be very difficult.

You achieve abstraction in a number of ways. For example, you can achieve abstraction by passing self-contained documents between systems. Passing a document does not instruct another system to perform a specific function, but it leaves that choice to the receiving system. Thus, if the receiving application processes the document in a different way, the originating system is not affected.

Maintaining State

Most integration solutions aim to streamline business processes such as placing an order or making a payment. These processes rely on the coordinated completion of a series of steps. When an order arrives, the order has to be validated, the inventory has to be checked, the sales tax has to be computed, and an invoice has to be generated. This type of integration requires some mechanism to track the current *state* of an order. For example, the mechanism might indicate whether the order has been validated yet and which step should be completed next. This state mechanism can be implemented in three ways:

- **Manually**. State can reside in the user's head or in a manual on the user's desk. Based on the information gathered, a user can decide which step should be performed next. This approach is less efficient and less reliable than more automated solutions, but it is also very flexible and easy to implement.

- **Inside existing applications**. The state can be kept inside existing applications. For example, after the inventory application has verified the number of items on hand, it can be programmed to send a message to the financial system to compute the sales tax. The financial system in turn might send a message to the fulfillment system to ship the goods. This approach is more efficient but also ties the applications more closely to each other.

- **In an integration layer**. You can insert a new integration layer to orchestrate the activities across multiple applications and to keep track of state. Such a layer is likely to require additional effort, but it manages all interactions from a central point without applications requiring information about each other.

Coupling

Loose coupling has become the standard of distributed applications. Loose coupling makes integrated systems less dependent on each other and allows them to evolve independently. However, loose coupling is not a panacea. Loosely coupled systems can often be difficult to understand and debug.

Semantic Dissonance

One of the key difficulties in building integration solutions is the notion of *semantic dissonance*. This term describes a situation where data that *appears* to be the same may not necessarily *mean* the same thing. For example, one system might treat a monetary figure for annual revenues as if it includes sales tax, while another system treats the monetary figure as if it does not include any taxes. Likewise, one system might define the Western Region, in the context of revenue breakdown, to include the state of Colorado. Meanwhile, another system may define Colorado as part of the Central Region. These types of semantic dissonance can be very difficult to detect and reconcile. Some rather elegant types of integration rely on the complete resolution of semantic dissonance, which might not be feasible in real-life situations. Other simpler forms of integration, such as *Portal Integration*, can accommodate ambiguity, but they do it at the expense of precision. For an in-depth discussion of data modeling and the perils of semantic dissonance, see *Data and Reality*, by William Kent [Kent00].

Choosing an Integration Layer Type

Based on these considerations, this guide identifies three approaches towards integrating layers. Each approach is presented as a pattern (see Figure 3.1):

- *Entity Aggregation*
- *Process Integration*
- *Portal Integration*

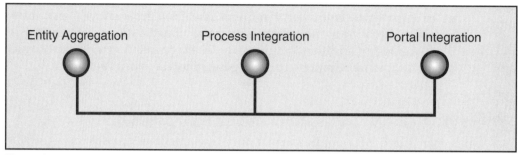

Figure 3.1
Three integration approaches

The following paragraphs briefly describe each approach to integration, in order from least to most complex.

Portal Integration

Portal Integration connects systems to provide a unified view to a user. *Portal Integration* can dramatically increase productivity because users no longer have to access multiple applications independently. Instead, they receive a comprehensive view across all systems in a visually consistent format that is illustrated in Figure 3.2. More sophisticated versions of *Portal Integration* also allow the user to make updates to individual systems or even across multiple systems.

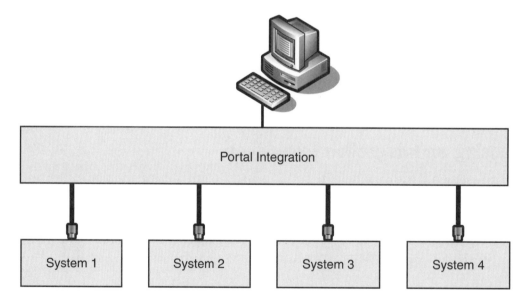

Figure 3.2
Portal Integration provides a unified view across systems

Portal Integration is often easier to implement than other, more automated alternatives. The disadvantage of the simplicity is that much of the business process and many of the rules still reside in a user's head as opposed to in a system. Nevertheless, *Portal Integration* is often a good first step towards integration.

Entity Aggregation

The main limitation of *Portal Integration* is that it aggregates information only for end users but not for applications. *Entity Aggregation* addresses this shortcoming by providing a unified data view to applications, as illustrated in Figure 3.3.

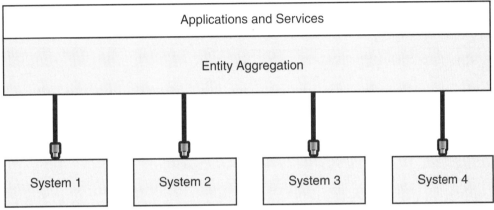

Figure 3.3
Entity Aggregation provides unified data access across systems

Entity Aggregation provides a logical representation of unified data entities across multiple data stores. Applications can interact with this representation as if it were a single data source. Thus, *Entity Aggregation* greatly simplifies the development of applications that need to access data across multiple data stores. The tradeoff for this increased integration is that the integration layer must now resolve any instances of semantic dissonance between the individual systems. Resolving such semantic dissonance and creating a unified data layer can be a major undertaking.

Process Integration

Process Integration focuses on the orchestration of interactions between multiple systems, as illustrated in Figure 3.4. As mentioned earlier, automated business processes such as straight-through processing often drive integration initiatives. It is often advisable to model these processes outside of the applications to avoid coupling the applications to each other. You can achieve this modeling by adding a *Process Integration* layer that manages the interaction across applications. This layer tracks the state of each business process instance and also enables centralized reporting. For example, this layer enables the Business Activity Monitoring (BAM) feature of Microsoft BizTalk® Server.

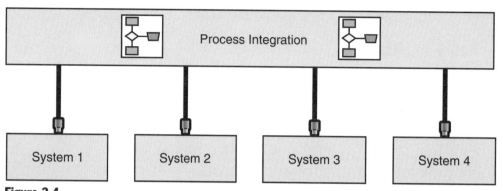

Figure 3.4
Process Integration orchestrates activities across systems

The three integration layer types are not mutually exclusive. An integration solution might use *Portal Integration* for some portions of the solution and *Process Integration* for others. Management reporting functions may be accomplished by using *Entity Aggregation*. All the approaches may be used in parallel.

Integrating Layer Patterns

The following table summarizes the three patterns just discussed and shows the corresponding implementation patterns.

Table 3.1: Integrating Layer Patterns

Pattern	Problem	Associated implementations
Entity Aggregation	How can enterprise data that is redundantly distributed across multiple repositories be effectively maintained by applications?	
Process Integration	How do you coordinate the execution of a long-running business function that spans multiple disparate applications?	*Implementing Process Integration with BizTalk Server 2004*
Portal Integration	How can users efficiently perform tasks that require access to information that resides in disparate systems?	

Entity Aggregation

Context

Enterprise-level data is distributed across multiple repositories in an inconsistent fashion. Existing applications need to have a single consistent representation of key entities which are logical groups of related data elements such as Customer, Product, Order, or Account. Moving data between these repositories may not be a viable option.

Problem

How can enterprise data that is redundantly distributed across multiple repositories be effectively maintained by applications?

Forces

The following forces have to be considered in this context:

- There may be multiple systems of record for the same entity. Business rules and processes could dictate the manner in which the system of record is determined for a given entity. For example, an employee entity is usually defined in human resource management system (HRMS) applications, in payroll applications, and in benefits applications, as well as in other systems. Each system defines its own view of an employee. However, if you are building an employee self-service portal, you need to have a complete view of what constitutes an employee and not just the bits and pieces.

- Often, semantic dissonance exists between the data values represented within the same entity across repositories. The same data element may not represent the same information in multiple repositories. For example, the data element NumberOfDaysRemaining for a project task might include all days including holidays in one repository, but it might include only workdays in another repository.

- Even when the data elements are semantically consistent, the information they represent might vary across parallel instances of the data element. In such cases, it may be difficult to determine which instance of the data element is accurate. For example, in a financial institution where there are dedicated repositories for various customer communication channels, the Available Balance entity in one repository may not be the same as the Available Balance in another repository. For example, the Available Balance in the ATM database may not be the same as the Available Balance in the repository serving the online banking channel.

- Invalid data might have crept in through other entry points into the repositories. All the entry points may not enforce all the business and data validation rules in a consistent fashion. This is typical of mainframe systems where the validation logic enforced in the screens may be outdated and therefore not enforced in the enterprise's newer applications.

- Referential integrity of data across multiple repositories may have been violated. This happens due to absent or malfunctioning data synchronization processes. In a manufacturing environment, it is critical that the product data management (PDM) system always be concurrent with the order management system. Orders entered in the order management system that have an invalid reference to a product can violate the referential integrity of the product data across the respective repositories.

- Applications may need logical subsets of the data elements that may not be available in a single repository. Therefore, business logic may have to be applied to properly group the data elements into the logical subset. For example, a banking customer maintains different kinds of information across various repositories. Personal information is stored in the customer information file repository; account balance is stored in a financial application repository; and loan information is stored in the mortgage lending repository. When the customer accesses the online banking site, the nature of the customer's request determines the subset of the information to be presented. An address change request needs data from the customer information file repository, but an inquiry on the outstanding balance for all accounts and loans requires specific data from all three repositories.

- Data synchronization processes may already exist between repositories that permit one repository to act as a front end to the other. In these cases, the synchronization mechanism is better left untouched. This is typical where database replication is used across two separate database instances that use the same underlying technology.

Solution

Introduce an *Entity Aggregation* layer that provides a logical representation of the entities at an enterprise level with physical connections that support the access and that update to their respective instances in back-end repositories.

This representation is analogous to the *Portal Integration* pattern, which presents to the end user a unified view of information that is retrieved from multiple applications. Similar to the portal layer that provides this view for the application front ends, the *Entity Aggregation* layer provides a similar view across the data in the back-end repositories as shown in Figure 3.5.

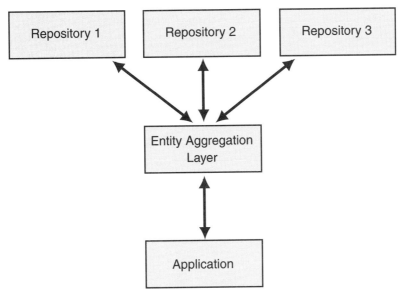

Figure 3.5
Entity Aggregation

Establishing *Entity Aggregation* involves a two-step process:

1. Defining the enterprise-wide representation that provides a consistent unified representation of the entity.

2. Implementing a physical bidirectional connection between this representation and its respective instances in the back-end repositories.

The following example explains this process in more detail.

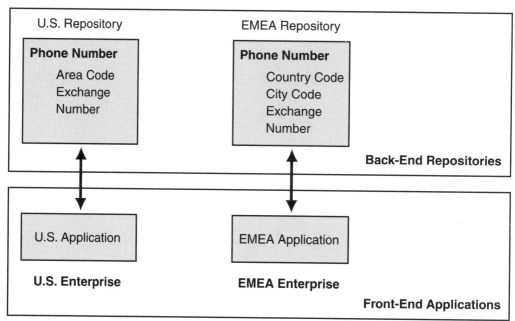

Figure 3.6
Environment without Entity Aggregation

Figure 3.6 shows two applications that access their respective back-end repositories for information about the Phone Number entity within two different enterprises: U.S. Enterprise and the Europe, Middle East, and Asia (EMEA) Enterprise. Both applications maintain the information about the phone number within their respective repositories.

Each application follows the respective domestic convention for representing phone numbers in its back-end repository. The U.S. representation of the entity includes the area codes, the exchanges, and the numbers. The EMEA representation, on the other hand, represents the same information using the country code, the city code, the exchange, and the number.

As part of a merger and acquisition exercise, these enterprises merge to form a new logical enterprise. Both applications have to access the information in both repositories. Therefore, the phone number now has to be represented at an enterprise-wide level that includes both the U.S. and the EMEA business units.

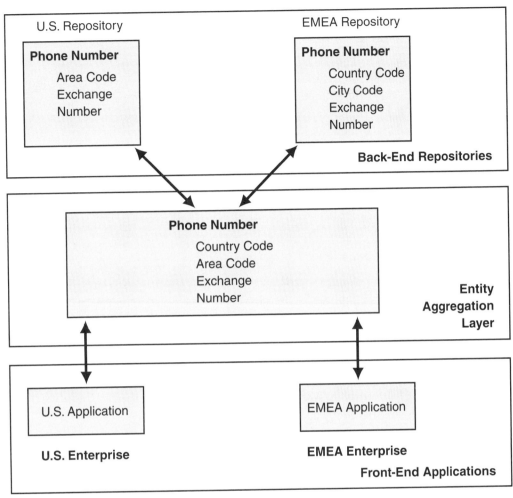

Figure 3.7
Environment with Entity Aggregation

Figure 3.7 shows the manner in which *Entity Aggregation* can facilitate the seamless representation of the Phone Number entity across both repositories.

The first step in establishing this layer involves defining the enterprise-wide representation of the Phone Number entity.

The Phone Number entity within the *Entity Aggregation* layer includes attributes that are unique to each enterprise. The Phone Number entity also includes attributes that are common across both enterprises. Thus, Country Code is included because it is an attribute unique to the EMEA enterprise. Similarly, because Exchange and Number are common attributes across both repository instances, they are also included. Even though Area Code and City Code are unique to each enterprise, their basic representation and purpose is identical. Therefore, the *Entity Aggregation* layer representation chooses to include the Area Code while using this field to store the City Code information from the EMEA repository.

The next step involves building the physical connections between the *Entity Aggregation* layer and the back-end U.S. and EMEA repositories. The technology driving these connections depends on the repository being accessed.

Approach

There are two architectural approaches to implementing *Entity Aggregation*:

- Straight-through processing
- Replication

Depending on the architectural characteristics of the entity instances to be integrated, a combination of these approaches may be required.

Straight-Through Processing

A straight-through processing approach fetches information from the respective back-end repositories in real time and correlates the information into a single unified view. This implies that the *Entity Aggregation* layer has real-time connectivity to the repositories and should be able to associate the disparate instances of the entity.

Replication

The replication of entities for use by the *Entity Aggregation* layer is required when the following conditions are true:

- Real-time connectivity to the repositories is absent.
- Complicated joins across multiple instances of the same entity across various repositories is required to provide a consistent representation.
- High performance is vital to the solution.

This approach requires a separate physical repository within the *Entity Aggregation* layer that stores data conforming to the enterprise-wide representation of the entity. The data in each back-end repository is replicated into the *Entity Aggregation* repository. This replication requires the implementation of supporting processes to enforce the business rules that validate the data being replicated. Replication should be performed both ways between the back-end repositories and the *Entity Aggregation* repositories.

In many respects, this approach offers capabilities very similar to those supported by a data warehouse. Data warehouses originally were built with the intent of summarizing transactional data that could be used for business intelligence and trends analysis. In many large enterprises today, data warehouses have transformed into yet another repository within the enterprise. They do not always serve as the enterprise-wide unified representation of the data. However, such data warehouses have a good baseline definition for enterprise-level entities, and the enterprise-wide representation of an entity can be built on top of this definition.

Design Considerations

Effective design of an *Entity Aggregation* layer requires several issues to be given due consideration. These issues may be broadly classified as follows:

- **Data representation**. Data representation includes *entity representation* and *schema reconciliation*. Entity representation is the definition of the enterprise-wide representation of the entity with its attributes and key relationships to other entities. Schema reconciliation involves reconciling the varied definitions of the underlying schema across repositories. In addition to the data representation being defined, the format in which the representation is stored must be established as well.

- **Data identification**. Introduction of a new layer of data representation requires the establishment of an appropriate mechanism that uniquely identifies each entity across all repositories, including the *Entity Aggregation* layer itself. An *entity reference* is one such mechanism.

- **Data operation**. Data operation includes the manner in which transactional operations are performed on the data. This includes Create, Read, Update, and Delete (CRUD) actions, and it includes any compensatory measures thereof. For more information about this consideration, see "Inquiry vs. Update" later in this pattern.

- **Data governance**. Data governance involves establishing ownership of ongoing maintenance and establishing *change management* processes to direct the ongoing maintenance of entities and their data elements. These processes also help refine the integration requirements by rationalizing the number of data repositories, if necessary.

Each of these issues is outlined in the following sections.

Entity Representation

There are several approaches that could be adopted to defining the enterprise-wide representation of the entity.

Entity representations may have to be custom developed to address the specific needs of the enterprise as whole. This may be the only viable option under the following circumstances:

- Existing representations within the enterprise represent only a small portion of the enterprise-wide representation of the entity and are not readily extensible to accommodate the needs of the enterprise.

- Characteristics that are unique to the enterprise cannot be properly reflected within any external representations of the entity.

However, custom representations are not always a financially viable option because they require a regeneration of the existing entities and their relationships.

Instead, a representation that is foreign to all the applications within the enterprise may be a viable approach as long as it still conforms to the core business processes. You could also use current representations that are specific to certain industries for this purpose. In other words, embracing an external representation does not necessarily entail the additional expense of procuring an application.

In other cases, you could choose the representation supported by one of the existing applications within the enterprise. ERP and CRM applications that support and drive the business processes for the enterprise are prime candidates for this approach.

While *Entity Aggregation* is all about having a single view of entities across the enterprise, entity representations within this layer might have to be adjusted to represent the nuances of individual business units. This is especially true for large international conglomerates that have been forced into being a logical enterprise through acquisitions and mergers of other enterprises that operate as autonomous business units.

Reaching a consensus on the representation within any one of these units can be a challenge. Therefore, reaching a similar consensus across all of these units can be an ambitious goal, if not an impossible one. In these cases, multiple representations (one for each operating unit) might be a more realistic and practical approach.

Schema Reconciliation

Even if the enterprise reaches consensus on the entity representation, the representation within each instance of the entity may still vary across different repositories. Different repositories can hold different schemas for the same entity. The *Entity Aggregation* layer must harmonize the subtle differences between these schemas in the following ways:

- Entity Aggregation must account for the representation of all entities held within the different repositories.

- Entity Aggregation must define a unified schema for all entities which represents a logical consolidation of all the views.

- Entity Aggregation must effect transformations between each repository's schema and the unified schema.

Note: Sometimes, the term *canonical schema* is used instead of *unified view*. This pattern uses the latter term, because canonical schema implies that all the representations share the same schema, which is not always necessary.

Figure 3.8 shows an example of customer information that is represented in more than one repository. Although the contact repository defines the contact information for a customer, the financial repository defines the credit card details for the customer. The *Entity Aggregation* layer defines a unified schema that contains all the attributes required for representing the customer entity. The *Entity Aggregation* layer also defines the mapping between the unified schema and those schemas held by the individual repositories.

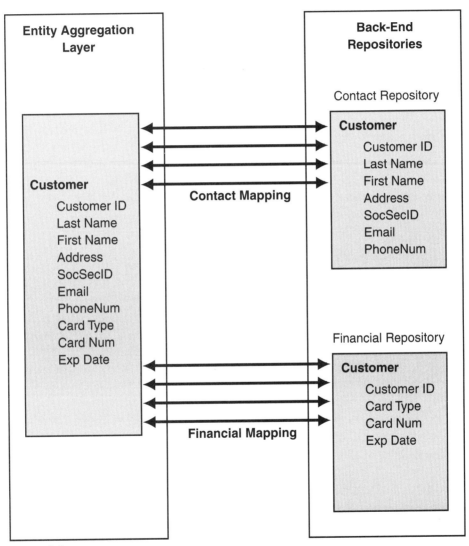

Figure 3.8
Schema reconciliation

References

Entity reference is the information required to uniquely identify an entity. Repositories that store instances of a given entity tend to maintain their own unique identifiers for their respective instances to ensure they have full control over internal data consistency. The *Entity Aggregation* layer should account for this and should be able to map references that point to a single instance. Apart from references that are held by other repositories, the *Entity Aggregation* layer might create its own reference for an entity instance. The idea here is that the *Entity Aggregation* layer maintains its own reference to an entity instance and maps this reference to the individual repository's reference. This reduces the coupling between the *Entity Aggregation* layer and individual repositories because new repositories can be introduced without affecting the *Entity Aggregation* layer's unified view.

Master Reference

Entity Aggregation layer uniquely identifies an entity instance by using a reference known as a master reference. A master reference could be:

- A reference held by one of the repositories. For example, you can designate the reference held by a CRM repository as the master reference for a customer entity.

- A new reference that the *Entity Aggregation* layer creates for the entity instance and maps to other references held by different repositories.

Inquiry vs. Update

The technological solutions available today are more robust for inquiring than they are for updating data in the back-end repositories. Updating has the inherent challenges of maintaining the synchrony of data across repositories.

Note: In the context of this pattern, deleting an entity is considered to be a form of update.

An update request usually contains two elements: a reference that uniquely identifies the instance and an update payload that contains information about the updated attributes and their respective values.

The *Entity Aggregation* layer uses entity references across all the repositories to perform the inquiries and updates. Although the *Entity Aggregation* layer maintains the entity reference, the references that are unique to each repository have to be determined before the update is made to the back-end repositories. For more information, see "References."

Compensation

The process of performing a compensating action can be manual or automatic. Business process owners have a strong influence on the manner in which compensating actions should be implemented.

If one of the systems fails to handle the update request, the *Entity Aggregation* layer should be able to handle this business exception by using one of the following approaches:

- Request a rollback on all the other updates that have already been made.
- Run a compensating transaction to reverse the effects of the successful updates that were already completed.

Ownership

Although the *Entity Aggregation* layer represents the unified view of an entity, it is certainly possible to store different fragments of an entity in different systems. Therefore, the system of record is not the same for all fragments.

For example, employee information could be distributed across the payroll and benefits repositories. It is also possible that some information may be owned by multiple systems. For example, attributes such as LastName and FirstName are probably represented in more than one system. In this case, the *Entity Aggregation* layer should designate a system as an *authoritative source* for attributes that are represented in more than one system.

This has several implications for the behavior that occurs during inquiries and updates. Attributes will always be fetched from the authoritative source. If the same attribute is represented by another system, those values will be ignored by the *Entity Aggregation* layer. Updates, on the other hand, have different semantics. When the *Entity Aggregation* layer receives an update request for an entity, the updates should be propagated to all the constituent systems of record.

Change Management

Processes have to be put in place to coordinate changes across all the repositories and the *Entity Aggregation* layer. In addition to ensuring active participation from the different business process owners and information technology (IT) representatives for each repository, a key step in this process is to ensure that the integrity of the enterprise-wide representation of the entity is not compromised.

Three types of changes to the underlying repositories can directly and significantly affect the *Entity Aggregation* layer:

- **Configuration**. The repository configuration could undergo changes. This would include redeployment of the repository to a new physical location or to a different server. Configuration parameters such as the scheduled downtime for maintenance could affect connectivity to the *Entity Aggregation* layer as well. In an ideal environment, only the *Entity Aggregation* layer is directly affected by this change because connections between repositories usually do not exist. However, the other repositories could be indirectly affected by these changes through their connectivity to the *Entity Aggregation* layer.

- **Data model**. The data model could undergo changes within the repository. The enterprise-wide representation of entities supported by the *Entity Aggregation* layer is significantly affected by these changes. Other repositories that store information in the same domain are affected also.

- **Data values**. Changes to transactional data in a repository have the least impact, if any, on the *Entity Aggregation* layer and on other repositories. However, changes to reference data that spans repositories or to reference data that is used by the *Entity Aggregation* layer have a significant impact.

Example

Figure 3.9 shows a scenario where the Stock Trade entity is partitioned across systems based on geographical constraints. Applications that analyze the trends in a given industry require a complete view of the trades across geographical boundaries and systems.

The *Entity Aggregation* layer consolidates the view across geographical boundaries so that the partitioning of data across the repositories is transparent to the applications that perform trends analysis.

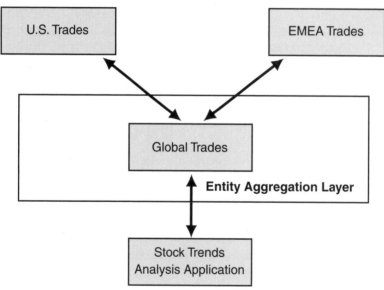

Figure 3.9
Stock trades scenario

Resulting Context

Entity Aggregation has the following benefits and liabilities:

Benefits

- **Consensus**. *Entity Aggregation* forces consensus across business and functional units on the manner in which entities are represented at an enterprise-level.
- **Single view**. *Entity Aggregation* enables a single view of key business entities such as Customer, Account, Product, and (in the case of healthcare) Patient.
- **Improved access to information**. An enterprise-level view of key business entities enables applications to have immediate access to the information pertinent to these entities. Access to information is not constrained by the repositories that house them.
- **Reduced semantic dissonance**. *Entity Aggregation* eliminates semantic dissonance across existing applications that work on the same data elements from multiple repositories.
- **Central location**. *Entity Aggregation* supports a central location for validating data that is populated into the repositories.
- **Reduced change impact**. *Entity Aggregation* reduces the potential impact of changes to the back-end repositories. Depending on the nature of the changes being made, the *Entity Aggregation* layer can continue to serve the needs of the applications while these changes are in progress.

Liabilities

- **Additional layer**. *Entity Aggregation* introduces an additional architectural layer that could adversely affect end-to-end performance of the solution.
- **Consensus**. *Entity Aggregation* requires consensus across business units on the definition of the enterprise-wide representation of entities.
- **Reengineering applications**. Existing applications that are tightly coupled to a given set of repositories would have to be reengineered to accommodate the new architectural layer. Additionally, it is not always possible to reengineer some applications—especially packaged solutions.

Testing Considerations

The following testing considerations apply when adding an *Entity Aggregation* layer:

- Depending on the degree to which the *Entity Aggregation* layer is adopted, all valid combinations of applications and their back-end repositories would have to be regression tested.

- Existing test cases may have to be revised to reflect the business rules being exercised in the *Entity Aggregation* layer.

- Test data available within a given repository must be repurposed to accommodate the enterprise-wide representation of entities in the *Entity Aggregation* layer.

- Simultaneous connectivity from the *Entity Aggregation* layer to all the back-end repositories has to be tested. In the absence of *Entity Aggregation*, connectivity would have been a requirement only between the various application-repository pairs.

Security Considerations

The *Entity Aggregation* layer is effective at providing access to information that is pertinent to business entities at an enterprise level. However, applications might be able to obtain access to repositories that may not have been available prior to the introduction of the *Entity Aggregation* layer. Even though applications might still operate on the same data elements, they might access new repositories through the *Entity Aggregation* layer. Access privileges for various roles within these applications have to be managed at the *Entity Aggregation* layer.

Operational Considerations

There are two separate operational aspects to the *Entity Aggregation* layer:

- The *Entity Aggregation* layer has to be operated and monitored as a repository that houses the enterprise-wide representation of entities. Less maintenance of the underlying data in the *Entity Aggregation* layer is required for the straight-through processing solution than for the replication solution. In the replication solution, the operational aspects that apply to the data in the repositories also apply to the *Entity Aggregation* layer. In either case, similar operational aspects apply if the *Entity Aggregation* layer maintains the entity references that are external to all the repositories.

- Network connectivity between the applications and the *Entity Aggregation* layer and network connectivity between the *Entity Aggregation* layer and the repositories are critical components of the overall solution. The straight-through processing solution, in particular, requires concurrent connectivity to all the repositories.

Known Uses

Enterprise Information Integration is another industry term that is used to identify the enterprise-wide representation of a logical data model that houses the key business entities that have bidirectional physical connections to the back-end repositories where data is stored.

Some companies provide a logical metadata modeling approach that allows enterprises to reuse models and data for real-time aggregation and caching with update synchronization. All these companies initially provided query-only capability, but they are slowly beginning to support bidirectional transfer of data between the *Entity Aggregation* layer and the back-end repositories.

Related Patterns

Given that the *Entity Aggregation* layer provides a view of data that is distributed across repositories, *Data Integration* is closely related to this pattern.

Process Integration

Context

You have multiple disparate systems, and each of those systems is part of an overall business function. For example, a business function such as processing an incoming order may require the participation of the customer management system, the inventory system, the shipping system, and one or more financial systems. The business could operate more efficiently if the systems could be integrated so that the business function could be completed automatically.

Problem

How do you coordinate the execution of a long-running business function that spans multiple disparate applications?

Forces

To solve this problem, you have to balance the following considerations and forces:

- To implement the overall business function, you could have one system directly call the system that performs the next step, as defined in the business function. However, this approach encodes the sequence of interactions into the individual systems. Creating this dependency in each system makes changing the sequence more error-prone and also limits your ability to reuse systems in multiple contexts.

- The change and maintenance cycle of a complex business function is likely to be different from the change cycle of the individual business functions that reside inside the applications. For example, financial functions such as computing sales tax or posting revenues are typically subject to infrequent, but mandatory, legal or regulatory changes. In contrast, the overall execution of a business function might be changed much more frequently based on business and marketing strategies.

- Complex business functions can often take days or weeks to complete. However, most functions that are available in existing applications are synchronous; that is, the caller has to wait while the application performs the requested function. This type of synchronous interaction is not well-suited to long-running business functions because one application could spend a significant amount of time waiting for another application to complete the requested function.

- A longer time span of execution increases the likelihood that an application might fail during the execution of the business function. If one application fails, portions of the overall function may have to be reverted so that all systems can be returned to a consistent state.

- Because a complex business function can take a long time to execute, it is likely that a new request will arrive while the previous one is still being serviced. To improve response times, the solution should be able to handle multiple concurrent executions of the function. Many applications are not designed for this type of concurrent execution.

- Modeling business processes inside a software component can be difficult if the processes are not well understood or documented. In many businesses, users make decisions based on experience rather than documented business rules.

Solution

Define a business process model that describes the individual steps that make up the complex business function. Create a separate process manager component that can interpret multiple concurrent instances of this model and that can interact with the existing applications to perform the individual steps of the process.

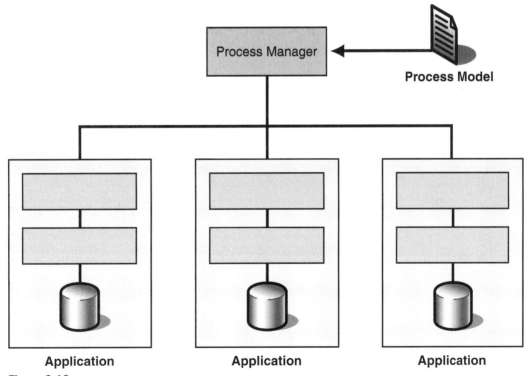

Figure 3.10

Process Integration with a process manager component directing applications according to a process model

For each incoming request for the business function, the process manager creates a new process instance based on the process model. Each instance maintains the current state of the process plus any additional information that is needed for the business process to continue. Creating individual process instances allows the process manager to execute many business functions in parallel.

After one application completes its business function, the process manager determines which function to execute next based on the state of the process instance. Therefore, each participating application can operate individually without any knowledge of the sequence of steps defined in the process model.

The process manager maintains this state even if a specific application is temporarily unavailable. As a result, the overall execution of the business function is not stopped if a specific application is temporarily unavailable. Instead, the business function can continue after the application is back online.

The process manager interacts with the individual applications by way of *Data Integration*, *Functional Integration*, or *Presentation Integration*, depending on the nature of the interaction and the architecture of the application. Therefore, *Process Integration* resembles a *composite application* built on top of existing business functions that reside in existing applications.

Process Integration provides a clean separation between the definition of the process in the process model, the execution of the process in the process manager, and the implementation of the individual functions in the applications. This separation allows the application functions to be reused in many different processes.

The separation of process model and process manager also allows the process manager to be domain independent because it only has to interpret the basic constructs that form a process model. These constructs manage the parallel execution of multiple steps, and they typically comprise sequences, decision points, forks, and joins. Using these constructs, enterprises can create a model at the business level without having to understand the internals of the process manager or the individual applications.

Process Integration involves collaboration between the components that are described in Table 3.2.

Table 3.2: Process Integration Components

Component	Responsibilities	Collaborations
Process model	Defines the sequence of steps that make up the business instances.	The process manager interprets the process model in separate process function.
Process manager	– Manages multiple instances of the process model and their current state. – Maps the steps defined in the process model to the business functions that reside in the applications.	– Interprets the process model. – Directs applications through steps according to the process model.
Application	Executes a specific business function.	None.

The process manager typically exposes an external interface so that the business process defined by the process model can be initiated by a user, by business partners, or by another application. Correspondingly, the interface can take the form of a user interface or the form of an application programming interface (API) that can be made available to other applications by using *Functional Integration,* making it essentially indistinguishable from a simple application. Therefore, this business process can be used as part of another overarching business process that is defined using a higher-level process model. As a result, process managers and applications can be linked in a recursive fashion. Figure 3.11 shows a hierarchy of process managers and applications.

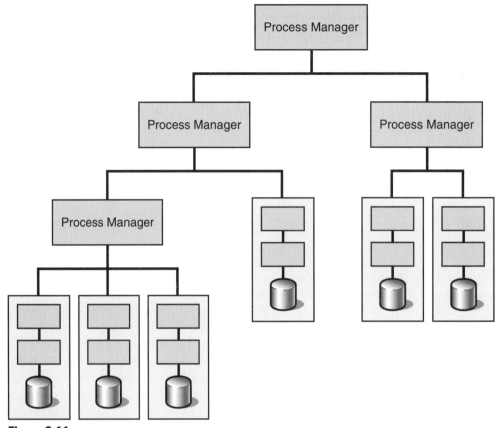

Figure 3.11
Hierarchy of process managers and applications

Implementation Details

At first glance, the process manager resembles a traditional application that implements business logic. The only difference is that the process manager takes advantage of functions implemented in existing systems. However, the fact that the execution of the business function can take hours or days places specific requirements on the process manager. Specifically, a process manager typically must be able to:

- Correlate messages from external systems with the instance of the business process they are intended for.
- Support long-running transactions.
- Handle exceptions raised by individual steps in the business process, and take appropriate action in the event of these exceptions.
- Provide compensation logic to undo actions committed earlier in the business process if a failure occurs in the business process.

Correlating Messages and Process Instances

Orchestration of processes involves messages sent to external systems and received from external systems. These external systems implement the actions that make up the business process. At any time, there are likely to be many instances of the business process running at once, and any message that is received must be correlated with the correct instance of the business process that it was intended for.

Transactions

Transactions provide encapsulation of individual atomic actions. A transaction is an action or a series of actions that transform a system from one consistent state to another. When dealing with long-running business functions, it is useful to distinguish between two kinds of transactions: atomic transactions and long-running transactions. When you use *Process Integration,* your design must support both kinds of transactions.

Atomic transactions are the same kind of transactions as those found in databases. They adhere to a set of properties, commonly called the Atomicity, Consistency, Isolation, and Durability (ACID) properties. This type of transaction requires transactional resources, such as a database update or the sending of a message, that permit you to automatically roll back changes if the transaction is stopped. Atomic transactions are suited only for short-running portions of the overall process.

Long-running transactions are used when one or more of the following conditions are true:

- The transactions must occur over an extended time period, and the transaction cannot be supported by atomic transactions.
- The actions involved in the transaction are not themselves transactional, but you want to group these actions into more granular atomic units of work that can exist across time, organizations, and applications.
- Other transactions are grouped within a transaction. Both atomic and long-running transactions may be grouped in a long-running transaction, but other transactions cannot be grouped in an atomic transaction.

For long-running transactions, you must allow the user to stop the process midstream. When the process stops, the system will persist data regarding the completed actions and the intermediate states. After the process restarts, the application will reload this intermediate state to allow the process to continue from the point where it stopped.

Handling Exceptions and Compensating Transactions

When external applications are invoked to implement a specific action, a variety of errors can occur. These errors cause error codes to be sent in messages that are returned by the external systems, and these errors cause exceptions to be thrown.

Status code errors can be handled by conditional logic inside the process model. This approach is natural, but can lead to an unwieldy control flow if all possible error conditions have to be covered. Errors in the form of exceptions can be handled by exception handlers attached to the scope in which the exception occurred. This scope can be the entire process model, or it can be a specific subsection. If an exception occurs within this scope, the exception handler is automatically invoked without the process designer having to explicitly model each individual error condition.

Some of these errors require the application to revert the transaction state to the state before the long-running transaction started. When these errors occur, the application issues a compensating transaction.

Example

Process Integration is commonly used to streamline the execution of a sequence of tasks. One popular application in the financial industry is the notion of straight-through processing (STP). STP describes the automated end-to-end processing of transactions such as trades from inception to settlement.

As described in the solution section, *Process Integration* can also be used to provide an aggregate service to other applications. For example, consider a service that makes concurrent updates to multiple data sources as defined in *Entity Aggregation*. The implementation of such a service requires *Process Integration* internally to manage transactional integrity, partial failure situations, and compensation actions.

Process Integration is such a common need that standards committees and working groups are defining standard languages to describe process models. Examples of such languages are:

- Business Process Modeling Language (BPML)
- Business Process Execution Language (BPEL)
- Web Services Choreography Interface (WSCI)

Resulting Context

Process Integration results in the following benefits and liabilities:

Benefits

- **Maintainability**. Creating a separate process integration layer allows users to define and maintain the business process independent from the implementation of the individual functions. This increases maintainability and reduces the skill set requirements for the personnel who maintain the process definition.

- **Reusability**. Because the existing applications are not dependent on the process management layer, the functions inside these applications can be reused in multiple process definitions.

- **Flexibility**. The process manager can support a variety of configurations that would be difficult to implement in many traditional programming models. For example, parallel execution of multiple tasks, synchronization points, timeouts, and escalations are all configurations that would be difficult to implement in a traditional programming model. Supporting a variety of configurations gives the process manager the flexibility to adapt to many different business requirements.

- **Reporting capability**. Because the process instances are maintained centrally, it becomes feasible to extract statistical information that spans multiple process steps and process instances. Such reports can provide answers to questions such as "How long does it take on average to fulfill an order?" or "How many orders are on hold due to insufficient inventory?" This type of reporting can be instrumental in making informed business decisions.

Liabilities

- **Potential bottleneck**. Managing a large number of process instances in a central process manager component can present a run-time bottleneck. However, in most cases, the parallel execution of multiple process manager instances can alleviate this threat while maintaining the benefit of central configurability.

- **Temptation to overuse**. This liability is the flip side of the flexibility inherent in *Process Integration* solutions. Because *Process Integration can* be used to solve nearly any integration problem, some people take this as an indication that each and every integration problem should be solved using *Process Integration*. This is not true. Using *Process Integration* frivolously can lead to overarchitected and sometimes inefficient solutions—for example, in cases where a *Message Broker* would be perfectly appropriate to address the requirements.

- **Complexity**. A generic process manager can be difficult to build because it has to deal with concurrency, checkpoints, and recoverability. For these reasons, a commercial process manager should be used whenever possible. If a commercial component is not available, the cost of building the process manager should be carefully weighed against the cost of making changes to the process model.

Testing Considerations

Separating the process definition from the functions provided by the applications allows you to test each function individually by creating a simple test driver that only calls one specific function and that verifies the results, as shown in Figure 3.12.

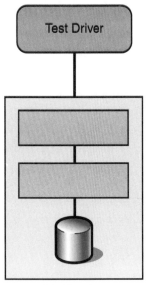

Application

Figure 3.12
Test driver

Likewise, you can test the process manager by creating placeholder implementations, or *stubs*, of the actual services while providing test triggers to the process manager (see Figure 3.13).

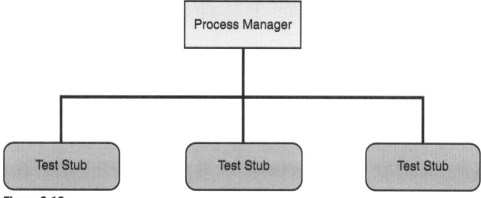

Figure 3.13
Using stubs to test the process manager

Related Patterns

For more information, see the following related patterns:

- *Implementing Process Integration with BizTalk Server 2004*. This pattern uses the Global Bank scenario to show how you can use BizTalk Server 2004 to implement *Process Integration*.

- *Process Manager* pattern [Hohpe04]. *Process Manager* describes the internal function and implementation of the process manager component.

Acknowledgments

[Hohpe04] Hohpe, Gregor; Bobby Woolf, *Enterprise Integration Patterns: Designing, Building, and Deploying Messaging Solutions*. Addison-Wesley, 2004.

[Ruh01] Ruh, William. *Enterprise Application Integration. A Wiley Tech Brief*. Wiley, 2001.

Implementing Process Integration with BizTalk Server 2004

Context

You are developing new solutions that reuse functionality provided by existing applications and systems in your enterprise. The individual mechanisms to integrate with each of these applications have already been defined, so now you use Microsoft BizTalk Server 2004 to implement *Process Integration* to coordinate and manage the overall interaction between all these systems.

Background

Global Bank is developing new banking solutions, including an electronic bill payment system. Global Bank wants to enable customers to schedule payments from their accounts. These scheduled payments will be batch-processed daily by the bank's systems.

The application to be built, which processes the customer's scheduled payments (Execute Scheduled Payments use case), will reuse functionality supplied by various bank systems including the Microsoft SQL Server database, various Web services, and the Microsoft Host Integration Server interface to the bank mainframe (see *Implementing Gateway with Host Integration Server 2004*). The Execute Scheduled Payments application will also interact with internal, external, and manual payment systems.

Global Bank has already defined the individual integration mechanisms for each of these applications and systems. Now Global Bank wants to use BizTalk Server 2004 orchestration to manage interactions across all the systems that constitute the composite electronic bill payment business process.

BizTalk Server orchestration is a good choice for describing complex process models. Orchestration is a .NET Framework language, just like C# and Microsoft Visual Basic® .NET. Orchestration provides programming constructs such as loops, decision statements, program scope, transactions, and exception processing semantics. Orchestrations are compiled to produce .NET Framework common language runtime (CLR) libraries that are hosted by the BizTalk Server runtime. The BizTalk Server runtime essentially acts as an application server for long-running business applications.

Implementation Strategy

Global Bank developers have already implemented the individual integration mechanisms required to interact with each of the systems that are involved in the Execute Scheduled Payments solution. You now define a process model that describes the sequence of steps that make up the overall application. This process model is defined and implemented as a BizTalk Server orchestration. Figure 3.14

shows the relationship between the orchestration (the process model), the existing systems, and the BizTalk Server runtime (the process manager).

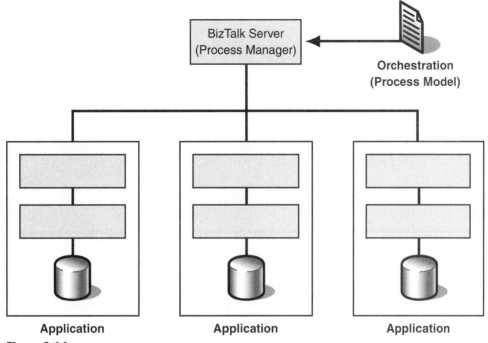

Figure 3.14
BizTalk Server orchestration directing applications according to a process model

To develop the Execute Scheduled Payments application, you use BizTalk Orchestration Designer to define the process model. Orchestration Designer presents a visual design and development environment that defines the process flow separately from the implementation of the individual steps in the process. You then link each action in the process flow with the implementation of that action. The implementation is usually represented as an interaction with an application that is external to the orchestration itself.

Each incoming request to execute a payment creates a new instance of the Execute Scheduled Payments orchestration. These orchestration instances run in parallel, maintain their own state, and maintain any additional information that is needed for execution. The orchestration engine uses the orchestration to determine the external applications to invoke and the sequence in which to call them. The external applications are invoked synchronously or asynchronously depending on the nature of the interaction and the architecture of the external application. For example, an external application is invoked synchronously when updating status information in the database and asynchronously when sending payment requests to external systems.

To completely model a process, an orchestration must do more than invoke each of the external applications in sequence. The orchestration must be able to do the following:

- Correlate messages from external systems with the instance of the business process they are intended for.
- Support long-running application instances.
- Handle exceptions raised by individual steps in the application and take appropriate action when these exceptions occur.
- Provide compensation logic to undo actions committed earlier in the business process if a failure occurs.

BizTalk Server orchestration provides functionality to support each of these requirements, as described in the following sections.

Correlating Messages and Process Instances

Orchestration of processes such as Execute Scheduled Payments involves messages sent to external systems and received from external systems. These external systems implement the actions that make up the business process. At any time, there are likely to be many instances of the business process running at the same time. Each instance maintains its own state, and any message that is received must be correlated with the correct instance of the business process that it was intended for. For example, Execute Scheduled Payments receives a payment acknowledgment message from a payment authority to indicate that a specific payment has been processed. For more information, see, "Step 6: Sending the Payment and Receiving an Acknowledgment," in the "Example" section.

To set up correlation within an orchestration, you start by defining a correlation type that specifies one or more message properties. The combination of these properties is guaranteed to be unique across all instances of the business process. These properties map to fields in the outgoing and incoming messages. For example, SSN could be a property that occurs in both the outgoing message and the incoming message, albeit in a different location in each message.

To map the properties to fields in the outgoing message, you create an instance of this correlation type called a *correlation set*. This correlation set is then initialized (unique values are assigned to the properties in the correlation type) by specifying this correlation set as the **Initializing Correlation Set** for a **Send** shape in the orchestration. This means that when a message is transmitted by way of this **Send** shape, the correlation set will be initialized using the correct fields in the message (SSN, for example).

Lastly, you configure the matching **Receive** shape to use this correlation set as the **Following Correlation Set**. This means that when a message is sent back to the orchestration, the message will be passed to the instance of the orchestration that has a correlation set with properties that match the properties in the message.

Long-Running Transactions

A long-running transaction contains persistence points that are also restart points if a failure occurs. BizTalk Server 2004 implements transactions, compensation, and exception handling within a **Scope** shape. The **Scope** shape supports both atomic and long-running transactions. For more information about atomic and long-running transactions, see "Transactions" in the *Process Integration* pattern.

The Execute Scheduled Payments orchestration uses long-running transactions to handle long-lived interactions with external systems that may fail or time out. For more information, see "Step 6: Sending the Payment and Receiving an Acknowledgment" in the "Example" section.

Handling Exceptions and Compensating Transactions

When external applications are invoked to implement a specific action, a variety of errors can occur. These errors may cause exceptions to be thrown. For example, when an orchestration calls a Web service, the Web service can raise an exception that is passed back to the BizTalk orchestration process. Exceptions are handled by exception handlers that are attached to the scope within which the exception occurred. The outermost scope in a BizTalk orchestration is that of the orchestration itself. Additional scopes can be nested within an orchestration by using the **Scope** shape.

Exception handling logic can be defined for the entire orchestration as a separate execution flow within the Orchestration Designer. It is also possible to encapsulate various action shapes within a **Scope** shape and to define an exception handling boundary around these shapes so that the shape has its own unique exception handling properties. An example of this is shown in "Step 4: Handling Exceptions."

When an error occurs, an orchestration may need to reverse the effects of transactions that occurred earlier in the orchestration, and that have already been committed. To achieve this, the orchestration executes a compensation block, which specifies how the transaction can be reversed. Compensation also reverses actions that are not transactional, such as sending a message.

For example, an orchestration contains a scope with an atomic transaction that commits and writes changes to a database. This first scope is followed by another scope with a long-running transaction. When an error occurs in this second scope, the error aborts the long-running transaction and then starts exception handling logic for the long-running transaction. However, the effects of the first atomic transaction cannot be rolled back, because they have already been committed.

Instead, a compensating transaction (series of actions which compensate for the original transaction) is required to remove the changes from the database.

Implementing the Execute Scheduled Payments Orchestration

The following steps form the general guidelines for implementing and deploying an orchestration like the Execute Scheduled Payments orchestration:

1. **Designing the orchestration**. You use BizTalk Orchestration Designer to lay out the sequence of actions that define the Execute Scheduled Payments application. No implementation is specified at this stage.

2. **Designing the schemas used by the orchestration**. You use the BizTalk Schema Editor in Visual Studio .NET to define schemas for all messages received or sent by the orchestration so that the message can be read or written by the orchestration.

3. **Adding implementation to actions in the orchestration**. You use BizTalk Orchestration Designer to link the steps in the orchestration with the implementation of those steps. This may involve sending and receiving messages by using **Send** and **Receive** shapes to and from external systems. Or, it may involve sending and receiving messages by specifying small code segments in **Expression** shapes.

4. **Adding error and exception handling**. You add error and exception handling by using **Decision** shapes or by using **Exception** blocks that are attached to **Scope** shapes.

5. **Building and deploying the orchestration**. An orchestration has to be deployed to the global assembly cache and to the BizTalk Management database before it can be executed. The orchestration is deployed by using the BizTalk Deployment Wizard.

6. **Setting up send and receive ports**. Before the orchestration can be started, you use BizTalk Explorer from within Visual Studio .NET to create BizTalk receive and send ports, and to bind them to the logical port definitions referenced by the orchestration.

7. **Setting up the receive adapter**. The SQL Server adapter is configured to periodically execute a stored procedure that returns XML records to the orchestration based on a specified query. The SQL Server Adapter is typically configured by using the BizTalk Explorer from within Visual Studio .NET.

8. **Starting the orchestration**. Starting the orchestration causes it to actively listen to incoming messages. The service is now live and executes an instance of the orchestration for each message that is delivered by the SQL Server Adapter.

Example

This example follows a Global Bank developer through the process of creating the Execute Scheduled Payments scenario and describes the specific configurations that are necessary to meet Global Bank's requirements.

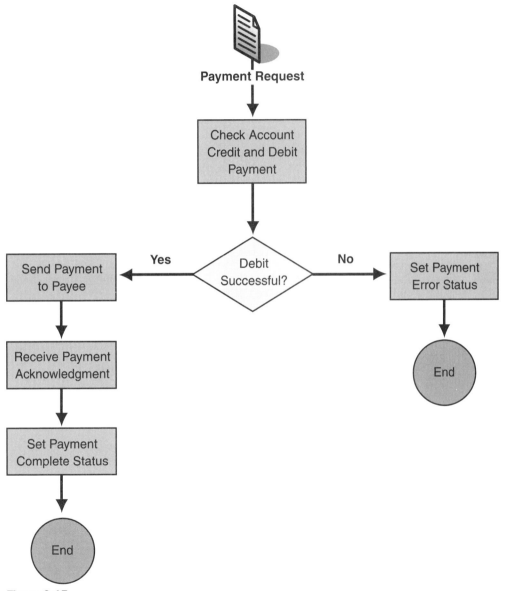

Figure 3.15
High-level view of the Execute Scheduled Payments business process

To implement the Execute Scheduled Payments process, the Global Bank developer starts by designing the process model that describes the solution. Figure 3.15 shows a high-level sketch of the process flow for this solution. The developer uses this process model design to develop the Execute Scheduled Payments orchestration in the BizTalk Server Orchestration Designer. Initially, the developer just specifies the process flow in the orchestration and then links the actions in the orchestration to the implementation of those actions. For example, actions may be implemented by a call to an external Web method.

The following steps describe in detail how the Execute Scheduled Payments orchestration implements the process model. They also describe how the completed orchestration is compiled and deployed in the Global Bank environment.

Note: Although the following steps adhere to the general implementation and deployment guidelines presented earlier in "Implementing the Execute Scheduled Payments Orchestration," the order and number of the steps vary slightly. The sample steps that follow reflect both the order in which the developer creates the orchestration in BizTalk Server and the order in which BizTalk Server presents the orchestration in the user interface. The developer also performs some steps such as error handling multiple times, according to accepted practices.

Step 1: Receiving a Payment Request

The first shape in the orchestration is a **Receive** shape, which receives payment messages (requests). This **Receive** shape is linked to an orchestration port called **ReceivePaymentRequest** (see Figure 3.16).

Figure 3.16
The first stage in the orchestration is receiving the Payment message

Whenever a payment request message is received, a new instance of the orchestration is created and the message is received by this port. For information about how these messages are generated, see "Step 10: Setting Up the SQL Server Adapter."

Step 2: Designing the Payment Message Schema

The developer needs to specify an XML schema that describes the payment message so that it can be processed by the orchestration. Normally, a developer would use the BizTalk Schema Editor to design a schema. However, in this case, the payment messages are generated by using a SQL query to create an XML record set (see "Step 10: Setting Up the SQL Server Adapter"). The developer can use the SQL Server Adapter Wizard to automatically generate a schema that is appropriate for this query. Figure 3.17 shows the Global Bank payment schema as viewed in the BizTalk Schema Editor.

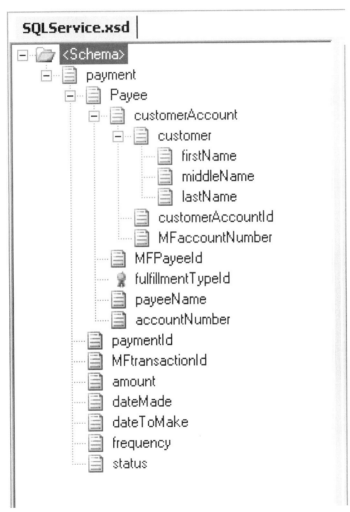

Figure 3.17
The generated payment schema in the BizTalk Schema Editor

When the SQL query is executed, multiple payment records are typically returned. The payment records must be split into separate records so that each payment can be handled individually. The developer uses the BizTalk Schema Editor to create another schema that is known as an envelope schema. The envelope schema represents the set of payments. When the receive port is configured to use these schemas, the XML recordset that is generated is automatically split into individual XML records.

Step 3: Calling a Web Service to Debit the Account

Next, the customer's account is checked to ensure that it has sufficient funds to pay the bill. The appropriate amount is then debited from the account. The functionality for these steps exists on the mainframe and has been exposed as a Web service through Host Integration Server (see *Implementing Gateway with Host Integration Server 2004*).

To implement this part of the orchestration, the developer uses the Add Web Reference Wizard to add a Web reference to the project, just as he or she would add a Web reference to any other .NET Framework application. Adding the Web reference creates an orchestration port that is bound to the Web service. Figure 3.18 shows the results of adding a Web reference to an orchestration; the DebitPort is the port bound to the Web service, and **CheckBalanceAndDebit** and **CreditAccount** represent some of the Web methods that this Web service implements.

In addition, the Add Web Reference Wizard generates XML schemas that represent the request-response messages for each of the Web methods exposed by the Web service. The Add Web Reference Wizard also creates corresponding orchestration message types. The developer then creates instances of the orchestration message types CheckBalanceAndDebit_request and CheckBalanceAndDebit_response. These instances are called DebitRequest and DebitResponse respectively.

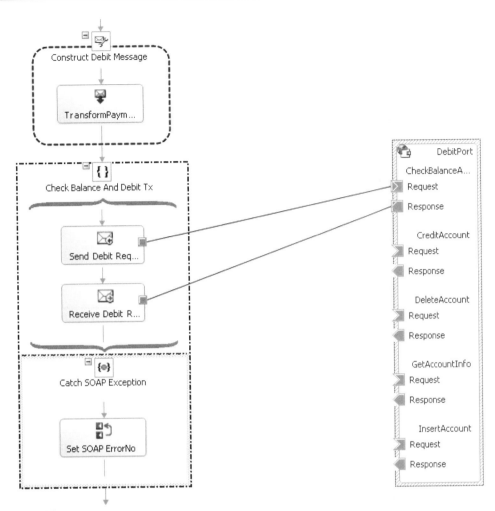

Figure 3.18
Preparing and sending a message to a Web method

The DebitRequest message is initialized using a **Transform** shape called **TransformPayment2DebitRequest** (see Figure 3.19). This shape applies an Extensible Stylesheet Language for Transformations (XSLT) transformation to the incoming Payment message and initializes the DebitRequest message.

The DebitRequest message is then sent to the Web method **CheckBalanceAndDebit** by the **SendDebitRequest** shape, which ensures the account has sufficient funds. The appropriate amount is then debited from the account. The Web method returns the DebitResponse message to the **ReceiveDebitResponse** shape. This message has fields that contain the new account balance and the status of the debit action.

Step 4: Handling Exceptions

Under some circumstances, the **CheckBalanceAndDebit Web** method may return an exception. For example, an exception is generated if a request to **CheckBalanceAndDebit** specifies an invalid account number. The orchestration must handle this exception by providing an exception handler that specifies an appropriate action under these conditions.

Exception handling can be set at various levels of scope within the orchestration. In this instance, the Web method request and response are enclosed by a **Scope** shape. The **Scope** shape has specific exception handling code attached (see **Catch SOAP Exception** in Figure 3.18).

In this example, the exception handling is simple. The code in the **Set Error Status Expression** shape sets the value of the errorStatus orchestration variable to 1, to indicate that a Web service exception has occurred. This value is checked later in the orchestration (see "Step 5: Checking for Errors").

> **Note:** This example assumes that if an exception is generated, no debit occurs. Therefore, no compensation logic is required in this case. For an example that requires compensation logic, see "Step 7: Compensating for Payment Errors."

Step 5: Checking for Errors

Step 4 described how the Web method can throw exceptions, and how these exceptions are caught and handled. Additionally, the Web method response message (DebitResponse) returns a status code that may also indicate an error such as insufficient funds in the account.

Exceptions and error status messages differ in their recoverability. An exception is reserved for situations where a fundamental error has occurred that is not likely to be recoverable. Step 4 provides an example of an exception being thrown for an invalid account number. This situation may indicate a significant problem (a data error) that is not likely to be recoverable.

An error status message is reserved for an error status that is returned by a Web method and that indicates a business error occurred where the business error is likely to be recoverable. An example of a business error that is likely to be recoverable is an attempt to execute a payment when there are insufficient funds in the account.

When the Web method returns a response message, the response message contains a Boolean status field. The orchestration checks the value of this field to determine if the Web method call was successful. In this case, the Web method call is successful if the appropriate amount was debited from the account. To check the value of the field, a **Decide** shape is used to test the value of the status field as shown in Figure 3.19.

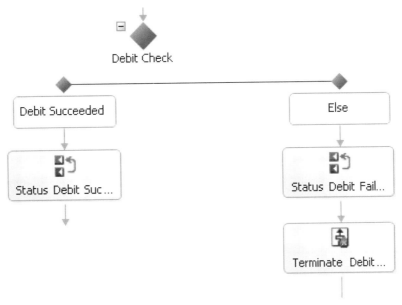

Figure 3.19
Checking the status in the Web method response

The following is the expression in the **Decide** shape.

```
(DebitResponse(ExecutePaymentSchemas.success) == true) && (errorNo == 0)
```

Notice that the **Decide** shape also checks the value of the global orchestration variable, **errorStatus**, which is set to 1 if an exception occurs. Assuming that both of these conditions are met, no error has occurred, so the orchestration proceeds to "Step 6: Sending the Payment and Receiving an Acknowledgment."

If either of the conditions is not met, an error occurs, and the orchestration writes status information back to the database. Specifically, the orchestration writes status information to the **Status** field of the appropriate record in the Payment table. The orchestration then terminates by using the **Terminate** shape. The **Terminate** shape sets an error message that which appears in the operations view of the BizTalk Server Health and Activity Tracking (HAT) console.

Step 6: Sending the Payment and Receiving an Acknowledgment

After the account has been checked for sufficient funds and the funds have been debited, a payment message is sent to the appropriate payment authority based on the value that is specified in the fulfillmentTypeId field in the payment. To simplify this process and to avoid having to change the Execute Scheduled Payments business process whenever the payment authorities make changes, the payment message is sent to a *Message Broker*. *Message Broker* is implemented with BizTalk Server also, For additional information, see *Implementing Message Broker with BizTalk Server 2004*.

Message Broker selects the appropriate payment authority based on the fulfillmentTypeId field, transforms the message to the appropriate format for that payment authority, and then sends the message. This series of events is shown in Figure 3.20.

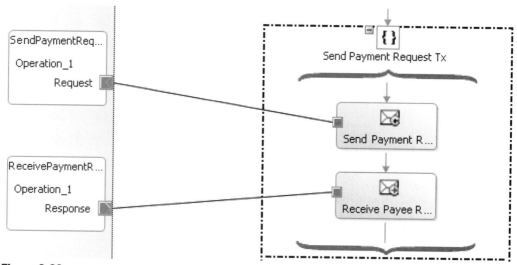

Figure 3.20
Sending the payment request and receiving a response

After the payment message is sent to the payment authority through the *Message Broker*, the payment authority sends an acknowledgement back to the **ReceivePaymentResponse** port. When these acknowledgement responses arrive, they need to be correlated to the correct instance of the payment orchestration for which they are intended.

To correlate the response message with the orchestration instance, the developer creates a correlation type that specifies certain fields in the message. These fields are guaranteed to be unique across all instances of the orchestration; this example uses the PaymentId field. The developer creates an instance of this correlation type called a correlation set. The correlation set is be initialized with the actual value of the PaymentId from the PaymentRequest message when that message is sent out the **SendPaymentRequest** orchestration port. Lastly, the developer configures the **Receive Payee Response** shape to wait for an acknowledgment message that matches this correlation set.

Now, when the payment authority sends an acknowledgment back, the acknowledgment includes the PaymentId. The BizTalk orchestration engine automatically passes the acknowledgment to the instance of the ReceivePaymentResponse port with a correlation set that equates to this PaymentId.

Step 7: Compensating for Payment Errors

At this stage in the orchestration, the following errors could have occurred:

- **No response was received from the payment authority**. This error could occur either because the payment authority never received the Payment message or because of some fault with the payment authority system.

- **The response indicated that payment could not be processed**. This error could occur for a number of reasons, such as invalid payee details or incorrect payment details.

Exceptions and errors are handled in the same way as in steps 4 and 5. One or more exception handlers catch exceptions, and a **Decide** shape checks the status fields in the response messages.

Note: The **Send Payment Request Tx** scope shape can have a timeout attached so that if no response is received within a certain time, the orchestration automatically generates an exception.

Compensation processing is also needed at this point. Compensation processing reverses the effects of earlier transactions that have occurred in the business process. In this example, the customer account is debited before the payment request is sent to the payment authority. It is not possible to roll back this transaction because it has already been committed and the money has been deducted from the customer's account balance. Because the bill has not been paid, the compensation processing must reverse the effects of this transaction by crediting the money back to the account.

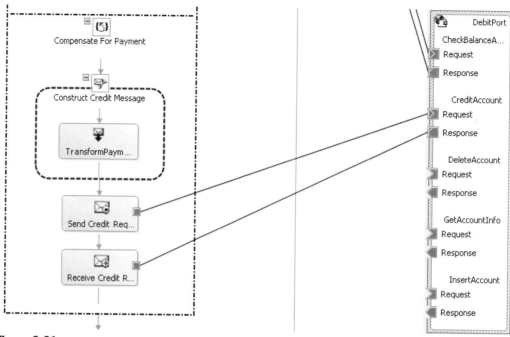

Figure 3.21
Compensation logic for failed payments

Figure 3.21 shows how the compensation is added to the **Scope** shape that sends the payment request message. The compensation logic transforms the payment message to create a Web method request that can be sent to the **CreditAccount** Web method.

Note: A real-world scenario would require additional error handling around the compensation code, but this has been excluded in this example for simplicity.

Step 8: Deploying the Orchestration

The orchestration, schemas, and maps now must be compiled to a .NET Framework assembly, and then the assembly must be deployed to the BizTalk Server Configuration database and to the global assembly cache. To deploy to the global assembly cache, the assembly must be signed with a strong name.

Before building the assembly, create a key file by using the following command at the command prompt.

```
>sn -k ExecutePayment.snk
```

Copy the file to the project folder, and then enter the file name in the **Assembly Key File** name property in the project properties. Next, build and deploy the solution.

Note: The developer can also use the scripts that ship with the BizTalk Server 2004 Software Development Kit (SDK) to perform these actions.

Step 9: Setting Up Send and Receive Ports

As well as the two sets of SOAP ports that are automatically negated when the orchestration is deployed, the orchestration has the following ports:

- **ReceivePaymentRequest**. This port receives messages from the SQL Server Adapter and initiates a new instance of the orchestration for each message that is received.

- **SendPaymentRequest**. This port sends the payment message to the *Message Broker*. The *Message Broker* then sends it to the payment authority.

- **ReceivePaymentResponse**. This port receives a payment response from the payment authority.

A physical BizTalk receive or send port is created for each of these and is bound to the appropriate orchestration port. The developer uses BizTalk Explorer inside Visual Studio .NET to create these ports. After the physical ports are set up, the orchestration is bound to these ports in BizTalk Explorer. The developer can also use the BTSdeploy command line utility and a binding file. The binding file is created by using the **Export BizTalk assembly binding to file** option in BizTalk Deployment Wizard to bind ports.

Note: The ReceivePaymentRequest port is configured to use the SQL Server Adapter to periodically execute a SQL query. This is covered in more detail in the next section, "Step 10: Setting Up the SQL Server Adapter."

Step 10: Setting Up the SQL Server Adapter

In this step, the developer creates a BizTalk Server receive port that is configured with the SQL Server Adapter. The SQL Server Adapter is configured to periodically execute a query that returns all payments to be processed as an XML recordset. Figure 3.22 shows how the SQL Server Adapter is configured to periodically call this query and to return the individual XML records.

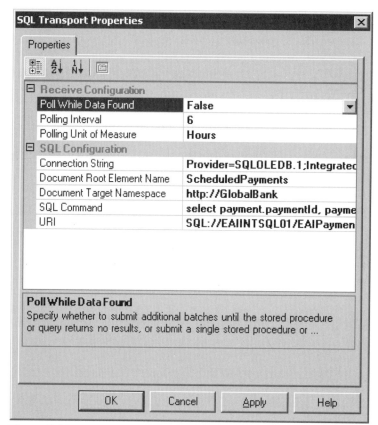

Figure 3.22
Configuring the SQL Server receive adapter

The following query returns all payments that need to be run now as an XML recordset that is based on scheduled time (**payment.dateToMake**) and status (**payment.status**).

```
SELECT payment.MFtransactionId, payment.amount, payment.dateMade,
payment.dateToMake, payment.frequency, payment.status, Payee.MFPayeeId,
Payee.fulfillmentTypeId, Payee.payeeName, Payee.accountNumber,
customerAccount.customerAccountId, customerAccount.MFaccountNumber,
customer.firstName, customer.middleName, customer.lastName
FROM payment, Payee, customerAccount, customer
WHERE payment.payeeId = Payee.PayeeId
AND payment.customerAccountId=customerAccount.customerAccountId
AND customerAccount.customerId=customer.customerId
AND payment.status='sc'
AND payment.dateToMake > getdate()
FOR XML AUTO, ELEMENTS
```

As described in steps 1 and 2, the record set returned is split into individual payment messages by using an XML envelope schema, and each of these messages creates a new instance of the orchestration.

Step 11: Starting the Orchestration

Finally, the developer uses BizTalk Explorer to bind the physical receive and send ports created in steps 9 and 10 to the ports in the orchestration. The developer then starts the orchestration. Now, the SQL Server Adapter should execute the SQL query every six hours, and one instance of the orchestration should be created for each payment record that is returned. These orchestrations execute the scheduled payment as described and terminate upon completion.

Resulting Context

This implementation of *Process Integration* results in the following benefits and liabilities.

Benefits

- **Maintainability**. Creating a separate process integration layer allows users to define and maintain the business process independent from the implementation of the individual functions. This increases maintainability and reduces the skill set requirements for the personnel who maintain the process definition. BizTalk Server orchestration supports this by defining the business process flow independently of the binding to individual actions that make up that flow.

- **Reusability**. Because the existing applications are not dependent on the process management layer, the functions inside these applications can be reused in multiple process definitions.

- **Flexibility**. BizTalk orchestration supports a variety of configurations that would be difficult to implement in many traditional programming models. For example, BizTalk orchestration supports parallel execution of multiple tasks, synchronization points, timeouts, and escalations. Supporting a variety of configurations gives the process manager the flexibility to adapt to many different business requirements.

- **Reporting**. Because the process instances are maintained centrally, it becomes feasible to extract statistical information that spans multiple process steps and process instances. Such reports can tell you the average length of time it takes to fulfill an order and the number of orders that are on hold because of insufficient inventory. BizTalk Server provides extensive real-time reporting, and in addition, it uses SQL Server Analysis Services to provide comprehensive reporting across aggregated business results.

Liabilities

- **Potential bottleneck**. Managing a large number of process instances in a central process manager component may present a run-time bottleneck. However, BizTalk Server provides mechanisms to manage the lifetime of a large number of concurrently running orchestrations. These mechanisms include dehydration and rehydration of business processes that are currently blocked.

- **Temptation to overuse**. This liability is the flipside of the flexibility inherent in *Process Integration* solutions. Because BizTalk orchestration can be used to solve nearly any integration problem, the temptation is to apply BizTalk orchestration to all integration problems. This can lead to overarchitected solutions and sometimes to inefficient solutions. For example, many developers might be tempted to use *Process Integration* in cases where *Message Broker* would be perfectly appropriate to address the requirements.

Testing Considerations

Separating the process definition from the functions provided by the applications means that you can test each business function (service) individually by creating simple test drivers that call the functions and verify the results. For example, you can test the Gateway Web service by using a.NET Framework application to call the Web service, by supplying various test parameters, and by validating the responses.

The advantage of using a commercial process manager such as BizTalk Server 2004 is that it is designed to handle complex issues that are related to throughput, threading, transactions, locking, and performance bottlenecks. This means that you only need to perform minimal testing of these aspects of the application. This also means that more testing effort can concentrate on the unit tests of the individual steps of the business process and on the integration of these steps into a complete business process.

Security Considerations

Applications built using BizTalk Server orchestration typically access multiple business systems that encapsulate the individual steps of the business process. These business systems often provide their own authentication mechanism, usually a user name and password. A common requirement when using BizTalk orchestration to access these systems is for the orchestration to supply credentials for the user who is represented by this instance of the business process.

For example, a business process may be initiated by many users filling out a Microsoft Office InfoPath™ form and sending it in a SOAP message to BizTalk Server. The messages initiate a new instance of the orchestration for each user. These instances then access business systems such as an Enterprise Resource Planning

(ERP) system by using the user's credentials for that system. Because it is not practical to request the credentials from the user, credentials are either encoded in the message itself or accessed by BizTalk from a secure store.

BizTalk Server provides the enterprise single sign-on (SSO) system to store credential information. SSO provides a secured store, which is based on the user's security context, and stores security and state information that is pertinent to that security context. In the earlier example, the security context of the user filling out the InfoPath form can be used to retrieve the user name and password for the ERP system from SSO. The orchestration can then access the ERP system on that user's behalf.

Operational Considerations

BizTalk Server orchestrations are bound to a BizTalk Server host. A BizTalk Server host is an engine for messaging and orchestration. An instance of a BizTalk Server host can be created on each BizTalk Server computer in the BizTalk Server group, which results in the creation of a process on a computer through a Windows service. The process then executes instances of the orchestration.

You can use the BizTalk Server Administration console to create additional hosts. You can then bind the additional hosts to orchestrations and map to servers in the BizTalk Server group. This allows orchestrations to be deployed to any combination of servers in the BizTalk Server group. Therefore, the business application can be distributed across the servers in your enterprise as needed.

Related Patterns

Process Manager [Hohpe04] describes the internal function and implementation of the process manager component.

Acknowledgments

[Hohpe04] Hohpe, Gregor, and Bobby Woolf, *Enterprise Integration Patterns: Designing, Building, and Deploying Messaging Solutions*. Addison-Wesley, 2004.

[Chapell03] David Chappell, Chappell & Associates. "Understanding BizTalk Server 2004." Microsoft Corporation, 2003. Available at *http://go.microsoft.com/fwlink/?LinkId=21313*.

Portal Integration

Context

Many business functions require users to access information that resides in multiple disparate systems. For example, a customer might call a service representative to place a new order. However, before the service representative accepts a new order, he or she has to verify the customer's payment history in the accounting system to ensure that the customer is in good standing. Switching between systems makes the service representative's work tedious and error-prone.

Problem

How can users efficiently perform tasks that require access to information that resides in multiple disparate systems?

Forces

To solve this problem, you need to consider the following forces:

- It is still very common for an end user to have to manually copy information from one system to another. This type of integration is often referred to humorously as "swivel chair integration" because the user has to access multiple systems, often from multiple terminal screens. The user views the information on one screen and then swivels to another screen to enter data based on the information from the first screen. Obviously, this type of manual integration is very inefficient and error prone.

- *Process Integration* can automate tasks that combine data and functions from multiple systems, thereby alleviating the need for users to access multiple systems directly. However, *Process Integration* requires a good understanding of the business process so that the business process can be accurately represented in a process model. This is often not the case because users make improvised decisions based on the information they see.

- *Entity Aggregation* allows multiple systems to share data, which enables the user to access all required information from a single point. However, *Entity Aggregation* is often impossible or not economical due to strong semantic dissonance between the individual systems and lack of a common vocabulary between systems and people.

- Reading data from an application is generally simpler and less risky than updating information. This is especially true in cases such as *Data Integration*, which directly accesses application data and bypasses the business and validation logic.

Solution

Create a portal application that displays the information retrieved from multiple applications in a unified user interface. The user can then perform the required tasks based on the information displayed in this portal.

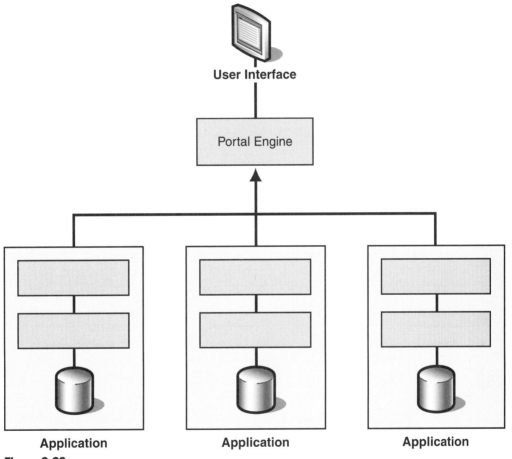

User Interface

Portal Engine

Application   Application   Application

Figure 3.23
Portal Integration

Portal Integration is a comparatively simple form of integration. It is popular because it is typically much easier to implement and less intrusive than more sophisticated types of integration, such as *Process Integration*. With *Portal Integration*, the business process that describes the sequence of tasks does not have to be represented in a precise process model, but instead resides in the user's head. This enables the end user to compensate for mismatches in semantics between the individual systems and to make a case-by-case decision. This approach is naturally less efficient than *Process*

Integration, but it gives the user flexibility and it is typically much faster to implement. In many cases, *Portal Integration* can be used as an intermediate solution until business processes are better understood and can be incorporated into a process model, thus enabling the transition to *Process Integration.*

The portal engine shown in Figure 3.23 interacts with the individual applications using *Data Integration, Functional Integration,* or *Presentation Integration.* Because the primary purpose of the portal is the display of information, *Portal Integration* works particularly well with simpler forms of connectivity, such as *Data Integration* or *Presentation Integration.*

Portal Integration comes in a variety of flavors from very simple to fairly complex. The following list categorizes the different variants:

- **Display-only**. The simplest form of *Portal Integration* simply displays data in different areas of the screen. Information from each application is mapped to a rectangular area of the screen, also referred to as a *pane*. This display allows the user to view information retrieved from multiple applications on a single screen. No other functionality is provided.

- **Simple post-processing**. Instead of presenting the data received from each individual system, many portals add simple rules that help the user make decisions. For example, if the billing system reports that a customer payment is overdue, the portal would list this as an exception in bold red letters at the top of the screen instead of showing the history of all payments received. This type of functionality helps turn raw data into useful information for the user.

- **Single application interaction**. This variant displays data in different areas of the screen, but it also allows the user to issue commands to one system at a time. This extra functionality enables the user to view information from multiple systems and use the resulting data to perform a business function that is limited to a single system.

- **Cross-pane interactivity**. In many cases, the information to be displayed in one pane depends on a user selection in another pane. For example, a list of customers might be retrieved from the customer relationship management (CRM) system. When the user selects a customer's name from the list, the portal retrieves the selected customer's payment history from the billing system and displays it in a separate pane. To automate these steps, basic interaction between different portal panes is required. This type of portal speeds up the user's tasks without requiring full integration between systems. However, this type of portal does require the availability of common keys, such as a customer identifier (ID), that function across multiple systems. With this type of portal, the development of the interaction is often difficult to test and reuse.

The *Portal Integration* solution relies on interplay between the solution components that are described in Table 3.3.

Table 3.3: Portal Integration Solution Components

Component	Responsibilities	Collaborators
Portal engine	– Extract information from existing applications – Render information into a unified user interface	Applications
Application	Host relevant business data	None

Example

Many customer service functions require access to a range of customer data. For example, a customer may call to place a new order, check whether a payment has been received, and change his or her phone number. Often, this type of information is stored in many different systems, such as the order management system, the billing system, or the complaint system. Giving a customer service representative a unified view of the various records for a customer can be enormously helpful in providing efficient and effective service to the customer. A similar or reduced version of the portal could also be presented directly to the consumer on the company's Web site.

Resulting Context

Portal Integration results in the following benefits and liabilities:

Benefits

- **Non-intrusiveness**. Because its primary function is the retrieval and display of information, *Portal Integration* can typically be added to existing systems without disturbing the existing functionality. This is particularly true if *Portal Integration* uses *Data Integration* for the retrieval of data from the individual systems.

- **Speed of implementation**. Adding a portal to existing applications can often be accomplished in a matter of days or weeks, whereas a full integration of the systems could take many months. Many vendors offer *Portal Integration* platforms in combination with a suite of prefabricated panes that integrate with many popular enterprise applications and data sources.

- **Flexibility**. Because the user makes the decisions, *Portal Integration* can be used in situations where business rules are not well understood or not agreed upon.

Liabilities

- **Inefficient**. *Portal integration* is best suited to the automation of simple tasks and processes because it still requires manual interaction by the user. For example, because most portals allow the user to interact with only one application at a time, the user might have to perform multiple manual actions in sequence to complete a complex business function. This makes *Portal Integration* unsuitable for high-volume applications. In these situations, *Process Integration* is generally a better solution because the sequence of steps can be encoded in a process model and run automatically by the process manager.

- **Error-prone**. When using *Portal Integration,* the user makes business decisions and determines the sequence of tasks to be performed. While this provides flexibility, it also introduces the risk of human error. Therefore, *Portal Integration* is not well suited to integrations that require strict repetition of a defined business process. *Process Integration* is generally a better choice in those scenarios.

4

System Connections

The previous chapter described different strategies for the design of an integration layer and the tradeoffs involved in choosing an alternative. After you decide to use an integrating layer, you must then decide exactly how you are going to connect each system that you intend to integrate.

As you consider how to connect to different information systems, you will encounter a mix of technical architectures. Each technical architecture is designed to allow certain types of access and to restrict others. These access restrictions constrain the set of integration options that are available to you. This chapter discusses a series of related patterns that will help you analyze the alternative methods and the tradeoffs to consider when you choose your system connections.

Connecting to Layered Applications

When trying to find connection points to an existing application, you need to study the way these applications are structured. The prevailing architectural style for business applications is *Layered Application*. Many applications fall into the more specific form of the *Three-Layered Services Application* pattern [Trowbridge03]. The components of this pattern are shown in Figure 4.1.

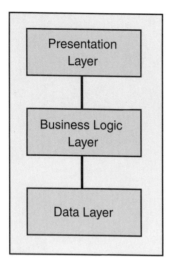

Figure 4.1
A three-layered services application

This architectural style defines three distinct layers:

- Presentation layer. The presentation layer displays information to the end user and allows for user input.
- Business logic layer. The business logic layer contains business functions that act on the business data
- Data layer. The data layer stores data persistently in a data store. This layer is also known as the resource layer.

Each application layer presents an opportunity for an application to interact with the integration layer, as shown in Figure 4.2.

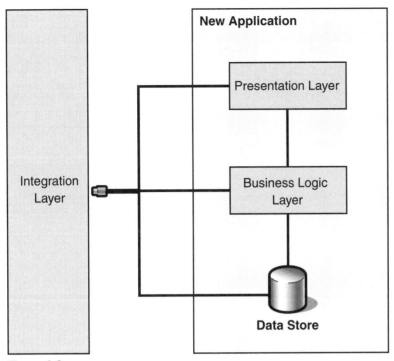

Figure 4.2
Multiple choices when connecting an application

Because each layer has different requirements and purposes, you face different challenges when connecting to each layer. Similarly, there are three primary patterns you can use to connect an application to an integration layer:

- *Presentation Integration.* The integration layer can extract information from the application's user presentation layer through a technique known as *screen scraping*.
- *Functional Integration.* The integration layer can interact with the business logic layer through application or service interfaces.
- *Data Integration.* The integration layer can move data in and out of the data layer.

To make an informed choice about which pattern to use, you must know the options that are viable, and you must evaluate their impact on the overall integration architecture. This chapter describes each pattern and elaborates on the benefits and liabilities of each one.

As in other chapters, this chapter uses visual models to show the associations between the patterns. Figure 4.3 shows the patterns as circles and simple associations between them as lines. As the discussion progresses, more complex pattern relationships build upon this basic diagram.

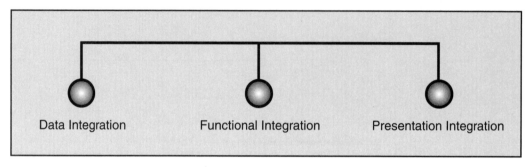

Figure 4.3
System connection patterns

The first kind of integration to consider is *Data Integration*.

Data Integration

Many applications keep large volumes of data in data stores such as flat files and relational, hierarchical, and object-oriented databases. Other applications that need this information can access it directly from these data stores.

Connecting applications through the data store is relatively simple. Usually, you use FTP, scheduled batch files, database management system (DBMS) utilities, extract transform and load (ETL) tools, and integration servers.

If you decide to integrate at the data layer, there are three patterns that represent the three types of data integration to consider: *Shared Database* [Hohpe04], *Maintain Data Copies* [Teale03], and *File Transfer* [Hohpe04]. These patterns are shown in Figure 4.4.

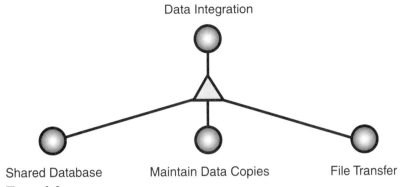

Figure 4.4
Three kinds of data integration

Figure 4.4 introduces a new pattern relationship to the visual model from Figure 4.3. The triangle indicates refinement between the base pattern (*Data Integration*) and the derivative patterns (*Shared Database*, *Maintain Data Copies*, and *File Transfer*). More precisely, this relationship is defined as follows:

"A specific pattern *refines* a more abstract pattern if the specific pattern's full description is a direct extension of the more general pattern. That is, the specific pattern must deal with a specialization of the problem the general pattern addresses, must have a similar (but more specialized) solution structure, and must address the same forces as the more general pattern, but may also address additional forces. To make an analogy with object-oriented programming ... the *refines* relationship is similar to inheritance." [Noble98]

Applying this relationship to the problem of data integration means that if you decide to integrate systems at the data layer, you must further refine your decision by choosing one of three alternatives. You could share a single instance of a database between multiple applications by using the *Shared Database* pattern, as shown in Figure 4.5.

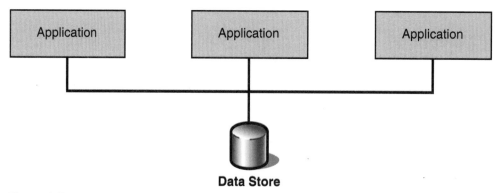

Figure 4.5
Multiple applications sharing the same data store

Another approach is to create multiple copies of a database and distribute them throughout your enterprise according to the *Maintain Data Copies* pattern. If you do this, you must then maintain these separate copies, which introduces synchronization and replication. Figure 4.6 shows the *Data Replication* pattern, which refines *Maintain Data Copies*.

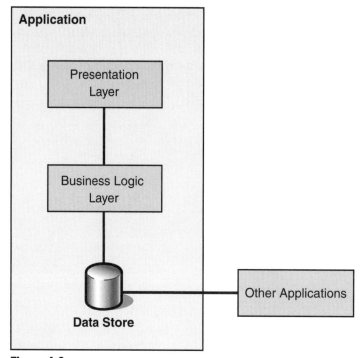

Figure 4.6
Data Replication, a refinement of Maintain Data Copies

Yet another approach is to use *File Transfer*. In this pattern, one application produces a file and transfers it so that other applications can consume it. Files can then be produced at regular intervals to synchronize two or more systems.

The *Data Integration* pattern, later in this chapter, describes these alternatives in detail and provides the benefits and liabilities of each approach. This discussion should help you choose the kind of data integration that is appropriate for your requirements.

Using *Data Integration* is made easier by the abundance of tool support provided by many companies. However, in spite of the low cost and the maturity of the tools, accessing the data store is not viable in some cases. A less invasive way of connecting applications is to connect through the presentation layer.

Presentation Integration

When applications that have user interfaces join an integration architecture, other applications can connect to them through the presentation byte stream as shown in Figure 4.7.

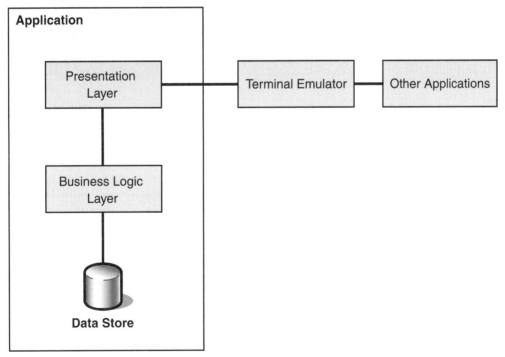

Figure 4.7
Connecting to an application through the presentation layer

Presentation connectivity represents the least invasive way of connecting applications because the other applications appear to the host application as humans who are interacting through the user interface. Therefore, this form of integration does not require any changes to the host. The disadvantage is that simulating user interaction is cumbersome and inefficient. It requires parsing the data or functionality out of the byte stream, which effectively reverses the transformations performed by the presentation logic. In addition, applications that connect through the presentation layer can only access what is also available to a human user. The granularity of the exposed data and functionality is very coarse; burying potentially-rich APIs.

One advantage of *Presentation Integration* is that it can be an inexpensive way to integrate applications. Although the connection is inexpensive, it is also easily disrupted. By its very nature, presentation integration is tightly coupled to the host application's presentation. If the application's presentation changes, the presentation integration solution must also change.

Instead of sharing data or parsing through a byte stream to access a system's functionality, it is often preferable to access a system's business logic directly through *Functional Integration*.

Functional Integration

By connecting directly to the business logic layer, *Functional Integration* enables other applications and services to take advantage of the business logic that is encapsulated in other systems, as shown in Figure 4.8.

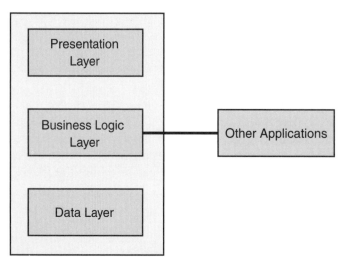

Figure 4.8
Integrating applications and services at the business logic layer

Functional Integration connects applications through interfaces and specifications. Unfortunately, not all applications in an integration architecture have interfaces and specifications. Quite often, the applications that have APIs do not expose their data and functions at a granularity level that is suitable for integration.

Functional Integration can be very effective in the right circumstances. A good example of when to use *Functional Integration* is for a credit scoring application or service.

Credit Scoring Example

Many financial applications require a credit score to qualify an applicant for a specific loan. Salespeople often want a quick and accurate response from a credit scoring system so they can quickly prequalify customers and steer them to an affordable alternative. In addition, credit scores depend on a number of dynamic factors, which means that credit scores can quickly become out of date.

Because credit scores are calculated values, sharing data means relying on credit scores that might be out of date or duplicating raw input data and forcing each application to implement the credit scoring algorithm independently. A better solution is to share the business logic encapsulated in the credit scoring system and to then expose it through some type of functional interface that other systems can consume. For this level of integration, you need *Functional Integration*.

Kinds of Functional Integration

After you choose to use *Functional Integration,* you must further refine your decision by choosing one of the three alternatives:

- *Distributed Object Integration. Distributed Object Integration* is also known as instance-based collaboration because it extends the model of object-oriented computing to distributed solutions. Objects inside one application interact with objects in another remote application in the same way they would interact locally with another object.

- *Message-Oriented Middleware Integration. Message-Oriented Middleware Integration* connects systems by using asynchronous message queues that are based on proprietary message-oriented middleware. The connected systems then communicate through messages that contain small packets of data. Because the communication is asynchronous and durable, there is little chance that the messages will be lost during a network or system failure.

- *Service-Oriented Integration. Service-Oriented Integration* connects systems by enabling them to consume and provide XML Web services. This type of integration uses standards to provide both a portable type system and an extensible messaging framework that is not coupled to a proprietary implementation or transport. In addition, *Service-Oriented Integration* recommends the WS-I Basic Profile to ensure interoperability between endpoints. The WS-I Basic Profile is a carefully chosen subset of XML, SOAP, HTTP, and other standards.

Note: The term *service* is used in many different ways in the context of software engineering. It is also used in at least seven levels of scope: operating system, process, object, distributed object, proprietary message-oriented middleware, logical, and XML Web services. This guide uses the term *service* to mean XML Web services unless indicated otherwise.

Figure 4.9 shows these three alternatives as distinct derivatives, or refinement patterns, of *Functional Integration*.

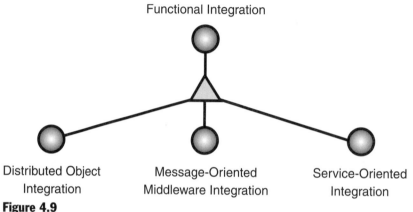

Figure 4.9
Three kinds of Functional Integration

Later in this chapter, the *Functional Integration* pattern describes these alternatives in detail and discusses the benefits and liabilities of each approach. This discussion should help you choose the kind of functional integration that is appropriate for your requirements.

System Connection Patterns

Data, presentation, and functional integration represent ways in which seasoned integration architects connect applications. But given your specific requirements, how do you connect applications within your integration architecture?

Sometimes the applications you are integrating limit your choices. If there is more than one way you can connect them, you must evaluate the tradeoffs associated with each potential choice. The *Data Integration*, *Presentation Integration*, and *Functional Integration* patterns later in this chapter distill the knowledge required to make an informed decision.

Two general points are worth noting. First, an application that uses one style of connection can communicate with another application that uses a different style. For example, *Presentation Integration* may be the only way to extract data from a preexisting application, but you can still insert this data into the target application using *Data Integration*. Second, despite sometimes similar names, a specific integration layer pattern can be used with any system connection pattern. For example, a *Portal Integration* solution can extract data from existing applications by using *Presentation Integration*, *Functional Integration*, or *Data Integration*.

Figure 4.10 shows three system connection patterns, with derivative patterns and associations.

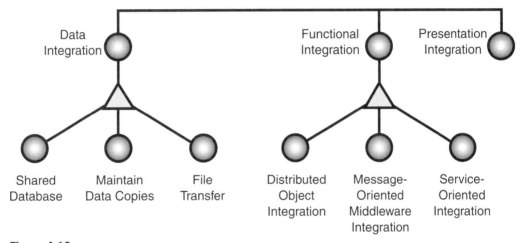

Figure 4.10
System connection patterns and their relationships

Table 4.1 summarizes these patterns and provides the problem/solution pairs they represent.

Table 4.1: System Connections Patterns

Pattern or pattlet	Problem	Solution	Associated implementations
Data Integration	How do you integrate information systems that were not designed to work together?	Integrate applications at the logical data layer. Use a *Shared Database*, *File Transfer*, or *Maintain Data Copies*.	
Shared Database [Hohpe04]	How can multiple applications work together and exchange information?	Have multiple applications store data in a single database. Define a schema that handles the needs of all relevant applications.	
Maintain Data Copies [Teale03]	How can multiple applications work together and exchange information?	Have multiple applications access multiple copies of the same data. Maintain state integrity between copies.	
File Transfer [Hohpe04]	How can multiple applications work together and exchange information?	At regular intervals, have each application produce files that contain the information that the other applications must consume. After you create it, do not maintain the file.	
Functional Integration	How do you integrate information systems that were not designed to work together?	Integrate applications at the logical business layer. Use *Distributed Object Integration*, (proprietary) *Message-Oriented Middleware Integration*, or *Service-Oriented Integration*.	
Distributed Object Integration (see also *Remote Procedure Invocation* [Hohpe04])	How do you integrate applications at the logical business layer?	Develop systems that have object interfaces that can be consumed remotely by other systems.	

Pattern or pattlet	Problem	Solution	Associated implementations
Message-Oriented Middleware Integration (see also *Messaging* [Hohpe04])	How do you integrate applications at the logical business layer?	Use proprietary message-oriented middleware to send messages asynchronously.	
Service-Oriented Integration	How do you integrate applications at the logical business layer?	Use Web services to expose interfaces that can be consumed remotely by other systems.	*Implementing Service-Oriented Integration with ASP.NET*, or *Implementing Service-Oriented Integration with BizTalk Server 2004.*
Presentation Integration	How do you integrate information systems that were not designed to work together?	Access the application's functionality through the user interface by simulating a user's input and reading data from the screen display.	

Data Integration

Context

Enterprise information systems are comprised of a variety of data storage systems, which vary in complexity and in the ways they access internal data. An example of a simple data storage system is a flat file. An example of a far more complex data storage system is a Database Management System (DBMS) server farm.

Problem

How do you integrate information systems that were not designed to work together?

Forces

- Most enterprises contain multiple systems that were never designed to work together. The business units that fund these information systems are primarily concerned with functional requirements rather than technical architectures. Because information systems vary greatly in terms of technical architecture, enterprises often have a mix of systems, and these systems have incompatible architectures.

- Many applications are organized into three logical layers: presentation, business logic, and data.

- When you integrate multiple systems, you usually want to be as noninvasive as possible. Any change to an existing production system is a risk, so it is wise to try to fulfill the needs of other systems and users while minimizing disturbance to the existing systems.

- Likewise, you usually want to isolate applications' internal data structures. Isolation means that changes to one application's internal structures or business logic do not affect other applications. Without isolated data structures, a small change inside an application could cause a ripple effect and require changes in many dependent applications.

- Reading data from a system usually requires little or no business logic or validation. In these cases, it can be more efficient to access raw data that a business layer has not modified.

- Many preexisting applications couple business and presentation logic so that the business logic is not accessible externally. In other cases, the business logic may be implemented in a specific programming language without support for remote access. Both scenarios limit the potential to connect to an application's business logic layer.

- When making updates to another application's data, you should generally take advantage of the application's business logic that performs validations and data integrity checks. You can use *Functional Integration* to integrate systems at the logical business layer.
- Direct access to an application's data store may violate security policies that are frequently implemented in an application's business logic layer.
- The availability of commercial tools can influence the integration strategy between applications. Commercial tools usually carry a lower risk and expense when compared to a custom solution.

Solution

Integrate applications at the logical data layer by allowing the data in one application (the source) to be accessed by other applications (the target), as shown in Figure 4.11.

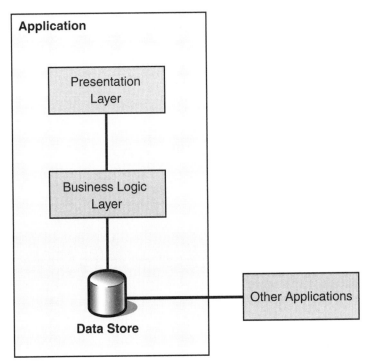

Figure 4.11
Integrating applications at the logical data layer

To connect applications at the logical data layer, use one or more of the following patterns:

- *Shared Database*. All applications that you are integrating read data directly from the same database.

- *Maintain Data Copies*. Maintain copies of the application's database so that other applications can read the data (and potentially update it).

- *File Transfer*. Make the data available by transporting a file that is an extract from the application's database so that other applications can load the data from the files.

When you are implementing *Data Integration*, you usually have to consider the following design tradeoffs:

- **Latency tolerance**. Some forms of data integration imply a delay between up-dates to the data that is used by multiple applications. For example, in the *Data Replication* pattern [Teale03], the data is extracted from the source system, and it is transported over a network. The data might then be modified, and then it is inserted in a target database. This delay means that one system may have access to data that is more up to date than another system. This latency in propagating data can play an important role in integration.

- **Push versus pull**. When accessing a data source's database, a system can either pull the data from the database or let the database itself push the data when a change occurs. Pull approaches are generally less intrusive, while push approaches minimize latency.

- **Granularity**. Getting a larger chunk of information at one time is generally more efficient than propagating each small change by itself. This requires an under-standing of the cohesion between multiple data entities. If one entity changes, are other entities also likely to be affected?

- **Master/subordinate relationships**. If updates are made only to one application's data, propagating these changes is relatively simple. However, if multiple appli-cations are allowed to update the information, you can run into difficult synchro-nization issues. For a more detailed description of synchronization issues, see the *Master-Master Replication* pattern [Teale03].

- **Synchronization logic versus latency**. For geographically dispersed applications, sharing a single database may cause excessive network latency. To overcome this problem, you can use distributed databases that contain copies of the same data. However, distributed databases add the additional complexity of synchronization and replication logic.

Example

There are many real-life examples of *Data Integration*. For example, an order entry application may store a copy of product codes that reside in the Enterprise Resource Planning (ERP) system. If product codes do not change very frequently, the data from the source (the ERP system) may be synchronized daily or weekly with the data on the target (the order-entry application).

Resulting Context

After you decide to use *Data Integration,* you must then choose a particular kind of data integration that is appropriate for your situation. Your choices are summarized by the following patterns:

● *Shared Database*
● *Maintain Data Copies*
● *File Transfer*

Shared Database

The *Shared Database* approach is shown in Figure 4.12. *Shared Database* aims to eliminate latency by allowing multiple applications to access a single physical data store directly. This approach is more intrusive because you usually have to modify some applications to use a common schema.

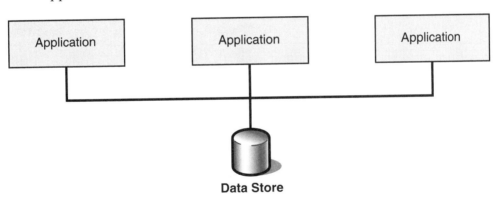

Figure 4.12
Shared Database

Reading data directly from a database is generally harmless, but writing data directly into an application's database risks corrupting the application's internal state. Although transactional integrity mechanisms protect the database from corruption through multiple concurrent updates, they cannot protect the database from the insertion of bad data. In most cases, only a subset of data-related constraints is implemented in the database itself. Other constraints are likely to be contained in the business logic. This distribution of data constraints allows other applications to leave the database in a state that the application logic considers to be invalid. For a more detailed description, see Martin Fowler's *Shared Database* pattern in Hohpe and Woolf's *Enterprise Integration Patterns* [Hohpe04].

Maintain Data Copies

Instead of sharing a single instance of a database between applications, you can make multiple copies of the database so that each application has its own dedicated store. To keep these copies synchronized, you copy data from one data store to the other.

This approach is common with packaged applications because it is not intrusive. However, it does imply that at any time, the different data stores are slightly out of synchronization due to the latency that is inherent in propagating the changes from one data store to the next. Figure 4.13 shows the *Data Replication* pattern, which is a derivative of *Maintain Data Copies*.

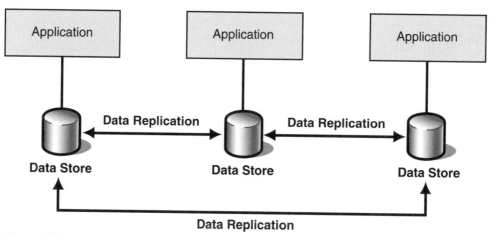

Figure 4.13
Data Replication

The mechanisms involved in maintaining these copies are complex. *Data Patterns* discusses these mechanisms in a cluster of 12 data movement patterns [Teale03] that use *Maintain Data Copies* as a root pattern. The other patterns in the guide include the following:

- *Move Copy of Data*
- *Data Replication*
- *Master-Master Replication*
- *Master-Slave Replication*
- *Master-Master Row-Level Synchronization*
- *Master-Slave Snapshot Replication*
- *Capture Transaction Details*
- *Master-Slave Transactional Incremental Replication*
- *Implementing Master-Master Row Level Synchronization Using SQL Server*
- *Implementing Master-Slave Snapshot Replication Using SQL Server*
- *Master-Slave Cascading Replication*

For more details about these patterns, see *Data Patterns* on MSDN *(http://msdn.microsoft.com/architecture/patterns/default.aspx?pull=/library/en-us/dnpatterns/html/Dp.asp)*.

File Transfer

In the *File Transfer* pattern, one application produces a file and transfers it so that other applications can consume it. Because files are a universal unit of storage for all enterprise operating systems, this method is often simple to implement. The disadvantage of this method is that two applications can lose synchronization with each other because each one is changing the file independently. For more information, see Martin Fowler's *File Transfer* pattern [Hohpe04].

Choosing Between Alternatives

There are many factors to consider when you choose the kind of data integration that is best for your particular requirements. Some of those factors include:

- Tolerance for data that is not current (*stale data*)
- Performance
- Complexity
- Platform infrastructure and tool support

After you pull data from a transactional system, the data is effectively stale. When you attempt to modify the data, you encounter potential contention and conflict resolution logic. If your conflict resolution logic is simple, and if you can accommodate relatively long time intervals with stale data, *File Transfer* may be the best way to integrate data.

If your conflict resolution logic is more complex, and if you have less tolerance for stale data, consider *Shared Database* or *Maintain Data Copies*. Before deciding on one or the other, consider your performance needs.

If your applications and databases are located in the same data center, then *Shared Database* enables you to use transaction managers to enforce data consistency. Using transaction managers to enforce data consistency limits stale data. However, if you have too many applications accessing the same data, the database may become a performance bottleneck for your system.

Maintaining multiple copies of the same data reduces the performance bottleneck of a single database, but it creates stale data between synchronizations. Also, if your application is geographically distributed, sharing one single database creates excessive network latency and affects performance. *Maintain Data Copies* also presents its own operations challenges. However, you can reduce the effort associated with maintaining multiple copies by using the synchronization and replication capabilities that are built into many DBMSs.

As you can see, each form of data integration has advantages and disadvantages. Choosing the right kind of data integration depends on the factors that are most important to your organization and on achieving the right balance among the tradeoffs.

Benefits

Regardless of the type of data integration you choose, the benefits are as follows:

- **Nonintrusive.** Most databases support transactional multiuser access, ensuring that one user's transaction does not affect another user's transaction. This is accomplished by using the Isolation property of the Atomicity, Consistency, Isolation, and Durability (ACID) properties set. In addition, many applications permit you to produce and consume files for the purpose of data exchange. This makes *Data Integration* a natural choice for packaged applications that are difficult to modify.

- **High bandwidth.** Direct database connections are designed to handle large volumes of data. Likewise, reading files is a very efficient operation. High bandwidth can be very useful if the integration needs to access multiple entities at the same time. For example, high bandwidth is useful when you want to create summary reports or to replicate information to a data warehouse.

- **Access to raw data**. In most cases, data that is presented to an end user is transformed for the specific purpose of user display. For example, code values may be translated into display names for ease of use. In many integration scenarios, access to the internal code values is more useful because the codes tend to more stable than the display values, especially in situations where the software is localized. Also, the data store usually contains internal keys that uniquely identify entities. These keys are critical for robust integration, but they often are not accessible from the business or user interface layers of an application.

- **Metadata**. Metadata is data that describes data. If the solution that you use for data integration connects to a commercial database, metadata is usually available through the same access mechanisms that are used to access application data. The metadata describes the names of data elements, their type, and the relationships between entities. Access to this information can greatly simplify the transformation from one application's data format to another.

- **Good tool support**. Most business applications need access to databases. As a result, many development and debugging tools are available to aid in connecting to a remote database. Almost every integration vendor provides a database adapter component that simplifies the conversion of data into messages. Also, Extract, Transform, and Load (ETL) tools allow the manipulation of larger sets of data and simplify the replication from one schema to another. If straight data replication is required, many database vendors integrate replication tools as part of their software platform.

Liabilities

Regardless of the type of data integration you choose, the liabilities are as follows:

- **Unpublished schemas**. Most packaged applications consider the database chema to be unpublished. This means that the software vendor reserves the right to make changes to the schema at will. A solution based on *Data Integration* is likely to be affected by these changes, making the integration solution unreliable. Also, many software vendors do not document their database schemas for packaged applications, which can make working with a large physical schema difficult.

- **Bypassed business logic.** Because data integration accesses the application data store directly, it bypasses most of the business logic and validation rules incorporated into the application logic. This means that direct updates to an application's database can corrupt the application's integrity and cause the application to malfunction. Even though databases enforce simple constraints such as uniqueness or foreign key relationships, it is usually very inefficient to implement all application-related rules and constraints inside the database. Therefore, the database may consider updates as valid even though they violate business rules that are encoded in the application logic. Use *Functional Integration* instead of *Data Integration* if you need the target application to enforce complex business rules.

- **No encapsulation.** Accessing an application's data directly provides the advantage of immediate access to raw data. However, the disadvantage is that there is little or no encapsulation of the application's functionality. The data that is extracted is represented in the format of an application-internal physical database schema. This data very likely has to be transformed before other applications can use it. These transformations can become very complex because they often have to reconcile structural or semantic differences between applications. In extreme scenarios, the data store may contain information in a format that cannot be used by other systems. For example, the data store might contain byte streams representing serialized business objects that cannot be used by other systems.

- **Simplistic semantics.** As the name suggests, *Data Integration* enables the integration of data only. For example, it enables the integration of data contained in entities such as "Customer XYZ's Address." It is not well-suited for richer command or event semantics such as "Customer XYZ Moved" or "Place Order." Instead, use *Functional Integration* for these types of integration.

- **Different storage paradigms.** Most data stores use a representation that is different from the underlying programming model of the application layer. For example, both relational databases and flat-file formats usually represent entities and their relationships in a very different way from an object-oriented application. The difference in representation requires a translation between the two paradigms.

- **Semantic dissonance.** Semantic dissonance is a common problem in integration. Even though you can easily resolve syntactic differences between systems, resolving semantic differences can be much more difficult. For example, although it is easy to convert a number into a string to resolve a syntactic difference, it is more difficult to resolve semantic differences between two systems that have slightly different meanings for the Time, Customer, and Region entities. Even though two databases might contain a Customer entity, the semantic context of both entities might be dramatically different.

Testing Considerations

Testing data integration solutions can be difficult for a number of reasons, including the following:

- The direct access to the data source and destination does not allow isolation of a specific function. For example, using a test stub or mock object does not allow isolation of a specific function. If the data exchange uses a file to transfer data, you can use test files to test the data insertion.

- Inserting data directly into the target database bypasses all or most business logic. Therefore, testing the insert itself may not be very meaningful because it is likely to succeed. Even if the data is inserted successfully into the database, the data may violate another application's business logic. As a result, the complete application may have to be regression tested after you insert data directly into the application data store.

- Because *Data Integration* puts few constraints on the data to be inserted into an application's data store, a large data set may be required to provide appropriate coverage of all test cases.

Security Considerations

Data Integration presents potential security issues that are worth considering:

- **Coarse-grained security**. Because *Data Integration* bypasses the application logic, it also bypasses any security rules that are enforced by the application logic. Many databases manage access privileges at the table level. At the table level, a user either has access to the Customer table or the user does not have access. Most applications enforce security at an object level. At the object level, a specific user has access only to those customer records that are associated with the user.

- **Privacy policies may not be enforced**. Many corporate databases are subject to privacy policies that are based on corporate or legal guidelines. Directly accessing these data stores may be in violation of these policies because it is difficult to control the ways the retrieved data may be used. In comparison, *Functional Integration* can offer restricted access to sensitive data to only allow queries that do not expose individual data. For example, a functional interface may allow the user to query the average compensation in a specific region but not individual compensation.

- **Data may be encrypted**. Data inside the database may be encrypted so that it is not accessible for data integration unless the integration solution obtains the key to decrypt the data. Providing the key to the data integration solution could present a security risk unless the key is properly protected.

Related Patterns

For more information, see the following related patterns:

- *Functional Integration*. *Data Integration* is used to extract data from or insert data into an existing application. If direct access to the data source must be avoided, use *Functional Integration* instead. *Functional Integration* interfaces with an application's business logic.

- *Data Consistency Integration* [Ruh01]. In cases where inserting data into an application is tied to specific business rules and validations, straight data integration might not be the best solution because the business logic has to be re-created for the data insert operation. In these cases, consider using *Functional Integration* to achieve data consistency.

Acknowledgments

[Britton01] Britton, Chris. *IT Architectures and Middleware – Strategies for Building Large, Integrated Systems*. Addison-Wesley, 2001.

[Hohpe04] Hohpe, Gregor, and Bobby Woolf. *Enterprise Integration Patterns: Designing, Building, and Deploying Messaging Solutions*. Addison-Wesley, 2004.

[Ruh01] Ruh, William. *Enterprise Application Integration. A Wiley Tech Brief*. Wiley, 2001.

[Teale03] Teale, Philip; Christopher Etz, Michael Kiel, and Carsten Zeitz. "Data Patterns." *.NET Architecture Center*. June 2003. Available at: *http://msdn.microsoft.com/architecture/patterns/default.aspx*.

Functional Integration

Context

Enterprise information systems contain a variety of applications that provide levels of interaction that range from simple to complex. The functions that are included in these systems offer a variety of capabilities and levels of access, from undocumented functions and silo applications to fully developed composite applications. In addition, the mechanism for invoking a function differs from one system to another.

Problem

How do you integrate information systems that were not designed to work together?

Forces

To correctly solve this problem, you need to consider the following forces:

- Most enterprises contain multiple systems that were never designed to work together. The business units that fund these information systems are primarily concerned with functional requirements rather than technical architectures. Because information systems vary greatly in terms of technical architecture, enterprises often have a mix of systems, and these systems have incompatible architectures.

- Many applications are organized into three logical layers: presentation, business logic, and data.

- Most commercial business applications developed in the last decade provide stable documented programming interfaces to allow access to the business functionality that is incorporated in the application. Software vendors provide these APIs specifically to support integration with external software.

- The functional interfaces provided by an application typically abstract from the underlying data representations so that they are more stable than the internal representations. For example, while a database schema might change in a new version of the software, the vendors keep the public APIs compatible with the previous version so that external applications accessing the API do not break.

- Accessing a function that resides in another application provides a natural extension of the application programming model that developers are used to. The semantics of accessing an external function that resides in another application are similar to making a local method call. This allows for natural integration with existing applications.

- Making direct updates to another application's data store through *Data Integration* bypasses all business and validation logic incorporated in the application's business logic layer. As a result, the risk of corrupting an application's data store is high.

- Exchanging messages between applications that include both data and behavior can provide for a more powerful conversation between systems. Instead of sending a message that only contains a customer's address, one system can instruct the other system to perform a specific function. For example, one system can instruct another system to validate the customer's address or to update a customer record with the customer's new address. More powerful conversations also allow an application to more specifically describe the functions and services it can provide to other applications.

- Many programming interfaces are programming language-specific and are not available remotely unless they have been developed on top of a specific remoting technology, such as Microsoft .NET Framework remoting or Common Object Request Broker Architecture (CORBA).

Solution

Integrate applications at the business logic layer by allowing the business function in one application (the source) to be accessed by other applications (the target), as shown in Figure 4.14.

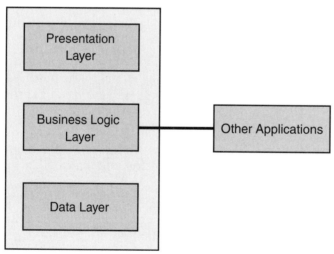

Figure 4.14
Integrating applications at the business logic layer

For an external application to integrate with the source application through *Functional Integration*, the following two conditions must be met:

● The business function that you want must be available inside the source application's business logic.
● The API of the source application must be accessible remotely.

If the desired business function is not available, you have to modify the source application to make the function available. If modifying the source application is not feasible, you should add the new function outside the source application and then communicate with the application through another form of integration, such as *Data Integration* or *Presentation Integration*. This approach has fewer side effects and is generally available for most types of applications.

Many applications only expose their business functions as a local API that is dependent on a specific programming language such as C++ or C#. In those cases, a local adapter or middleware interface has to be created that translates incoming messages from other applications into local API calls. Likewise, results from API calls are translated back into messages. In most cases, such an adapter can be generic enough to support a variety of different functions without having to be modified for each individual function that you want to make available externally.

Functional Integration is very versatile because many different operations can be performed though an API. A functional interface can retrieve data, update data entities (change an address), or perform business functions (validate a credit card). In fact, one common use of *Functional Integration* is to ensure data consistency between applications [Ruh01].

Functional Integration is based on the interaction between the components that are described in Table 4.2.

Table 4.2: Functional Integration Components

Components	Responsibilities	Collaborators
Business logic	Executes local business functions	Middleware interface
Middleware interface	– Converts incoming messages into method invocations of functions that reside in the business logic – Converts return data back into messages that can be transported across the network	Business logic and remote application
Remote application	Consumes functions that reside in the application	Middleware interface

Resulting Context

After you decide to use *Functional Integration,* you must choose a particular kind of integration that is appropriate for your situation. Your choices are summarized by the following patterns:

- *Distributed Object Integration*
- *Message-Oriented Middleware Integration*
- *Service-Oriented Integration* (through XML-based Web services)

Distributed Object Integration

Distributed Object Integration is also known as instance-based collaboration because it extends the model of object-oriented computing to distributed solutions. Objects inside one application interact with objects in another remote application in the same way that they would interact locally with another object. This implies that the interaction occurs with a specific object instance and that the client application often manages the lifetime of the object it is accessing. This type of interaction usually seems natural to application developers, but it can result in a complex and tightly-coupled interaction model between the components. This tight coupling is not a problem as long as the components are part of a single distributed application. However, it is generally not a good choice when integrating multiple stand-alone applications.

Great examples of distributed component middleware are technologies such as .NET remoting, COM+, or CORBA. For more information, see the *Remote Procedure Invocation* pattern [Hohpe04] or the "Distributed Systems" chapter in *Enterprise Solution Patterns Using Microsoft .NET* [Trowbridge03].

Message-Oriented Middleware Integration

Message-Oriented Middleware Integration connects systems by using asynchronous message queues that are based on proprietary message-oriented middleware. The connected systems then communicate by using messages that contain small packets of data. Because the communication is asynchronous and durable, there is little chance of the messages being lost during network or system failure.

To share request/response type functionality, the consuming system must create a request message and send it by way of the message queue to the system that provides the functionality. The provider then takes the message from the queue, interprets it as a request, and processes it. Upon completion, the provider creates a response message and sends it back to the functional consumer by way of the message queue. Of course, not all functionality is shared by using a request/response style collaboration, but similar principles apply. For more information, see the *Messaging* pattern [Hohpe04].

Service-Oriented Integration

Service-Oriented Integration connects systems by enabling them to consume and provide XML-based Web services. The interfaces to these systems are described through Web Services Definition Language (WDSL) contracts. Systems interact with each other by using SOAP messages. SOAP messages are usually conveyed through HTTP by using XML serialization.

Note: The term *service* is used in many different ways in the context of software engineering. It is also used in at least seven levels of scope: operating system, process, object, distributed object, proprietary message-oriented middleware, logical, and XML Web services. This guide uses the term *service* to mean XML Web services unless indicated otherwise.

A *Service Interface* [Trowbridge03] exposes functionality as a Web service, and, a *Service Gateway* encapsulates the logic necessary to consume services (see Figure 4.15).

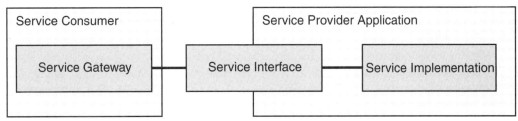

Figure 4.15
Using a service gateway and service interface to connect a Web service consumer and provider

Using *Service-Oriented Integration* increases interoperability by using XML and XML Schema as the basis of message exchange and by using SOAP as an extensible messaging framework. XML Schema provides for a type system that is portable between disparate technical architectures. In contrast, SOAP can be bound to a number of different transport mechanisms. For more information, see *Service-Oriented Integration*.

Choosing Between Alternatives

There are many factors to consider when choosing the kind of *Functional Integration* that is best for your particular requirements. Some of these factors include:

- Reliability and latency of the network between endpoints
- Interfaces exposed by your current systems
- Need for interoperability between disparate technical architectures
- Performance

- Fragility, if incompatible updates are introduced to any participant
- Expertise of the technical team
- Existing infrastructure

Choosing Distributed Objects

If your team is proficient with object-oriented development and if you use a platform infrastructure that offers a *Broker* such as .NET Framework remoting, *Distributed-Object Integration* can be fairly simple to implement. Although the remote interface is almost as easy to manipulate as the local interface, you must always consider network latency, network failure, and distributed systems failures. You must develop a significant amount of error detection and correction logic to anticipate these impacts. With high-latency network round trips, you want to avoid a large number of fine-grained method invocations. Therefore, use *Remote Facade* [Fowler03] and *Data Transfer Object* [Trowbridge03] to optimize call granularity and payload size.

This kind of integration works best when the systems that you want to connect are located in the same data center and when those systems have fairly reliable and high-speed connections. This kind of integration does not work well across slow and unreliable connections, including any connection that uses the Internet. This kind of integration is fragile if incompatible updates are introduced to any of the participants. Of course, if the target system you want to integrate with only exposes object-based APIs, you must use this method or an adapter to connect.

Choosing Message-Oriented Middleware Integration

Message-Oriented Middleware Integration is an excellent choice when systems are not reliably connected because there is the potential for network failure or distributed systems failure. Because *Message-Oriented Middleware Integration* works by placing messages asynchronously into a durable queue, there is little chance that the messages could be lost during a system or network failure. In addition, using asynchronous communication decouples the sender from the receiver. The application that sends the messages will continue to function even if the receiver fails, and the failed message receiver will continue processing messages from the queue after the receiver is restored.

The sender and the receivers are also decoupled from each other because they use a common message format. This makes it easier to separate the message from the set of intended receivers in the enterprise. After a message is sent from a source, you can design an integration network that uses the *Message Broker* pattern, the *Message Bus* pattern, the *Publish/Subscribe* pattern, or a host of other message receivers without modifying the original message sender. This allows the source, distribution, and consumption of the message to vary independently, thus improving flexibility.

Of course, there are tradeoffs involved with using *Message-Oriented Middleware*. Although the programming model is fairly simple for *Distributed-Object Integration*, the programming model becomes much more complex for *Message-Oriented Middleware*. Messages arriving at endpoints become events; therefore, the programming model is event driven. In addition, these events arrive across networks that may be unreliable and that do not have implicit correlation between them. The order of message arrival is not necessarily guaranteed and there may be duplicate messages. Sometimes, processing duplicate messages (also known as *idempotent messages*) does not adversely affect your system. Other times, processing duplicate messages is a serious flaw, for example, when you are transferring money. The security context of the message must be established, policies must be applied, and trust boundaries must be established. Your particular requirements must anticipate and justify this additional complexity. In addition, using proprietary message-oriented integration binds you to a particular message-oriented middleware implementation. It must be installed on the endpoint you want to communicate with, which may not always be the case inside your enterprise or between trading partners.

Service-Oriented Integration

Most enterprises have heterogeneous technical architectures and want to take advantage of system-based collaboration over the Internet. The most competitive enterprises want flexible and automated business processes that may require technology independence. All of these factors contribute to an urgent requirement for interoperability between different technical architectures. The best way to design for interoperability is by using *Service-Oriented Integration*.

Like *Message-Oriented Middleware Integration*, *Service-Oriented Integration* uses messages to communicate between senders and receivers. Unlike *Message-Oriented Middleware*, *Service-Oriented Integration* uses XML Schema and SOAP to transport and resolve messages. These two standards provide a portable type system and an extensible messaging framework that is not coupled to any proprietary implementation or transport. In addition, *Service-Oriented Integration* recommends the Web Services Integration (WS-I) Basic Profile to ensure interoperability between endpoints.

Service-Oriented Integration enables interoperability and allows you to send both synchronous and asynchronous messages (for more information, see the *Service-Oriented Integration* pattern). As a result, you can have the same kind of complex programming model as *Message-Oriented Middleware*. In addition, you have the complexity of a new and still emerging set of standards to understand and comply with. Therefore, make sure your requirements justify this level of complexity.

After you build these interoperable systems, there is one more tradeoff to consider: performance. Using XML incurs the cost of serializing, deserializing, and parsing XML documents. In addition, XML documents are often much larger than their binary equivalents because they contain metadata. This can increase the size of the payload that must be processed during message exchanges. However, because processing power is relatively inexpensive and because processors get faster every year, the issue of payload size can be addressed though hardware. Also, you can selectively trade interoperability for performance by using binary encoding inside your SOAP message as needed. Finally, given the support of major vendors, it is likely that new platform infrastructure will evolve in a way that will optimize Web services–based performance.

Combining Distributed Objects, Message-Oriented Middleware, and Services

It is likely you will use some combination of all three types of integration in your enterprise. Start by identifying services at a level of granularity that is meaningful to the business, such as steps within a business process. This will help you define service boundaries where interoperability is important. For interactions across these boundaries, use *Service-Oriented Integration*. For an example of service identification, see Chapter 9, "Integration Examples." To implement a service within these boundaries, you may want to use *Distributed-Object Integration*, *Message-Oriented Middleware Integration*, or *Service-Oriented Integration*. If you need to do two-phase commits across distributed databases, using *Distributed-Object Integration* permits you to take advantage of platform infrastructure that supports two-phase commits across distributed databases. Just ensure that you keep these transactions inside your service boundaries.

Any time you connect with systems and networks that you consider to be unreliable, consider using *Message-Oriented Middleware* to provide a durable buffer between connected systems. Using messages as your means of communication, either through *Message-Oriented Middleware* or *Service-Oriented Integration*, permits you to construct more advanced integration architectures that use *Message Broker* and *Message Bus* to communicate. As needed, you can always connect these integration architectures by using object-based APIs as described by the *Adapter* pattern [Gamma95].

Regardless of the kind of *Functional Integration* you use, you will encounter the following benefits and liabilities.

Benefits

- **Flexibility**. *Functional Integration* is very flexible. The abstraction, in the form of a function call, permits many different types of interchanges, such as data replication, shared business functions, or business process integration. This also implies that a generic mechanism for *Functional Integration* can be used in many different integration scenarios.

- **Encapsulation**. A functional interface provides an abstraction from an application's internal workings. This isolates users of the programming interface from variations in the application's internal workings or data representations.

- **Robust**. Executing a function through an application's business logic layer ensures that only well-defined functions can be executed. It also ensures that all validations built into the application logic are executed. This ensures that other applications cannot perform invalid functions or corrupt the application's internal state.

- **Familiar programming model**. *Functional Integration* provides a programming model that is more aligned with widespread application programming models. *Functional Integration* is therefore familiar to most application developers. Other styles of integration, such as *Data Integration* or *Presentation Integration*, require developers to learn a new style of development.

Liabilities

- **Tighter coupling**. One application that sends a command directly to another application results in tighter coupling compared to publishing data to a common *Message Bus* because the requesting application requires information about the location of the application that is providing the service. However, inserting a *Message Broker* can alleviate this type of coupling.

- **Requires business layer to be exposed**. Naturally, *Functional Integration* is limited to scenarios where the affected applications expose a suitable functional interface. This is the case for most contemporary business applications, but it may not be true for older monolithic applications or for Web applications hosted by external entities. In those cases, *Presentation Integration* may be the only option.

- **Limited to available functions**. In most cases, *Functional Integration* is limited to the functions that are already implemented in the application's business logic. Extending the application's logic with new functions usually involves significant development and may outweigh the other benefits of *Functional Integration*. In such cases, implementing the new function externally might be a more efficient approach.

- **Inefficient with large datasets**. Existing functional interfaces are generally designed to execute individual functions. This typically makes them inefficient for the transmission of large datasets because many individual requests must be made.

- **Programming-language specific**. Many functional interfaces are tied to a specific programming language or technology because the stronger semantics of the conversation require a more detailed contract that includes the representation of method names, complex data structures, return values, exceptions, and other elements.

Testing Considerations

Functional Integration is easier to test than other integration approaches for the following reasons:

- The additional abstraction provided by the separation of the exposed functional interface and the internal execution of the function permits the creation of mock objects and test stubs. These constructs work with the external applications in the same way the full application does because they implement the same interface. However, the test stub or mock object usually does not perform actual business functions that may be slow or that may require many external resources. Instead, the stub fabricates response data, or it logs data into a logging mechanism that can be monitored by the test tools.

- Because *Functional Integration* is based on the same programming model as the application itself, tests of the integration are easier to tie to the testing of the application itself. This type of testing is also generally well-supported by test tools such as NUnit that target application testing.

However, you must consider the following considerations. Your ability to test depends on how well the functional interface of the existing application is structured. If the interface exposes functions that are well-defined and that are free of side effects free, testing should be relatively easy. If the functional interface consists of a blur of poorly defined functions that are full of side effects, then testing will be difficult.

Security Considerations

The richer semantics of *Functional Integration* allow for a more finely grained security model. Many applications enforce security rules based on user identity, and they control permissions on an object level. For example, a user is only allowed to access the accounts that belong to that user and to access related accounts. This type of permission checking is typically not available with *Data Integration*.

The disadvantage of this more complex security model is that the integration solution has to acquire the proper user credentials to access data or to invoke functions. Because other applications are generally unaware of the security context used in another application, the security context has to be established by the middleware. You can establish the security context either by using a fixed user or by using an explicit translation of security contexts between applications.

Acknowledgments

[Hohpe04] Hohpe, Gregor, and Bobby Woolf, *Enterprise Integration Patterns: Designing, Building, and Deploying Messaging Solutions*. Addison-Wesley, 2004.

[Linthicum04] Linthicum, David. *Next Generation Application Integration*. Addison-Wesley, 2003.

[Ruh01] Ruh, William. *Enterprise Application Integration. A Wiley Tech Brief*. Wiley, 2001.

[Trowbridge03] Trowbridge, David; Dave Mancini, Dave Quick, Gregor Hohpe, James Newkirk, and David Lavigne. *Enterprise Solution Patterns Using Microsoft .NET*. Microsoft Press, 2003. Also available on the *MSDN Architecture Center* at: *http://msdn.microsoft.com/architecture/patterns/default.aspx?pull=/library/en-us /dnpatterns/html/Esp.asp*

[W3C04] "Web Services Architecture W3C Working Draft 11 February 2004." Available on the W3C Web site at: *http://www.w3.org/TR/2004/NOTE-ws-arch-20040211/*

Service-Oriented Integration

Context

You've decided to use the *Functional Integration* pattern to integrate information systems that were not designed to work together. You need interoperability among systems built with different technical architectures. In addition, the systems that you want to integrate may not be reliably connected.

Problem

How do you integrate applications at the business logic layer?

Forces

Integrating systems at the business logic layer involves balancing the following forces:

- **Machine boundaries are important**. The idea that you can take a local object interface and extend it across machine boundaries to create location transparency is flawed. Although it is true that both the remote objects and the local objects have the same interface from the perspective of the calling process, the behavior of the called interface is quite different depending on location. From the client perspective, a remote implementation of the interface is subject to network latency, network failure, and distributed system failures that do not exist with local implementations. A significant amount of error detection and correction logic must be written to anticipate the impacts of using remote object interfaces.

- **Coupling affects interoperability**. Integrating at the logical business layer involves sharing functionality. Sharing functionality implies some level of coupling between the consumer and the provider of the functionality. There are many forms of coupling. These forms of coupling include the following:

  - **Temporal coupling**. Temporal coupling occurs during the request for functionality. If the request is synchronous, the calling system must wait for the provider to finish processing the request before it can continue. If the request is asynchronous, the calling system can continue processing after it makes the request while the providing system independently continues to process the request. In terms of time, the asynchronous call is more loosely coupled than the synchronous call.

- **Type-system coupling**. Type-system coupling occurs when a process must associate the name of a type with its binary representation on the host computer. This association may be as simple as an integer, meaning a big-endian 4-byte primitive on one computer and a 2-byte little-endian primitive on another. Of course, user-defined types such as a customer object become much more complex. When two systems interoperate, they must share a common type representation; in this sense they are coupled together. Most implementation platforms do not share the same type representation.

- **Dependency coupling**. Dependency coupling occurs when one executable depends on other executables to run. If the executable cannot resolve its dependencies at run time, the executable fails. In this sense, the executable and its dependencies are coupled together.

To integrate disparate systems, you must resolve potential differences in type systems and execution dependencies. You must also decide whether you want the calling thread of execution to block when making a request to the provider.

- **Coupling and Interface Definition Language**. Even when the type system is described using an Interface Definition Language (IDL), platform infrastructure code must be installed on the host computer that interprets the IDL. For example, if you are using Common Object Request Broker Architecture (CORBA), infrastructure such as an Object Request Broker (ORB) must be installed on the host computer for a system to resolve the CORBA IDL types. Two CORBA-based systems that are installed on different hardware platforms and operating systems can interoperate, but they both remain coupled to the CORBA type specification and binary mappings.

- **Coupling and message-oriented middleware**. Type-system coupling also occurs when using proprietary message-oriented middleware. To resolve message formats, each endpoint must contain an installation of the appropriate message-oriented middleware. Although a particular message-oriented-middleware product may be ported to multiple platforms, any endpoint you want to communicate with must also have the same message-oriented middleware product installed.

- **Portable type system**. Most enterprise systems can process XML. From the perspective of type-system coupling, the only primitive that must be agreed upon is a string. After the incoming byte stream is interpreted as a string buffer, the string can be parsed according to XML specifications, including XML schema. In turn, the schema provides a type system that is highly portable between disparate hardware and operating systems.

- **Contracts**. Contracts have proven to be an excellent means of specifying behavior between a consumer and a provider of services.

Solution

To integrate applications at the business logic layer, enable systems to consume and provide XML-based Web services. Use Web Services Description Language (WSDL) contracts to describe the interfaces to these systems. Ensure interoperability by making your implementation compliant with the Web Services family of specifications (for example, the Web Services Security [WS-Security] specification). For more information about the Web Services specifications, see "Specifications" in the Web Services Developer Center on MSDN (*http://msdn.microsoft.com/webservices/understanding/specs/default.aspx*). Whenever possible, use the document message style and literal serialization (see "Use Document/Literal SOAP Styles and Encoding" later in this pattern).

Note: The term *service* is used in many different ways in the context of software engineering. It is also used in at least seven levels of scope: operating system, process, object, distributed object, proprietary message-oriented middleware, logical, and XML Web services. This guide uses the term *service* to mean XML Web services unless indicated otherwise.

To expose existing functionality as a Web service, use the *Service Interface* pattern [Trowbridge03]. To encapsulate the logic necessary to consume services, use the *Service Gateway* pattern [Trowbridge03]. Figure 4.16 shows the design elements involved in this interaction.

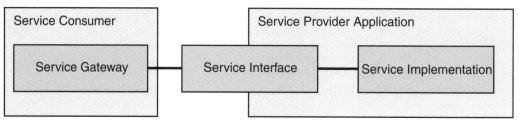

Figure 4.16
Using Service Gateway and Service Interface to connect a Web service consumer and provider

In addition to following the Web Services specifications, you should also refer to the Web Services Interoperability (WS-I) profiles when you design and build Web services. For more information about WS-I, see the Web Services Interoperability Organization Web site (*http://www.ws-i.org*). For guidance about how to build Web services that are compliant with the WS-I basic profile, see *Building Interoperable Web services: WS-I Basic Profile 1.0* on MSDN (*http://msdn.microsoft.com/library /default.asp?url=/library/en-us/dnsvcinter/html/wsi-bp_msdn_landingpage.asp*).

Web Services

What exactly is a Web service? According to the World Wide Web Consortium (W3C),

> "a Web service is a software system designed to support interoperable machine-to-machine interaction over a network. It has an interface described in a machine-processable format (specifically WSDL). Other systems interact with the Web service in a manner prescribed by its description using SOAP-messages, typically conveyed using HTTP with an XML serialization in conjunction with other Web-related standards." [W3C04]

In terms of interaction, two systems use Web services to communicate when a requesting application creates an XML document in the form of a message and sends it over the network to a provider of Web services. Optionally, the provider sends a reply to the requester in the form of an XML document. Web services standards specify the interface that the message is sent to, the format of the message, the mapping of the message contents to service implementations, the optional headers, and the means by which services can publish and discover other Web services.

Resolving the Forces

How does using Web services to integrate systems resolve the forces mentioned earlier? First, basing your messages on XML and XML Schema definition language (XSD) results in a highly portable type system as explained earlier. A portable type system dramatically reduces type-system coupling. Type-system coupling is a major impediment to cross-platform integration. However, to take full advantage of this portable type system, you must understand SOAP styles and encoding.

Use Document/Literal SOAP Styles and Encoding

The WSDL 1.1 specification identifies two message styles (document and Remote Procedure Call [RPC]) and two means of serializing the message onto the transport mechanism (SOAP encoding and XML Schema). Choosing the right combination of style and serialization have major impact on the interoperability of your Web service.

The document message style indicates that the message body contains an XML document. It is up to the service consumer and the service provider to agree on the document exchanged. The RPC style indicates that the message body will contain an XML representation of an RPC.

To serialize the message data, the XML Schema–based serialization simply uses the definitions contained in the XML Schema specification. Because using XML Schema results in a highly portable type system, the messages are highly interoperable. However, the SOAP-encoded serialization uses encoding rules that require RPC-style communication. Since the details of RPC communication can vary significantly between implementations, the resulting messages are not as easily interoperable.

As a result of these interoperability concerns, use document-style messages with literal encoding (doc/literal) whenever possible. For more information about this topic, see "Understanding Soap" on MSDN (*http://msdn.microsoft.com/webservices /understanding/webservicebasics/default.aspx?pull=/library/en-us//dnsoap/html /understandsoap.asp*).

Combine Synchronous and Asynchronous Behavior to Address Temporal Coupling

To address temporal coupling, it is possible to invoke Web services both synchronously and asynchronously. To understand how to do this in the context of Web services, you must understand parts of the WSDL, SOAP, and Web Service Architecture specifications.

To abstract communication away from implementation notions such as synchronous and asynchronous calls, WSDL uses the concept of message exchange patterns (MEP) to describe generic patterns of message exchange between endpoints. There are four kinds of MEP described in WSDL 1.1, as shown in Table 4.3.

Table 4.3: Four Kinds of Message Exchange Patterns (MEP)

MEP name	Description	Type
Request-response	The endpoint receives a message and then sends a correlated message.	Synchronous*
One-way	The endpoint receives a message.	Asynchronous
Solicit-response	The endpoint sends a message and then receives a correlated message.	Synchronous*
Notification	The endpoint sends a message.	Asynchronous

* This MEP emulates synchronous behavior with HTTP POST/GET SOAP binding.

SOAP provides an extensible one-way messaging framework between sender and receiver. To implement SOAP, however, you must bind it to a specific protocol. HTTP POST/GET is the most common protocol. Because HTTP is a synchronous protocol, if you use the SOAP/HTTP binding, you get the synchronous/asynchronous behavior shown in Figure 4.17.

In cases where there are long-running transactions across enterprises, a Web service exchanges messages synchronously while the larger business process that it runs within executes asynchronously. For example, consider the Global Bank scenario.

Global Bank's Asynchronous Business Process

In the Execute Scheduled Payment use case (see Chapter 2 for more details), Global Bank sends international payments through a Society for Worldwide Interbank Financial Telecommunication (SWIFT) payment gateway by using Web services over the Internet. The message sent is an XML document containing the information necessary for the payment gateway to electronically pay the payee identified in the document. This message is sent synchronously through HTTP, and the response only acknowledges a successful transmission. When the successful transmission occurs, the payment gateway processes the message, and the calling system does not wait for a response. After the payment gateway has finished processing the payment, it sends another message to Global Bank confirming the payment status. This message is a synchronous HTTP request/response, and the response information only acknowledges a successful message transmission.

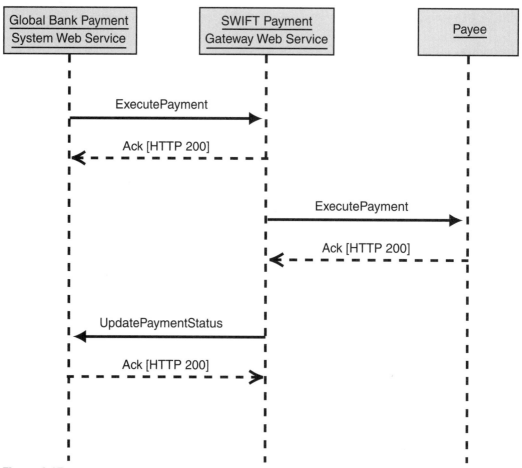

Figure 4.17
SWIFT payment gateway combining synchronous exchanges to simulate asynchronous behavior

In the Execute Scheduled Payment use case, two synchronous message exchanges participate in an asynchronous business collaboration. This effectively decouples the systems.

Recognize Explicit Boundaries

Because Web services pass documents instead of RPC calls, there is no attempt to consider that the location of the service is transparent. Indeed, the boundary between the two services is explicitly recognized. With explicit boundaries, the connection is not treated as reliable and available, as it would be treated with *Distributed Object Integration*. You can use other patterns such as *Server Clustering*, *Load-Balanced Cluster*, and *Failover Cluster* [Trowbridge03] to meet operational requirements when traversing these boundaries.

Treat Services as Autonomous

When using services to integrate systems, you should consider two key elements: service interfaces and service implementations. Service interfaces describe the functionality, messages, and results that the consumers of the service can expect. Contracts provide these interfaces in the form of WSDL files. Service implementations contain the software that implements the service and all its execution dependencies, with the possible exception of other services.

Collaborations through service interfaces facilitate a high degree of interoperability in your enterprise. The services should be capable of being independently versioned, managed, and deployed. As these services are deployed, all the appropriate execution dependencies (except other services) should be deployed with the service and contained within the service boundary.

Example

For detailed examples, see *Implementing Service-Oriented Integration with ASP.NET* and *Implementing Service-Oriented Integration with BizTalk Server 2004*.

Resulting Context

As a result of implementing the *Service-Oriented Integration* pattern, the following tenets apply [Box04]:

- **Boundaries are explicit**. Crossing service boundaries can be costly. For example, you may need to span geography, trust boundaries, or execution environments.. You should therefore explicitly opt into service orientation by formally passing defined messages between services. The explicit boundaries allow you to formally express implementation-independent interaction so that your interactions do not depend on the different platform, middleware, or coding language choices used to implement other services.

- **Services are autonomous**. There is no presiding authority in a service-oriented environment. Services are independently deployed, versioned, and managed. The topology in which a service executes evolves over time. The service should expect that peer services will fail and that it will receive malformed or malicious messages. The services should be built by using techniques such as redundancy and failover so that the services do not fail.

- **Services share schema and contract, not class**. Services interact solely on their expression of structures through schemas and behaviors through contracts. The service's contract describes the structure of messages and ordering constraints over messages. The formality of the expression allows machine verification of incoming messages. Machine verification of incoming messages allows you to protect the service's integrity. Contracts and schemas must remain stable over time, so building them flexibly is important.

- **Service compatibility is based on policy**. Services express their capabilities and requirements in terms of a machine readable policy expression. Policy assertions are identified by a stable, globally unique name. Individual policy assertions are opaque to the system as a whole; services must simply be able to satisfy each other's policy requirements.

Benefits

The key benefit of using *Service-Oriented Integration* is interoperability between disparate technical architectures. Interoperability at the level of technical architecture helps to decouple an enterprise's business architecture from its information technology. This decoupling gives an enterprise a great deal of flexibility in terms of how it implements specific business capabilities.

Although an enterprise contains processes, resources, goals, business rules, and relationships [Eriksson00], it is the business processes that define how work actually is done. Technical architectures enable work to be done efficiently by incorporating business processes.

Without interoperable systems, the cost of process change is relatively high because it may involve crossing technology boundaries. When using interoperable systems, however, the cost of process change is dramatically lowered. This is especially true when services are designed at a level of granularity that is meaningful to the business, such as steps within a process. Businesses that have interoperable systems and that use services that are relevant to business process are in a better position to sense and respond to market changes and opportunities. These businesses become more agile as a result of creating interoperable systems and using services that are relevant to business practices.

Liabilities

The key liability of using *Service-Oriented Integration* is the performance cost of serializing, deserializing, and parsing XML documents. In addition, XML documents are much larger than their binary equivalents because they contain metadata. This increases the size of the payload that must be processed during message exchange.

Security Considerations

Security is critical to services. Given its complex and technology-specific nature, you must consider security individually for each implementation.

Related Patterns

For more information, see the following related patterns:

- *Implementing Service-Oriented Integration with ASP.NET.*

- *Implementing Service-Oriented Integration with BizTalk Server 2004.*

- *Broker* [Buschmann96]. To discover and publish services, Web services use an implementation of the Universal Description, Discovery, and Integration of Web Services (UDDI) specification. UDDI is an implementation of the *Indirect Broker* pattern. The *Indirect Broker* is a specialized kind of *Broker* [Buschmann96]. *Indirect Broker* enables one endpoint to locate another. After the other endpoint is located, the two endpoints communicate directly with each other. In comparison, *Direct Broker* also helps make the initial connection, but it maintains central control over the communication. For an example of a *Direct Broker*, see *Message Broker*.

- *Service Gateway* [Trowbridge03]. This pattern contains the code that implements the consumer portion of the contract into its own *Service Gateway* component.

- *Service Interface* [Trowbridge03]. This pattern designs an application as a collection of software services. Each software service has a service interface that consumers of the application can interact through.

Acknowledgments

[Box04] Box, Don. "Code Name Indigo: A Guide to Developing and Running Connected Systems with Indigo." *MSDN Magazine*. January 2004. Available from the MSDN Windows Code-Named "Longhorn" Developer's Center at: *http://msdn.microsoft.com/longhorn/understanding/pillars/indigo/default.aspx?pull=/ msdnmag/issues/04/01/Indigo/default.aspx.*

[Buschmann96] Buschmann, Frank; Regine Meunier, Hans Rohnert, Peter Sommerlad, and Michael Stal. *Pattern-Oriented Software Architecture, Volume 1: A System of Patterns.* John Wiley & Sons Ltd, 1996.

[Erikkson00] Eriksson, Hans-Erik, and Magnus Penker. *Business Modeling with UML: Business Patterns at Work*. John Wiley & Sons, Inc., 2000.

[Newcomer02]. Newcomer, Eric. *Understanding Web Services: XML, WSDL, SOAP, and UDDI*. Addison-Wesley, 2002.

[Skonnard03-2] Skonnard, Aaron. "Understanding SOAP." *MSDN Web Services Developer Center*, March 2003. Available at:
http://msdn.microsoft.com/webservices/understanding/webservicebasics/default.aspx?pull=/library/en-us//dnsoap/html/understandsoap.asp.

[Trowbridge03] Trowbridge, David; Dave Mancini, Dave Quick, Gregor Hohpe, James Newkirk, and David Lavigne. *Enterprise Solution Patterns Using Microsoft .NET*. Microsoft Press, 2003. Also available on the *MSDN Architecture Center* at:
http://msdn.microsoft.com/architecture/patterns/default.aspx?pull=/library/en-us/dnpatterns/html/Esp.asp.

[W3C04] "Web Services Architecture W3C Working Draft 11 February 2004." Available on the W3C Web site at:
http://www.w3.org/TR/2004/NOTE-ws-arch-20040211/

[Wanagel03] Wanagel, Jonathan, et al. "Building Interoperable Web Services: WS-I Basic Profile 1.0." *MSDN Library*, August 2003. Available at:
http://msdn.microsoft.com/library/default.asp?url=/library/en-us/dnsvcinter/html/wsi-bp_msdn_landingpage.asp.

Implementing Service-Oriented Integration with ASP.NET

Context

You are connecting two systems by using *Service-Oriented Integration* so that one system can consume functions provided by the other. The service provider is implemented by using the Microsoft .NET Framework.

Background

In the Global Bank scenario, the Web application server accesses the mainframe computer through a gateway service to retrieve a customer's account balance. Figure 4.18 illustrates how the interaction between the two systems is implemented as *Service-Oriented Integration* by using Microsoft ASP.NET Web services.

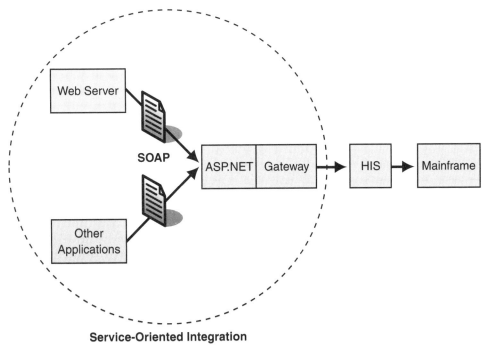

Figure 4.18

Two applications using Service-Oriented Integration to access the gateway

This implementation describes how to expose functionality that resides on a mainframe computer as a Web service so that it can be accessed through *Service-Oriented Integration*. The gateway is a custom C# application that connects to the banking mainframe computer through Microsoft Host Integration Server (HIS). The mainframe computer manages the account balances for the customer accounts and provides functions such account balance retrieval, account credits, and account debits.

Note: This implementation focuses on the interaction between the Web server and the *Gateway* component. For a more detailed description of the interaction between the *Gateway* and the mainframe computer, see *Implementing Gateway with Host Integration Server 2004*.

The mainframe gateway exposes a number of different methods to get account balances, to credit and debit accounts, and to perform other functions. This implementation describes only the use of the **GetAccountInfo** method to return the name and balance of an account.

Implementation Strategy

As already mentioned, the strategy is to enable *Service-Oriented Integration* by exposing mainframe functionality as an ASP.NET Web service. Before discussing detailed steps, it is helpful to review the concept of *Service-Oriented Integration* as well as some details about ASP.NET Web services.

Service-Oriented Integration

Service-Oriented Integration connects applications through the exchange of documents, usually in the form of XML documents. Figure 4.19 shows *Service-Oriented Integration* passing documents between a service consumer and a service provider.

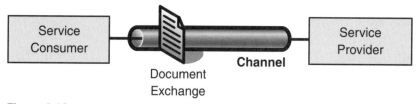

Figure 4.19
Document exchange in Service-Oriented Integration

The document exchange in Figure 4.19 does not imply interaction with a specific instance of a remote object. Instead, when the document is passed from the consumer to the provider, it triggers the execution of a specific function or service that is self-contained and stateless. This is an important difference between *Service-Oriented Integration* and *Distributed Object Integration* (also known as instance-based integration), which allows the client to manage the lifetime of a specific remote object instance.

The following example shows an XML document passed inside a SOAP envelope.

```
<?xml version="1.0" encoding="utf-8"?>
<soap:Envelope xmlns:xsi="http://www.w3.org/2001/XMLSchema-instance"
               xmlns:xsd="http://www.w3.org/2001/XMLSchema"
               xmlns:soap="http://schemas.xmlsoap.org/soap/envelope/">
  <soap:Body>
    <GetAccountInfoRequest xmlns="http://msdn.microsoft.com/patterns/">
      <AccountID xmlns="">12345678</AccountID>
    </GetAccountInfoRequest>
  </soap:Body>
</soap:Envelope>
```

ASP.NET Web Services

When you use ASP.NET to implement a Web service, the function that processes the incoming document is implemented as a method of a .NET Framework class. The .NET Framework manages the instantiation of a specific instance of that class.

The .NET Framework does quite a bit of work behind the scenes when it receives an incoming SOAP request, as shown in Figure 4.20. Understanding the functions that the .NET Framework performs internally is not strictly necessary, but it is very helpful when designing ASP.NET Web services. It also gives you a good appreciation of the amount of functionality that resides in the .NET Framework.

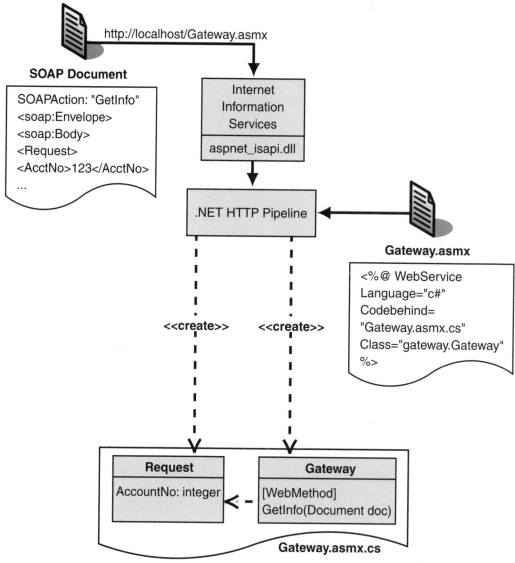

Figure 4.20
ASP.NET Web services handling

When a document reaches a specified endpoint, the server has two main pieces of information to work with: the contents of the document and the URL of the endpoint. With those two pieces of information, the server has to complete the following steps:

1. Determine the .NET Framework class that should handle the request.
2. Determine the method to invoke inside that class.
3. Instantiate data transfer objects to pass data from the incoming document to the method.
4. Invoke the method.
5. Return the results.

Internet Information Services (IIS) uses the file extension of the incoming URL to map requests to the appropriate Internet Services API (ISAPI) handler. ASP.NET Web services endpoints carry an .asmx extension in the URL. The .asmx extension in the URL causes IIS to map the request to the standard .NET Framework HTTP pipeline. Based on default computer configuration settings, the .NET Framework HTTP pipeline hands control over to a **WebServiceHandler**. The **WebServiceHandler** in turn determines the .NET Framework class that is associated with the URL by reading the .asmx file referenced by the URL. In Figure 4.21, the Gateway.asmx file specifies the class **Gateway** as the class servicing requests. This class is defined inside a code-behind page named Gateway.asmx.cs.

The Web service handler still has to determine the method to invoke for the incoming document. By default, it determines the method to invoke based on the value of the SOAPAction field that is part of the HTTP header. The following is a sample of that part of an HTTP header.

```
SOAPAction: "http://msdn.microsoft.com/patterns/GetAccountInfo"
```

After the Web service handler has determined the method to invoke, it parses the incoming XML document and creates an instance of the matching .NET Framework objects to be passed to the method. This step is referred to as deserialization and is performed by the .NET Framework XML Serializer. The method performing the function does not even have to know that the parameters were originally passed as an XML document wrapped inside a SOAP envelope. Lastly, the Web service handler creates an instance of the class that implements the service function and invokes the appropriate method, passing instances of the applicable data transfer objects.

For a more detailed description of ASP.NET Web service internals, see "How ASP.NET Web Services Work" on MSDN (*http://msdn.microsoft.com/library/ default.asp?url=/library/en-us/dnwebsrv/html/howwebmeth.asp*) [Skonnard03].

Building an ASP.NET Web Service

XML Web services expose the service contract to potential consumers as a Web Services Description Language (WSDL) document. To simplify development of Web services, the .NET Framework offers a variety of capabilities, including the automatic generation of WSDL documents based on a service implementation. As a result, you have a number of options when creating a new service interface:

- **Develop the code first**. Write the service implementation code first, and then let the .NET Framework create the WSDL document from the code.

- **Specify the XML schemas first**. Develop message schemas as XML Schema definition language (XSD) schemas first, generate code from the schemas, and then let the .NET Framework create the WSDL document.

- **Develop the WSDL first**. Develop the WSDL definition first, and then let the .NET Framework generate skeleton code matching the definition.

Each approach has advantages and limitations. Generally, the choice is among the amount of control you need, the effort required, and the ease of integrating with other platforms.

Developing the Code First

The easiest way to expose code as a Web service is to label a .NET Framework class with the **[WebService]** attribute and to label the affected method with a **[WebMethod]** attribute. The .NET Framework then takes care of all the details. For example, it generates the WSDL document to give potential clients a description of the service. To perform this conversion without any additional information, the .NET Framework derives the names of SOAP body elements from the name of the method and its arguments. The advantage of this approach is clearly its simplicity. With two lines of extra "code," a method can become a Web service that can be invoked remotely. The limitation lies in the fact that the service interface exactly resembles the code, including variable names. The .NET Framework allows you to override the default naming choices by specifying additional attributes, but the specification for the service still resides in application code. This can be undesirable, for example, if an enterprise wants to keep a global repository of all message definitions independent of the platform that implements a particular service. Another potential pitfall, however, is that this approach can generate a service that will not function properly. For example, if a method returns a non-serializable object, any service invocation will fail even though the code compiled without errors.

Specifying XML Schemas First

A Web services call typically requires two separate messages: a request message and a response message. These messages play roles similar to the roles played by the parameters and the return value of a regular method. Just as defining the signature of a method is an important first step in the creation of a new method, defining the request and return message formats is a logical first step in the creation of a Web services interface. After the message format has been specified, it can be compiled into a C# classes automatically without incurring additional effort. At run time, the .NET Framework still renders the WSDL document and eliminates the need for hand-coding.

XML Web services use XSD documents to define message formats. Defining these documents by using a standard format such as XSD has advantages over generating them from the code. XSD documents are platform-independent and can be used to define message formats independent of the technology implementing the service, whether it is the .NET Framework, the Java 2 Platform, Java 2 Enterprise Edition (J2EE), or any in a range of other technologies. This makes it feasible to keep a global repository of all message types in an enterprise. Creating XML schemas also gives the interface designer exact control over the look of SOAP messages that are sent to and from a particular service.

Potential disadvantages of developing the XSD schemas first include the fact that a new specification language (XML Schema) and tool has to be used. However, many modern development environments, including Microsoft Visual Studio .NET, include powerful and easy-to-use XML Schema editors. Creating XSD documents first also requires additional development and build steps because the XSD document first has to be converted into C# classes. This step has to be repeated whenever the XSD document changes, presenting the risk that the document and the implementation of the service can get out of synchronization.

Developing WSDL First

The specification of a service contract depends on factors other than just the format of inbound and outbound messages. For example, to be accessible, the service has to be bound to a port that can be addressed by using a specified Uniform Resource Identifier (URI). A WSDL document specifies these additional contract terms, such as ports and binding. Starting with the creation of a WSDL document ensures that all details of the service contract (at least to the extent that they are supported by WSDL) can be specified directly and in a technology-neutral manner. The biggest drawback of starting with a WSDL document is that the verboseness of WSDL makes the manual creation tedious.

Example: Building an ASP.NET Web Service to Access the Mainframe Gateway

As described in the Global Bank scenario, the Web application server accesses the mainframe computer through a gateway service to retrieve a customer's account balance. This example creates an ASP.NET Web service that accesses the gateway to the mainframe.

The ASP.NET page framework supports the development of both service providers and service consumers. This implementation begins with the design and development of the service provider. In the example, the mainframe gateway is the service provider. Fortunately, most of the work that the .NET Framework performs is hidden from the developer of an ASP.NET Web service. The developer's main task is to create the interface definition of the service and to fill out the implementing code with the correct attributes to configure the behavior of the ASP.NET internals.

As mentioned in the previous section, there are several approaches to developing a Web service by using ASP.NET. This implementation begins by defining XSD documents for the request and response messages. This approach gives you good control over the published service interface while sparing you from having to hand-code full-blown WSDL documents.

To expose an existing function as an ASP.NET Web service, follow these steps:

1. Develop an XSD document for the request and the response message.
2. Generate data transfer classes from the schema.
3. Define the operations that the service exposes.
4. Connect the service interface to the service implementation.
5. Build and run the service.
6. Create a test client that invokes the Web service.

Figure 4.21 illustrates this process. Each numbered step is explained in detail in the sections that follow.

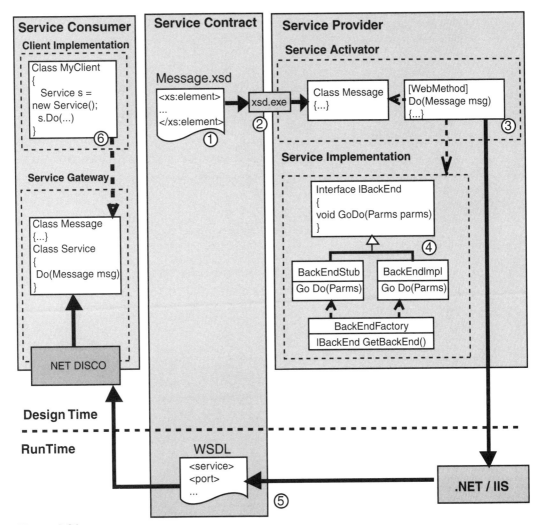

Figure 4.21
Building an ASP.NET Web service

Step 1: Develop XSD Documents

The first step is to define the format of the request and response messages by creating two XSD files. The following are the XSD files for the **GetAccountInfo** method generated using the Microsoft Visual Studio .NET XSD Editor. To ensure maximum interoperability between the gateway service and the consumers, this implementation uses only standard data types and avoids using .NET Framework–specific data types such as **DataSet**.

The XML schema for the request message (GetAccountInfoRequest.xsd) looks like the following example. (To improve readability, the namespace declarations have been omitted.)

```
<xs:schema … >
  <xs:element name="GetAccountInfoRequest">
    <xs:complexType>
      <xs:sequence>
        <xs:element name="AccountID" type="xs:string" />
      </xs:sequence>
    </xs:complexType>
  </xs:element>
</xs:schema>
```

You will notice that the document for the request is quite simple; it contains only a single string data element named **<AccountID>**.

The following sample is what the XML schema response (GetAccountInfoResponse.xsd) looks like.

```
<xs:schema … >
  <xs:element name="GetAccountInfoResponse">
    <xs:complexType>
      <xs:sequence>
        <xs:element name="AccountID" type="xs:string" />
        <xs:element name="Balance" type="xs:decimal" />
        <xs:element name="Name" type="xs:string" />
        <xs:element name="Description" type="xs:string" />
      </xs:sequence>
    </xs:complexType>
  </xs:element>
</xs:schema>
```

After creating the XSD files, the next step is to generate the data transfer classes.

Step 2: Generate Data Transfer Classes

The XML Schema Definition tool (xsd.exe) in the .NET Framework can create a .NET Framework class from an XSD file. To create the data transfer files, run the following commands from the command prompt in the directory where the XSD files reside:

```
xsd /n:GatewayWS /c GetAccountInfoRequest.xsd
xsd /n:GatewayWS /c GetAccountInfoResponse.xsd
```

These commands generate the GetAccountInfoRequest.cs and GetAccountInfoResponse.cs files. Using the **/namespace** option (or the short form, **/n**) enables you to specify the namespace to be used for the generated class. Otherwise, the global namespace is used as the default namespace, which could lead to conflicting namespaces.

The generated class file GetAccountInfoRequest.cs is shown in the following sample.

```
namespace GatewayWS {
    using System.Xml.Serialization;
    ...
    public class GetAccountInfoRequest {
        [System.Xml.Serialization.XmlElementAttribute
            (Form=System.Xml.Schema.XmlSchemaForm.Unqualified)]
        public string AccountID;
    }
}
```

The attribute in front of the AccountID field instructs the XML Serializer that no namespace qualifier is required in the XML string for this element.

The generated class has no functionality, but rather it is a simple data holder class that acts as a *Data Transfer Object* [Trowbridge03] between the .NET Framework and the service implementation. This class is the .NET Framework representation of the XML document that is embedded in a SOAP request to the gateway service. As described previously, at run time the XML Serializer parses the incoming SOAP document, creates an instance of this object, and populates all fields with the values from the incoming SOAP XML document.

Step 3: Define the Operations That the Service Exposes

Now that you have data transfer objects, you can define the methods and operations that the service is going to expose. As described in "ASP.NET Web Services" earlier in this pattern, an ASP.NET Web service endpoint is created from the combination of an .asmx file and an associated code-behind page that contains the actual class definition. Because the Visual Studio .NET tool set generates the .asmx file for you, you can focus on the **Gateway** class itself, which is contained in the file Gateway.asmx.cs. This implementation follows the *Service Interface* [Trowbridge03] approach and separates the public service interface from the implementation.

The class **Gateway** inherits from the base class **WebService**. To keep things simple, the class exposes only a single method, **GetAccountInfo**, as a service.

```
namespace GatewayWS
{
    [WebService(Namespace="http://msdn.microsoft.com/patterns/")]
    public class Gateway : System.Web.Services.WebService
    {
    ...
        [WebMethod]
        [SoapDocumentMethod(ParameterStyle=SoapParameterStyle.Bare)]
        public GetAccountInfoResponse GetAccountInfo(
            GetAccountInfoRequest GetAccountInfoRequest)
        {
            return null;
        }
    }
}
```

For now, leave the method body empty and only return a null value. You will tie this method to the service implementation in the next step.

Note that both the method and the class are encoded with special attributes. The **[WebMethod]** attribute of the **GetAccountInfo** method makes the method accessible as part of the Web service. The additional **[SoapDocumentMethod(...)]** attribute customizes the way the XML Serializer parses incoming SOAP messages. By default, the XML Serializer expects method parameters to be wrapped inside an additional element, which is in turn contained in the **<soap:Body>** element. Changing the **ParameterStyle** setting to **SoapParameterStyle.Bare** makes these method parameters appear immediately under the **<soap:Body>** element, rather than encapsulated in an additional XML element.

The following example shows a SOAP message that causes the **GetAccountInfo** method of the Gateway.asmx Web service to be invoked.

```
...
<soap:Envelope xmlns:xsi="http://www.w3.org/2001/XMLSchema-instance"
               xmlns:xsd="http://www.w3.org/2001/XMLSchema"
               xmlns:soap="http://schemas.xmlsoap.org/soap/envelope/">
  <soap:Body>
    <GetAccountInfoRequest xmlns="http://msdn.microsoft.com/patterns">
      <AccountID xmlns="">1234567</AccountID>
    </GetAccountInfoRequest>
  </soap:Body>
</soap:Envelope>
```

The **<soap:Body>** element contains a **<GetAccountInfoRequest>** element. This element corresponds to the single parameter that the **GetAccountInfo** method receives.

Without the **ParameterStyle** setting, the SOAP request for the same method would look like the following sample. Note that an additional **GetAccountInfo** node beneath the **<soap:Body>** element wraps the method parameters.

```
...
<soap:Envelope xmlns:xsi="http://www.w3.org/2001/XMLSchema-instance"
               xmlns:xsd="http://www.w3.org/2001/XMLSchema"
               xmlns:soap="http://schemas.xmlsoap.org/soap/envelope/">
  <soap:Body>
    <GetAccountInfo xmlns="http://msdn.microsoft.com/patterns/">
      <GetAccountInfoRequest xmlns="http://msdn.microsoft.com/patterns">
        <AccountID xmlns="">1234567</AccountID>
      </GetAccountInfoRequest>
    </GetAccountInfo>
  </soap:Body>
</soap:Envelope>
```

Because the method receives all the necessary data elements inside a single data transfer object, the additional wrapping is not required and makes the SOAP message unnecessarily verbose. Therefore, set the **ParameterStyle** to **Bare**.

Step 4: Connect the Service Interface to the Service Implementation

Now that you have built the service interface and have encoded it with the necessary Web service attributes, you need to link the still-empty **GetAccountInfo** method to the actual service implementation. One option is to insert the code that implements the service into the **GetAccountInfo** method of the **Gateway** class. However, this approach has a number of drawbacks.

First, the **Gateway** class inherits from the **WebService** base class. That means that the class cannot be part of a separate inheritance tree that the service implementation may require.

Second, tying together the Web service interface and the implementation makes it harder to test the implementation outside the Web services context.

Third, the functions that the service implementation provides may not exactly match the service interface definition. For example, the service implementation may require multiple calls to fine-grained methods, whereas the Web service interface should expose coarse-grained functions. Or, the service implementation may use .NET Framework–specific data types, such as **DataSets**, that you are seeking to avoid in the public Web service interface. As a result, the service may need to contain logic to arbitrate between the public Web service interface and the internal implementation.

Finally, tying the Web service directly to the implementation means that the Web service can be functional only when the service implementation is running and is available. That may not always be the case if the actual service implementation resides in an existing system. For example, many mainframe systems have offline times when they are not available for online requests. As the Web service is weaved into a larger solution, these outages could hinder testing. For testing purposes, it would be very convenient to be able to replace the service implementation with a dummy implementation without affecting the service interface.

All these problems can be solved with a combination of well-known design patterns that is shown in Figure 4.22. The first step is to separate the interface of the service functionality from the implementation—for example, the mainframe access. You can do so by applying the *Separated Interface* pattern [Fowler03]. The interface **IGlobalBank** is a generic interface that represents the functions provided by the mainframe system, but it has no dependency on the server running HIS. The class **GlobalHIS** implements the methods specified in this interface by connecting to the mainframe through HIS.

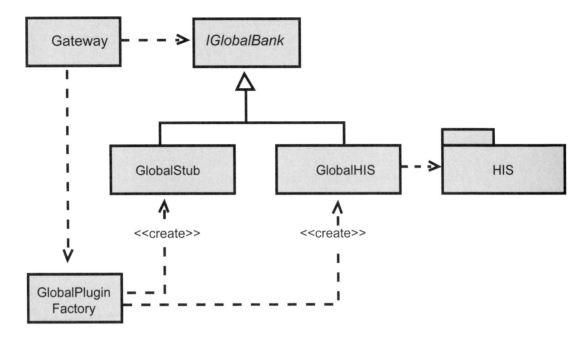

Figure 4.22
Separating the service implementation from the service interface

After you have separated the interface from the implementation, you can create a *Service Stub* [Fowler03]. A service stub is a dummy implementation of an external service that reduces external dependencies during testing. The **GlobalStub** service stub implements the same **IGlobalBank** interface but does not actually connect to the mainframe computer. Instead, it simulates the mainframe functions internally.

Now that you have two implementations, you have to decide which one to use. You want to be able to switch between the dummy implementation and the real implementation without having to change any code or having to recompile. Therefore, this example uses a *Plugin* [Fowler03]. *Plugin* links classes during configuration rather than compilation. You implement the *Plugin* inside the **GlobalPlugInFactory** class. The factory class reads the name of the implementing class from a configuration file so that you can switch between **GlobalStub** and **GlobalHIS** at run time by changing the application configuration file.

What is left for the **Gateway** class to do? It has to call the **GlobalPlugInFactory** class to obtain a reference to an implementation of the **IGlobalBank** interface. Next, it has to invoke the appropriate method in the interface. The names and types of the parameters of the service implementation may differ from the XML schemas that you created, so the **Gateway** class may have to perform simple mapping functions between the two data representations.

Even though the implementation of these extra classes is not strictly necessary to create a working Web service, these patterns simplify testing tremendously and are well worth the additional coding effort. It turns out that the implementation of each class is actually quite simple. The implementation involves the following steps:

1. Create an interface.
2. Create service implementations.
3. Create the plug-in factory.
4. Implement the Web service method.

Let's walk through these steps one by one.

Step 4.1: Create an Interface

First, create an interface for the service implementation. The following code is from the IGlobalBank.cs file. The code references the **AccountInfo** class. The **AccountInfo** class is used by the service implementation. Note that this interface and the data transfer class have no dependency on a specific service implementation.

```
public interface IGlobalBank
{
    // Throws ArgumentException if account does not exist.
    AccountInfo GetAccountInfo (string AccountID);
}

public class AccountInfo
{
    public string accountID;
    public string name;
    public string description;
    public decimal balance;

    public AccountInfo(string accountID, string name,
                       string description, decimal balance)
    {
        this.accountID = accountID;
        this.name = name;
        this.description = description;
        this.balance = balance;
    }
}
```

Step 4.2: Create the Service Implementations

Next, create two implementations of the interface as shown. Create one that is a simple stub, and create another one that connects to the mainframe system through HIS.

The two implementation classes are named **GlobalHIS** and **GlobalStub**. **GlobalHIS** connects to the external system. In the example, the mainframe gateway is the external system. The class implements the **IGlobalBank** interface.

```
public class GlobalHIS : IGlobalBank
{
    ...
    public AccountInfo GetAccountInfo(string accountID)
    {
        decimal balance = 0.00m;
        string name = "";
        object [] contextArray = null;

        TCP_LinkTRM_NET.GlobalBank bank = new TCP_LinkTRM_NET.GlobalBank ();
        bank.cedrbank (ref name ,ref accountID ,ref balance,
                       ref contextArray);
        AccountInfo info = new AccountInfo(accountID, "","", balance);
        return info;
    }
}
```

The **GlobalStub** class provides another implementation of the **IGlobalBank** interface but is a simple stub without any dependency on external systems. It uses an internal **accounts** collection to simulate account balances. For testing purposes, the class constructor initializes this collection by using hard-coded values.

```
public class GlobalStub : IGlobalBank
{
    static IDictionary accounts = (IDictionary) new Hashtable();

    public GlobalStub()
    {
        if (accounts.Count == 0)
        {
            accounts.Add("123",
                new AccountInfo("123", "TestAccount", "TestDescription", 777.12m));
        }
    }

    public AccountInfo GetAccountInfo(string accountID)
    {
        if (!accounts.Contains(accountID))
            throw new ArgumentException("Account does not exist");
        return (AccountInfo)accounts[accountID];
    }
}
```

Step 4.3: Create the Plug-in Factory

Now that you have created two implementations of the **IGlobalBank** interface, you need to decide the implementation that you want to use at run time. This is the purpose of the **GlobalBankPlugInFactory** class. The class reads the name of the class to be used from the configuration file and then creates an instance of that class. It returns a reference to the newly created object to the service interface, but the reference is cast to the **IGlobalStub** interface. This way the service interface is not dependent on the implementation that was chosen.

```
public class GlobalBankPlugInFactory
{
    static string globalBankImplName =
System.Configuration.ConfigurationSettings.AppSettings["GlobalBankImpl"];

    static public GlobalBank.IGlobalBank GetGlobalBankImpl()
    {
        Type globalBankImplType = Type.GetType(GetImplementationClassName());
        if (globalBankImplType == null)
            throw new TypeLoadException("Cannot load type " + globalBankImplName);
        GlobalBank.IGlobalBank bank =
(GlobalBank.IGlobalBank)Activator.CreateInstance(globalBankImplType);
        return bank;
    }

    static public string GetImplementationClassName()
    {
        if (globalBankImplName == null)
            globalBankImplName = "GlobalBank.GlobalStub";
        return globalBankImplName;
    }
}
```

For the **Plugin** class to be functional, you need to add the following entry to the Web.config file.

```
<appSettings>
    <add key="GlobalBankImpl" value="GlobalBank.GlobalStub"/>
</appSettings>
```

Step 4.4: Implement the Web Service Method

Now that you have defined the implementation classes, you can finally fill in the implementation code to the **GetAccountInfo** method of the Gateway.asmx Web service as follows.

```
[WebMethod]
[SoapDocumentMethod(ParameterStyle=SoapParameterStyle.Bare)]
public GetAccountInfoResponse GetAccountInfo(
        GetAccountInfoRequest GetAccountInfoRequest)
    {
        GlobalBank.IGlobalBank bank =
GlobalBank.GlobalBankPlugInFactory.GetGlobalBankImpl();

        GlobalBank.AccountInfo globalAccountInfo =
bank.GetAccountInfo(GetAccountInfoRequest.AccountID);

        return BuildAccountInfo(globalAccountInfo);
    }

private GetAccountInfoResponse BuildAccountInfo(GlobalBank.AccountInfo
globalAccountInfo)
    {
        GetAccountInfoResponse response = new GetAccountInfoResponse();
        response.AccountID = globalAccountInfo.accountID;
        response.Balance = globalAccountInfo.balance;
        response.Name = globalAccountInfo.name;
        response.Description = globalAccountInfo.description;
        return response;
    }
```

The preparation you have done pays off. The implementation of the Web service interface method now consists of three easy steps:

1. Obtain a reference to the **IGlobalBank** interface.

2. Invoke the service implementation by using the reference.

3. Construct the correct response format to return to the consumer.

Each step can be implemented in a single line of code. Step 3 is implemented in a **BuildAccountInfoResponse** private helper method. In this contrived example, it might appear unnecessary to use separate structures for **GetAccountInfoResponse** and **GlobalBank.AccountInfo** because they are essentially identical. However, each structure is likely to undergo a different change cycle over time. Including this translation step allows the gateway to accommodate changes to either the HIS interface or to the gateway interface without affecting both interfaces.

Step 5: Build and Run the Web Service

Now you are ready to build and run the Web service. In Visual Studio .NET, click the **Build** menu, and then click **Build Solution**. Visual Studio then compiles the Web service. Browse the Web service by typing the URL in the Microsoft Internet Explorer Address bar. For the example, the URL is *http://localhost/GatewayWS /Gateway.asmx*.

A key aspect of a service is the service contract. XML Web services use WSDL documents to describe the contract between a service consumer and the provider. A WSDL document is quite comprehensive. Fortunately, the .NET Framework automatically renders the WSDL document that describes the service. The following example shows the definitions section of the WSDL document.

```xml
<?xml version="1.0" encoding="utf8"?>
<definitions …>
    <types>…</types>
    <message name="GetAccountInfoSoapIn">
        <part name="GetAccountInfoRequest" element="s0:GetAccountInfoRequest"/>
    </message>
    <message name="GetAccountInfoSoapOut">
        <part name="GetAccountInfoResult" element="s0:GetAccountInfoResult"/>
    </message>
    <portType name="GatewaySoap">
        <operation name="GetAccountInfo">
            <input message="tns:GetAccountInfoSoapIn"/>
            <output message="tns:GetAccountInfoSoapOut"/>
        </operation>
    </portType>
    <binding>…</binding>
    <service name="Gateway">
        <port name="GatewaySoap" binding="tns:GatewaySoap">
            <soap:address location="http://localhost/GatewayWS/Gateway.asmx"/>
        </port>
    </service>
</definitions>
```

The other major sections of the WSDL document include the following:

- Types
- Messages
- Bindings
- Service

Note: For the sake of clarity, some sections of the document have been condensed here; they are discussed in more detail later in this chapter.

Types

The **<types>** element specifies the request and response messages. The content of the element reflects the XSD documents that you created in step 1.

```
<types>
  <s:schema elementFormDefault="qualified"
            targetNamespace="http://msdn.microsoft.com/patterns">
    <s:element name="GetAccountInfoRequest" type="s0:GetAccountInfoRequest"/>
    <s:complexType name="GetAccountInfoRequest">
      <s:sequence>
        <s:element minOccurs="0" maxOccurs="1" form="unqualified"
                   name="AccountID" type="s:string"/>
      </s:sequence>
    </s:complexType>
    <s:element name="GetAccountInfoResult" type="s0:GetAccountInfoResponse"/>
    <s:complexType name="GetAccountInfoResponse">
      <s:sequence>
        <s:element minOccurs="0" maxOccurs="1" form="unqualified"
                   name="AccountID" type="s:string"/>
        <s:element minOccurs="1" maxOccurs="1" form="unqualified"
                   name="Balance" type="s:decimal"/>
        <s:element minOccurs="0" maxOccurs="1" form="unqualified"
                   name="Name" type="s:string"/>
        <s:element minOccurs="0" maxOccurs="1" form="unqualified"
                   name="Description" type="s:string"/>
      </s:sequence>
    </s:complexType>
  </s:schema>
</types>
```

Messages

The next section of the WSDL document specifies the operations that the service supports. For each operation, the request and response message format is specified through the types declared in the <types> section of the WSDL document. As you can see in the condensed WSDL listing, the Web service you are building provides a single operation named **GetAccountInfo**. The operation takes a **GetAccountInfoRequest** as an argument and returns a message of type **GetAccountInfoResult**. The .NET Framework derives the name of the operation directly from the name of the method that implemented it.

Bindings

The third major section of the WSDL document defines the binding of the operation to a transport protocol and a message format. The style attribute of the **<soap:binding>** element is set to **document**, indicating that the operation is document-oriented and not remote procedure call–oriented. The **[soapAction]** attribute of the **<soap:operation>** element specifies the action string to be used in the

SOAPAction HTTP header. As explained in "ASP.NET Web Services," the .NET Framework uses this string to determine the method to execute.

The **soap:body** elements describe that the message format will be **literal**, meaning that the body portion of an incoming SOAP request looks exactly as specified in the **types** section of the document without any additional wrapping or encoding. The specified style of SOAP message exchange is also referred to as **doc/literal**.

```
<binding name="GatewaySoap" type="tns:GatewaySoap">
    <soap:binding transport="http://schemas.xmlsoap.org/soap/http"
                  style="document"/>
    <operation name="GetAccountInfo">
        <soap:operation style="document"
               soapAction="http://msdn.microsoft.com/patterns/GetAccountInfo" />
        <input>
            <soap:body use="literal"/>
        </input>
        <output>
            <soap:body use="literal"/>
        </output>
    </operation>
</binding>
```

Service

The last part of the WSDL document specifies an address for the service. The service in the example is available through the URL *http://localhost/GatewayWS/Gateway.asmx*.

As you can see, you can save a significant amount of work by having the .NET Framework generate the WSDL document for you rather than coding it manually.

Step 6: Create a Test Client

Now that the service is available online and it is properly described by a service contract in the form of a WSDL document, you are ready to create a client application that consumes the service.

To create a test client that accesses the Web service, create a new ASP.NET project. Use the Add Web Reference Wizard in Visual Studio .NET Solution Explorer to create a reference to the gateway Web service. You can also use the Web Services Description Language tool (Wsdl.exe). This command-line tool creates proxy classes from WSDL. Compiling this proxy class into an application and then calling the method of this proxy class causes the proxy class to package a SOAP request across HTTP and to receive the SOAP-encoded response.

You can use these proxy classes later to generate automated test cases by using test tools such as NUnit (*http://www.nunit.org*).

Resulting Context

Evaluate the following benefits and liabilities to decide whether you should implement and use *Service-Oriented Integration* with ASP.NET.

Benefits

- **Efficient**. ASP.NET does a lot of the work involved in exposing functions as Web services.
- **Flexible**. If you want, you can still control the exact behavior declaratively through the use of attributes. This approach provides a good combination of simplicity without being unnecessarily restrictive. If you need even finer-grained control, you can replace the standard **WebServiceHandler** with a custom class.

Liabilities

- **Geared towards custom applications**. Even though the .NET Framework does a lot of the Web service coding and configuration, you still have to code the service implementation in C# or Visual Basic .NET by hand. ASP.NET does not offer built-in support for process modeling and orchestrations that might be needed for the creation of more complex composite services. If this type of functionality is required, consider using *Implementing Service-Oriented Integration with BizTalk Server 2004* instead.
- **Synchronous interaction**. By default, this approach supports only synchronous interaction. The client has to wait until the service completes. In distributed service-oriented environments, asynchronous communication is often the preferred approach.

Testing Considerations

Two design decisions significantly improve your ability to test the service provider in this implementation:

- The separation of the service interface from the service implementation
- The use of a plug-in to dynamically substitute a service stub for the implementation

Service Interface Separation

The separation of the service interface from the service implementation makes it easy to test the service implementation without having to deal with the Web service aspect of the gateway component. You can create unit test cases as you would for any application. Do this by creating test cases for the service implementation and by circumventing the service interface, as shown in Figure 4.23).

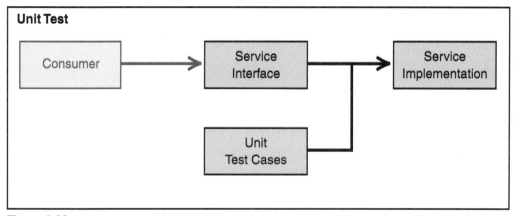

Figure 4.23
Unit testing of Service-Oriented Integration

Automating the unit test cases has a very desirable side effect: you can apply the same test cases to both the real implementation and the dummy implementation. Applying the same test cases ensures that the **GlobalStub** class is a true rendering of the mainframe functionality. It also allows you to use the stub implementation to run all functional tests with confidence.

Service Stub

The service stub, in combination with the plug-in factory, allows you to switch between the real service implementation and a dummy implementation at run time by changing a configuration file. This allows you to test consumers of the service more easily, reliably, and quickly because you eliminate any dependencies to the mainframe service (see Figure 4.24).

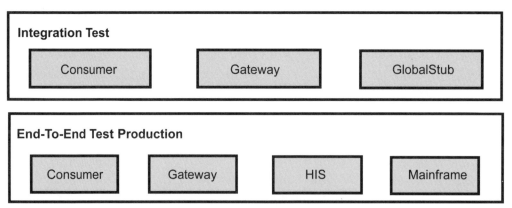

Figure 4.24
Replacing the implementation of the gateway for testing

You can be assured that the switch does not affect the behavior of the gateway because both the dummy (stub) implementation and the Host Integration Server interface have been unit-tested by using the same suite of unit tests.

Security Considerations

The Web service implementation presented here does not incorporate any security considerations. This may be undesirable because the Web service exposes sensitive account data that resides in the bank's mainframe computer. Even though the Web service resides behind the firewall, you would not want anyone with Visual Studio .NET and a little programming skill to create a client to this service to retrieve customers' account balances.

Security has been widely recognized as a critical element for the success of Web services. Microsoft has partnered with IBM and VeriSign to develop the Web Services Security (WS-Security) specification. This specification describes how SOAP messages can be augmented with security certificates. The WS-Security specification is currently implemented by Web Services Enhancements (WSE) for Microsoft .NET.

Acknowledgments

[Fowler03] Fowler, Martin. *Patterns of Enterprise Application Architecture*. Addison-Wesley, 2003.

[Skonnard03] Skonnard, Aaron. "How ASP.NET Web Services Work." *MSDN Library*, May 2003. Available at:
http://msdn.microsoft.com/library/default.asp?url=/library/en-us/dnwebsrv/html /howwebmeth.asp.

[Trowbridge03] Trowbridge, David; Dave Mancini, Dave Quick, Gregor Hohpe, James Newkirk, and David Lavigne. *Enterprise Solution Patterns Using Microsoft .NET*. Microsoft Press, 2003. Also available on the *MSDN Architecture Center* at: *http://msdn.microsoft.com/architecture/patterns/default.aspx?pull=/library/en-us /dnpatterns/html/Esp.asp.*

Implementing Service-Oriented Integration with BizTalk Server 2004

Context

You are connecting two or more systems by using *Service-Oriented Integration*. The service implementation requires the orchestration of multiple functions.

Background

In the Global Bank scenario, the customer can view his or her balances for all accounts, including loan accounts, on a single page. To provide this function, the Web application server interacts with multiple systems to retrieve the required information. The loan accounts may reside on multiple external loan systems that are operated by subsidiaries that were acquired over time. Figure 4.25 shows how the Web application server interacts with the multiple systems to display the account information in the customer's Web browser.

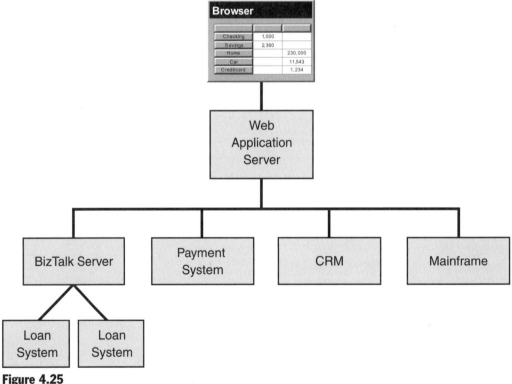

Figure 4.25
Aggregated account balances from multiple banks

To hide the complexity of interacting with external loan systems, you want to design a service that the Web application server can easily access by using a single GetOtherLoans request.

Implementation Strategy

This pattern implements a Microsoft BizTalk Server 2004 orchestration and exposes it as a Web service. Before discussing detailed steps, it is helpful to review the concept of *Service-Oriented Integration* and to review some details about BizTalk Server orchestrations.

Service-Oriented Integration

Service-Oriented Integration connects applications by exchanging documents. In many cases, these documents are represented in XML format. The following code shows a document passed in a SOAP envelope.

```
)<?xml version="1.0" encoding="utf-8"?>
<soap:Envelope>
  <soap:Body>
    <LoanBalanceRequest>
      <MasterCustomerID>12345678</MasterCustomerID>
      <CorrelationID>1100222</CorrelationID>
    </LoanBalanceRequest>
  </soap:Body>
</soap:Envelope>
```

Service-Oriented Integration hides the complexity of the underlying service very well. For example, the service might execute a complex process internally that has many parallel threads of activity. However, the complex internal process does not affect the service interface at all (see Figure 4.26).

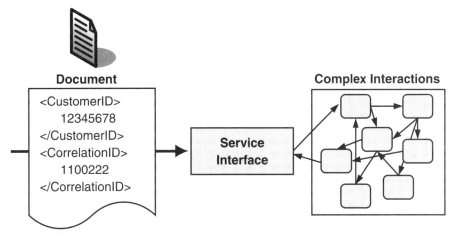

Figure 4.26
Complexity hidden behind a service-oriented interface

Exposing a BizTalk Orchestration as a Web Service

You can use BizTalk Server 2004 to model complex processes by using the BizTalk Orchestration Designer. BizTalk orchestrations interact with the outside world through logical ports as shown in Figure 4.27. An orchestration can interact with logical ports through send and receive ports that are incorporated into the orchestration graph. Messages received from a receive port can start a new instance of an orchestration or interact with an existing orchestration instance. An orchestration can send messages to any output port through the send port. A sent message can either be the response to a previously received message or to a standalone message.

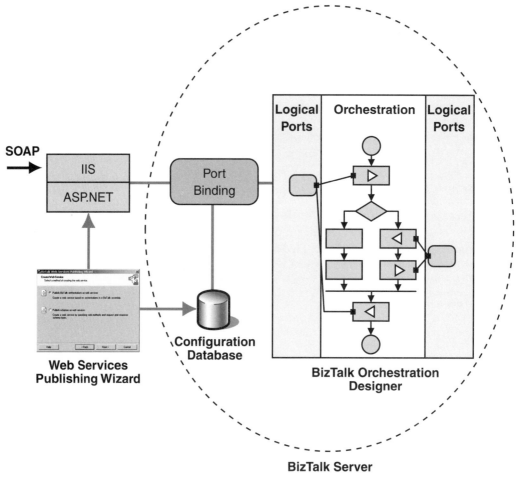

Figure 4.27
An orchestration invoked by a Web service call

Logical ports can be bound to physical ports at design time or at deployment time. Physical ports specify a transport type, such as File, File Transfer Protocol (FTP), HTTP, or SOAP. Physical ports also specify a physical location, such as a directory name or a URL. This separation of logical and physical ports allows you to create and reuse orchestrations without being tied to specific directory names or URLs. You can specify a physical Web port by selecting the SOAP transport protocol and by specifying a URL.

After you design an orchestration in BizTalk Server, you can expose it as a Web service to be invoked from other applications. The BizTalk Web Services Publishing Wizard supports this task, generating both a physical port definition and an ASP.NET Web service that invokes the orchestration when it receives a SOAP request. For a more detailed description of ASP.NET Web services, see *Implementing Service-Oriented Integration with ASP.NET*.

The following steps are necessary to create a BizTalk orchestration and to expose it as a Web service to be consumed by other applications. To illustrate this procedure, all steps here are performed manually. However, you can automate some steps by scripting to the BizTalk Windows Management Instrumentation (WMI) interface.

▶ **To expose a BizTalk orchestration as a Web service**

1. **Define the message schemas for inbound and outbound messages**. The message schemas define the format of the messages that the orchestration receives and sends. Ultimately, the Web Services Description Language (WSDL) document generated by the ASP.NET Web service uses these message schemas to specify the required format for inbound and outbound SOAP messages.

2. **Define logical request-response ports**. A logical port is required so that the orchestration can receive and send messages. A request-response port is a port that receives a request message and that sends a response within the same interaction.

3. **Define the orchestration and connect it to the logical port**. The orchestration encapsulates the tasks that the service needs to execute internally. Connecting to the logical port starts a new instance of the orchestration every time a new message arrives on the port.

4. **Build and deploy the orchestration**. An orchestration has to be built and deployed to the global assembly cache and to the BizTalk Management database before it can be executed. You use the BizTalk Deployment Wizard to deploy the orchestration.

5. **Run the BizTalk Web Services Publishing Wizard**. The wizard creates and compiles a Microsoft Visual Studio project for an ASP.NET Web service. If you select the **Create BizTalk Receive Location** option, the wizard also creates a physical port definition in the BizTalk configuration database.

6. **Bind the orchestration's logical port to the physical port**. Before you can start the orchestration, you must bind the logical port definition referenced by the orchestration to a physical port. To do this, you usually use BizTalk Explorer from within Microsoft Visual Studio .NET. In this case, you bind the logical port to the physical port that the Web Services Publishing Wizard created.

7. **Start the orchestration**. When you start the orchestration, it begins to actively listen to incoming messages. In this case, the incoming messages are SOAP requests. The service is now live and executes the orchestration for each incoming SOAP request.

8. **Create a test client that invokes the Web service**. The ASP.NET Web service generated by the Web Services Publishing Wizard renders the necessary WSDL document that describes the public service contract. This means that you can use the Web Services Description Language tool (Wsdl.exe) or Visual Studio .NET to easily create applications that consume the newly created Web service.

Example

The following example explains the architectural decisions involved and the steps performed in building the Global Bank solution.

Asynchronous Interaction

In the Global Bank scenario, customers can view their account balances, including loan balances, on a single page. The loan balances, however, must be retrieved from external systems that may not always be available or that may have slow response times. Users indicated that quick response times for the Web site were more important than complete information. Therefore, given that the system cannot guarantee quick response times, the user requirements state that loan balances are optional for display on the View Scheduled Payments page.

This optional user requirement is reflected in the solution architecture by making the request for the loan balances asynchronous. This means that the Web application server requests the loan balances first, and then it retrieves data from the mainframe and payment systems. After all other data has been retrieved, the application server checks whether the loan balances were retrieved. If so, they are incorporated into the page display. If not, the page is rendered without the loan balance portion. Figure 4.28 shows the concurrent action in Unified Modeling Language (UML). The interaction between BizTalk Server and the individual loan systems is not shown.

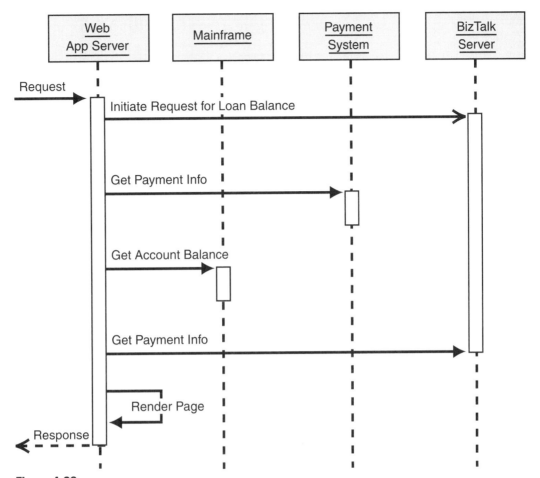

Figure 4.28
Asynchronous interaction between the Web application server and BizTalk Server

Implementing Asynchronous Web Services

To make the interaction between the Web application server and BizTalk Server asynchronous, you have three implementation choices. The three implementation choices are illustrated in Figure 4.29.

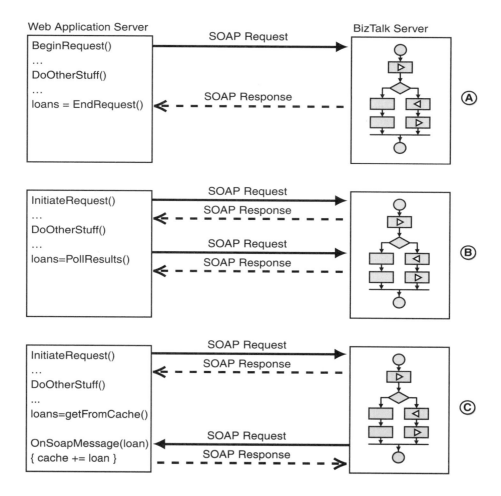

Figure 4.29

Implementation choices for asynchrony between the Web application server and BizTalk Server

The three implementation choices from Figure 4.29 can be summarized as follows:

A. **Client-side asynchrony**. The Web server issues a single SOAP request by using the asynchronous Web service API. This API permits the client (in this case, the client is the Web application server) to continue with other processing and to read the results of the request at a later time. This approach permits the client to operate asynchronously while the interaction with BizTalk Server is synchronous.

B. **Asynchronous interaction with polling**. The Web server makes two SOAP requests to BizTalk Server. One of the SOAP requests initiates the request for loan information. This first request only initiates processing on the BizTalk Server side and returns immediately. Subsequently, the Web server issues a second SOAP request to poll for the results. BizTalk Server returns the results if they are available or returns a blank message if they are not yet available. BizTalk Server discards the loan balance results if they become available after the Web server polled for them.

C. **Asynchronous interaction with callback**. The Web server issues a single SOAP request to initiate the retrieval of loan information. As with option B, control is returned immediately to the Web server. The Web server then goes on to other work. After BizTalk Server has retrieved the loan information, it sends a SOAP request back to the Web server to pass the loan information. It is important to note that for this part of the interaction, the Web server has to be able to service incoming SOAP messages. Therefore, the Web server has to act as the server. The Web server stores the loan information in a global cache that is accessible to the threads that generated the requests. Before the Web server renders the HTML page, it checks the global cache to see whether any loan information has arrived while it was interacting with the mainframe and the Customer Relationship Management (CRM) systems.

To choose the best option, you need to evaluate the advantages and disadvantages of each option. Table 4.4 compares the different options.

Table 4.4: Comparison of the Implementation Choices for Asynchronous Interaction

	Option A: client-side asynchrony	Option B: asynchronous interaction with polling	Option C: asynchronous interaction with callback
Client-side implementation effort	Low	Medium	High
Server-side implementation effort	Low	Medium	Medium/low
Network traffic	Low	Higher	Higher
Efficient use of resources	Poor (for long-running interactions)	Good	Good
Where state is kept	Connection	Server	Client

As you can see, each option has its advantages and disadvantages. Therefore, you must make your decision based on the priorities that you assign to the individual criteria.

Although option A may be the easiest to construct, it is essentially a synchronous SOAP interaction that just appears to be asynchronous to the client code because the connection between the client and the service remains active throughout the whole interaction. The use of long-standing connections can quickly deplete system resources and can be one of the biggest impediments to a solution's scalability. Because the loan balance service has to access external loan systems over slow and unreliable connections, the interaction can definitely be long running. Therefore, you should eliminate option A.

The choice between option B and C is more difficult and depends on whether you want to maintain the state on the client (the Web application server) or on the server running BizTalk Server. Both servers are multithreaded and quite efficient at keeping state for many concurrent requests. The choice also depends on where you want to allocate the additional development effort. Do you prefer to put additional effort into the ASP.NET code on the Web server or into the orchestration design on the server running BizTalk Server? Option B requires a little extra work on the BizTalk Server to ensure proper correlation and to allow the concurrent servicing of multiple requests. Option C requires additional coding effort in the Web server to maintain and to clear the global cache. Overall, option B offers the best results for the smallest amount of development effort and is the first choice. However, this discussion highlights that architectural decisions are not only based on technical considerations alone but also on development resource constraints and skills preferences.

Building the Solution

Based on the tradeoffs discussed in the previous section, Global Bank decided to use option B, asynchronous interaction with polling. The next step was to start building the solution. The rest of this example shows you the steps required to build the Global Bank solution. Due to the large number of steps involved in creating the solution, some steps are not covered in full detail.

Step 1: Define the Message Schemas for Inbound and Outbound Messages

To define the format of the request and response messages, create two XML Schema (XSD) files in the Visual Studio .NET XSD Editor. The XSD schema for the LoanBalanceRequest.xsd request message looks like the following schema. To improve readability, the namespace declarations are omitted.

```
<xs:schema...>
  <xs:element name="LoanBalanceRequest">
    <xs:complexType>
      <xs:sequence>
        <xs:element minOccurs="1" maxOccurs="1" name="MasterCustomerID"
                    type="xs:string" />
      </xs:sequence>
    </xs:complexType>
  </xs:element>
</xs:schema>
```

The document specifies a single MasterCustomerID data field for the request message. The MasterCustomerID field is common across all systems and can be used to locate all the customer's accounts.

In response to the request, the application returns the following acknowledgement (Ack.xsd).

```
<xs:schema...>
  <xs:element name="Ack">
    <xs:complexType>
      <xs:sequence>
        <xs:element name="CorrelationID" type="xs:string" />
      </xs:sequence>
    </xs:complexType>
  </xs:element>
</xs:schema>
```

The only field in this schema is a unique correlation identifier. The orchestration assigns an ID to this field and uses it later to match (or *correlate*) the request and response messages across the asynchronous communication. For more information, see the *Correlation Identifier* pattern in *Enterprise Integration Patterns* [Hohpe04].

After receiving the acknowledgment response from the orchestration, the client polls the orchestration for the result.

The client application copies the correlation identifier returned in the acknowledgment message (Ack.xsd) into PollReq.xsd. PollReq.xsd has only one field (CorrelationID), as shown in the following schema.

```
<xs:schema...>
  <xs:element name="PollReq">
    <xs:complexType>
      <xs:sequence>
        <xs:element name="CorrelationID" type="xs:string" />
      </xs:sequence>
    </xs:complexType>
  </xs:element>
</xs:schema>
```

The XSD code for the LoanBalanceResponse.xsd response message looks like the following.

```
<xs:schema …>
  <xs:element name="LoanBalanceResponse">
    <xs:complexType>
      <xs:sequence>
        <xs:element name="Loan">
          <xs:complexType>
            <xs:sequence>
              <xs:element name="Name" type="xs:string" />
              <xs:element name="AccountID" type="xs:string" />
              <xs:element name="Amount" type="xs:decimal" />
            </xs:sequence>
          </xs:complexType>
        </xs:element>
      </xs:sequence>
    </xs:complexType>
  </xs:element>
</xs:schema>
```

The response message schema defines a list of account names and balances. This list is filled in by the Web service (through the orchestration). The completed message is then sent back to the client.

Step 2: Define Logical Request-Response Ports

In BizTalk Orchestration Designer, add a port to the orchestration, and then use the Port Configuration Wizard to configure a public request-response port. Figure 4.30 indicates the **Request-Response** option.

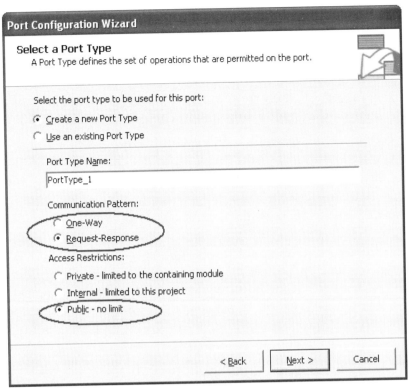

Figure 4.30
Using the BizTalk Port Configuration Wizard to add a request-response port

In addition to selecting the **Request-Response** setting, you must change the **Access Restrictions** setting to **Public – no limit**.

Step 3: Define the Orchestration and Connect It to the Logical Port

As described in "Implementing Asynchronous Web Services," the interaction between the Web server and the BizTalk Server orchestration consists of two parts:

- The Web server requests loan information from BizTalk Server.
- The Web server polls for results. The BizTalk Server orchestration returns a response immediately with the results it retrieved up to that point.

Based on Global Bank requirements, the orchestration must:

a. **Receive the initial request from the Web server**. The orchestration creates a new instance of the orchestration for each request.

b. **Generate a unique correlation identifier to pass back to the client**. The orchestration returns the correlation identifier back to the Web server so that it can use this identifier to poll later for the results.

c. **Request the loan balance from multiple backend loan systems**. These requests can be made concurrently. The results from each loan system have to be combined into a single message. In this example, both loan systems are accessible through prebuilt Web services.

d. **Service the polling request**. The orchestration has to be able to receive a polling request from the Web server at any time. When it receives a polling request, the orchestration returns the loan balances if they have been obtained already. Otherwise, the orchestration returns a blank result. The polling request can arrive at any time after the initial request.

e. **Time out**. If the orchestration does not receive a polling request after an extended period of time (for example, 60 seconds), the orchestration is terminated. This function keeps orchestration instances from staying active indefinitely while they are waiting for a polling request.

Figure 4.31 shows these tasks modeled inside a BizTalk Server orchestration.

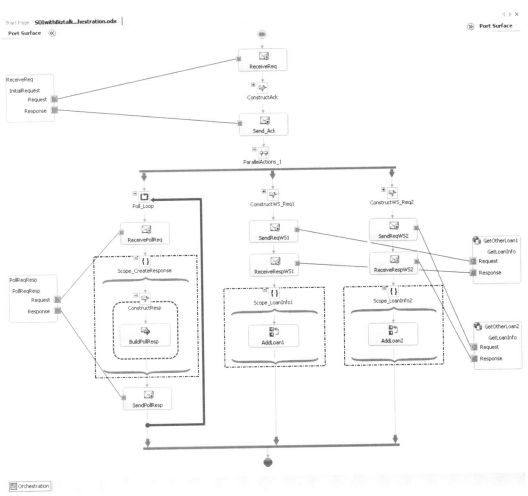

Figure 4.31
The BizTalk Server orchestration for loan balances

Now, let's examine the orchestration tasks in more detail. The letters in the following list correlate to the letters in Figure 4.31.

A: Receive the Initial Request from the Web Server

In the Global Bank scenario, the ASP.NET client sends a request for a customer's loan balances (GetOtherLoans) to BizTalk Server. LoanBalanceRequest.xsd defines the format of the request. The request contains only the MasterCustomerID field (see "Step 1: Define the Message Schemas for Inbound and Outbound Messages").

The request is received through the **ReceiveReq** port in the orchestration (see Figure 4.31). After the message is received, the port forwards it to the **ReceiveReq Receive** shape. The **Activate** property of the **ReceiveReq Receive** shape is set to **True**, which activates the orchestration.

B: Generate a Correlation Identifier and Send Acknowledgment

After the ASP.NET client sends the initial request to BizTalk Server, it receives an acknowledgment message (Ack.xsd). This message contains the CorrelationID field. The CorrelationID field identifies the orchestration instance associated with the initial request. This field guarantees that incoming messages are associated with the correct instance of the orchestration.

To create the correlation ID, you can use a custom C# class that uses **System.Random** to generate and return an ID. That ID is assigned to the CorrelationID field of the Ack.xsd message, and it is returned to the client. Alternatively, you can assign one of the BizTalk Server message context properties (**BTS.MessageID**) as a unique ID to the CorrelationID field of the Ack.xsd message. This is accessible within an **Expression** shape in the orchestration.

For the CorrelationID field to be accessible to the code in the Expression Editor window, you must use the BizTalk Schema Editor to promote it, as shown in Figure 4.32.

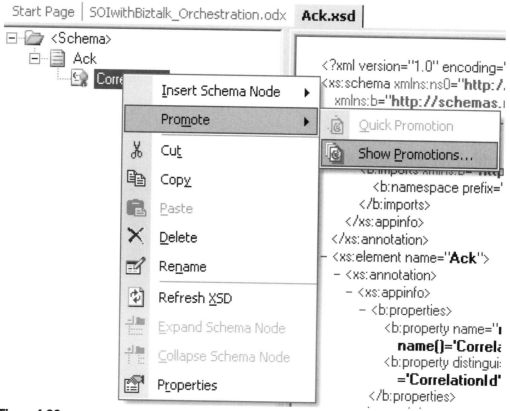

Figure 4.32
Promoting a schema field

After the acknowledgment response is created, the **Send_Ack** send shape sends the response to the receive-request port, and the receive-request port then returns it to the client. The **Send** shape should be configured to initialize the orchestration correlation set. To accomplish this, add a correlation type and a correlation set in the Orchestration Viewer, and then set the **Initialize Correlation** property of the **Send** shape to the new correlation type you created. When the orchestration sends the message to the client, the correlation set is automatically initialized with the value in the CorrelationID field.

C: Request the Loan Balances

The initial request from the client activated the orchestration. The orchestration then synchronously returned an acknowledgment containing the CorrelationID to the client. Now, to retrieve the customer's loan balance, the orchestration needs to call the external systems that are implemented as two Web services, GetOtherLoans1.asmx and GetOtherLoans2.asmx. The request and response messages to these Web services are fairly simple. Each takes a customer ID as a request and returns the loan information that corresponds to that customer ID. This is shown in the following selection from the GetOtherLoan1.asmx external Web service request schema.

```
<?xml version="1.0" encoding="utf-16" ?>
<xs:schema ..>
<xs:element name="Request">
<xs:complexType>
<xs:sequence>
 <xs:element name="CustomerId" type="xs:string" />
 </xs:sequence>
 </xs:complexType>
 </xs:element>
 </xs:schema>
```

Note: The namespace information in these examples is omitted here for brevity.

At this stage, the client's request must be transformed into the message format that the external Web services require. Each external Web service can have a different schema, although both schemas are identical in this example. The following is the key portion of the GetOtherLoans1.asmx external Web service response schema.

```
<?xml version="1.0" encoding="utf-16" ?>
    <xs:schema …>
        <xs:element name="Response">
<xs:complexType>
        <xs:sequence>
<xs:element name="Name" type="xs:string" />
<xs:element name="Amount" type="xs:string" />
<xs:element name="AccountNo" type="xs:string" />
```

```
    </xs:sequence>
            </xs:complexType>
    </xs:element>
    </xs:schema>
```

To transform one schema into another, **Transform** shapes in ConstructWS_Req1 and ConstructWS_Req2 map the CustomerId fields of the two schemas. You use the BizTalk Mapper to map the MasterCustomerID field of LoanBalanceRequst.xsd to the CustomerId field of the Web service's request schema (see Figure 4.33).

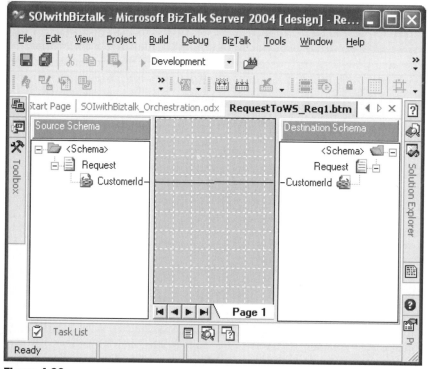

Figure 4.33
Using BizTalk Mapper to map request fields

Now that the Web services' request messages have been constructed, the response messages have to be parsed and consumed. In BizTalk Solution Explorer, open the Web service's Reference.xsd file. Using the **Promote** option, distinguish the **Name**, **AccountNo**, and **Amount** elements of the Web service response schema (see Figure 4.32). Distinguishing these fields allows the code in the **AddLoan1** and **AddLoan2 Expression** shapes to reference their values and use them to construct the response document.

Next, you use the response from each Web service to construct a LoanBalanceResponse.xsd response that is returned to the client. To accomplish this, **AddLoan1** and **AddLoan2 Expression** shapes use a custom C# class (**LoanInfoCollection**) to collect the results returned by each Web service. Each Web service returns the **Name**, **AccountNo**, and **Amount** for the customer's loan. The custom class aggregates the responses into an XML document which is returned to the polling client as the LoanBalanceResponse.xsd response. The following is the code from the **Expression** property of **AddLoan1**.

```
LoanInfoCollection.AddLoan(
msgWebServ1_Resp.GetLoanInfoResult.Name,
msgWebServ1_Resp.GetLoanInfoResult.Amount,
msgWebServ1_Resp.GetLoanInfoResult.AccountNo);
```

Because all three branches of the parallel action use the **LoanInfoCollection** class, the **AddLoan1** and **AddLoan2 Expression** shapes are inside synchronized blocks (**Scope_LoanInfo1** and **Scope_LoanInfo2** respectively). The **Transaction Type** property of the synchronized blocks is set to **Atomic** to protect the class from concurrent access. For more information about transactions in BizTalk Server, see *Implementing Process Integration with BizTalk Server 2004*.

D: Service Polling Request

At this point, the response message has been constructed and is ready to be delivered to the client. The client polls the orchestration by sending a SOAP message to BizTalk Server. The message contains the correlation ID that identifies the instance of the orchestration that is associated with this request.

The **PollReqResp** port is linked to the **ReceivePollReq** receive shape. The **ReceivePollReq** receive shape has an important property, **Following Correlation Sets**. This property is set to the correlation type created earlier in step B, and it allows BizTalk Server to associate the polling request to the correct instance of this orchestration.

The request message is then assigned the loan information gathered from Web services by the **LoanInfoCollection** class within the **Construct Response** shape of **Scope_CreateResponse**.

As the final step, the **SendPollResp Send** shape sends the constructed response message that is mentioned earlier to the **PollReqResp** port. The **PollReqResp** port then sends the constructed response message to the polling client.

E: Time Out

With respect to the polling request, there are two potential scenarios that you have to design the orchestration to handle properly. In the first scenario, the client may poll too early, before the orchestration has received a response from external Web services and constructed the response message. In the second scenario, the client may not poll at all. If the client does not poll at all, the orchestration instance is left in an active state forever.

To handle early polling, you must allow the client to poll again if no results are returned. To accomplish this, you add a loop and set it to run indefinitely. In this case, add a **Poll_Loop**. Note, however, that the loop is limited by the **Timeout** property value of the orchestration.

To set the **Timeout** value for the orchestration, set the **Transaction Type** property to **Long Running**, and set the **Timeout** property value to **60 seconds** or another appropriate value. This allows the client enough time to poll for the result and eliminates the possibility that an orchestration could run indefinitely.

Step 4: Build and Deploy the Orchestration

Before you build the orchestration, create an assembly key file by typing **sn –k SOIwithBizTalk.snk** at the command prompt. Copy the file to the project folder, and then enter the file name in the **Assembly Key File** name property of the project properties.

Note: You need to build the **LoanInfoCollection** assembly that is referenced by the project by using a strong name assembly key file. You then must deploy it to the global assembly cache.

From the Visual Studio .NET menu, build the solution. This creates a .NET Framework assembly called **SOIwithBizTalk**. You then deploy the **SOIwithBizTalk** assembly by using the BizTalk Server Deployment Wizard or by using the scripts that are included with the BizTalk 2004 SDK.

Step 5: Run the BizTalk Web Services Publishing Wizard

To expose the **SOIwithBizTalk** assembly that you deployed in step 5 as a Web service, run the BizTalk Web Services Publishing Wizard. The wizard creates the SOIwithBiztalk_Proxy Web service. The SOIwithBiztalk_Proxy Web service exposes Web services corresponding to the **ReceiveReq** and **PollReqResp** ports.

Step 6: Bind the Orchestration's Logical Port to the Physical Port

The Web Services Publishing Wizard that you ran in step 4 also created two receive ports for the **ReceiveReq** and **PollReqResp** ports, which you can access through BizTalk Explorer.

Note: The **Receive Pipeline** property of these ports should be set to **XmlReceive**. To set this property in BizTalk Explorer, select the port, right-click the port name, and then click **Edit** on the context menu.

Next, you need to add two send ports for the **GetOtherLoan1** and **GetOtherLoan2** Web ports. The **Receive Pipeline** properties of these ports also should be set to **XmlReceive** instead of the default **PassThrough** setting.

After you set up the physical ports, bind the orchestration to these ports in BizTalk Explorer. Note that there are two inbound ports and two outbound ports in the Port Binding Properties window of the orchestration. You can also use the BTSDeploy command line utility and a binding file to bind ports. Use the **Export BizTalk assembly binding to file** option in BizTalk Deployment Wizard to create the binding file.

Step 7: Start the Orchestration

After binding the logical ports to physical ports, start the orchestration in BizTalk Explorer.

Step 8: Create a Test Client That Invokes the Web Service

To test the orchestration, you need to create a client that consumes the Web service created from the orchestration in step 4. As you saw in step 4, the wizard created two Web services that correspond to the two request-response ports of the orchestration. The following code shows part of the WSDL file for PollReqResp.asmx. For the sake of clarity, some parts of the file are not shown here.

```
  <types>
    + <s:schema elementFormDefault="qualified" targetNamespace="http://
msdn.microsoft.com/soi">
    - <s:schema elementFormDefault="qualified" targetNamespace="http://
SOIwithBiztalk.PollReq">
        <s:element name="PollReq" type="s1:PollReq" />
      - <s:complexType name="PollReq">
        <s:sequence>
          <s:element minOccurs="0" maxOccurs="1" form="unqualified"
name="CorrelationId" type="s:string" />
        </s:sequence>
      </s:complexType>
    </s:schema>
    - <s:schema elementFormDefault="qualified" targetNamespace="http://
SOIwithBiztalk.PollResp">
        <s:element name="PollResp" type="s2:PollResp" />
      - <s:complexType name="PollResp">
      - <s:sequence>
          <s:element minOccurs="0" maxOccurs="1" form="unqualified"
name="Loans" type="s2:ArrayOfPollRespLoan" />
        </s:sequence>
      </s:complexType>
    - <s:complexType name="ArrayOfPollRespLoan">
      - <s:sequence>
          <s:element minOccurs="0" maxOccurs="unbounded" form="unqualified"
```

```
name="Loan" type="s2:PollRespLoan" />
        </s:sequence>
      </s:complexType>
    - <s:complexType name="PollRespLoan">
    -   <s:sequence>
          <s:element minOccurs="0" maxOccurs="1" form="unqualified"
name="Amount" type="s:string" />
          <s:element minOccurs="0" maxOccurs="1" form="unqualified"
name="Name" type="s:string" />
          <s:element minOccurs="0" maxOccurs="1" form="unqualified"
name="AccountNo" type="s:string" />
        </s:sequence>
      </s:complexType>
    </s:schema>
  </types>
+ <message name="PollReqRespSoapIn">
+ <message name="PollReqRespSoapOut">
+ <portType name="SOIwithBiztalk_SOIwithBiztalk_Orchestration_PollReqRespSoap">
+ <binding name="SOIwithBiztalk_SOIwithBiztalk_Orchestration_PollReqRespSoap"
type="s0:SOIwithBiztalk_SOIwithBiztalk_Orchestration_PollReqRespSoap">
- <service name="SOIwithBiztalk_SOIwithBiztalk_Orchestration_PollReqResp">
    <documentation>BizTalk assembly "SOIwithBiztalk, Version=1.0.0.0,
Culture=neutral, PublicKeyToken=c6495a1a84cf8ad3" published web service.</
documentation>
  - <port name="SOIwithBiztalk_SOIwithBiztalk_Orchestration_PollReqRespSoap"
binding="s0:SOIwithBiztalk_SOIwithBiztalk_Orchestration_PollReqRespSoap">
      <soap:address location="http://localhost/SOIwithBiztalk_Proxy/
SOIwithBiztalk_SOIwithBiztalk_Orchestration_PollReqResp.asmx" />
    </port>
  </service>
</definitions>
```

The test client is a Windows Form application that uses the NUnit test tool. For more information about this tool, see *www.nunit.org*. The following test case sends a request to BizTalk Server, waits, and then polls for the result.

```
[Test]
   public void TestRequestAndPollLater()
   {
        RequestWS.SOIwithBiztalk_SOIwithBiztalk_Orchestration_ReceiveReq
ws = new
TestSOIwithBiztalk.RequestWS.SOIwithBiztalk_SOIwithBiztalk_Orchestration_ReceiveReq();
   RequestWS.Request req = new RequestWS.Request();
   req.MasterCustomerID = "1234";
   RequestWS.Ack resp = ws.InitialRequest(req);

   string corId = resp.CorrelationId;
   //wait for external services to return response
   System.Threading.Thread.Sleep(6000);
   //poll for result
PollWS.SOIwithBiztalk_SOIwithBiztalk_Orchestration_PollReqResp pollws = new
```

```
TestSOIwithBiztalk.PollWS.SOIwithBiztalk_SOIwithBiztalk_Orchestration_PollReqResp();
    PollWS.PollReq pollreq = new TestSOIwithBiztalk.PollWS.PollReq();
    pollreq.CorrelationId = corId;

    PollWS.PollResp pollresp = pollws.PollReqResp(pollreq);

    Assertion.AssertEquals(2, pollresp.Loans.Length);
    //test results
    ValidateLoanEntry(pollresp.Loans[0]);
    ValidateLoanEntry(pollresp.Loans[1]);
}

    private void ValidateLoanEntry(PollWS.PollRespLoan entry)
    {
        // note: the responses do not have to be in order
        if (entry.AccountNo.Equals("1234"))
        {
            Assertion.AssertEquals("1000", entry.Amount);
        }
        else if (entry.AccountNo.Equals("5678"))
        {
            Assertion.AssertEquals("2000", entry.Amount);
        }
        else
        {
            Assertion.Fail("Wrong account number");
        }
    }
```

Resulting Context

This implementation of *Service-Oriented Integration* results in the following benefits and liabilities:

Benefits

- **Powerful**. You can use BizTalk Server 2004 to model complex processes comprising multiple parallel interactions. You can even build a hierarchy of orchestrations where one orchestration invokes other orchestrations. BizTalk Server also imports important concepts that are critical when developing asynchronous, event-driven solutions. These solutions include correlation, synchronization, timeouts, long-running transactions, and compensating actions.

- **Integrated development tools**. The BizTalk Server 2004 visual modeling tools are integrated into Visual Studio .NET. This greatly enhances the development experience for mixed development consisting of actual C# or Visual Basic .NET code and visual models from maps and orchestrations.

- **Operational support**. Monitoring and operating Web services solutions can be difficult. BizTalk Server 2004 includes sophisticated tools to monitor the flow of messages and the execution of orchestrations through the Health and Activity Tracker (HAT) tool.

Liabilities

- **Complexity.** Although BizTalk Server 2004 provides many useful features, it also introduces a series of new concepts, a large number of moving parts, and a different development environment than what developers are used to. This can increase the learning curve for application developers.

Testing Considerations

There are several possible options available when testing this implementation. First, the Web service as a whole can be tested by writing a test client in the .NET Framework. To create the test client, create a new C# console application, and use the **Add Web Reference** command in Visual Studio Solution Explorer to create a reference to the orchestration Web service. You can then write test code that invokes the Web service. Subsequently, you can add automated test cases to this test client by using test tools such as NUnit.

After running the test client, you can use the Orchestration Debugger to examine traces of the orchestration execution. You can access the Orchestration Debugger from the HAT tool and use the Orchestration Debugger in two modes: reporting mode and interactive mode. Reporting mode tracks the execution of each shape in the orchestration as it occurs. In reporting mode, you can replay the steps or set breakpoints on the class of orchestration so that you can then debug new instances in interactive mode. Interactive mode enables you to debug a currently running instance. To debug a process interactively, set a breakpoint within an orchestration while in reporting mode, and then submit a new message (create a new instance of an orchestration). The orchestration will stop at the breakpoint, and you can then attach the orchestration debugger to that instance.

Security Considerations

The Web service implementation presented here does not address security considerations. Appropriate security measures are essential in this scenario because the Web service exposes sensitive account data that resides in the bank's mainframe computer. Even though the Web service resides behind the firewall, you would not want unauthorized users to create a client to this service to retrieve customers' account balances.

Security is implemented at multiple levels when exposing an orchestration as a Web Service:

- **Transport security.** The BizTalk Web Services Publishing Wizard creates an ASP.NET virtual directory like any other ASP.NET Web service. SOAP messages sent to this virtual directory can be sent by using HTTPS (encrypted). Additionally, the virtual directory can be configured to require basic authentication, NTLM authentication, or even client certificates.

- **SOAP security**. Microsoft has partnered with IBM and VeriSign to develop the Web Services Security (WS-Security) specification. The WS-Security specification describes how SOAP messages can be augmented with security certificates. The WS-Security specification is currently implemented by Web Services Enhancements (WSE) for Microsoft .NET. The current version of the SOAP adapter does not support WS-Security, but this functionality can be supported by using custom pipeline components in the BizTalk receive and send pipelines.

- **Receive adapter security**. The SOAP adapter is run by a BizTalk Server Isolated Host instance within a specific Microsoft Windows security context. If the BizTalk Isolated Host was installed as trusted, then the user that acquires authentication when running the Web service must be a member of the BizTalk Isolated Host Users group (this is often the IUSR_*computer name* account). If the BizTalk Isolated Host was not installed as trusted, the ASP.NET account must be a member of the BizTalk Isolated Host Users group.

- **Receive port security**. You can configure the receive port to require messages to be authenticated before they are processed. Messages are authenticated in the ResolveParty stage of the receive pipeline by using a client certificate or by using a Security Identifier (SID). Messages that are not authenticated can either be dropped or saved, but they are not processed.

Operational Considerations

Many of the BizTalk receive adapters, including the HTTP and the SOAP adapters, perform batching to optimize throughput and server resource utilization by minimizing polling. The default batch size is 10, and there is a delay between polls of one second. This means that a single synchronous HTTP post or SOAP call is processed, but because it is not a complete batch, the adapter waits for one second before polling again. Therefore, successive calls may be delayed. This is appropriate behavior in high-transaction situations, but it is not appropriate behavior for a highly responsive system.

To make the HTTP and SOAP adapters more responsive, you can set the registry **HttpBatchSize** subkey **DWORD** value in the **HKLM\CurrentControlSet\BtsSvc 3.0\HttpReceive** registry key to **1**. Setting this value to **1** affects the maximum throughput that the adapter is capable of handling.

Acknowledgments

[Hohpe04] Hohpe, Gregor, and Bobby Woolf, Enterprise Integration Patterns: Designing, Building, and Deploying Messaging Solutions. Addison-Wesley, 2004.

Presentation Integration

Aliases

Screen scraping

Context

You have multiple independent applications that are organized as functional silos. Each application has a user interface.

Problem

How do you integrate information systems that were not designed to work together?

Forces

To correctly solve this problem, you need to consider the following forces:

- When integrating multiple applications, you should minimize changes to existing systems because any change to an existing production system represents a risk and might require extensive regression testing.

- Because many computer systems are designed according to the *Layered Application* pattern, some of the layers are typically deployed in physical tiers that are not externally accessible. For example, security policy may require the database tier of an application to reside on a separate physical server that is not directly accessible to other applications. Most Web applications allow external access only to the user interface and protect the application and database tiers behind firewalls.

- Many applications feature little or no separation between business and presentation logic. The only remote components of these applications are simple display and input devices. These display terminals access the central mainframe computer, and the central mainframe computer hosts all business logic and data storage.

- The business logic layer of many applications is programming-language specific and is not available remotely, unless it was developed on top of a specific remoting technology such as DCOM or Common Object Request Broker Architecture (CORBA).

- Directly accessing an application's database layers can cause corruption of application data or functionality. In most applications, important business rules and validations reside in the business logic, and they often reside in the presentation layer also. This logic is intended to prevent erroneous user entry from affecting the integrity of the application. Making data updates directly through the data store bypasses these protection mechanisms and increases the risk of corrupting the application's internal state.

Solution

Access the application's functionality through the user interface by simulating a user's input and by reading data from the screen display. Figure 4.34 shows the elements of a solution that is based on the *Presentation Integration* pattern.

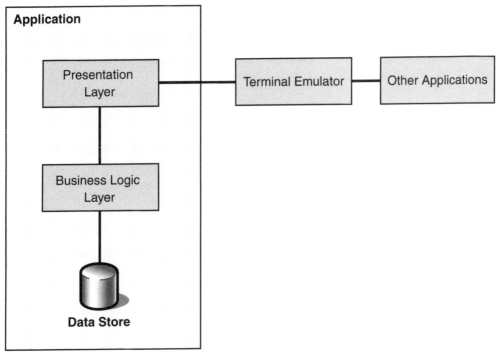

Figure 4.34
Presentation Integration connects to an existing application through the presentation layer

The *Presentation Integration* pattern is sometimes disparagingly called *screen scraping* because the middleware collects (or *scrapes*) the information from the information that is displayed on the screen during a user session. Collecting information from the screen of the user session tends to be the simpler part of the integration. The more difficult part tends to occur when the middleware has to locate the correct screen in the application in the same way a human user has to.

To simulate user interaction, the integration solution has to use a terminal emulator that appears to the application as a regular terminal, but that can be controlled programmatically to simulate user input. Such a terminal emulator is usually specific to the exact type of user interface device that is supported by the application. Fortunately, in the mainframe world, IBM's 3270 terminal standard is so widespread that many commercial 3270 terminal emulators are available. Instead of displaying information to the user, these emulators make the screen data available through an API. In the case of 3270 emulators, a standard API exists that is called the High Level Language Application Program Interface (HLLAPI). The emulator can send data to the application to simulate keystrokes that a user would make on a real 3270 terminal. Because the terminal emulator mimics a user's actions, it usually does not depend on the specific application that it is interacting with. Additional middleware logic must encode the correct keystrokes and extract the correct fields from the virtual screen.

The widespread trend of equipping applications with Web-based interfaces has revived interest in using *Presentation Integration* as a vital integration approach. Web applications are easily accessible over the Internet. However, the only accessible portion is the user interface that is accessed through the relatively simple HTTP protocol. Web applications transmit presentation data in HTML. Because HTML is relatively easy to parse programmatically, *Presentation Integration* is a popular approach.

Unfortunately, the ease of collecting information from a provider's Web page over the Internet has caused some application providers to intentionally exploit the biggest weakness of *Presentation Integration*: brittleness. Because *Presentation Integration* usually depends on the exact geometric layout of the information, rearranging data fields can easily break a *Presentation Integration* solution. The graphical nature of HTML allows a provider to easily modify the HTML code that describes the layout of the information on the screen. The layout changes then block any attempt to collect information from the Web page.

Presentation Integration is based on the interaction between the components that are described in Table 4.5.

Table 4.5: Presentation Integration Components

Component	Responsibilities	Collaborators
Presentation layers	– Render a visual presentation to be displayed on a user terminal – Accept user input and translate it into commands to be executed by the business logic	Terminal emulator
Terminal emulator	– Impersonates a user session to the presentation layer – Makes screen information available through an API – Allows other applications to issue commands to the presentation tier	Presentation layer and other applications
Other applications	– Consume application data – Issue commands	Terminal emulator

Example

A big challenge faced by government agencies is the lack of integrated data across multiple state agencies. For example, integrated data gives an income tax agency a more holistic view of a business because the integrated data might show the number of employees that the business has and the amount of sales tax that the business reports, if any. This type of information can be used to identify businesses where there is a difference between the tax owed and the tax actually collected; this common issue is referred to as a *tax gap*. However, integrating information from multiple state agencies is often constrained by political and security concerns. In most cases, it is easier for an agency to obtain end-user access to another agency's data as opposed to obtaining direct database access. In these situations, you can use *Presentation Integration* to gain end-user access to a remote data source in the context of an automated integration solution.

Resulting Context

Presentation Integration is almost always an option and has certain advantages, but also suffers from a number of limitations:

Benefits

- **Low-risk**. In *Presentation Integration,* a source application is the application that the other applications extract data from. It is unlikely that the other applications that access the source application can corrupt it because the other applications access the data the same way that a user accesses the data. This means that all business logic and validations incorporated into the application logic protect the internal integrity of the source application's data store. This is particularly important with older applications that are poorly documented or understood.

- **Non-intrusive**. Because other applications appear to be a regular user to the source application, no changes to the source application are required. The only change that might be required is a new user account.

- **Works with monolithic applications**. Many applications do not cleanly separate the business and presentation logic. *Presentation Integration* works well in these situations because it executes the complete application logic regardless of where the logic is located.

Liabilities

- **Brittleness**. User interfaces tend to change more frequently than published programming interfaces or database schemas. Additionally, *Presentation Integration* may depend on the specific position of fields on the screen so that even minor changes such as moving a field can cause the integration solution to break. This effect is exacerbated by the relative wordiness of HTML.

- **Limited access to data**. *Presentation Integration* only provides data that is displayed in the user interface. In many cases, other applications are interested in internal codes and data elements such as primary keys that are not displayed in the user interface. *Presentation Integration* cannot provide access to these elements unless the source application is modified.

- **Unstructured information**. In most cases, the presentation layer displays all data values as a collection of string elements. Much of the internal metadata is lost in this conversion. The internal metadata that is lost includes data types, constraints, and the relationship between data fields and logical entities. To make the available data meaningful to other applications, a semantic enrichment layer has to be added. This layer is typically dependent on the specifics of the source application and may add to the brittleness of the solution.

- **Inefficient**. *Presentation Integration* typically goes through a number of unnecessary steps. For example, the source application's presentation logic has to render a visual representation of the data even though it is never displayed. The terminal emulation software in turn has to parse the visual representation to turn it back into a data stream.

- **Slow**. In many cases, the information that you want to obtain is contained in multiple user screens because of limited screen space. For example, information may be displayed on summary and detail screens because of limited screen space. This requires the emulator to go to multiple screens to obtain a coherent set of information. Going to multiple screens to obtain information requires multiple requests to the source application and slows down the data access.

- **Complex**. Extracting information from a screen is relatively simple compared to locating the correct screen or screens. Because the integration solution simulates a live user, the solution has to authenticate to the system, change passwords regularly according to the system policy, use cursor keys and function keys to move between screens, and so on. This type of input typically has to be hard-coded or manually configured so that external systems can access the presentation integration as a meaningful business function, such as "Get Customer Address." This translation between business function and keystrokes can add a significant amount of overhead. The same issues of complexity also affect error handling and the control of atomic business transactions.

Testing Considerations

One advantage of using *Presentation Integration* is that most user interfaces execute a well-defined and generally well-understood business function. This can be an enormous advantage when dealing with monolithic systems that might be poorly documented or understood.

Unfortunately, this advantage is often offset by the fact that testing usually depends on the ability to isolate individual components so that they can be tested individually with a minimum of external dependencies. Such a testing approach is generally not possible when using *Presentation Integration*.

Security Considerations

Presentation Integration uses the same security model as an end user who logs into the application. This can be an asset or a liability depending on the needs of the applications that are participating in the integration solution. An end-user security model typically enforces a fine-grained security scheme that includes the specific data records or fields that a user is permitted to see. This makes exposing the functions through presentation integration relatively secure.

The disadvantage of the fine-grained security scheme is that it can be difficult to create a generic service that can retrieve information from a variety of data sources. In those cases, a special user account has to be created that has access rights to all the data resources that are needed by the external applications.

Acknowledgments

[Ruh01] Ruh, William. *Enterprise Application Integration. A Wiley Tech Brief.* Wiley, 2001.

5

Integration Topologies

"Always design a thing by considering it in its next larger context — a chair in a room, a room in a house, a house in an environment, an environment in a city plan." —Eliel Saarinen, a Finnish-American architect and city planner

Earlier chapters covered integration layers and the various approaches used to connect layered applications. Making these connections and creating integration layers are important parts of your integration design. Equally important, however, is the larger context that these connections and layers form as you join them together. The design of this integration context should specify the locations, structure, and channels that you use to connect these elements together to form a coherent whole. This context is called an *integration topology*.

As you consider integration designs, you will notice key differences between designing for conventional applications and designing for integration. During application design, you are usually in control of synchronous request and reply interactions, message flow, and the multiplicities of messages. You have a fairly straightforward programming model that you can use to coordinate elements, exceptions, and retries. This is not always true when you design for integration.

As you design for integration, your application becomes a computational resource that provides and consumes services as part of a larger integration architecture. And while your system may be simply connected point-to-point with another service, your system may also be a provider or publisher of business events to other systems. If your system is a provider or publisher, your event message might be sent to a message broker or to a message bus. These components may then send copies of the message to many other subscribed applications or systems. Other systems may be connected or removed from these message brokers or message buses without any modifications to your system. In fact, your system may not have any direct knowledge of these other systems at all.

To understand how to design systems as service providers and consumers, it is important to have a working knowledge of integration topologies. These topologies cover the flow of messages though an integration architecture, and they introduce elements such as message brokers and message buses. Although topics like physical topologies may seem unimportant at this level of abstraction, it turns out that some integration elements, such as message buses, are tightly coupled to lower-level topologies. Therefore, it is important to understand how these lower levels work in order to fully understand the higher-level topologies.

This chapter starts, as many integration architectures do, by considering a basic *Point-to-Point Connection* pattern. It then progresses to a more complex integration pattern – the *Broker* (and its variants). Unlike the coupled endpoints in a *Point-to-Point Connection*, the *Broker* decouples the source from the target by inserting intermediaries. After the *Broker*, the next pattern is the *Message Bus*. The *Message Bus* pattern further decouples endpoints by using agreed-upon message schemas, command messages, and shared infrastructure. Finally, the chapter examines another pattern used by all three of the previous patterns to notify interested subscribers – *Publish/Subscribe*. After describing these four patterns, the chapter takes a more detailed look at logical and physical topologies to help you better understand the collaborations within the *Point-to-Point Connection*, the *Broker*, and the *Message Bus* patterns.

Point-to-Point Connection

Many integration projects start with the need to connect two systems, and the easiest way to do so is to use the *Point-to-Point Connection* pattern. A point-to-point connection ensures that only one receiver receives a particular message. For this to work, the sending system must know the location of the receiving node. The sending system often must translate the message into a format that the receiving system understands.

When you use point-to-point connections, each system determines the address of all the other nodes that it needs to communicate with. When target addresses or protocol details change, all the systems that communicate with the target server must be updated. As the size of your integration network grows and as the frequency of change increases, the operational cost associated with this approach becomes significant.

Most integration scenarios require you to transform the data between the source system and the target systems. Additionally, in many scenarios, developers want to take advantage of some conditional logic when they configure message routing. If you use point-to-point connections, this logic is often duplicated on each server that requires transformation and routing. Duplicate code is expensive to write, and it is difficult to maintain, to extend, to test, and to manage.

The strength of the *Point-to-Point Connection* pattern is how simple it is to implement. The weakness of the *Point-to-Point Connection* pattern is the duplication of transformation and routing code between systems, and the high configuration cost of endpoint address changes. To minimize these weaknesses, you can add another layer of indirection between endpoints that contains a broker.

Broker

The *Broker* pattern and its variants are often used in both application design and integration design. The foundation work for this pattern is contained in *Pattern-Oriented Software Architecture, Volume 1: A System of Patterns* [Buschmann96]. The original pattern presented in this work is rather large in scope and contains four themes of particular interest for integration:

- Creating client-side proxies, server-side proxies, and the related infrastructure to encapsulate the complexities of distributed communication
- Providing a means for systems to register services with a broker so they can be consumed by other systems
- Providing a means for systems to locate necessary services
- Describing how brokers and endpoints can collaborate using both direct and indirect communication

In the first work in this pattern series, *Enterprise Solution Patterns using Microsoft .NET* [Trowbridge03], *Broker* is discussed in the context of client proxies and server proxies using *Distributed Object Integration*. However, that discussion did not emphasize direct and indirect communication or naming services. This chapter breaks the primary *Broker* pattern down to a hierarchy of specialized patterns where each specialized pattern has particular responsibilities that refine the responsibilities of the primary *Broker* pattern.

The intent of a broker is to decouple source systems from target systems. In the context of *Distributed Object Integration*, the source system may send a marshaled set of parameters when the source system requests a method invocation from the target system. In the context of *Service-Oriented Integration*, the source system may send a message that requests a service from a target system. While the contexts vary significantly, both use a *Broker* pattern to decouple the source systems and the target systems.

A broker decouples source systems and target systems by assuming responsibility for coordinating communication between endpoints. There are three responsibilities that are involved in communication. These three responsibilities include the following:

- **Routing**. Routing involves determining the location of a target system, and it is performed by using direct and indirect communication.

- **Endpoint registration**. Endpoint registration is the mechanism that a system can use to register itself with the *Broker* so that other systems can discover that system.

- **Transformation**. Transformation is the process where an element is converted from one format to another.

In this case, the source element is the message that is sent by the source system, and the target element is the message that is received by the target system. Figure 5.1 shows the *Broker* pattern and the three related patterns that refine the basic *Broker* pattern: *Direct Broker, Indirect Broker,* and *Message Broker* [Hohpe04].

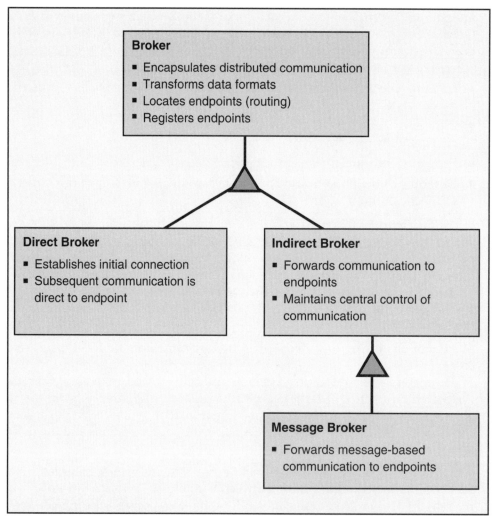

A pattern refinement

Figure 5.1
Broker and related patterns

A direct broker establishes initial communication between endpoints. After the initial communication, the two endpoints communicate directly by using client-side and server-side *Proxies* [Gamma95]. Figure 5.2 illustrates a *Direct Broker* implementation.

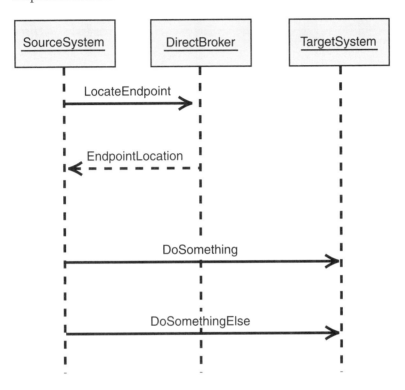

Figure 5.2
Sequence diagram for a Direct Broker implementation

In contrast, an indirect broker is a middleman, and all the communication between endpoints passes through it. Using an indirect broker allows a sender to be unaware of target details and provides central control of the message flow. In this way, *Indirect Broker* is similar to *Mediator* [Gamma95]. *Mediator* "keeps objects from referring to each other explicitly, and it lets you vary their interaction independently" [Gamma95]. Figure 5.3 shows how an indirect broker acts as a mediator between source systems and target systems.

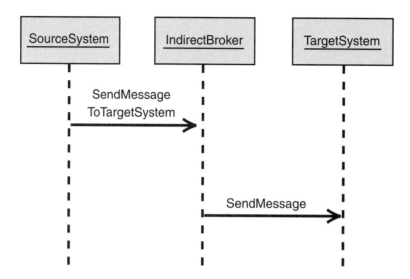

Figure 5.3

Sequence diagram for an Indirect Broker implementation

While the *Indirect Broker* pattern is useful when you need to control communications, *Direct Broker* offers better performance, especially when an additional intermediary is not needed for all communications.

The *Message Broker* pattern is a specialized version of the *Broker* pattern [Buschmann96, Trowbridge03]. A message broker communicates exclusively by using messages and indirect communication. The *Message Broker* is an important and frequently used integration pattern. It is often referred to as a *hub-and-spoke* architecture.

Let's examine several *Broker* implementations to see how this pattern and its variations work in practice.

Broker Examples

To illustrate how the *Broker* pattern is used, let's look at the following five examples of the *Broker* pattern in action:

- Microsoft Distributed Common Object Model (DCOM)
- Microsoft .NET Framework Remoting
- Common Object Request Broker Architecture (CORBA)
- Universal Description Discovery and Integration (UDDI)
- Microsoft BizTalk Server 2004

DCOM

Microsoft's Distributed Common Object Model (DCOM) is an example of *Distributed Object Integration* that uses a direct broker. When a calling application on a source server wants to create and use an object on a target server, DCOM coordinates communications between these endpoints. To coordinate this communication, DCOM first locates the target server by using configuration information that is stored in the registry. DCOM then creates a client proxy on the source system and a server proxy (stub) on the target system. Subsequent communication occurs directly between the client proxy and the server proxy (stub) using point-to-point connections as shown in Figure 5.4.

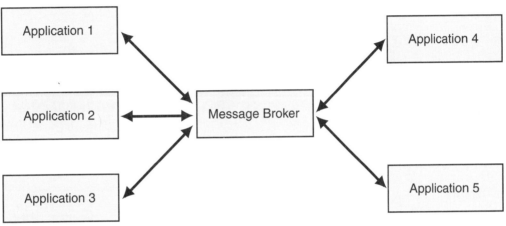

Figure 5.4
Sequence diagram showing DCOM acting as a direct broker

.NET Framework Remoting

.NET Framework remoting is another example of *Distributed Object Integration* that uses *Direct Broker.* The collaboration is the same as the collaboration that is shown in Figure 5.4. However, unlike DCOM, .NET Framework remoting does not retrieve the server location from the registry. Instead, the URL for the server is passed as a parameter to the **Activator.GetObject()** method call. This call then sets up communication between proxies. After the channels are registered and the proxies have been set up, subsequent communication occurs directly between proxies by using a point-to-point connection. This implementation uses the server and client proxies' portion of the *Broker* pattern, but does not directly use a naming service to register and to locate endpoints.

The programming model for both the client and the server is very straightforward. For more information, see *Implementing Broker with .NET Remoting Using Server-Activated Objects* [Trowbridge03] and *Implementing Broker with .NET Remoting Using Client-Activated Objects* [Trowbridge03].

CORBA

The Common Object Request Broker Architecture (CORBA) is a specification that has multiple implementations. While these implementations vary in practice, this section focuses on an implementation that uses *Distributed Object Integration* with a direct broker.

Upon startup, an object request broker (ORB) acting as a client sends a User Datagram Packet (UDP) broadcast on its local subnet to find a naming service. The ORB then stores the location of the first naming service that responds to this request. Because this is a broadcast, the communication uses a bus-based logical topology. (See the topology section later in this section for more information about topologies.)

Using this naming service, the ORB requests the location of the target server on behalf of the client. Assuming the server has previously registered with the naming service, the naming service then returns the server location to the ORB. After the ORB obtains the server location, it sets up a client proxy and a server proxy (skeleton). All subsequent communication occurs directly between the client proxy and the server proxy by using a point-to-point connection.

UDDI

The Universal Description Discovery and Integration (UDDI) specification defines a SOAP-based Web service for finding and registering Web services. UDDI is also a publicly accessible set of implementations of the specification. These implementations enable businesses to register and to discover Web services. UDDI implementations can be either private or public.

At run time, a UDDI server can act as a *Direct Broker* between two Web services. The interaction starts with the consuming service. The consuming service then contacts the UDDI server. The UDDI server locates the target service and returns it to the consuming service. After receiving the target's location in the UDDI binding template and after receiving the target's configuration, the consuming service communicates directly with the providing service.

For more information about how to use UDDI at run time, see "Using UDDI at Run Time, Part I" and "Using UDDI at Run Time, Part II" by Karsten Januszewski [Januszewski01, Januszewski02].

BizTalk Server 2004

BizTalk Server 2004 is a versatile platform infrastructure component that you can configure in many different ways. Most importantly, you can use BizTalk Server 2004 as the component that implements *Message Broker.* Unlike the previous examples that used direct brokers, *Message Broker* is a refinement of the *Indirect Broker* pattern. Systems that use *Indirect Broker* do not communicate directly with each other. Instead, they communicate through a middleman — the indirect broker. The source system communicates the logical name of the target to the indirect broker. The indirect broker then looks up the target system that is registered under the logical name and passes the communication to the target system. A message broker is a specialized type of indirect broker that communicates by using messages. For a detailed example, see *Implementing Message Broker with BizTalk Server 2004.*

The preceding five examples demonstrate that the *Broker* pattern and its variants are frequently used for systems integration. Compared to *Point-to-Point Connection*, it effectively decouples source systems and target systems by adding another level of indirection. There are situations, however, that call for even greater decoupling. In these situations, you often want a data format and a message structure that are common across multiple systems. You also want a shared infrastructure that can communicate these common messages to any interested system. At this point, it is time to consider *Message Bus.*

Message Bus

The notion of a bus originated in the field of electrical engineering where a common bus is used to carry current of a specific voltage and frequency. This notion is extended with the buses that are found in computer hardware systems so that it includes not only common voltages, but also agreed-upon messages such as a data bus and an address bus. A message bus extends this concept to provide a common communication mechanism between disparate systems. To provide this common mechanism, the systems must have three elements:

- A set of agreed-upon message schemas
- A set of common command messages [Hohpe04]
- A shared infrastructure for sending bus messages to recipients

This shared infrastructure can be achieved either by using a *Message Router* [Hohpe04] or by using a *Publish/Subscribe* mechanism. In this book, the focus is on message buses that use *Publish/Subscribe* mechanisms. For details on how to design a message bus that uses message-oriented middleware and a message router, see *Enterprise Integration Patterns: Designing, Building, and Deploying Messaging Solutions* [Hohpe04].

Figure 5.5 shows a *Message Bus* associated with a *Publish/Subscribe* implementation.

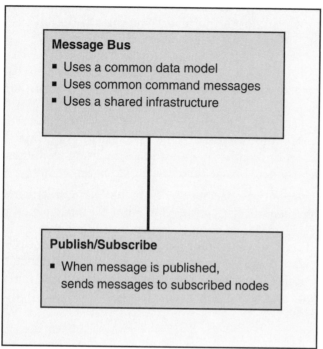

Figure 5.5
Message Bus associated with a Publish/Subscribe pattern implementation

The *Publish/Subscribe* pattern describes a collaboration where one system subscribes to change messages or to event messages that are produced by another system. In the *Message Bus* context, a system can subscribe to bus messages. After the system subscribes, the system is then sent all the messages that are addressed to this common bus. Although message buses often use *Publish/Subscribe* implementations, these implementations are used by other topologies as well. For example, *Point-to-Point Connection* and *Message Broker* can also use *Publish/Subscribe* collaborations.

The advantage of a message bus is that once it is established, the cost of adding new applications is minimal. A new application can subscribe to bus messages without affecting other subscribers. Because all systems, including the new system, understand common message schemas and command messages, there is no need for additional translation. However, as you add a new system to the bus, it may be useful to use an *Adapter* [Gamma95] to encapsulate any translation needed to initially connect with the message bus.

The disadvantage of a message broker is the significant amount of work that is involved in creating common message schemas, command messages, and shared infrastructure within an enterprise. Because these systems typically cross organizational boundaries and systems, gaining agreement on these key areas may be extremely difficult, time consuming, or impossible.

Message Bus implementations vary significantly depending on the kind of *Publish/ Subscribe* mechanism they employ. Because a *Publish/Subscribe* mechanism is such an integral part of a *Message Bus* implementation, the next section looks at this pattern more closely.

Publish/Subscribe

At a high level, the *Publish/Subscribe* [Buschmann96] pattern helps keep cooperating systems synchronized by one-way propagation of messages because one publisher sends a message to any number of intended subscribers. However, there are significant differences in the next level of design within the pattern. These differences lead to three refinements of the *Publish/Subscribe* pattern: *List-Based Publish/Subscribe*, *Broadcast-Based Publish/Subscribe*, and *Content-Based Publish/Subscribe*.

List-Based Publish/Subscribe

A *List-Based Publish/Subscribe* pattern advises you to identify a subject and to maintain a list of subscribers for that subject. When events occur, you have the subject notify each subscriber on the subscription list. A classic way to implement this design is described in the *Observer* [Gamma95] pattern. When you use this pattern, you identify two classes: subjects and observers. Assuming you use a push model update, you add three methods to the subject: **Attach()**, **Detach()**, and **Notify()**. You add one method to the observer — **Update()**.

To use an observer, all interested observers register with the subject by using the **Attach()** method. As changes occur to the subject, the subject then calls each registered observer by using the **Notify()** method. For a detailed explanation of the *Observer* pattern, see *Design Patterns: Elements of Reusable Object-Oriented Software* [Gamma95].

An observer works fine if you have created instances of objects that reify all your observers and subjects. An observer is especially well suited to situations where you have one-to-many relationships between your subjects and your observers. However, in the context of integration, you often have many observers that are linked to many subjects, which complicates the basic *Observer* pattern. One way to implement this many-to-many relationship is to create many subjects and to have each subject contain a list of observers.

If you use this object structure to implement *Publish/Subscribe*, you must write these relationships to persistent storage between process executions. To do so within a relational database, you must add an associative table to resolve the many-to-many dependencies between subject and observer. After you write this information to persistent storage in a set of tables, you can directly query the database for the list of subscribers for a topic.

Maintaining lists of published topics (subjects) and subscribers (observers) and then notifying each one individually as events occur is the essence of *List-Based Publish/ Subscribe* implementations. A very different means of achieving the same result is a *Broadcast-Based Publish/Subscribe* implementation.

Broadcast-Based Publish/Subscribe

When you use a *Broadcast-Based Publish/Subscribe* approach [Tannebaum01, Oki93], an event publisher creates a message and broadcasts it to the local area network (LAN). A service on each listening node inspects the subject line. If the listening node matches the subject line to a subject that it subscribes to, the listening node processes the message. If the subject does not match, the listening node ignores the message.

Subject lines are hierarchical and may contain multiple fields that are separated by periods. Listening nodes that are interested in a particular subject can subscribe to these fields by using wildcards, if required.

Although this *Broadcast-Based Publish/Subscribe* implementation is an effective method for decoupling producers from consumers, it is sometimes useful to identify particular topic subscribers. To identify topic subscribers, a coordinating process sends a message that asks listening nodes to reply if they subscribe to a particular topic. Responses are then returned by each listening node to the provider to identify the subscribers.

Because all messages are sent to all listening nodes, and because each node is responsible for filtering unwanted messages, some authors refer to this as a publish/ subscribe channel with reactive filtering [Hohpe04].

Content-Based Publish/Subscribe

Both *Broadcast-Based Publish/Subscribe* implementations and *List-Based Publish/ Subscribe* implementations can be broadly categorized as topic-based because they both use predefined subjects as many-to-many channels. *Publish/Subscribe* implementations have recently evolved to include a new form — *Content-Based Publish/ Subscribe*. The difference between topic-based and content-based approaches is as follows:

In a topic-based system, processes exchange information through a set of pre-defined subjects (topics) which represent many-to-many distinct (and fixed) logical channels. Content-based systems are more flexible as subscriptions are related to specific information content and, therefore, each combination of information items can actually be seen as a single dynamic logical channel. This exponential enlargement of potential logical channels has changed the way to implement a pub/sub system. [Baldoni03]

The practical implication of this approach is that messages are intelligently routed to their final destination based on the content of the message. This approach overcomes the limitation of a broadcast-based system, where distribution is coupled to a multicast tree that is based on Transmission Control Protocol (TCP). It also gives the integration architect a great deal of flexibility when deciding on content-based routing logic.

A More Detailed Look at Topologies

To fully understand how collaborations that are based on *Point-to-Point Connection*, *Broker*, and *Message Bus* work together with other parts of your technical architecture, it is useful to view your system's topologies from three discrete topology levels: physical, logical, and integration.

Note: This section discusses low-level layers of the Open Systems Interconnection (OSI) stack. It then moves on to discuss the top layer (Application), bypassing many important layers. This is intentional because this section only discusses the relationship between these low-level layers and the integration topology pattern choices. It does not mean that these layers are not important. However, they are not architecturally significant for this particular discussion.

Topology Levels

Because the terms point-to-point, bus, and hub were first defined at the physical level, this section starts with a review of the physical network topology level. In addition to a physical connection, you also need a logical communication protocol. That logical communication protocol also implies a topology. After logical and physical topology levels are established, it is possible to establish patterns of communication between the collaborating nodes. These patterns of communication and collaboration form an integration topology level that is described by the *Point-to-Point Connection*, the *Broker*, and the *Message Bus* patterns.

In some cases, the topology used at the integration topology level and the topology used at the physical topology level may be the same topology. In other cases, a system may use different topologies at the integration topology level, the logical topology level, and the physical topology level. It therefore is useful to separate topologies from topology levels to avoid potential confusion. This section discusses the physical, logical, and integration topology levels in more detail.

Note: The term *topology* is used within the industry to refer to both the arrangement of nodes within a network (for example, bus or hub) and to the physical and logical network levels of elements. However, the remainder of this chapter uses the following convention. *Topology* describes the arrangement of elements (for example, bus or hub). *Topology level* is used to indicate the levels of elements, such as the physical versus the logical levels. This convention permits clarity if, for example, the chapter refers to a system that uses a bus-based topology at the physical topology level.

Physical Topology Level

The first level to consider is the physical topology. The physical topology level describes the way that each system node physically connects to the network. The topology choices are point-to-point, bus, hub, and ring. These four topologies are illustrated in Figure 5.6.

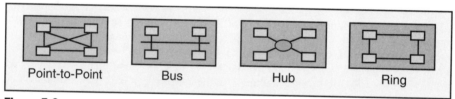

Figure 5.6
Four physical topologies

You can determine the topology that is used at the physical topology level of any set of hardware nodes by observing the arrangement of the network cables and the devices that connect the nodes. Logical network protocols use this topology to facilitate communication between the nodes. Because these protocols assume a particular sequence of communication and a logical structure between nodes, these collaborations form topologies at the physical topology level.

Logical Topology Level

A logical topology level describes the means, the sequence, and the protocol that physical nodes use to communicate. The most popular network protocol today is the Ethernet standard (IEEE 802.3). Ethernet uses a bus-based topology at the logical topology level. Ethernet is bus based because the original protocol was designed so that all packets on a network or on a subnetwork were sent to all nodes on the same network segment. This configuration requires each listening node to filter unwanted packets. The protocol provides for collisions that may occur if more than one node transmits simultaneously. Since the original protocol was developed, advances in network hardware have enabled devices to route messages to selected nodes to improve performance. One such advance is the development of switches. The Ethernet protocol also has evolved to take advantage of these developments, but it still supports a bus-based logical topology.

A less-used network protocol is token passing (IEEE 802.5). Token passing uses a ring-based topology at the logical topology level. With this topology, each node connects to the next node in the ring and passes a message in a circular fashion until it arrives at the intended destination.

As shown in Figure 5.7, the topology of the logical topology level and the topology of the physical topology level correspond exactly in some cases.

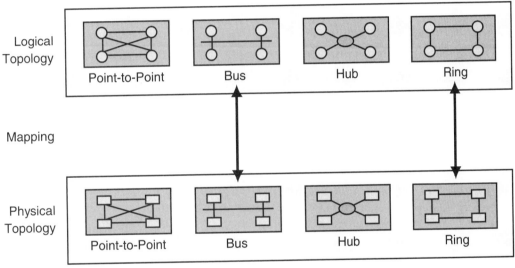

Figure 5.7
Direct mapping of topologies at the logical and physical topology levels

For example, a set of nodes that are connected with a bus-based topology at the physical topology level might also be connected with a bus-based topology at the logical topology level. This topology is the topology that often exists when you use the Ethernet protocol. Or, a set of nodes that are connected with a ring-based topology at the physical topology level might also be connected with a ring-based topology at the logical topology level. This is the topology that exists when you use token passing. However, it is important to understand that the topologies used at the physical and logical topology levels do not have to be the same. In practice, they are often different.

For example, multiple nodes might be connected in a hub-based topology (100Base-T) at the physical topology level, and a bus-based topology (Ethernet) might be used at the logical topology level. In this case, an incoming packet is broadcast to all the nodes that are physically connected to the hub, and the hub effectively acts as a bus. Each listening node is then responsible for filtering the unwanted messages. Figure 5.8 shows a bus-based topology at the logical topology level. The bus-based topology is mapped to both a bus-based topology and to a hub-based topology at the physical topology level.

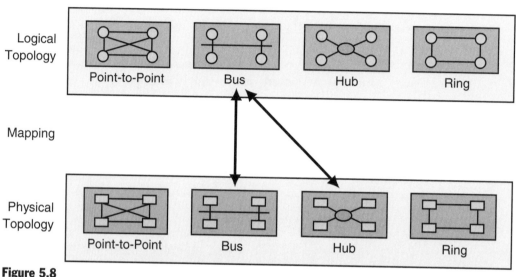

Figure 5.8

A bus-based topology at the logical topology level mapped to both a bus-based topology and a hub-based topology at the physical topology level

Another example of different topologies at the logical and physical topology levels is a ring-based topology at the logical topology level that runs on top of a bus topology at the physical topology level. This configuration is described in IEEE 802.4. In this configuration, messages are passed in the logical topology level through a ring of nodes, but the nodes are connected by using a bus-based or a hub-based topology at the physical topology level.

As you analyze a set of connected systems in detail, it is useful to clarify the topology level you are referring to. This helps to separate the logical issues from the physical issues. Above the logical level, the integration topology level describes the arrangement of integrated systems.

Integration Topology Level

The integration topology level describes the arrangement of channels, collaborations, and mechanisms that different systems and services use to communicate. This topology level consists of different combinations of three patterns: *Point-to-Point*

Connection, *Broker*, and *Message Bus*. These patterns, along with the related *Publish/ Subscribe* pattern, are illustrated in Figure 5.9 by using circles.

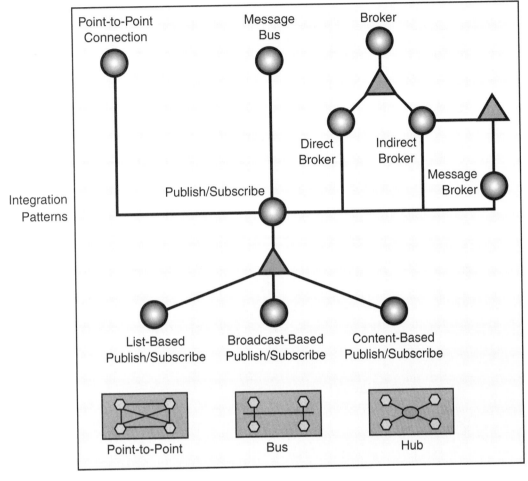

A pattern refinement

Figure 5.9
Integration patterns related to topologies

Now let's look at how integration topologies interact with logical and physical topologies in more detail.

Using Topologies Together

To design an integration architecture, you must decide on high-level collaborations in the integration topology level. These collaborations use other combinations of collaborations and topologies in the logical topology level. In turn, these collaborations use, and in some situations are constrained by, the topologies used in the physical topology level. Note that each level has its own set of concerns and responsibilities. Let's now look at these collaborations in more detail.

Point-to-Point Connection

Figure 5.10 shows how to implement the *Point-to-Point Connection* pattern. Given the popularity of Ethernet, point-to-point connections are often connected by a bus in the logical topology level. Using common network devices like routers, hubs, and switches, the physical topology level is usually either hub based or bus based. Regardless of the topologies used at the physical and logical topology levels, from an integration pattern perspective, the nodes are using a *Point-to-Point Connection* pattern if both of the following are true:

- Exactly one message is sent to and received by one target node.
- The responsibility for determining the target location and protocol lies with the sender.

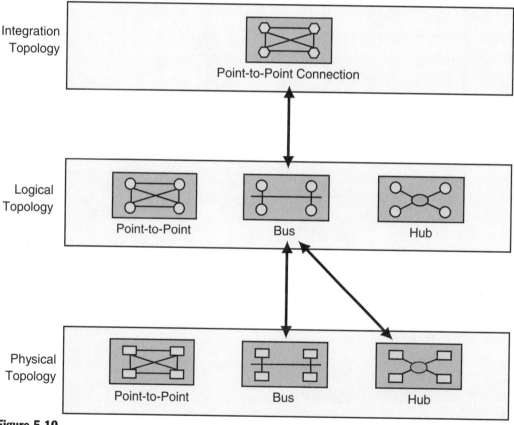

Figure 5.10
Topologies stack for a Point-to-Point Connection integration pattern

Breaking these topologies into discrete levels lets you qualify topology discussions by using a frame of reference. For example, using the configuration that is shown in Figure 5.10, you might have a *Point-to-Point Connection* topology at the integration topology level that is connected to a bus topology at the logical topology level and to a bus or hub topology at the physical topology level.

Broker

The collaboration described in the *Broker* pattern uses a combination of many other topologies. For example, let's review the CORBA direct broker example that is discussed earlier in this chapter.

"Upon startup, an object request broker (ORB) acting as a client sends a UDP broadcast on its local subnet to find a naming service."

Here, a broker uses a bus topology at the logical topology level to send a broadcast to all the systems that are connected to its subnet. In this case, the topology used at the physical topology level is irrelevant, but it is likely to be hub based or bus based due to the ubiquity of Ethernet. Note that the naming service must be located on the same subnet as the ORB for this scheme to work.

"Using this naming service, the ORB requests the location of the target server on behalf of the client."

This is a standard broker collaboration. The main requirement here is that the source system be able to connect point-to-point with the naming service. Therefore, the topologies used at the logical and physical topology levels are less important. Again, due to the ubiquity of Ethernet, the topology used at the logical topology level is likely to be bus based, but the topology used at the physical topology level is likely to be either hub based or bus based.

"All subsequent communication occurs directly between the client proxy and the server proxy by using a point-to-point connection."

Again, the main requirement is that the source system be able to connect point-to-point to the target. This also is likely to be a bus topology at the logical topology level and a hub or bus topology at the physical topology level.

Although the *Broker* collaboration may have some amount of coupling to underlying topologies at both the physical and logical topology levels, the amount of coupling is much more pronounced when you use *Message Bus* in conjunction with a *Publish/Subscribe* implementation.

Message Bus and Publish/Subscribe

Message Bus implementations can vary greatly depending on the *Publish/Subscribe* mechanism that they employ. Now let's examine the practical implications of using the three *Publish/Subscribe* variations together with *Message Bus*.

Message Bus with Broadcast-Based Publish/Subscribe

To use a *Message Bus* implementation that contains a *Broadcast-Based Publish/Subscribe* implementation, a system sends a command message to the message bus. The message bus broadcasts the message to all the nodes that are listening to the bus. The message bus makes no attempt to determine the appropriate subscribers. Instead, each listening node filters any unwanted messages and processes only the messages that it is interested in. Any data associated with the messages is in a common format so that all systems can interpret the command message and the data, and then respond appropriately.

From a topology perspective, this combination of the *Message Bus* pattern and the *Publish/Subscribe* patterns uses a bus-based topology at the logical topology level (Ethernet) to make a bus-based broadcast communication from the message bus to all the listening nodes. The physical topology at this point is irrelevant, but it is usually either hub based or bus based.

Message Bus with List-Based Publish/Subscribe

To use a message bus that contains *a List-Based Publish/Subscribe* implementation, a system sends a command message to the message bus. The message bus then looks up all interested bus subscribers and sends each one a copy of the original message. Any data associated with the message is in a common format so that all systems can interpret the command message and the data, and then respond appropriately.

From a topology perspective, this combination of the *Message Bus* and *Publish/ Subscribe* patterns is likely to use (but not to be coupled to) a bus topology at the logical topology level (Ethernet) to make point-to-point connections from the message bus to the subscribing nodes, as shown in Figure 5.11. At this point, the topology used at the physical topology level is irrelevant, but it is usually either hub based or bus based.

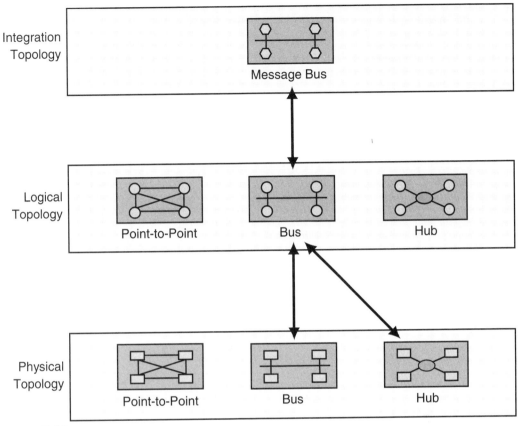

Figure 5.11
A message bus using a bus topology at the logical topology level and a bus or hub topology at the physical topology level

Message Bus with Content-Based Publish/Subscribe

To use a *Message Bus* pattern that contains a *Content-Based Publish/Subscribe* implementation, a system sends a command message to the message bus. After the message bus receives the message, it is responsible for matching the message against a set of subscribers. The message bus then forwards the message to each of the appropriate subscribers.

To match the message against a set of subscribers, the message bus must determine if there are any subscribers interested in this particular message. If an interested subscriber exists, the subscriber matches a particular message field or fields and a set of values. If a match exists between the message content and a subscriber, the message is then forwarded to each matching subscriber.

After a subscribing system receives a bus message, the subscribing system is able to process the message because the message contains the common command message and the agreed-upon message schemas.

Although the *Message Bus using List-Based Publish/Subscribe* and the *Message Bus using Content-Based Publish/Subscribe* patterns both check for subscriptions before forwarding messages, there are key differences. The list-based approach matches subscriptions on subjects. The content-based approach allows you to identify one or more fields in the message and to identify a set of acceptable values for each field. As a result, you can create very intelligent routing capabilities. This makes the content-based approach more flexible than the list-based approach.

To make *Content-Based Publish/Subscribe* work, you need a high performance infrastructure component that can read each message, query a set of potential subscribers, and efficiently route the message to each subscriber. In practice, you can think of this as a message switch. This is exactly how Microsoft BizTalk Server 2004 is designed.

Figure 5.12 shows the *Message Bus* pattern using a *Publish/Subscribe* pattern or one of the *Publish/Subscribe* variants.

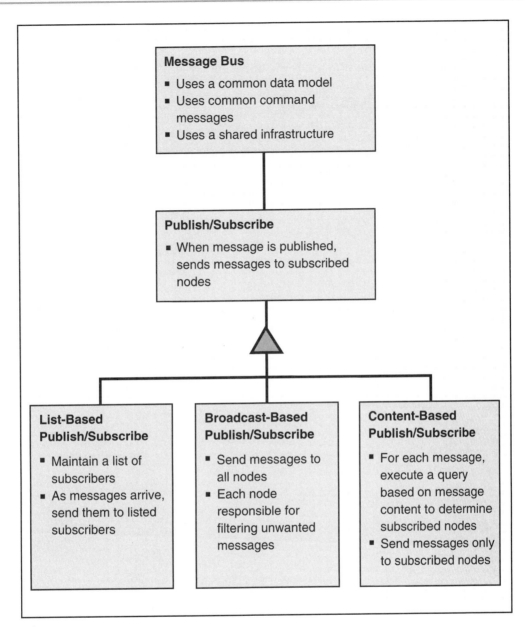

△ A pattern refinement

Figure 5.12

Message Bus using a Publish/Subscribe pattern

Integration Topology Level Patterns

The following table summarizes the integration patterns that are discussed in this chapter.

Table 5.1: Integration Network Patterns

Pattern	Problem	Associated implementations
Message Broker	How do you integrate applications without enforcing a common interface and also allow each application to initiate interactions with several other applications?	*Implementing Message Broker with BizTalk 2004*
Message Bus	As an integration solution grows, how can you lower the cost of adding or removing applications?	
Publish/Subscribe	How can an application in an integration architecture only send messages to the applications that are interested in receiving the messages without knowing the identities of the receivers?	

Message Broker

Aliases

Hub and Spoke

Context

You have an online store that integrates several systems, such as the Web-based front-end system, the credit card verification system, the retail system, and the shipping system. The control flow usually originates in the front end. For example, a customer placing an order causes the online store to send a request message to the credit card verification system. If the credit card information is validated, the online store sends request messages to the various retail systems, depending on the ordered items. An order for books translates into a purchase order message for the book retailer; an order for electronics translates into a purchase order message for the electronics retailer; and an order for gardening supplies translates into a purchase order message for the home and garden supplier.

The control flow could also originate in a retail or shipping system. For example, when a retailer updates a catalog, the retail system sends catalog update messages to the store so that the store can display the new items. When a shipper changes the shipping rates, the shipping system sends a rate update message to the store so that the store can compute the correct shipping charges. Similarly, when a shipper changes pickup times, the shipping system sends update messages to all the retailers the system serves so that they can have the shipments ready in time.

Problem

How do you integrate applications without enforcing a common interface and also allow each application to initiate interactions with several other applications?

Forces

To integrate applications without changing their interfaces, you must balance the following forces:

- Point-to-point integration requires a large number of connections between applications. Many connections usually translate into many interfaces.
- *Message Bus* integration facilitates adding new applications, but it requires a common bus interface. Because integration solutions usually involve applications that have proprietary interfaces provided by multiple vendors, *Message Bus* integration is difficult.

- Run-time control of qualities such as availability and performance may require dynamic reconfiguration.
- The applications in an integration solution could have conflicting quality of service (QoS) requirements.
- The applications in an integration solution could belong to different security realms.

Solution

Extend the integration solution by using *Message Broker*. A message broker is a physical component that handles the communication between applications. Instead of communicating with each other, applications communicate only with the message broker. An application sends a message to the message broker, providing the logical name of the receivers. The message broker looks up applications registered under the logical name and then passes the message to them.

Communication between applications involves only the sender, the message broker, and the designated receivers. The message broker does not send the message to any other applications. From a control-flow perspective, the configuration is symmetric because the message broker does not restrict the applications that can initiate calls. Figure 5.13 illustrates this configuration.

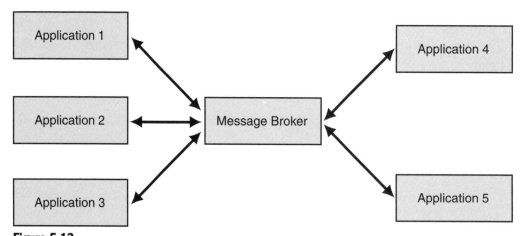

Figure 5.13
A message broker mediating the collaboration between participating applications

The message broker can expose different interfaces to the collaborating applications, and it can translate messages between these interfaces. In other words, the message broker does not enforce a common interface on the applications.

Prior to using a message broker, you must register the applications that receive communications so that the message broker can dispatch requests to them. The message broker may provide its own registration mechanism, or it may rely on an external service such as a directory.

Placing the message broker between the sender and the receiver provides flexibility in several ways. First, the message broker allows the integration solution to dynamically change its configuration. For example, if an application must be shut down for maintenance, the message broker could start routing requests to a failover application. Likewise, if the receiver cannot keep up with the incoming messages, the message broker could start load balancing between several receivers.

Second, the message broker can choose between applications that have different QoS levels. This resembles the dynamic configuration, but the message broker selects the application based on specified criteria. For example, an application for premium accounts may fulfill requests quickly, but an application for general use may have a longer processing time.

Third, the message broker allows the sender and the receiver to reside in different security realms. In other words, the message broker can reside on the boundary between two security realms and bridge requests between those two realms. Table 5.2 shows the responsibilities and collaborations of a message broker.

Table 5.2: Message Broker Responsibilities and Collaborations

Responsibilities	Collaborations
– Receive message – Determine the message recipients and perform the routing – Handle any interface-level differences – Send the message to the recipients	– Senders: applications that send messages to the message broker – Receivers: applications that receive messages from the message broker

Example

Consider an online store that allows shoppers to browse a variety of retail catalogs and to place orders. When an order is placed, the online store groups the shopping cart items by retailer and places appropriate orders with each retailer. As each retailer fulfills and ships the order, it sends the online store a tracking number. The online store updates its records so that this information is presented on the Check Order Status page. If the customer has configured e-mail alerts, the store also sends an e-mail message that contains the tracking information.

The online store that is illustrated in Figure 5.14 uses a message broker to communicate with the individual retailers. The broker knows how to reach each retailer and how to place orders, to cancel orders, and to check the order status. Likewise, the retailers communicate with the broker when they send tracking numbers. Each retailer must know how to reach the broker and how to send the tracking number. In other words, both the store side and the retailer side can initiate a communication, and the data flows in both directions.

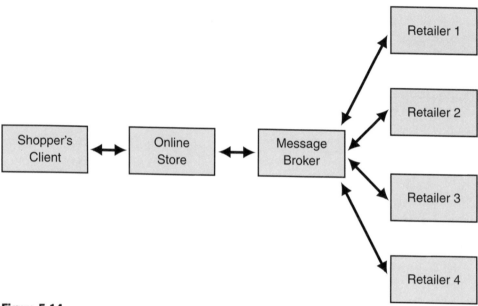

Figure 5.14
Online store communicating with retailers through a message broker

Resulting Context

The decision to use a message broker for integration entails balancing the benefits of removing inter-application coupling against the effort associated with using the message broker. Use the following benefits and liabilities to evaluate the balance:

Benefits

- **Reduced coupling**. The message broker decouples the senders and the receivers. Senders communicate only with the message broker, and the potential grouping of many receivers under a logical name is transparent to them.

- **Improved integrability**. The applications that communicate with the message broker do not need to have the same interface. Unlike integration through a bus, the message broker can handle interface-level differences. In addition, the message broker can also act as a bridge between applications that are from different security realms and that have different QoS levels.

- **Improved modifiability**. The message broker shields the components of the integration solution from changes in individual applications. It also enables the integration solution to change its configuration dynamically.

- **Improved security.** Communication between applications involves only the sender, the broker, and the receivers. Other applications do not receive the messages that these three exchange. Unlike bus-based integration, applications communicate directly in a manner that protects the information without the use of encryption.

- **Improved testability**. The message broker provides a single point for mocking. Mocking facilitates the testing of individual applications as well as of the interaction between them.

Liabilities

- **Increased complexity**. Communicating through a message broker is more complex than direct communication for the following reasons:
  - The message broker must communicate with all the parties involved. This could mean providing many interfaces and supporting many protocols.
  - The message broker is likely to be multithreaded, which makes it hard to trace problems.

- **Increased maintenance effort**. Broker-based integration requires that the integration solution register the applications with the broker. Bus-based integration does not have this requirement.

- **Reduced availability**. A single component that mediates communication between applications is a single point of failure. A secondary message broker could solve this problem. However, a secondary message broker adds the issues that are associated with synchronizing the states between the primary message broker and the secondary message broker.

- **Reduced performance**. The message broker adds an intermediate hop and incurs overhead. This overhead may eliminate a message broker as a feasible option for solutions where fast message exchange is critical.

Testing Considerations

A mock message broker can receive requests and send back canned responses. In effect, the mock message broker allows system testers to verify individual applications without removing the individual applications from the integration solution.

Likewise, a mock message broker that emulates some of the message broker's functionality allows testers to verify and to profile the interplay between a few applications, for example, a subset of the integration solution. In other words, a mock message broker allows you to test individual applications and to test subsystems.

Figure 5.15 shows these configurations; the shading indicates the areas under test.

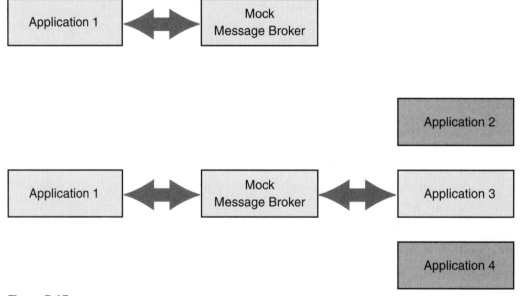

Figure 5.15
Using a mock message broker to test applications and subsystems

Security Considerations

Integration by using a message broker places a component between senders and receivers. On one hand, this configuration accommodates management of the security context through consolidation as well as impersonation. On the other hand, the message broker represents a central point of attack. Compromising the message broker compromises the communication between all the applications that use it.

Operational Considerations

The message broker can dynamically change the configuration. It can direct messages to a failover application if necessary or perform load balancing between applications, or the message broker can do both.

Known Uses

Broker-based integration products such as Microsoft BizTalk Server 2004 extend the traditional broker functionality with additional features. For example, BizTalk Server 2004 provides orchestration services, messaging services, and other features associated with these services such as business activity monitoring, transaction and exception handling, correlation, and graphic editing.

Variants

A message broker variant trades ease of integration for performance. The performance-optimized message broker looks up the receiver and then connects it to the sender, thus allowing the sender and the receiver to communicate directly. The direct connection eliminates the performance penalty that is associated with an intermediary between the communicating parties. However, this performance optimization only works if the sender and the receiver have the same interface.

Related Patterns

For more information, see the following related patterns:

- *Broker* [Buschmann96]. In a distributed setting, the *Broker* pattern tries to make distribution transparent. Client-side and server-side proxies mediate between the broker and the clients and server.

- *Implementing Message Broker with BizTalk Server 2004*. This pattern uses the Global Bank scenario to show how you can use BizTalk Server 2004 to implement *Message Broker*.

- *Client-Dispatcher-Server* [Buschmann96]. The *Client-Dispatcher-Server* pattern is a *Broker* variant that uses the direct communication optimization mentioned earlier in "Variants."

- *Content-Based Router* [Hohpe04]. The *Content-Based Router* pattern is a *Broker* variant that specializes in routing communications to different applications based on the content of the communication.

- *Mediator* [Gamma95]. The *Mediator* pattern separates objects so that they are only aware of the mediator but not each other. The *Broker* deals with similar concerns, but it can only be used in the context of enterprise applications.

Acknowledgments

[Buschmann96] Buschmann, Frank; Regine Meunier, Hans Rohnert, Peter Sommerlad, and Michael Stal. *Pattern-Oriented Software Architecture, Volume 1: A System of Patterns*. John Wiley & Sons Ltd, 1996.

[Gamma95] Gamma, Erich; Richard Helm, Ralph Johnson, and John Vlissides. *Design Patterns: Elements of Reusable Object-Oriented Software*. Addison-Wesley, 1995.

[Hohpe04] Hohpe, Gregor, and Bobby Woolf. *Enterprise Integration Patterns: Designing, Building and Deploying Messaging Solutions*. Addison-Wesley, 2004.

[Trowbridge03] Trowbridge, David; Dave Mancini, Dave Quick, Gregor Hohpe, James Newkirk, and David Lavigne. *Enterprise Solution Patterns Using Microsoft .NET*. Microsoft Press, 2003. Also available on the *MSDN Architecture Center* at: *http://msdn.microsoft.com/architecture/patterns/default.aspx?pull=/library/en-us/dnpatterns/html/Esp.asp*.

Implementing Message Broker with BizTalk Server 2004

Context

Your application is interacting with multiple other applications through a *Message Broker* so that each application only needs to communicate with the *Message Broker*, rather than all the other applications. The *Message Broker* is implemented by using Microsoft BizTalk Server 2004.

Background

Global Bank is implementing an Execute Scheduled Payment business process that customers can use to schedule payments. Each payment is transacted through a payment authority. The payment authority is determined when that payee is first configured. Currently, there are three different payment authorities:

- There is an internal payment authority that Global Bank uses to handle payments itself.

- There is an external payment authority where payment requests are sent to an external bill payment authority.

- There is a manual payment authority where payment requests are handled manually.

Bank growth, acquisitions, and mergers may increase the number of payment authorities.

To implement the Execute Scheduled Payment business process, Global Bank chose to use Microsoft BizTalk Server 2004 as an implementation of the *Message Broker* pattern. As Figure 5.16 shows, requests for payment are sent directly to the message broker, and the message broker then sends the request to the correct payment authority.

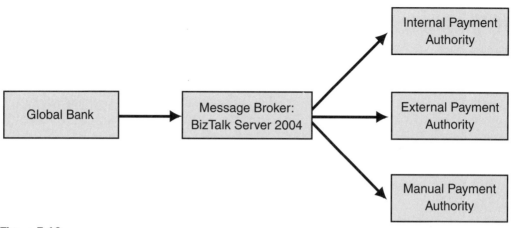

Figure 5.16
BizTalk Server 2004 as Message Broker in Global Bank

Apart from sending any message received to the appropriate recipient, the *Message Broker* implementation also must do the following:

- The implementation must parse the message to determine where to send it.
- The implementation must convert the message from the source format to the destination format.
- The implementation must allow receivers (applications) to register with the broker so that the broker can send messages to them.

Implementation Strategy

BizTalk Server 2004 uses a *Publish/Subscribe* messaging architecture that can easily be used to implement *Message Broker*. BizTalk Server 2004 uses *Pipes and Filters* for the message transformation.

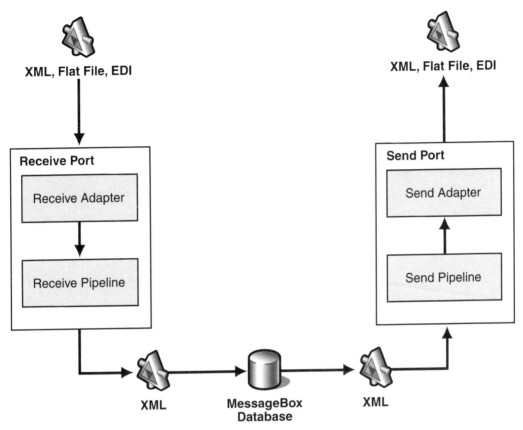

XML, Flat File, EDI

Receive Port

Receive Adapter

Receive Pipeline

XML, Flat File, EDI

Send Port

Send Adapter

Send Pipeline

XML   **MessageBox Database**   **XML**

Figure 5.17
BizTalk Server 2004 internal publish-subscribe architecture

Figure 5.17 shows how BizTalk Server 2004 receives, processes, routes, and sends messages. A client application (the publisher) sends a message to a receive port through a predefined protocol. For example, the publisher may send a message to the message broker by writing a file into a directory on the server. The message is received by the receive adapter. The following two types of adapters are available:

- **Transport adapters**. Transport adapters receive messages by using standard transport mechanisms. BizTalk Server 2004 includes many standard transport adapters such as HTTP, Simple Mail Transfer Protocol (SMTP), File, and File Transfer Protocol (FTP).

- **Application adapters**. Application adapters connect with common business applications. You usually purchase these adapters from a vendor, or you develop them yourself.

The receive adapter passes the message to a receive pipeline, and the receive pipeline then parses and converts the incoming message to XML (except when using the pass-through pipeline). XML is the format that BizTalk Server 2004 uses internally. As the receive adapter receives the message and as the receive pipeline processes it, additional data about the message is collected. This message metadata includes information about the transport the message was received on, such as the original name of the file in the case of a file transport. It also includes information from each of the components in the pipeline. For example, the Party Resolution component stores information it receives from a digital certificate attached to the message. This metadata is known as the *context properties*.

The receive pipeline uses an XML schema that the developer created. This schema disassembles and converts the message to XML and then validates the message against the schema specification. The schema describes the type, the cardinality, and the other attributes of every record and every field that is contained in the message. As the receive pipeline parses the message, it collects data from within the message itself. To do this, the developer creates a second schema that is known as a *property schema*. The property schema allows specific portions of the message to be promoted as additional metadata. This metadata is known as the *promoted properties*. For an example of how promotion occurs, see the "Example" section later in this pattern. After preprocessing in the receive pipeline, the message is submitted to the MessageBox database complete with all additional metadata.

The MessageBox database sends the message to the message recipients by using a message subscription. To implement a message subscription, the developer creates a send port that represents the message recipient. A send port usually consists of a send pipeline for post-processing of the message, a send adapter that transmits the message to its destination, and a filter expression that defines whether the message will be sent through this send port. The filter expression is a query against the context properties of messages in the MessageBox database. A copy of the message is only sent to this send port if there is a match between the filter expression and the context properties. For example, the filter expression on the send port might state, *"send all documents that are of type ExecutePayment.Payment, where the fulfillmentTypeId is equal to 1."*

The MessageBox database sends a copy of the messages to each send port that has a filter expression that matches the context properties. The message is received by the send port (the subscriber process), processed by the send pipeline, and then transmitted through the send adapter. The send adapter can be a transport adapter such as File, FTP, HTTP, BizTalk Message Queuing (MSMQT), SMTP, SOAP, or MQSeries. Or, the send adapter can be an application adapter that connects directly to the destination application.

To implement the *Message Broker*, the Global Bank developer must do the following:

1. The developer must define the format of the message sent by the source application to the *Message Broker*.

2. The developer must define the formats of the messages sent from the *Message Broker* to each of the external systems and specify how the source message is translated to the formats that are required by the external systems.

3. The developer must define how messages are sent from the *Message Broker* to each external system.

Example

Figure 5.18 shows the Global Bank *Message Broker* implementation based on BizTalk Server 2004. The numbers mark the areas that the following implementation steps focus on.

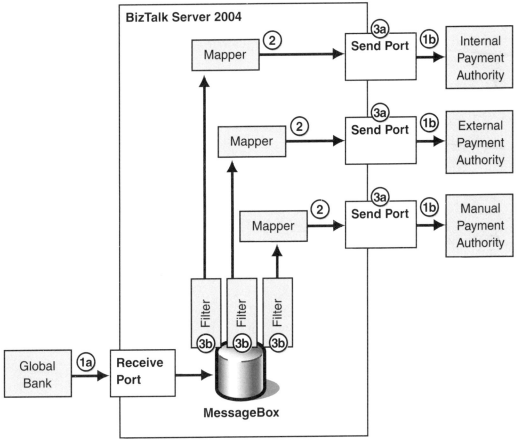

Figure 5.18
Global Bank Message Broker implementation with BizTalk Server 2004

Step 1: Create the Receive Port and Define Message Schemas

The first step in the implementation of the *Message Broker* is to create the receive port in BizTalk Explorer. This receive port defines the location that the client application will send messages to so that the messages are published to the message broker. Virtually any transport can be used to send messages from the client to the message broker. This example uses the BizTalk Message Queuing (MSMQT) adapter because MSMQT provides guaranteed delivery.

▶ **To create the receive port for the message broker**

1. Create a receive port called Payment Broker RP.

2. Create a receive location on this receive port called Payment Broker RL.

3. Set the transport for the receive location to MSMQT with a queue named Payments.

4. Specify the BizTalkServerApplication as the receive handler, and specify XML Receive as the receive pipeline.

5. After following the remaining steps to implement the message broker, enable the receive location.

This completes the creation of the receive port.

Next, the payment messages sent by Global Bank and the messages going to each of the three payment channels have to be defined. The payment messages are marked 1a in Figure 5.18, and the payment channels are marked 1b. BizTalk Server uses these definitions (XML schemas) to parse and to convert messages into XML if they are not already in XML. A disassembler component in the receive pipeline parses and converts these messages.

For the Execute Scheduled Payment implementation, the schema is actually generated automatically by the SQL Transport Schema Generation Wizard (see *Implementing Process Integration with BizTalk Server 2004*). Figure 5.19 shows the generated schema in the BizTalk Server Schema Editor.

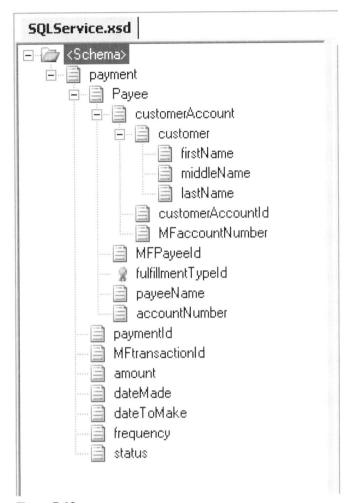

Figure 5.19
The Payment schema in the BizTalk Server 2000 Schema Editor

You can also create a special second schema that is known as a *property schema*. This property schema defines one or more fields that are linked to specific fields in the message schema. Linking fields in this way is known as promoting properties. This link between the message schema and the property schema is established in the **Promote Properties** dialog box in the BizTalk Server Schema Editor. In Figure 5.19, the unique symbol next to the fulfillmentTypeId field denotes a promoted property field.

Figure 5.20 shows the **Promote Properties** dialog box where you promote the fulfillmentTypeId field that is in the payment message. The value of the fulfillmentTypeId field is used later to determine the payment authority that the message is sent to.

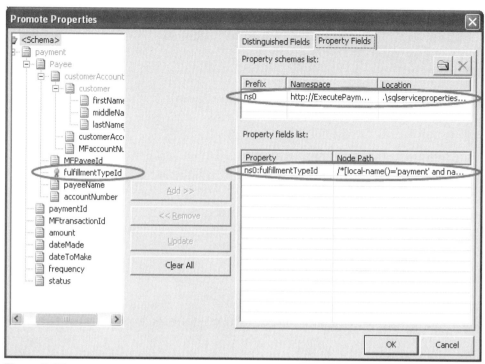

Figure 5.20
Creating a promoted property field

The format of the message that is sent to the message broker is specified by the XML schema shown in Figure 5.19. The format of the messages for each of the payment authorities is likely to be different from the source format. The format of the messages is also likely to vary between different payment authorities. Therefore, schema definitions for each of the outgoing message formats also have to be built. For brevity, these schema definitions are not presented here.

Step 2: Define Maps to Convert Between Message Formats

For each of the destination message formats specified in the previous section, an XSLT map must be developed. This XSLT map specifies how the source message format is translated to the destination message format (number 2 in Figure 5.18). These message format translations may be merely structural. For example, converting an XML message to a comma-separated-values (CSV) message is structural. Or, the translation may require the generation of new message content. For example, the source message may not contain any information about the time or date that the message was sent, but this information may be required in the destination format. New message content also has to be generated when a field in the source message is used as a key to a specific row in a database table, and fields in the destination message are filled from fields in this database row. This is a common requirement.

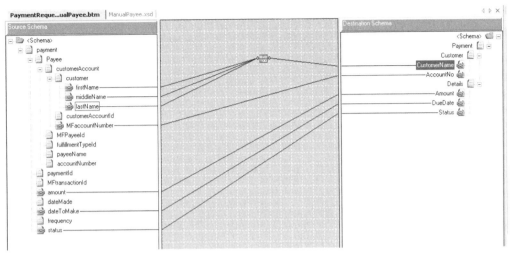

Figure 5.21
Payment authority map in the BizTalk Mapper

You can use the BizTalk Mapper to create the XSLT maps. The BizTalk Mapper provides a graphical view of source and destination schemas and of the conversion from one to the other. The output from the BizTalk Mapper is the XSLT map. Figure 5.21 shows the development of a payment authority map from the source XML schema in the BizTalk Mapper. Three separate maps are created, one for each of the payment authorities:

- PaymentRequest2InternalPayee.btm is created for the internal payee.
- PaymentRequest2ExternalPayee.btm is created for the external payee.
- PaymentRequest2ManualPayee.btm is created for the manual payee.

Step 3: Create Subscriptions to Messages

To configure the BizTalk Server message broker for the Execute Scheduled Payment scenario, three send ports must be configured. Each send port is configured with its own specific transport type and transport address, send pipeline, and BizTalk map (number 3a in Figure 5.18). In addition, the port filter has to be specified appropriately on each send port to set up the correct subscription for this payment authority to the MessageBox database (number 3b in Figure 5.18).

▶ **To configure one of the send ports (Internal Payment)**

1. Create a new send port that is called InternalPayee_SP.

2. Select **SOAP (Web Services)** for the transport type. Use the following as the transport address (the Uniform Resource Identifier [URI]):

    http://EAIPayee/InternalPayee/Payee.asmx

    Depending on the transport chosen, different transport address information can be specified.

3. Specify **XML Pipeline** as the send pipeline. The send pipeline defines the post-processing that is performed on the message just before the message is sent, such as attachment of a digital signature to the message.

4. Specify **PaymentRequest2InternalPayee.btm** as the XSLT map to be applied to the source messages.

5. Specify the filters for this send port. These filters define the subscription for this send port in the MessageBox database, and they control the criteria that the MessageBox database uses to determine the messages that are sent to this port. For the Execute Scheduled Payment scenario, the filter specifies the following two criteria as shown in Figure 5.22:

   ● All messages of type *http://GlobalBank#payment*.

   ● Messages that have a promoted **fulfillmentTypeId** property that is equal to 1 (internal fulfillment).

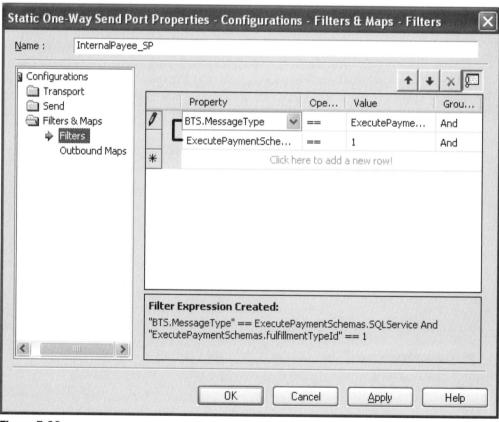

Figure 5.22
Specifying the filter (subscription) for a send port

With this configuration, all messages of type *http://GlobalBank#payment* that have a **fulfillmentTypeId** property that is set to 1 (internal fulfillment) are sent to this send port. This send port is configured to transmit the payment authorization to the internal payment application by using a SOAP call.

6. Configure the remaining ports in a similar way. Each port has its own unique transport address and its own unique XSLT map. In addition, the filters on these two ports specify a different value for the **fulfillmentTypeId** property. A value of 2 denotes external fulfillment, and a value of 3 denotes manual fulfillment.

7. Finally, enlist and then start each of the send ports.

Resulting Context

The implementation of the *Message Broker* pattern with BizTalk Server 2004 results in the following benefits and liabilities:

Benefits

- **Message routing is determined at run time**. Destination applications can be added or deleted from the system at run time without affecting the source application or other destination applications.

- **Message tracking and archiving**. All messages transmitted through the message broker can be automatically tracked and archived. The tracking, archiving, and reporting functionalities are implemented only once, and they are shared by all applications that use the message broker. In BizTalk Server 2004, these functionalities are provided by the BizTalk Server Health and Activity Tracker (HAT).

- **Centralized management**. The messaging for an application is configured and managed from a central location and is not coded into the applications.

Liabilities

- **Additional message processing steps**. This *Message Broker* implementation adds extra steps in the processing of a message. These extra steps could prevent some fully synchronous messaging scenarios from being implemented, and they could lead to higher latency than a straight-through processing solution. BizTalk Server 2004 has an alternate message processing mechanism that is known as a request-response port. The request-response port is specifically designed to solve problems caused by these synchronous messaging scenarios.

- **Routing rules are not centralized**. Decentralized routing rules are an inherent weakness in this *Message Broker* solution. The routing rules are spread between all the send port configurations in the filter rules that are specified. Therefore, configuration errors are harder to debug, and the configuration is more complex to manage.

Testing Considerations

You can use several strategies to test the *Message Broker* implementation:

- Create a mock destination application (in other words, set up a send port) that subscribes to all messages of a specific type sent to the message broker. These messages are written to a test directory. This process allows the message schemas and message maps to be validated.

- Enable or disable send ports to test individual subscribers in isolation.

- Use the HAT to track all incoming and outgoing messages, to analyze the message flow through the MessageBox database, to report exception conditions, and to analyze message throughput.

- Use the Microsoft Visual Studio .NET environment to test schemas and maps by validating sample documents, or use the schemas and maps to generate sample message instances.

Security Considerations

The following security considerations apply when implementing *Message Broker*:

- **Controlling the visibility of messages in the message broker**. If many different groups in an organization are using the message broker, it may be necessary to implement access security to control who can view messages that are sent to the message broker and to control who can set up subscriptions to messages. Remember that these messages may all be tracked and held in the Microsoft SQL Server database. BizTalk Server 2004 provides a very detailed security model that allows this type of access security to be enforced. For example, message traffic can be partitioned across multiple host instances, where each host instance runs by using different security credentials.

- **Passing digitally signed messages**. In a point-to-point processing scenario, a message originator may digitally sign and encrypt a message by using a certificate issued by the receiver of the message. However, if this message is transmitted through a message broker, the message broker usually cannot decrypt the message. To overcome this problem, the encrypted message can be wrapped in a clear text envelope. The envelope contains metadata about the message, such as the address. The metadata allows the message broker to pass the message to the intended recipient.

- **Validating senders and receivers**. Under some circumstances, the message broker may need to validate the publishers or the subscribers. This means the message broker must be able to validate a message that has been digitally signed and then attach a digital signature to a message. BizTalk Server 2004 provides these capabilities.

Operational Considerations

The following operational considerations apply when implementing *Message Broker*:

- **Dynamic configuration**. One of the big benefits of the *Message Broker* pattern is that it is easy to configure dynamically at run time. New publishers can easily be added at run time, and subscribers can be added or removed easily.

- **Load-balancing and fault tolerance**. As *Message Broker* becomes central to an organization's integration solution, it is essential for the message broker to be fault-tolerant and for the message processing workload to be spread across multiple nodes. BizTalk Server 2004 works in conjunction with Microsoft SQL Server 2000 so that all the configuration information, the messages, and the tracking data are held within SQL Server 2000. BizTalk Server 2004 also works in conjunction with Microsoft SQL Server 2000 so that all processing is distributed across all the servers running BizTalk Server 2004 that are part of the same BizTalk Server 2004 group. (A BizTalk Server 2004 group is a group of servers that share the same set of SQL Server tables).

- **Store and forward**. Rather than send a message immediately, some message brokers can hold onto a message until a subscriber requests it. This is useful in situations where subscribers are not connected all the time, or where network issues cause problems. BizTalk Server 2004 does not provide this functionality directly, although it can easily be implemented by using database staging tables or Microsoft Message Queuing (MSMQ).

Variants

Using promoted properties in the message and using filters on the send port is the simplest way to implement a message broker by using Microsoft BizTalk Server 2004. However, other more complex implementations may be preferable in certain circumstances.

Business Rule Engine

In some situations, the logic used to determine where the message is sent is more sophisticated than the simple example used here, or the logic is subject to frequent change. For example, a business may use a number of suppliers. The business may determine which supplier to send a purchase order to based on the current relationship of the business with that supplier. For example, the business might select the supplier based on the level of discounts. This cannot be calculated by using information in the message, so business logic has to be written to determine this. This logic could be coded in a Microsoft .NET Framework assembly and referenced from a map, but if the business rule is subject to frequent change, each time the rules change a new version of the business component must be deployed.

BizTalk Server 2004 solves this issue by providing a Business Rules Engine. The Business Rules Engine enables a user to define a vocabulary that is based on information contained in the message and in a database, and that is held in .NET Framework components. This vocabulary may then be used to define a series of business rules. These rules can implement sophisticated business logic, and this business logic can then be changed and deployed easily.

Roles and Parties

As the number of publishers and subscribers increases, it becomes increasingly difficult to manage and to maintain the receive ports, the send ports, and the subscriptions. In a scenario where there are thousands of potential subscribers for a message, BizTalk Server 2004 uses roles and parties. For example, you may have configured thousands of subscribers (suppliers) to send purchase orders to in your order processing system.

For this example, the Supplier role is created, and a port type is associated with this role. In this case, that is the PurchaseOrderToSupplierType port type. The outgoing message is then sent to an abstract PurchaseOrderToSupplierType port type.

Independently of this, parties are created to represent individual suppliers. After parties are created, a party can be enlisted in a role. For example, a party called Northwind Traders may be created and then enlisted in the Supplier role. When this is done, a physical port of type PurchaseOrderToSupplier must be configured to send the document to the actual supplier.

The roles and parties implementation is more complex and requires the message broker to use BizTalk Orchestration instead of using BizTalk Messaging. However, when many potential message recipients are involved, it provides a much simpler mechanism for maintaining the recipients in the system.

Related Patterns

Of particular note among related patterns, *Enterprise Integration Patterns* [Hohpe04] examines the difference between the *Publish/Subscribe* implementation (reactive filtering) and a content-based router. A content-based router examines the message and sends it to a recipient by using a process that is known as *predictive routing*. For more information, see the following patterns:

- *Broker* [Buschmann96]. In a distributed setting, the *Broker* pattern tries to make distribution transparent. Client-side and server-side proxies mediate between the broker and the clients and server.

- *Content-Based Router* [Hohpe04]. The *Content-Based Router* pattern is a *Broker* variant that specializes in routing communications to different applications based on the communication's content.

- *Mediator* [Gamma95]. The *Mediator* pattern separates objects so that they are only aware of the mediator but not each other. The *Broker* deals with similar concerns, but it can only be used in the context of enterprise applications.

Acknowledgments

[Buschmann96] Buschmann, Frank; Regine Meunier, Hans Rohnert, Peter Sommerlad, and Michael Stal. *Pattern-Oriented Software Architecture, Volume 1: A System of Patterns.* John Wiley & Sons Ltd, 1996.

[Gamma95] Gamma, Erich; Richard Helm, Ralph Johnson, and John Vlissides. *Design Patterns: Elements of Reusable Object-Oriented Software.* Addison-Wesley, 1995.

[Hohpe04] Hohpe, Gregor, and Bobby Woolf, *Enterprise Integration Patterns: Designing, Building, and Deploying Messaging Solutions.* Addison-Wesley, 2004.

Message Bus

Context

You have an integration solution that consists of applications that are provided by different vendors. These applications run on a variety of platforms. Some of these applications generate messages and many other applications consume the messages.

For example, consider a financial application that integrates trading tools, portfolio management applications, modeling and risk analysis tools, trend indicators, and tickers. Market activity causes interaction between these systems. For example, a trading system communicates the completion of a sell transaction by sending a message to all other trading applications. The trading system could have individual connections to each trading application. This works well for a few applications, but becomes a burden as the number of applications increases. Managing the addition or removal of trading applications should not interfere with processing trades.

Problem

As an integration solution grows, how can you lower the cost of adding or removing applications?

Forces

Adding an application to an integration solution or removing an application from an integration solution entails balancing the following forces:

- Communication between applications usually creates dependencies between the applications. The sender must communicate with the receivers. The receiver must recognize the messages from all the senders. These dependencies translate into coupling between the participants.

- In a configuration where point-to-point connectivity exists, the coupling has a quadratic (or $O[n^2]$) growth with the number of applications [Chandra03, Levine03]. For example, three fully connected applications need three connections, but 10 applications need 45 connections. This quadratic growth hampers maintainability, modifiability, and integrability.

- Usually, the applications of an integration solution have different interfaces. Changing the interfaces of proprietary applications is difficult. Even if you change the interface of one application, it is not feasible to change the interface for all the applications of your integration solution.

- Some integration solutions consist of a fixed set of applications. An integration solution that has low extensibility and modifiability requirements typically does not need to accommodate new applications.

Solution

Connect all applications through a logical component known as a message bus. A message bus specializes in transporting messages between applications. A message bus contains three key elements:

- A set of agreed-upon message schemas
- A set of common command messages [Hohpe04]
- A shared infrastructure for sending bus messages to recipients

When you use a message bus, an application that sends a message no longer has individual connections to all the applications that must receive the message. Instead, the application merely passes the message to the message bus, and the message bus transports the message to all the other applications that are listening for bus messages through a shared infrastructure. Likewise, an application that receives a message no longer obtains it directly from the sender. Instead, it takes the message from the message bus. In effect, the message bus reduces the fan-out of each application from many to one.

Usually, the bus does not preserve message ordering. Internal optimizations, routing, buffering, or even the underlying transport mechanism might affect how the messages travel to the receiving applications. Therefore, the order in which messages reach each receiver is nondeterministic. Preserving the order of messages requires additional logic. This additional logic can be provided by the participating applications. For example, the sending application could insert sequence numbers into the outgoing messages, and the receivers could use those numbers to reorder the incoming messages. The logic could also be provided by the bus, and the logic could therefore be transparent for the participating applications. However, this additional logic is not required.

Figure 5.23 shows an integration solution that uses a message bus. An application that sends messages through the bus must prepare the messages so that the messages comply with the type of messages the bus expects. Similarly, an application that receives messages must be able to understand (syntactically, although not necessarily semantically) the message types. If all applications in the integration solution implement the bus interface, adding applications or removing applications from the bus incurs no changes.

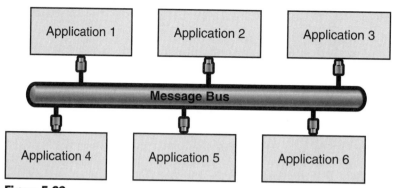

Figure 5.23

Applications communicating through a message bus

The shared infrastructure between a message bus and the listening applications can be achieved by using a *Message Router* [Hohpe04] or by using a *Publish/Subscribe* mechanism. This book focuses on message buses that use *Publish/Subscribe* mechanisms. For details on how to design a message bus that uses message-oriented middleware and a *Message Router*, see *Enterprise Integration Patterns* [Hohpe04].

Figure 5.24 shows the *Message Bus* pattern associated with the *Publish/Subscribe* pattern.

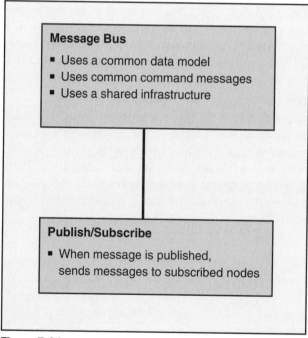

Figure 5.24

The Message Bus pattern associated with the Publish/Subscribe pattern

The kind of *Publish/Subscribe* implementation that you decide to use with a particular message bus has a profound impact on the message bus architecture. There are three types of *Publish/Subscribe* implementations: *List-Based Publish/Subscribe*, *Broadcast-Based Publish/Subscribe*, and *Content-Based Publish/Subscribe*.

> **Note:** Although the *Publish/Subscribe* pattern is an important part of a message bus, *Publish/Subscribe* implementations are also used independently of message buses. For example, *Publish/Subscribe* mechanisms are used with the *Point-to-Point Connection* and *Message Broker* patterns. See the *Publish/Subscribe* pattern for more details.

Message Bus with List-Based Publish/Subscribe

Maintaining lists of published topics (subjects) and subscribers (observers) and then notifying each one individually as events occur is the essence of *List-Based Publish/Subscribe* implementations.

To use a message bus that contains *a List-Based Publish/Subscribe* implementation, a system sends a command message to the message bus. The message bus then looks up all interested message bus subscribers and sends each message bus subscriber a copy of the original message. Any data that is associated with the message is in a common format so that all systems can interpret the command message and the data, and then respond appropriately.

Message Bus with Broadcast-Based Publish/Subscribe

To use a *Message Bus* implementation that contains a *Broadcast-Based Publish/Subscribe* implementation, a system sends a command message to the message bus. The message bus broadcasts the message to all the nodes that are listening to the bus. The message bus makes no attempt to determine the appropriate subscribers. Instead, each listening node filters any unwanted messages and processes only the messages that it is interested in. Any data that is associated with the message is in a common format so that all systems can interpret the command message and the data, and then respond appropriately.

Message Bus with Content-Based Publish/Subscribe

To use a *Message Bus* pattern that contains a *Content-Based Publish/Subscribe* implementation, a system sends a command message to the message bus. After the message bus receives the message, it is responsible for matching the message against a set of subscribers and then forwarding the message to each of the appropriate subscribers. To match the message against a set of subscribers, the message bus must determine if there are any subscribers interested in this particular message. If an interested subscriber exists, the subscriber matches a particular message field or fields and a set of values. If a match exists between the message content and a subscriber, the message is then forwarded to each matching subscriber.

After a subscribing system receives a bus message, the subscribing system is able to process the message because the message contains the common command message and the agreed-upon message schemas.

While the *Message Bus using List-Based Publish/Subscribe* and the *Message Bus using Content-Based Publish/Subscribe* patterns both check for subscriptions before forwarding messages, there are key differences. The list-based approach matches subscriptions on subjects. However, the content-based approach is much more flexible. Because the content-based approach allows you to identify one or more fields in the message and a set of acceptable values for each field, you can create very intelligent routing capabilities.

To make *Content-Based Publish/Subscribe* work, you need a high-performance infrastructure component that can read each message, query a set of potential subscribers, and efficiently route the message to each subscriber. In practice, you can think of this as a message switch. This is exactly how Microsoft BizTalk Server 2004 is designed.

Figure 5.25 shows the *Message Bus* pattern using a *Publish/Subscribe* pattern or one of the *Publish/Subscribe* variants.

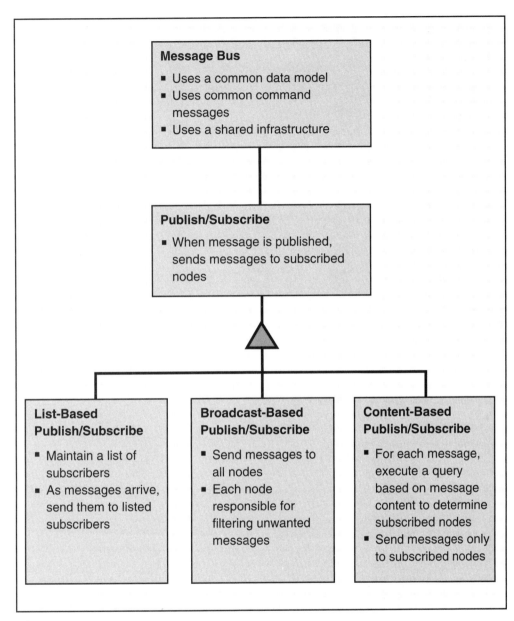

△ A pattern refinement

Figure 5.25
Message Bus pattern using a Publish/Subscribe pattern or one of the Publish/Subscribe variants

Table 5.3 shows the responsibilities and collaborations that are associated with the message bus.

Table 5.3: Message Bus Responsibilities and Collaborations

Responsibilities	Collaborations
– Provides a common set of message formats to the participating applications. – Transports messages from the sender to the other applications that are connected to the bus.	– Senders tag outgoing messages and pass them to the bus. – Receivers inspect the incoming messages and discard the messages that are of no interest to any application.

Choosing a message bus for communication between the components of an integration solution lowers the coupling, but it introduces other problems. The following are some questions you should ask when considering a message bus for an integration solution:

- **Bus latency**. How long does it take the message bus to deliver a message to all the applications that are connected to it? What happens if a sender tries to pass a message to the bus before the bus completes message delivery?

- **Bus contention**. How do you prevent some applications from monopolizing the message bus? If some applications monopolize the message bus, other applications cannot use it.

- **Bus arbitration**. How do you deal with multiple applications that want to pass messages to the message bus at the same time?

Example

Consider an integration solution that integrates two trading systems, a portfolio manager, a risk analysis application, a modeling application, a trend indicator, and a stock ticker. The trading systems communicate with each other whenever they process a transaction. They also send updates to the other applications.

A point-to-point configuration requires individual connections between each trading system and all six applications. In other words, integrating the participating applications involves 11 connections between the participating applications. Figure 5.26 shows this topology (top) and the connections that are required to extend the solution to include an additional trading system (bottom). The dotted lines represent the new connections.

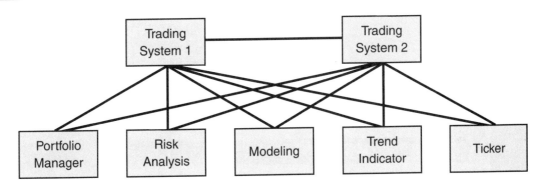

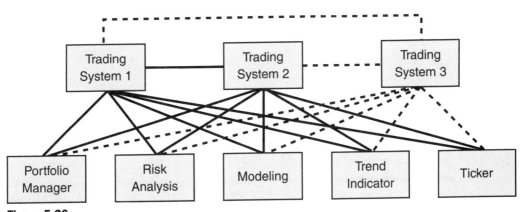

Figure 5.26
Trading applications that use point-to-point connectivity

A message bus reduces the number of connections between the trading applications; Figure 5.27 (top) shows this topology. As you can see from the figure, each trading application has a single connection to the bus. Each trading system is unaware of how many applications are interested in its transactions. With this topology (bottom), adding a new trading system requires a single connection and does not affect the existing applications.

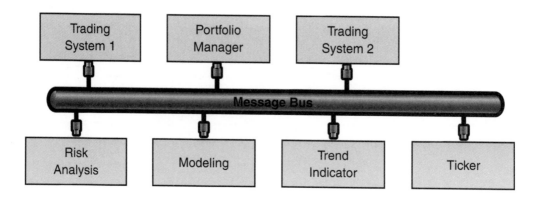

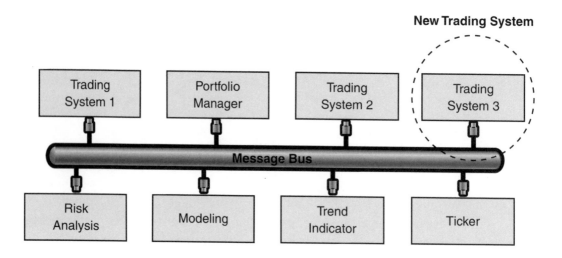

Figure 5.27

Trading systems communicating through a message bus

Resulting Context

When considering integration through a message bus, you should weigh the following benefits and liabilities that are associated with it:

Benefits

- **Improved modifiability**. Each application has a single connection to the message bus instead of multiple dedicated connections to each of the other applications. Adding or removing an application has no impact on the existing applications. In addition, upgrading the bus interface does not require changing any applications as long as the messages remain compatible with existing ones. For example, this is the case when you add new message types.

- **Reduced application complexity**. The message bus transports messages between senders and receivers. Senders no longer interact with all the receivers that they need to send messages to.

- **Improved performance**. There are no intermediaries between the communicating applications. Communication latency depends only on how fast the message bus can move messages.

- **Improved scalability**. Adding applications has a constant low cost. In addition, you can add applications to the message bus until the message bus is saturated. A message bus is saturated when it cannot keep up with the data that it has to move between applications.

Liabilities

- **Increased complexity**. Integrating through a message bus increases the complexity of the integration solution for the following reasons:

  - **Architectural mismatch**. The applications of an integration solution typically make conflicting architectural assumptions [Garlan95]. Designing the message bus interface and solving the mismatch around the data model is a difficult endeavor.

  - **Message bus access policies**. Communication through a shared resource such as a message bus requires you to implement policies that ensure fair access and that resolve concurrency conflicts.

- **Lowered modifiability when the bus interface breaks compatibility**. Changing the message bus interface in a way that breaks compatibility typically affects all the applications that use the bus. In other words, the bus interface represents an extreme example of a published interface. Designing it requires foresight.

- **Lowered integrability**. All the applications that are hooked to the message bus must have the same message bus interface. Applications that have incompatible interfaces cannot use the message bus. Because the message bus interface includes a common set of command messages, message schemas, and shared infrastructure, these elements together define a common subset that may somewhat restrict the operation of the participating applications.

- **Lowered security**. A message bus that uses the *Broadcast-Based Publish/Subscribe* pattern reaches all the applications that are connected to the bus, regardless of the applications that the message is intended for. Broadcasting to all participants may not be acceptable if the messages contain sensitive data.

- **Low tolerance for application unavailability**. The receiver must be able to process messages when the sender passes the messages to the bus. This solution does not tolerate receiver downtime. In addition, it does not provide direct support for disconnected operation.

Security Considerations

Before you use a message bus that uses *Broadcast-Based Publish/Subscribe*, you should consider whether this configuration meets your security requirements. The applications that are connected to the bus receive every message that goes through the message bus. Participants that require a private conversation must encrypt their communication. Also, applications that communicate through the message bus do not have intermediate components between them. In other words, no physical component exists for mapping between different security contexts. Consequently, this configuration is appropriate when the security context is managed through impersonation.

Operational Considerations

When a message bus becomes saturated, message delivery may take a long time or even fail. Saturation could occur after you add new applications or after you make changes to the communication profile of existing applications. For example, changes to the communication profile include changes in the message size and rate. Because both situations are common in bus-centered integration solutions, it is important to prevent saturation. This translates into monitoring the operation of the message bus and proactively keeping the message volume below the maximum capacity of the message bus.

Related Patterns

For more information, see the following related patterns:

- *Publish/Subscribe.* This pattern helps keep cooperating systems synchronized by one-way propagation of messages; one publisher sends a message to any number of intended subscribers.

- *Message Bus Architecture* [Hohpe04]. This pattern revolves around a messaging infrastructure, and it relies on a canonical data model and a common command set that is mentioned earlier in "Liabilities."

- *Blackboard* [Buschmann96]. The *Blackboard* pattern describes a shared storage area that the components of the pattern use to communicate. Consumer components monitor the blackboard and grab the data that matches their interest. Producers put their output on the blackboard so that it becomes available to the others. Typically, integration applications such as rule engines and expert systems use this pattern.

Acknowledgments

[Buschmann96] Buschmann, Frank; Regine Meunier, Hans Rohnert, Peter Sommerland, and Michael Stal. *Pattern-Oriented Software Architecture, Volume 1: A System of Patterns.* John Wiley & Sons Ltd, 1996.

[Chandra03] Chandra, David; Anna Liu, Ulrich Roxburgh, Andrew Mason, E. G. Nadhan, Paul Slater. *Guidelines for Application Integration,* Microsoft *Patterns & Practices,* December 2003. Available on MSDN at: *http://msdn.microsoft.com/library/default.asp?url=/library/en-us/dnpag/html/eappint.asp.*

[Garlan95] Garlan, David; Robert Allen, and John Ockerbloom. "Architectural Mismatch: Why Reuse Is So Hard," in *IEEE Software,* Volume 12, Issue 6, November 1995: 17-26.

[Hohpe04] Hohpe, Gregor and Bobby Woolf, *Enterprise Integration Patterns: Designing, Building, and Deploying Messaging Solutions.* Addison-Wesley, 2003.

[Levine03] Levine, Russell. "The Myth of the Disappearing Interfaces," in *Business Integration Journal,* November 2003.

Publish/Subscribe

Aliases

Pub/Sub

Context

You have an integration architecture consisting of several applications. A communication infrastructure connects these applications in a bus, broker, or point-to-point topology. Some applications send multiple message types. Other applications are interested in different combinations of these types.

For example, consider a financial system where several applications maintain customer information. A Customer Relationship Management (CRM) application holds the master customer information. However, a typical situation for integration scenarios exists — customer information also resides in other systems that perform their own customer information management functions. A customer-facing application generates update messages for changes to customer information, such as changes to customer addresses. The messages must reach the CRM application as well as the other applications that manage customer information. However, this message type is meaningless to the integrated applications that do not manage customer information.

Problem

How can an application in an integration architecture only send messages to the applications that are interested in receiving the messages without knowing the identities of the receivers?

Forces

Integrating applications so that they receive only the messages they are interested in involves balancing the following forces:

- The applications in an integration architecture consume different message types. For example, applications that manage customer information are interested in customer information updates. Trading applications are interested in buy and sell transactions. Applications that participate in two-phase commit transactions are interested in commit messages.

- An application in an integration architecture may send several message types. For example, the application may send customer information messages and operational messages about its status. (Status is also referred to as *health* in this context). Likewise, an application in an integration architecture is usually interested only in a subset of the messages that are sent by the other applications. For example, a portfolio manager is interested only in the financial transactions that affect the stocks that it manages.

- The extent to which applications let you add information to their messages varies widely. Fixed binary messages usually provide no flexibility or limited flexibility in this area. In contrast, it is usually easy to extend SOAP messages through envelope elements.

- Most integration architectures integrate proprietary applications. These applications often make strong assumptions about the messages that they use to communicate with other applications in the environment. Even with a flexible message format, it may be difficult to insert or to process message elements that the application does not know about.

Solution

Extend the communication infrastructure by creating topics or by dynamically inspecting message content. Enable listening applications to subscribe to specific messages. Create a mechanism that sends messages to all interested subscribers. The three variations of the *Publish/Subscribe* pattern you can use to create a mechanism that sends messages to all interested subscribers are *List-Based Publish/Subscribe*, *Broadcast-Based Publish/Subscribe*, and *Content-Based Publish/Subscribe*.

List-Based Publish/Subscribe

A *List-Based Publish/Subscribe* pattern advises you to identify a subject and to maintain a list of subscribers for that subject. When events occur, you have the subject notify each subscriber on the subscription list. A classic way to implement this design is described in the *Observer* [Gamma95] pattern. When you use this pattern, you identify two classes: subjects and observers. Assuming you use a push model update, you add three methods to the subject: **Attach()**, **Detach()**, and **Notify()**. You add one method to the observer — **Update()**.

To use an observer, all interested observers register with the subject by using the **Attach()** method. As changes occur to the subject, the subject then calls each registered observer by using the **Notify()** method. For a detailed explanation of the *Observer* pattern, see *Design Patterns: Elements of Reusable Object-Oriented Software* [Gamma95].

An observer works fine if you have created instances of objects that reify all your observers and subjects. An observer is especially well suited to situations where you have one-to-many relationships between your subjects and your observers. However, in the context of integration, you often have many observers that are linked to many subjects, which complicates the basic *Observer* pattern. One way to implement this many-to-many relationship is to create many subjects and to have each subject contain a list of observers.

If you use this object structure to implement *Publish/Subscribe*, you must write these relationships to persistent storage between process executions. To do so within a relational database, you must add an associative table to resolve the many-to-many dependencies between subject and observer. After you write this information to persistent storage in a set of tables, you can directly query the database for the list of subscribers for a topic.

Maintaining lists of published topics (subjects) and subscribers (observers) and then notifying each one individually as events occur is the essence of *List-Based Publish/Subscribe* implementations. A very different means of achieving the same result is a *Broadcast-Based Publish/Subscribe* implementation.

Broadcast-Based Publish/Subscribe

When you use a *Broadcast-Based Publish/Subscribe* approach [Tannebaum01, Oki93], an event publisher creates a message and broadcasts it to the local area network (LAN). A service on each listening node inspects the subject line. If the listening node matches the subject line to a subject that it subscribes to, the listening node processes the message. If the subject does not match, the listening node ignores the message.

Subject lines are hierarchical and may contain multiple fields that are separated by periods. Listening nodes that are interested in a particular subject can subscribe to these fields by using wildcards, if required.

Although this *Broadcast-Based Publish/Subscribe* implementation is an effective method for decoupling producers from consumers, it is sometimes useful to identify particular topic subscribers. To identify topic subscribers, a coordinating process sends a message that asks listening nodes to reply if they subscribe to a particular topic. Responses are then returned by each listening node to the provider to identify the subscribers.

Because all messages are sent to all listening nodes, and because each node is responsible for filtering unwanted messages, some authors refer to this as a publish/subscribe channel with reactive filtering [Hohpe04].

Content-Based Publish/Subscribe

Both *Broadcast-Based Publish/Subscribe* implementations and *List-Based Publish/Subscribe* implementations can be broadly categorized as topic-based because they both use predefined subjects as many-to-many channels. *Publish/Subscribe* implementations have recently evolved to include a new form — *Content-Based Publish/Subscribe*. The difference between topic-based and content-based approaches is as follows:

> In a topic-based system, processes exchange information through a set of predefined subjects (topics) which represent many-to-many distinct (and fixed) logical channels. Content-based systems are more flexible as subscriptions are related to specific information content and, therefore, each combination of information items can actually be seen as a single dynamic logical channel. This exponential enlargement of potential logical channels has changed the way to implement a pub/sub system. [Baldoni03]

The practical implication of this approach is that messages are intelligently routed to their final destination based on the content of the message. This approach overcomes the limitation of a broadcast-based system, where distribution is coupled to a multicast tree that is based on Transmission Control Protocol (TCP). It also gives the integration architect a great deal of flexibility when deciding on content-based routing logic.

Applying Publish/Subscribe

Figure 5.28 shows an integration solution that consists of four applications. The sender (also called a *publisher*) uses a topic-based approach to publish messages to topic A and to topic B. Three receivers (also called *subscribers*) subscribe to these topics; one receiver subscribes to topic A, one receiver subscribes to topic B, and one receiver subscribes to both topic A and to topic B. The arrows show messages flowing from the publisher to each subscriber according to these subscriptions.

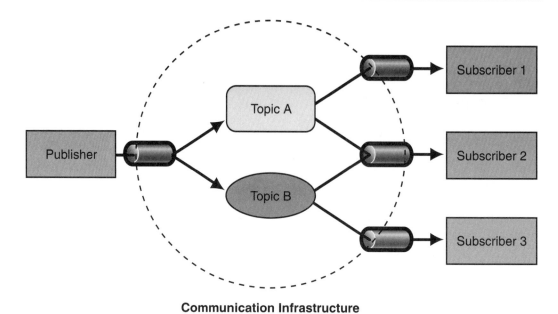

Communication Infrastructure

Figure 5.28
Subscription to topics controls the message types that reach each subscriber

Implementing *Publish/Subscribe* usually affects the messages, the integrated applications, and the communication infrastructure.

First, you must identify the topics or the content of interest to the receiving applications. This translates into partitioning the set of message types into different subsets. For example, consider the types of messages that are sent by a trading system. Some trading applications track buy transactions, some track sell transactions, and other applications track both types of transaction. Separating the message by creating a buy topic and a sell topic partitions the trading system messages into subsets aimed at these applications.

Next, you must add information to the messages that indicates the topic or that identifies specific content information. Sometimes you can store the topic-related information in an unused message field. Alternatively, you may be able to add a new field for the topic. For example, you may be able to insert a new element in a SOAP header. If you can neither use an existing field nor add a new one, you must find other ways to encode the topic into the message, or you must use a content-based approach instead.

You must then extend the communication infrastructure so that it delivers messages according to each subscriber's subscription. The approach that you use depends on the topology of the integration solution. For example, consider the three common topologies. For bus integration, you can implement the subscription mechanism in the bus interface. For broker integration, you can implement the mechanism through subscription lists to the broker. For point-to-point integration, you can implement the mechanism through subscription lists in the publisher.

Finally, you must modify the integrated applications. The publisher must add the topic-related information to each message that it publishes. For example, if the topic is encoded as a header element, the publisher must insert the topic-related information into the appropriate element. Likewise, the subscriber must specify the topics of interest.

Subscriptions can be either fixed or dynamic. With fixed subscriptions, the integration architect sets the topics that an application subscribes to. Applications have no control over their subscriptions. Usually, the subscriptions are specified when each application is added to the integration solution. Figure 5.29 shows a fixed subscription to Topic A.

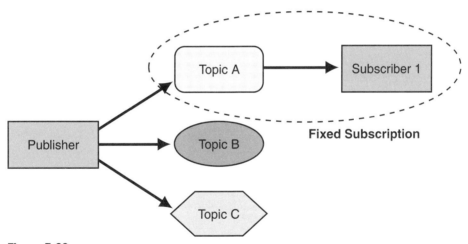

Figure 5.29
Publish/Subscribe with fixed subscription

In contrast, dynamic subscriptions enable applications to control their own subscriptions through a set of control messages. Applications can remove existing subscriptions by sending messages to the communication infrastructure that remove the application from the subscription list. Applications can add new subscriptions by sending messages to the communication infrastructure that add the application to a subscription list. Most communication infrastructures that have *Publish/Subscribe* capabilities provide this feature. However, supporting dynamic subscriptions is not a requirement.

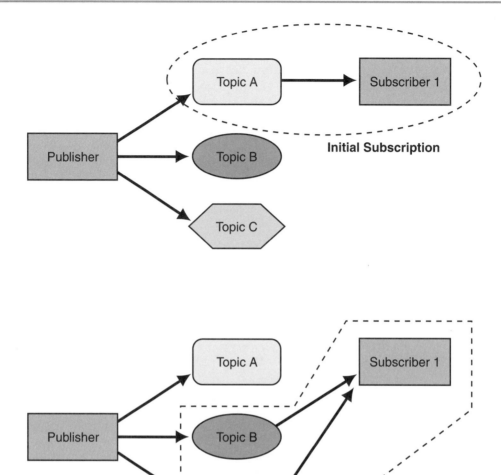

Figure 5.30
Publish/Subscribe with dynamic subscriptions

Figure 5.30 shows how dynamic subscriptions function. The top part of Figure 5.30 shows the initial subscription to topic A. The application then sends a message that removes it from the subscription list for topic A. The application then sends two messages that subscribe the application to topic B and topic C. The bottom part of Figure 5.30 shows the final subscription after these control messages are sent.

Related Decisions

After you decide to use *Publish/Subscribe,* you must make the following decisions:

- **Initial subscription**. You must decide how subscribers communicate their subscriptions to the communication infrastructure when they are first added to the solution.
- **Wildcard subscriptions**. You must decide if your publish/subscribe mechanism needs to support wildcard subscriptions. Wildcard subscriptions enable subscribers to subscribe to multiple topics through one subscription.
- **Static or dynamic subscriptions**. You must decide if the applications in your integration solution need to change their subscriptions dynamically.
- **Topic discovery**. You must decide how subscribers discover the available topics if the solution supports dynamic subscriptions.

Responsibilities and Collaborations

Table 5.4 summarizes the responsibilities and collaborations of the parties involved in *Publish/Subscribe.*

Table 5.4: Responsibilities and Collaborations Among Publish/Subscribe Components

Components	Responsibilities	Collaborations
Communication infrastructure	– Maintains the subscribers' subscriptions. – Inspects the topic-related information or the content information that is included in each published message. – Transports the message to the subscribed applications.	– The publisher publishes messages. – The subscriber subscribes to topics and receives messages.
Publisher	– Inserts topic-related information or content information in each message. – Publishes the message to the communication infrastructure.	– The communication infrastructure transports messages to subscribers.
Subscriber	– Subscribes to one or more topics or message content types. – Consumes messages published to the subscribed topics.	– The communication infrastructure transports published messages from the publisher.

Example

Microsoft BizTalk Server 2004 uses the *Publish/Subscribe* pattern internally to receive, to route, and to send messages. BizTalk Server receives messages through input ports and stores them in the MessageBox database. Orchestration ports and send ports consume messages from this database based on their subscriptions. Figure 5.31 illustrates this arrangement.

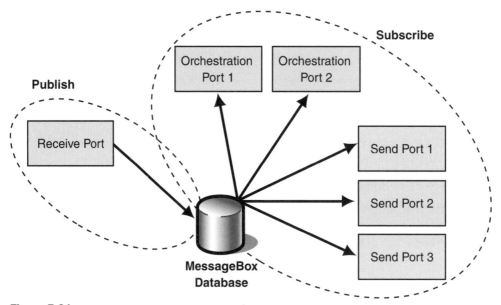

Figure 5.31
Publish/Subscribe in BizTalk Server 2004

Resulting Context

Using *Publish/Subscribe* has the following benefits and liabilities. Evaluate this information to help you decide whether you should implement *Publish/Subscribe*:

Benefits

- **Lowered coupling**. The publisher is not aware of the number of subscribers, of the identities of the subscribers, or of the message types that the subscribers are subscribed to.
- **Improved security**. The communication infrastructure transports the published messages only to the applications that are subscribed to the corresponding topic. Specific applications can exchange messages directly, excluding other applications from the message exchange.
- **Improved testability**. Topics usually reduce the number of messages that are required for testing.

Liabilities

- **Increased complexity.** *Publish/Subscribe* requires you to address the following:
  - You have to design a message classification scheme for topic implementation.
  - You have to implement the subscription mechanism.
  - You have to modify the publisher and the subscribers.

- **Increased maintenance effort.** Managing topics requires maintenance work. Organizations that maintain many topics usually have formal procedures for their use.

- **Decreased performance.** Subscription management adds overhead. This overhead increases the latency of message exchange, and this latency decreases performance.

Testing Considerations

The topics of a *Publish/Subscribe* implementation facilitate the testing of an integration solution. Subscriptions provide isolation by segmenting the message space. By subscribing only to the topics or to the content of interest, testers and testing tools have fewer messages to sift through. Likewise, by subscribing to other topics or content, testers can catch messages that are published to the wrong topic.

Security Considerations

An integration solution that uses *Publish/Subscribe* can restrict the participants of a message exchange, thus enabling applications to have private message exchanges. Depending on the topology, the messages may still be physically transported to all the applications in the integration architecture. For example, all the messages are transported to all the applications if your integration solution uses the *Message Bus using Broadcast-Based Publish/Subscribe* pattern. However, the interface between the communication infrastructure and the application enforces filtering according to each application's subscriptions.

Operational Considerations

Many integration solutions that use *Publish/Subscribe* have topics or content that is dedicated to messages about the applications' health. This separation facilitates your ability to monitor various operational parameters and to control the applications in the integration solution.

Related Patterns

For more information about *Publish/Subscribe*, see other similar patterns:

- *Message Bus* and *Message Broker* describe two common integration topologies.
- *Observer* [Gamma95] provides a mechanism for decoupling dependencies between applications.
- *Publisher-Subscriber* [Buschmann96] facilitates state synchronization between cooperating components.
- *Publish-Subscribe Channel* [Hohpe04] provides a way to broadcast events to all the receivers (subscribers) that subscribe to a specific topic.

Acknowledgments

[Baldoni03] Baldoni, R.; M. Contenti, and A. Virgillito. *"The Evolution of Publish/Subscribe Communication Systems." Future Directions of Distributed Computing.* Springer Verlag LNCS Vol. 2584, 2003.

[Buschmann96] Buschmann, Frank; Regine Meunier, Hans Rohnert, Peter Sommerlad, and Michael Stal. *Pattern-Oriented Software Architecture, Volume 1: A System of Patterns.* John Wiley & Sons Ltd, 1996.

[Gamma95] Gamma, Erich; Richard Helm, Ralph Johnson, and John Vlissides. *Design Patterns: Elements of Reusable Object-Oriented Software.* Addison-Wesley, 1995.

[Hohpe04] Hohpe, Gregor, and Bobby Woolf. *Enterprise Integration Patterns: Designing, Building and Deploying Messaging Solutions.* Addison-Wesley, 2004.

[Oki93] Oki, B.; M. Pfluegel, A. Siegel, and D. Skeen. "The Information Bus - An Architecture for Extensive Distributed Systems." *Proceedings of the 1993 ACM Symposium on Operating Systems Principles*, December 1993.

[Tannebaum01] Tannebaum, Andrew. *Modern Operating Systems.* 2nd ed. Prentice-Hall, 2001.

6

Additional Integration Patterns

This chapter completes this investigation of integration patterns by exploring the *Pipes and Filters* pattern and the *Gateway* pattern. Both patterns are simple but valuable for resolving integration problems.

Even though this chapter completes this discussion, you can obtain information about additional integration patterns in the Appendix.

Pipes and Filters

Pipes and Filters provides a solution for moving the output of one system into another system. The pipe is the portion of the code that is connected to the source system and to the sink or the receiving system. The filter is the portion of the code that transforms the data so that the sink program can process it.

This pattern is useful when you need to transform the data from one system into a different format to integrate that data into another system. A simple example is the conversion of data from ASCII to Extended Binary Coded Decimal Interchange Code (EBCDIC) that occurs when data moves from a desktop computer to a mainframe.

Figure 6.1 shows a source system integrated with a sink system. The source system uses multiple filters to transform the data to the format that the sink system requires.

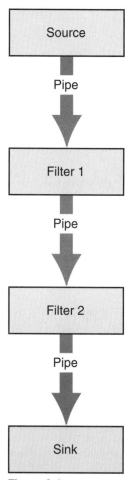

Figure 6.1

A source system integrated with the sink system through Pipes and Filters

In the Global Bank scenario, the *Pipes and Filters* pattern is used to handle the communication between Microsoft BizTalk Server 2004 and external payment channels.

Gateway

The *Gateway* pattern abstracts the access to an external system to a single interface. The pattern eliminates the need for multiple systems to understand how to connect to the external system. Therefore, the *Gateway* pattern simplifies the development and maintenance processes that are related to accessing external systems.

Common uses for the *Gateway* pattern include accessing mainframe programs and processing credit card transactions. For each of these common uses, the gateway replaces direct access to the external resource or system, as shown in Figure 6.2.

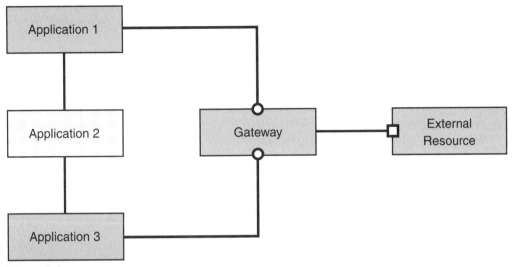

Figure 6.2
Gateway replaces direct access to the external resource

In the Global Bank scenario, the *Gateway* pattern is implemented by using Microsoft Host Integration Server 2004. Host Integration Server 2004 provides the solution for integrating the mainframe to the enterprise.

Integration Layers Patterns

The following table summarizes the two patterns just discussed and shows the corresponding implementation patterns.

Table 6.1: Integration Layers Patterns

Pattern	Problem	Associated implementations
Gateway	How can you make the applications of an integration solution access an external system without introducing many-to-one coupling between the applications and the external system?	*Implementing Gateway with Host Integration Server 2004*
Pipes and Filters	How do you implement a sequence of transformations so that you can combine and reuse them independently?	*Implementing Pipes and Filters with BizTalk Server 2004*

Pipes and Filters

Aliases

Data Flow Architecture

Context

You have an integration solution that consists of several financial applications. The applications use a wide range of formats—such as the Interactive Financial Exchange (IFX) format, the Open Financial Exchange (OFX) format, and the Electronic Data Interchange (EDI) format—for the messages that correspond to payment, withdrawal, deposit, and funds transfer transactions.

Integrating these applications requires processing the messages in different ways. For example, converting an XML-like message into another XML-like message involves an XSLT transformation. Converting an EDI data message into an XML-like message involves a transformation engine and transformation rules. Verifying the identity of the sender involves verifying the digital signature attached to the message. In effect, the integration solution applies several transformations to the messages that are exchanged by its participants.

Problem

How do you implement a sequence of transformations so that you can combine and reuse them independently?

Forces

Implementing transformations that can be combined and reused in different applications involves balancing the following forces:

- Many applications process large volumes of similar data elements. For example, trading systems handle stock quotes, telecommunication billing systems handle call data records, and laboratory information management systems (LIMS) handle test results.

- The processing of data elements can be broken down into a sequence of individual transformations. For example, processing XML messages typically involves a series of XSLT transformations.

- The functional decomposition of a transformation $f(x)$ into $g(x)$ and $h(z)$ (where $f[x]=g[x]?h[z]$) does not change the transformation. However, when separate components implement g and h, the communication between them (that is, passing the output of $g[x]$ to $h[z]$) incurs overhead. This overhead increases the latency of a $g(x)?h(z)$ implementation compared to an $f(x)$ implementation.

Solution

Implement the transformations by using a sequence of filter components, where each filter component receives an input message, applies a simple transformation, and sends the transformed message to the next component. Conduct the messages through *pipes* [McIlroy64] that connect filter outputs and inputs and that buffer the communication between the filters.

The left side of Figure 6.3 shows a configuration that has two filters. A source application feeds messages through the pipe into filter 1. The filter transforms each message it receives and then sends each transformed message as output into the next pipe. The pipe carries the transformed message to filter 2. The pipe also buffers any messages that filter 1 sends and that filter 2 is not ready to process. The second filter then applies its transformation and passes the message through the pipe to the sink application. The sink application then consumes the message. This configuration requires the following:

- The output of the source must be compatible with the input of filter 1.
- The output of filter 1 must be compatible with the input of filter 2.
- The output of filter 2 must be compatible with the input of the sink.

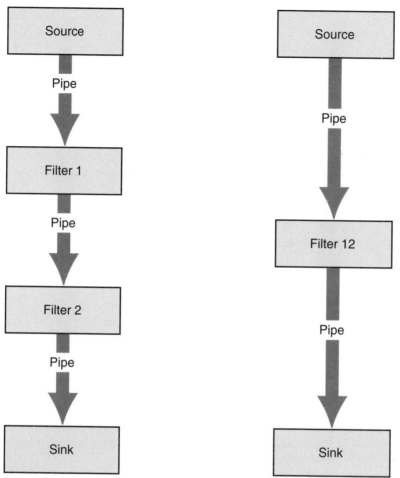

Figure 6.3
Using Pipes and Filters to break processing into a sequence of simpler transformations

The right side of Figure 6.3 shows a single filter. From a functional perspective, each configuration implements a transfer function. The data flows only one way and the filters communicate solely by exchanging messages. They do not share state; therefore, the transfer functions have no side effects. Consequently, the series configuration of filter 1 and filter 2 is functionally equivalent to a single filter that implements the composition of the two transfer functions (filter 12 in the figure).

Comparing the two configurations illustrates their tradeoffs:

- The two-filter configuration breaks the transformation between the source and the sink into two simpler transformations. Lowering the complexity of the individual filters makes them easier to implement and improves their testability. It also increases their potential for reuse because each filter is built with a smaller set of assumptions about the environment that it operates in.
- The single-filter configuration implements the transformation by using one specialized component. The one hop that exists between input and output and the elimination of the interfilter communication translate into low latency and overhead.

In summary, the key tradeoffs in choosing between a combination of generic filters and a single specialized filter are reusability and performance.

In the context of pipes and filters, a transformation refers to any transfer function that a filter might implement. For example, transformations that are commonly used in integration solutions include the following:

- Conversion, such as converting Extended Binary Coded Decimal Interchange Code (EBCDIC) to ASCII
- Enrichment, such as adding information to incoming messages
- Filtering, such as discarding messages that match a specific criteria
- Batching, such as aggregating 10 incoming messages and sending them together in a single outgoing message
- Consolidation, such as combining the data elements of three related messages into a single outgoing message

In practice, the transfer function corresponds to a transformation that is specific enough to be useful, yet simple enough to be reused in a different context. Identifying the transformations for a problem domain is a difficult design problem.

Table 6.2 shows the responsibilities and collaborations that are associated with pipes and filters.

Table 6.2: Responsibilities and Collaborations of Pipes and Filters

Responsibilities	Collaborations
– A filter takes a message from its input, applies a transformation, and sends the transformed message as output.	– A filter produces and consumes messages.
– A pipe transports messages between filters. (Sources and sinks are special filters without inputs or outputs.)	– A pipe connects the filter with the producer and the consumer. A pipe transports and buffers messages.

Example

Consider a Web service for printing insurance policies. The service accepts XML messages from agency management systems. Incoming messages are based on the ACORD XML specification, an insurance industry standard. However, each agency has added proprietary extensions to the standard ACORD transactions. A print request message specifies the type of document to be generated, for example, an HTML document or a Portable Document Format (PDF) document. The request also includes policy data such as client information, coverage, and endorsements. The Web service processes the proprietary extensions and adds the jurisdiction-specific information that should appear on the printed documents, such as local or regional requirements and restrictions. The Web service then generates the documents in the requested format and returns them to the agency management system.

You could implement these processing steps as a single transformation within the Web service. Although viable, this solution does not let you reuse the transformation in a different context. In addition, to accommodate new requirements, you would have to change several components of the Web service. For example, you would have to change several components if a new requirement calls for decrypting some elements of the incoming messages.

An implementation that is based on *Pipes and Filters* provides an elegant alternative for the printing Web service. Figure 6.4 illustrates a solution that involves three separate transformations. The transformations are implemented as filters that handle conversion, enrichment, and rendering.

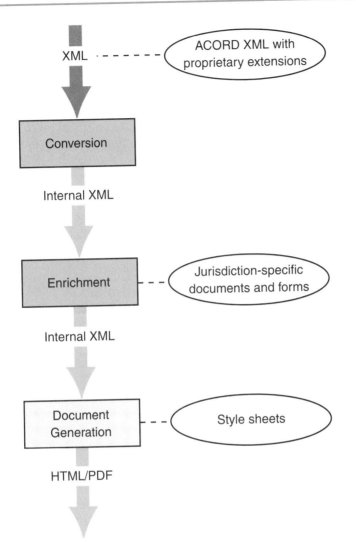

Figure 6.4
Printing Web service that uses Pipes and Filters

The printing service first converts the incoming messages into an internal vendor-independent format. This first transformation lowers the dependencies on the proprietary ACORD XML extensions. In effect, changing the format of the incoming messages only affects the conversion filter.

After conversion, the printing service retrieves documents and forms that depend on the jurisdiction and adds them to the request message. This transformation encapsulates the jurisdiction-specific enrichment.

When the message contains all the information that comprises the final electronic document, a document generation filter converts the message to HTML or PDF format. A style sheet repository provides information about the appearance of each document. This last transformation encapsulates the knowledge of rendering legally binding documents.

In this example, the *Pipes and Filters* implementation of the printing Web service has the following benefits that make it preferable to implementing the Web service as a single monolithic transformation:

- **Separation of concerns**. Each filter solves a different problem.
- **Division of labor**. ACORD XML experts implement the conversion of the proprietary extensions into an internal vendor-independent format. People who specialize in dealing with the intricacies of each jurisdiction assist with the implementation of the filter that handles those aspects. Formatters and layout experts implement document generation.
- **Specialization**. Document-rendering is CPU intensive and, in the case of a PDF document, uses floating point operations. You can deploy the rendering to hardware that meets these requirements.
- **Reuse**. Each filter encapsulates fewer context-specific assumptions. For example, the document generator takes messages that conform to some schema and generates an HTML or PDF document. Other applications can reuse this filter.

Resulting Context

Using *Pipes and Filters* results in the following benefits and liabilities:

Benefits

- **Improved reusability**. Filters that implement simple transformations typically encapsulate fewer assumptions about the problem they are solving than filters that implement complex transformations. For example, converting a message from one XML encapsulation to another encapsulates fewer assumptions about that conversion than generating a PDF document from an XML message. The simpler filters can be reused in other solutions that require similar transformations.
- **Improved performance**. A *Pipes and Filters* solution processes messages as soon as they are received. Typically, filters do not wait for a scheduling component to start processing.
- **Reduced coupling**. Filters communicate solely through message exchange. They do not share state and are therefore unaware of other filters and sinks that consume their outputs. In addition, filters are unaware of the application that they are working in.

- **Improved modifiability**. A *Pipes and Filters* solution can change the filter configuration dynamically. Organizations that use integration solutions that are subject to service level agreements usually monitor the quality of the services they provide on a constant basis. These organizations usually react proactively to offer the agreed-upon levels of service. For example, a *Pipes and Filters* solution makes it easier for an organization to maintain a service level agreement because a filter can be replaced by another filter that has different resource requirements.

Liabilities

- **Increased complexity**. Designing filters typically requires expert domain knowledge. It also requires several good examples to generalize from. The challenge of identifying reusable transformations makes filter development an even more difficult endeavor.

- **Lowered performance due to communication overhead**. Transferring messages between filters incurs communication overhead. This overhead does not contribute directly to the outcome of the transformation; it merely increases the latency.

- **Increased complexity due to error handling**. Filters have no knowledge of the context that they operate in. For example, a filter that enriches XML messages could run in a financial application, in a telecommunications application, or in an avionics application. Error handling in a *Pipes and Filters* configuration usually is cumbersome.

- **Increased maintainability effort**. A *Pipes and Filters* configuration usually has more components than a monolithic implementation (see Figure 6.4). Each component adds maintenance effort, system management effort, and opportunities for failure.

- **Increased complexity of assessing the state**. The *Pipes and Filters* pattern distributes the state of the computation across several components. The distribution makes querying the state a complex operation.

Testing Considerations

Breaking processing into a sequence of transformations facilitates testing because you can test each component individually.

Known Uses

The input and output pipelines of Microsoft BizTalk Server 2004 revolve around *Pipes and Filters*. The pipelines process messages as they enter and leave the engine. Each pipeline consists of a sequence of transformations that users can customize. For example, the receive pipeline provides filters that perform the following actions:

- The filters decode MIME and S/MIME messages.

- The filters disassemble flat files, XML messages, and BizTalk Framework (BTF) messages.
- The filters validate XML documents against XML schemas.
- The filters verify the identity of a sender.

The BizTalk Pipeline Designer allows developers to connect and to configure these filters within the pipeline. Figure 6.5 shows a pipeline that consists of Pre-Assemble, Assemble, and Encode filters. The toolbox shows the filters than can be dropped into this configuration.

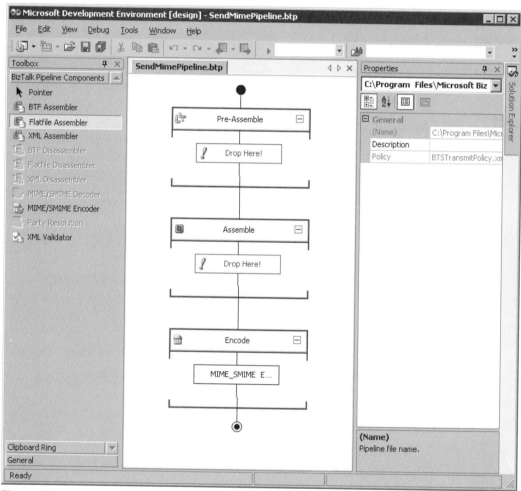

Figure 6.5

A Microsoft BizTalk Server2004 send pipeline in Pipeline Designer

Many other integration products use *Pipes and Filters* for message transformation. In particular, XML-based products rely on XSL processors to convert XML documents from one schema to another. In effect, the XSL processors act as programmable filters that transform XML.

Related Patterns

For more information about *Pipes and Filters*, see the following related patterns:

- *Implementing Pipes and Filters with BizTalk Server 2004*. This pattern uses the Global Bank scenario to show how you can use BizTalk Server 2004 to implement *Pipes and Filters*.
- *Pipes and Filters* [Shaw96, Buschmann96, Hohpe03].
- *Intercepting Filter* [Trowbridge03]. This version of *Intercepting Filter* discusses the pattern in the context of Web applications built using the Microsoft .NET Framework. Developers can chain filters to implement preprocessing and post-processing tasks such as extracting header information and rewriting URLs.
- *In-band and Out-of-band Partitions* [Manolescu97]. This pattern remedies the lack of a component that has a global context in *Pipes and Filters* systems. The out-of-band partition is context-aware; therefore, it can configure the filters and handle errors.

Acknowledgments

[Buschmann96] Buschmann, Frank; Regine Meunier, Hans Rohnert, Peter Sommerland, and Michael Stal. *Pattern-Oriented Software Architecture*. John Wiley & Sons Ltd, 1996.

[Hohpe04] Hohpe, Gregor and Bobby Woolf, *Enterprise Integration Patterns: Designing, Building, and Deploying Messaging Solutions*. Addison-Wesley, 2004.

[Manolescu97] Manolescu, Dragos. "A Data Flow Pattern Language," in *Proceedings of the 4th Pattern Languages of Programming*, September 1997, Monticello, Illinois.

[McIlroy64] The fluid-flow analogy dates from the days of the first UNIX systems and is attributed to Douglas McIlroy; see *http://cm.bell-labs.com/cm/cs/who/dmr/mdmpipe.html*.

[Trowbridge03] Trowbridge, David; Dave Mancini, Dave Quick, Gregor Hohpe, James Newkirk, and David Lavigne. *Enterprise Solution Patterns Using Microsoft .NET*. Microsoft Press, 2003. Also available on the *MSDN Architecture Center* at: *http://msdn.microsoft.com/architecture/patterns/default.aspx?pull=/library/en-us /dnpatterns/html/Esp.asp*.

[Shaw96] Shaw, Mary, and David Garlan, *Software Architecture: Perspectives on an Emerging Discipline*. Prentice Hall, 1996.

Implementing Pipes and Filters with BizTalk Server 2004

Context

You are implementing *Pipes and Filters* by using Microsoft BizTalk Server 2004.

Background

The Global Bank scenario includes the Execute Scheduled Payment use case. This use case permits Global Bank to transfer funds from a customer's account to a specified target account. The target account can reside in one of three systems:

- An internal banking system that uses an internal Global Bank payment channel.
- An external banking system that uses encrypted and signed e-mail messages to transfer funds. One such system is the Society for Worldwide Interbank Financial Telecommunication (SWIFT) payment channel.
- An external banking system that cannot accept an electronic funds transfer and therefore has to receive a paper check. This is an external manual payment channel.

This pattern describes how to implement the Execute Scheduled Payment use case in the Global Bank scenario by using the *Pipes and Filters* pattern that is described earlier in this guide. This implementation uses BizTalk Server 2004 to transform and to route funds to the target accounts by using the correct channel, as shown in Figure 6.6.

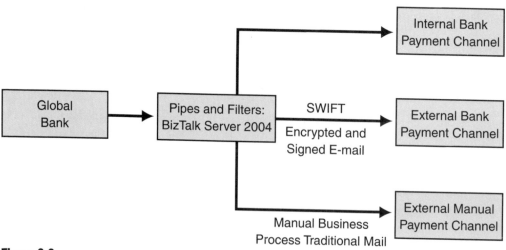

Figure 6.6
BizTalk Server2004 as Pipes and Filters

Specifically, this pattern focuses on how to implement BizTalk Server 2004 to send payment information to target accounts through channels such as the SWIFT bank payment channel. The communication on the external payment channel sends confidential information across public networks; that information should be protected against unauthorized use. To address this issue, the business requirements require you to encrypt the messages to avoid eavesdropping by third parties. The business requirements also require you to add a certificate to ensure the authenticity of messages. A certificate prevents third parties from generating false messages that are designed to credit bank accounts.

This implementation uses the S/MIME protocol and the Triple Data Encryption Standard (DES3) encryption algorithm. Signing and encrypting the messages for the external payment channel involves applying a pair of transformations to the message data. One transformation digitally signs the message by computing a checksum. Another transformation uses a 168-bit secret key to encrypt the message.

Implementation Strategy

When BizTalk Server 2004 receives a message, the incoming data can be processed by a receive pipeline before it enters the MessageBox database, as shown in Figure 6.7. The typical functions that are performed in a receive pipeline include the following:

- Decoding and parsing of incoming data such as an XML file or a flat file
- Validation; for example, verifying the incoming data against an XML schema
- Party resolution

Likewise, any message subscriber can configure a send pipeline to preassemble the message data before it is transferred out on the physical send port. Typical functions that are performed in a send pipeline include the following:

- Validation
- Assembly of an XML document
- Encoding
- Digital signing

Figure 6.7
BizTalk Server 2004 MessageBox database architecture

Even though all the *filters* (transformation components) in a pipeline have the same interface, some filters function independently and do not depend on other filters. For example, a filter may be used to transform data or to filter for a consuming service. In contrast, some filters inherently depend on other filters. For example, in some cases a message cannot be decoded by a filter until it has been encoded by another filter first. To make it easier to manage the semantic dependencies between filters, BizTalk Server 2004 defines *stages* for each pipeline. A stage is the portion of a pipeline that is dedicated to a certain type of work. Each available filter is assigned to a specific stage of the pipeline. A receive pipeline consists of the following stages:

- Decode
- Disassemble
- Validate
- Resolve Party

A send pipeline contains the following stages:

- Pre-Assemble
- Assemble
- Encode

Naturally, decoding the message is the first step that is performed in the receive pipeline, and encoding is the last step that is performed in the send pipeline. This design ensures that all other filters in the pipeline can work on messages that are not encoded.

BizTalk Server 2004 supplies default pipelines for frequently recurring needs, such as parsing an incoming XML message. If you need a more tailored functionality, you have the following options:

- You can configure a custom pipeline by using the pipeline components (also known as filters) that are supplied in BizTalk Server 2004.
- You can configure a custom pipeline by writing custom filters in C# or Microsoft Visual Basic .NET.

This pattern focuses on the first option because the standard BizTalk Server 2004 pipeline components provide the functionality that is required for the Global Bank scenario without any custom coding. To assemble a custom pipeline that uses the pipeline components that are included in BizTalk Server 2004, you have to complete the following steps:

1. Create a custom send pipeline.

First, you have to define a new pipeline. A pipeline definition is stored as a separate project file in Microsoft Visual Studio .NET.

2. **Assign and configure the filters**.

The Pipeline Designer in BizTalk Server 2004 enables you to drag filters into the new pipeline. You can configure each filter by using the properties editor.

3. **Build and deploy the pipeline**.

Pipeline definitions are compiled into a .NET Framework assembly. Before you can configure a send port or a receive port by using the custom pipeline definition, you have to deploy the assembly.

4. **Assign a certificate to BizTalk Server 2004**.

This step is needed because the business requirement includes signing the outbound message with a certificate. Such a certificate is usually obtained from an outside certificate authority and is loaded into the certificate store of the local operating system. After the certificate is loaded, the certificate *thumbprint* has to be entered into the BizTalk Administration console. The thumbprint is a unique identifier.

For a detailed description of certificates, see "Certificate Stores" in *Windows XP Professional Product Documentation* [Microsoft04].

5. **Configure the send port to use the custom pipeline**.

After the custom pipeline is deployed, you can reference the custom pipeline in the configuration settings of a send port.

Example

To make the communication on Global Bank's external payment channel secure, you must create a custom send pipeline that signs and encrypts the outbound messages. This pipeline is used in conjunction with the *Message Broker* described in *Implementing Message Broker with BizTalk Server 2004*.

Based on the implementation strategy, you have to complete the following steps to implement the new custom pipeline by using BizTalk Server 2004.

Step 1: Create a Custom Send Pipeline

Pipeline definitions are created in Visual Studio .NET and are compiled into a .NET Framework assembly by using the Pipeline Designer. First, create a new BizTalk Server 2004 solution in Visual Studio .NET. Next, select **Send Pipeline** in the item list, and then add it to the solution. This opens the Pipeline Designer.

Step 2: Assign and Configure the Filters

In this step, you use the Pipeline Designer to drag predefined filter components from the **Toolbox** into the pipeline, as shown in Figure 6.8.

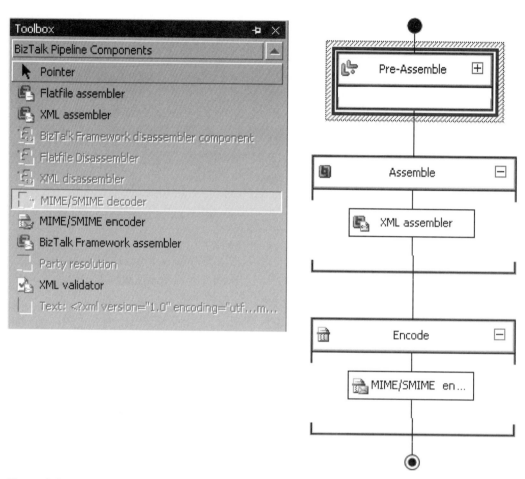

Figure 6.8
BizTalk Server 2004 Pipeline Designer and Toolbox

A send pipeline has three predefined stages: Pre-Assemble, Assemble, and Encode. The Global Bank solution requires only the Assemble and Encode stages, so leave the Pre-Assemble stage empty. The Assemble stage contains filters that convert message data from the BizTalk Server 2004 internal format to an external format, such as a flat file structure or an XML document. Because you want to send XML messages to the external bank payment system, add the XML assembler filter to this stage. You can use the default configuration for this filter.

The encryption and signing occurs in the Encode stage. This stage is the last stage. Add a MIME/SMIME encoder filter to this stage so that you can configure the encryption properties. Configure the properties as shown in Table 6.3.

Table 6.3: Properties for the MIME/SMIME Encoder Filter

Property	Value
Enable encryption	True
Encryption algorithm	DES3
Add signing certification to message	True
Signature type	BlobSign

The filter has built-in capability for DES3 and enables you to sign the message simply by selecting **True** for the **Add signing certification to message** property. The **BlobSign** value means that a signature is appended to the message and that the signature is encoded. When a message passes through this pipeline, the MIME/ SMIME encoder uses the certificate to sign the message.

Step 3: Build and Deploy the Pipeline

Save the pipeline definition. Then, build and deploy the project from Visual Studio .NET to make the pipeline definition available for port configuration.

Step 4: Assign Certificates to BizTalk Server 2004

BizTalk Server 2004 uses two distinct certificate stores in this scenario. A certificate store is the system area where certificates are stored. To sign outgoing documents, BizTalk Server 2004 uses certificates from the Personal certificate store. For a detailed description of how to import certificates, see "Certificate Stores" in *Windows XP Professional Product Documentation* [Microsoft04]. Each certificate has a thumbprint that is generated by running a hash algorithm across the public key portion of the certificate.

First, view the thumbprint on the **Details** tab in the **Certificate** dialog box for the certificate, as shown in Figure 6.9.

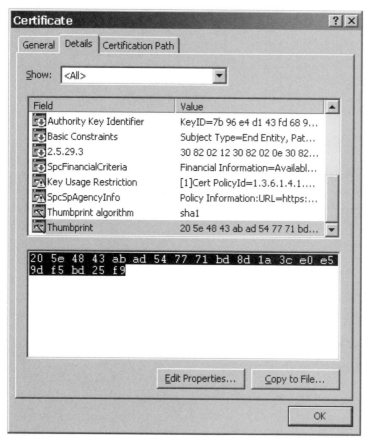

Figure 6.9
A certificate thumbprint

Next, configure the server running BizTalk Server 2004 with the certificate thumb-print. To do so, start the BizTalk Administration console. Then, configure the signing certificate thumbprint on the **General** tab in the **Microsoft BizTalk Server 2004 (Local) Properties** dialog box, as shown in Figure 6.10.

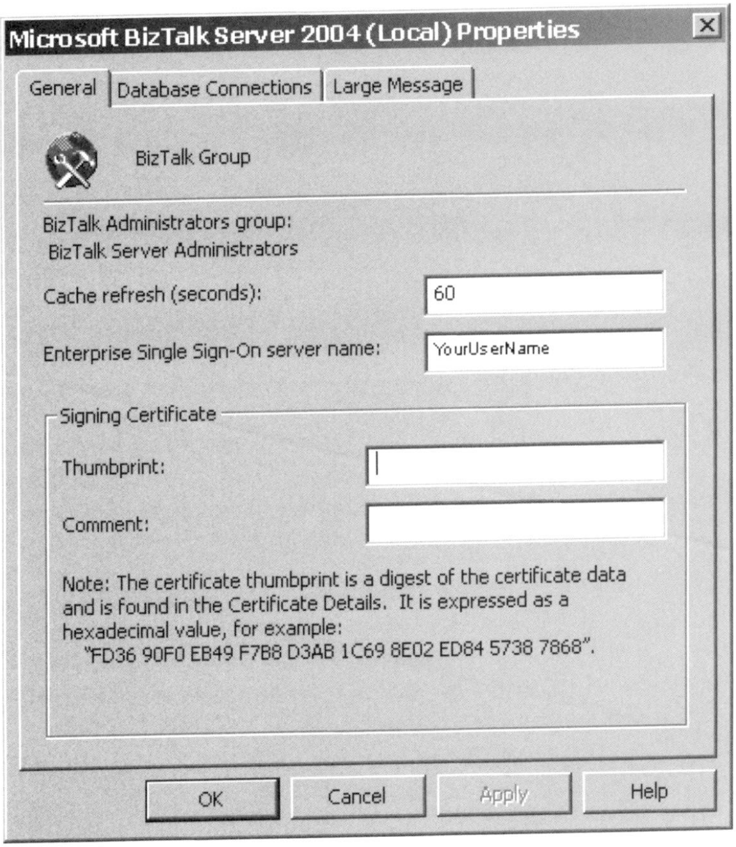

Figure 6.10
BizTalk Server 2004 properties

Use the same certificate to sign outgoing messages for all servers in the BizTalk Server 2004 group.

To encrypt outgoing messages, BizTalk Server 2004 uses the Local Machine\Other People certificate store. This certificate store holds public key certificates. Multiple certificates can be stored and then used to encrypt messages to specific parties. The certificate used to encrypt the message is specified in the send port configuration.

Step 5: Configure the Send Port to Use the Custom Pipeline

Now that the custom pipeline definition is deployed in a global assembly, you can use it in the configuration of the send port, as shown in Figure 6.11.

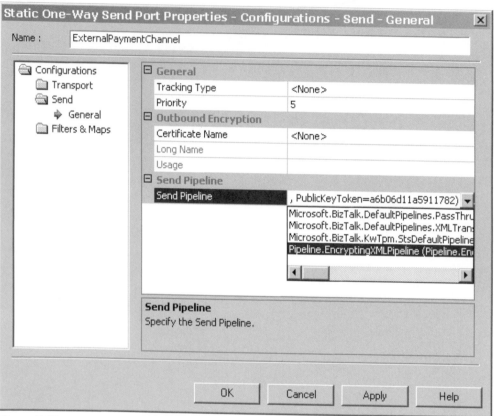

Figure 6.11
BizTalk Server 2004 send port properties

You can now connect the new send port to the MessageBox database as described in *Implementing Message Broker with BizTalk Server 2004.*

Resulting Context

Using *Pipes and Filters* with BizTalk Server 2004 results in the following benefits and liabilities:

Benefits

- **Filter reuse**. BizTalk Server 2004 users can reuse both the pipeline definitions and the set of pipeline filters across different ports. For example, the MIME/SMIME encoder filter is suitable for any application that needs to send MIME or S/MIME messages.
- **Amenable for graphical tools**. Programming the pipeline involves connecting and configuring filters by dragging components rather than by writing source code.
- **Developer specialization**. *Pipes and Filters* fosters the division of labor between different types of users. For example, C# developers build filters by using the Microsoft Small Business Customer Manager Filter SDK. Business users and developers who use BizTalk Server 2004 can assemble them without any programming.

Liabilities

- **Restricts the filter types**. BizTalk Server 2004 pipelines use filters that have a single input and a single output. This implementation of *Pipes and Filters* cannot accommodate filters that do not fit within this constraint.
- **Overhead cost**. BizTalk Server 2004 pipelines are very powerful when there are business rules and other types of processes on the data. However, the business rules and processes on the data are overhead if all that is required is a simple pipe between applications.

Testing Considerations

There are two main test scenarios when you use BizTalk Server 2004 to implement *Pipes and Filters.* The test scenario that applies to you depends on the customization option that you choose as your implementation strategy:

- **Configure a custom pipeline by using the filters that are supplied with BizTalk Server 2004**. In this case, you build the custom pipeline and configure the filters by using the Pipeline Designer. You then create a test configuration that uses this custom pipeline in either a receive port or a send port. You can then submit test messages and validate the resulting output.

- **Configure a custom pipeline by writing custom filters in C# or Visual Basic .NET.** In this case, you can test the pipeline component by creating a test configuration that uses the component in a custom pipeline as described earlier. You can also use Microsoft Visual Studio .NET to review the pipeline component code.

Security Considerations

In addition to security features that are provided by the transports, such as encryption when using HTTPS, BizTalk Server 2004 provides security at the message level. BizTalk Server 2004 can receive decrypted messages and validate digital signatures that are attached to these messages. Similarly, BizTalk Server 2004 can encrypt messages and attach digital signatures to messages before sending them. You can also purchase or develop custom security components as required.

Note: The BizTalk Server 2004 host instance runs the send pipelines and the receive pipelines within a specific security context. Therefore, any processing that the pipeline components perform operates within this security context. This security context may impose constraints on the way that the custom component accesses a database. The security context may also impose constraints on the location in the certificate store that the component can access a digital signature from.

Operational Considerations

BizTalk Server 2004 provides extensive support for application monitoring. Users can monitor the messages that are going through each pipeline. Users can therefore also monitor the ports the pipeline uses. BizTalk Server 2004 users can configure each send port or receive port to track messages, as shown in Figure 6.12.

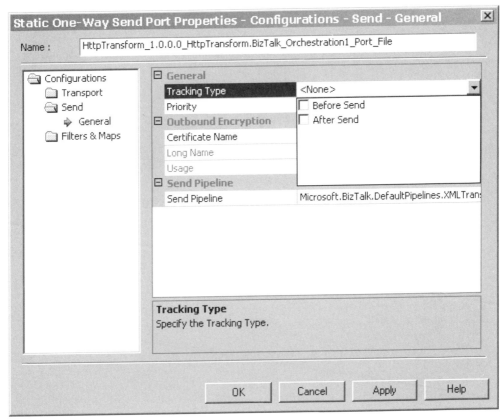

Figure 6.12
BizTalk Server 2004 port-level tracking

The Health and Activity Tracker (HAT) tool in BizTalk Server 2004 provides access to port-level tracking information that allows you to see what is happening in the system. It also allows you to examine archived data for patterns or trends.

Acknowledgments

[Microsoft04] Microsoft Corporation. "Certificate Stores." *Windows XP Professional Product Documentation*. Available from Microsoft.com at *http://www.microsoft.com/resources/documentation/windows/xp/all/proddocs/en-us /sag_cmuncertstor.mspx*.

Gateway

Context

You have an integration solution that consists of several applications that are provided by different vendors and that run on a variety of platforms. Some applications use an external resource and therefore have to communicate with it.

For example, consider the software that insurance carriers use to rate insurance policies. Although many carriers have upgraded to client-server or service-oriented architectures, some still rely on mainframe code for lines of business and for jurisdictions where the upgrade is not feasible. For example, quoting uses mainframe rating code to quote premiums. Endorsing uses the mainframe rating code to endorse policies. Renewal also uses the mainframe rating code to renew policies. In other words, several applications must integrate with the mainframe code.

Problem

How can you make the applications of an integration solution access an external system without introducing many-to-one coupling between the applications and the external system?

Forces

Accessing an external resource from an integration solution involves balancing the following forces:

- All applications that communicate directly with the external resource must have intimate knowledge of communication details such as application protocols, messaging protocols, and communication protocols. Each connection to the external resource adds dependencies between the integration solution and the resource.

- The external resource may use a different communication protocol than the communication protocol that the applications support natively. Implementing communication protocols and protocol translators is difficult and error-prone.

- Testing the integration solution involves both the external resource and the internal applications. However, because the external resource may not be accessible from the testing environment, it may not be possible to involve the external resource in tests. Also, including the external resource in tests may prevent testing error or boundary conditions.

Solution

Add a *Gateway* component that abstracts the access to the external resource. The gateway presents a single interface to the integrated applications while hiding the external resource interface. In addition, the gateway encapsulates any protocol translation that may be necessary to communicate with the external resource.

Figure 6.13 shows the gateway replacing direct access to the external resource. The applications that collaborate with the gateway and with the external resource are highlighted in blue, and the shapes at the end of the connectors denote different interfaces.

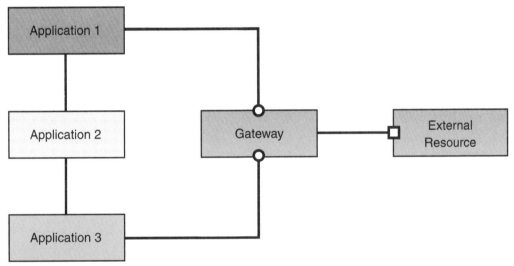

Figure 6.13
Gateway abstracting access to the external resource

The applications that need to communicate with the external resource do so by sending messages to the gateway interface. The gateway handles any protocol translation that is needed and then passes the message to the external resource. In effect, the gateway encapsulates all access to the external resource. Consequently, the applications do not require information about what it takes to communicate with the external resource.

The gateway also catches errors signaled by the external resource. The gateway may be able to handle errors such as communication timeouts and retries internally. Otherwise, it passes any errors that it cannot handle locally to the appropriate application. In effect, the gateway centralizes some error processing, but it probably does not centralize all that error processing. This frees applications from dealing with these errors. Moving the error handling logic from applications to the gateway guarantees consistency.

The communication through the gateway is asymmetric. The control flows from the applications to the external resource. In other words, the gateway only provides a point through which applications call the external resource. The gateway does not support inbound access to the applications. Table 6.4 shows the responsibilities and collaborations of the gateway.

Table 6.4: Gateway Responsibilities and Collaborations

Responsibilities	Collaborations
– To provide an internal interface through which the applications access the external resource. – To perform message transformations (if any). – To relay the message to the external resource and to return the reply message to the sending application (if there is a reply message). – To handle errors signaled by the external resource or to pass them to the appropriate component.	– Applications send requests addressed to the external resource. – External resource fulfills requests coming from the applications.

After you decide to use a gateway, you have to decide where the gateway will reside. The following are two possibilities:

- **Internal gateway for enterprise integration**. An internal gateway resides in the same jurisdiction as the applications. Therefore, external applications do not use the gateway, and you have full control over it.

- **External gateway for business-to-business (B2B) integration**. An external gateway serves other enterprise applications. An external gateway may even be provided by a third party, such as the resource owner. This configuration, which is shown in Figure 6.14, means that you no longer have to implement the gateway. However, using an external gateway adds a dependency on an outside component.

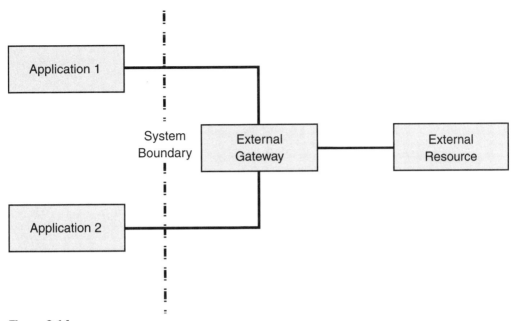

Figure 6.14
An external gateway that resides outside system boundaries (B2B integration)

An internal gateway provides the most flexible solution. You make the decisions about its interface, about the protocol translations it performs, and about the errors it handles. If you have an external gateway, and you want to reduce the coupling with it, you can use an internal gateway and regard the external gateway as the resource. This configuration is known as *gateway chaining*. Figure 6.15 illustrates this configuration.

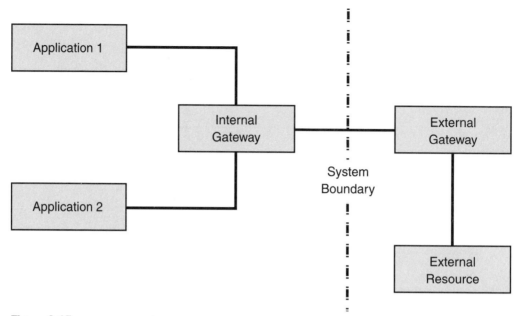

Figure 6.15

Gateway chaining: removing dependencies between applications and an external gateway

Gateway chaining translates into functional composition. If you have several gateways, and each gateway is specialized to handle a different aspect such as protocol translation or encryption, you can chain them together to create a composite gateway that handles each aspect sequentially. Chaining gateways might be complicated if the gateways make conflicting assumptions about tasks in the environment such as error handling.

Example

Consider a property and casualty system where separate applications implement policy management, general ledger, accounts payable, billing, and claims functionalities. The policy management, the claims, and the billing applications connect through sockets to an external print system to print policies, claims, and statements. This configuration is illustrated in Figure 6.16.

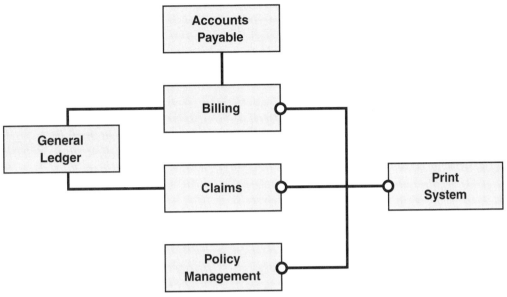

Figure 6.16
Property and casualty system without a gateway

In Figure 6.16, the billing, claims, and policy management applications access the print system directly. The round connectors denote a socket-based interface. Print system upgrades, such as replacing the socket-based interface with a Web service interface, require upgrading three systems: the policy management system, the claims system, and the billing system. These changes are expensive. Additionally, if the print system belongs to a different organization, the owners of the property and casualty system cannot control the timing of the upgrade. An upgrade during the peak renewal season would have a negative impact on the business.

Figure 6.17 shows the property and casualty system modified to use a gateway. The billing, claims, and policy management applications no longer access the print system directly. Instead, the billing, claims, and policy management applications access the print system through a gateway. The round connectors denote a socket-based interface, and the square connectors denote a Web services-based interface. This configuration reduces the costs that are associated with a print system upgrade.

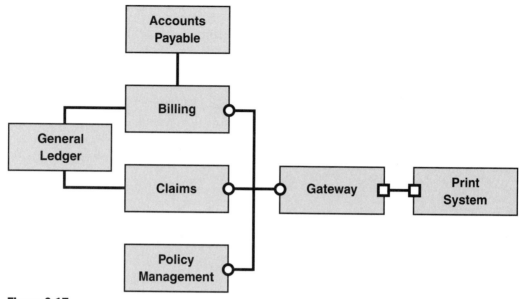

Figure 6.17
Property and casualty system with a gateway

Resulting Context

Using a gateway to provide a single point of access to an external resource has the following benefits and liabilities:

Benefits

- **Reduced coupling.** The gateway encapsulates access to the external resource. Applications that use the resource no longer require information about how to access that external resource.

- **Reduced application complexity.** Individual applications do not have to implement the communication protocols required to communicate with the external resource. In addition, the gateway can implement some of the error handling that each application would otherwise have to perform.

- **Improved integrability.** The gateway provides a single point of access for the external resource. This facilitates integration with external resources such as an Enterprise Resource Planning (ERP) system, a Customer Relationship Management (CRM) system, or another similar system.

- **Improved security.** A single point of access represents a single point of control. You can use this single point of access to implement security policies and to bridge between different security realms. It also allows you to meter access to the external resource and to implement business rules that control access.

- **Improved performance through optimization**. The gateway provides a logical place to optimize the communication protocol for use with the external resource. Optimization might include batching similar requests or caching results.

Liabilities

- **Reduced performance through overhead**. The gateway replaces direct communication, adding an intermediate layer. This translates into increased latency compared to direct communication.

- **Increased maintainability effort**. A gateway extends your integration solution with another component. This translates into additional implementation, configuration, testing, deployment, and management work.

- **Dependency of the gateway interface**. Designing the gateway requires foresight about the interactions between the applications and the external resource. If you have to change the gateway's interface in a way that breaks compatibility, you have to change all the applications that access it.

- **Reduced availability**. All access to the external resource passes through the gateway. From an availability perspective, the gateway represents a single point of failure.

Testing Considerations

Using a gateway improves testability on both sides in the following ways:

- Applications access the external resource solely through the gateway. A mock gateway can receive messages, return predefined responses, and exercise error handling logic. In other words, you can test the system without accessing the external resource.

- Because the external resource receives requests from the gateway, you can test the gateway by relaying requests to the external resource independent of the applications.

Figure 6.18 shows these test areas. The top diagram shows a mock gateway for testing the interaction with the applications. The bottom diagram shows a mock gateway for testing the interaction with the external resources. The shaded arrows indicate the test areas.

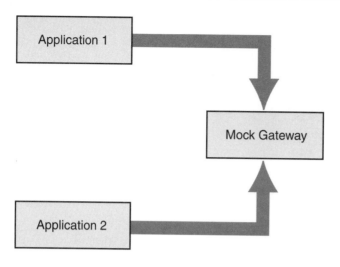

Figure 6.18
Using a mock gateway for testing

A gateway also facilitates load testing. Testers can use the gateway to insert test loads into the integration solution to measure the external resource's performance.

Security Considerations

Accessing an external resource through a gateway has the following security implications:

- A single point of access facilitates enforcement of a uniform security policy. However, it also represents a central point of attack.

- A gateway allows bridging between different security realms. For example, a gateway can mix different security context management policies, such as impersonation on one side and consolidation on the other. However, the gateway only provides a place where the mapping between the two can be handled. You must implement the mapping separately.

Operational Considerations

A gateway represents a single point of access and may cause contention among the applications that communicate with the external resource. You should monitor access to the external resource and act proactively when the first signs of contention appear. This single point of access also helps you to meter access to the external resource, to monitor the external resource, and to audit the external resource.

Related Patterns

The *Gateway* pattern described here relates to the following patterns:

- *Implementing Gateway with Host Integration Server 2004.* This pattern uses the Global Bank scenario to show how you can use Host Integration Server 2004 to implement *Gateway*.

- *Gateway* [Fowler03]. Martin Fowler discusses *Gateway* in the context of enterprise applications. He also covers the relationship with *Façade* and *Adapter* [Gamma95]. Fowler's *Gateway* is fine-grained at the object level. However, in the context of integration, *Gateway* is coarse-grained at the platform level.

- *Messaging Gateway* [Hohpe04]. *Messaging Gateway* wraps message-specific method calls, exposes domain-specific methods, and encapsulates access to the messaging system. Hohpe and Woolf also explain how to create composite gateways by using gateway chaining. A composite gateway permits you to use a gateway that encapsulates a single aspect together with other gateways to deal with several aspects.

- *Remote Proxy* [Buschmann96]. *Gateway* can be regarded as a refinement of the *Remote Proxy* pattern. *Remote Proxy* deals with distributed components in the general sense and provides the interprocess communication (IPC) mechanisms for communication with remote objects. *Gateway* is designed for integration solutions and therefore assumes that the integration infrastructure is available.

- *Service Interface* [Trowbridge03]. *Service Interface* exposes functionality as a service and provides an entry point for inbound requests. In effect, the control flows in the opposite direction compared to *Gateway*.

Acknowledgments

[Buschmann96] Buschmann, Frank; Regine Meunier, Hans Rohnert, Peter Sommerlad, and Michael Stal. *Pattern-Oriented Software Architecture, Volume 1: A System of Patterns.* John Wiley & Sons Ltd, 1996.

[Fowler03] Fowler, Martin. *Patterns of Enterprise Application Architecture.* Addison-Wesley, 2003.

[Gamma95] Gamma, Erich; Richard Helm, Ralph Johnson, and John Vlissides. *Design Patterns: Elements of Reusable Object-Oriented Software.* Addison-Wesley, 1995.

[Hohpe04] Hohpe, Gregor, and Bobby Woolf. *Enterprise Integration Patterns: Designing, Building, and Deploying Messaging Solutions.* Addison-Wesley, 2004.

[Trowbridge03] Trowbridge, David; Dave Mancini, Dave Quick, Gregor Hohpe, James Newkirk, and David Lavigne. *Enterprise Solution Patterns Using Microsoft .NET.* Microsoft Press, 2003. Also available on the *MSDN Architecture Center* at: *http://msdn.microsoft.com/architecture/patterns/default.aspx?pull=/library/en-us /dnpatterns/html/Esp.asp.*

Implementing Gateway with Host Integration Server 2004

Context

Most medium-sized to large-sized organizations rely on a distributed environment where business logic operates on many different computing technologies.

To the dismay of the software developers in these organizations, two of the most commonly used technologies can be difficult to integrate. These technologies are the Microsoft .NET Framework and the IBM Customer Information Control System (CICS) application subsystem. Implementing the *Gateway* pattern allows developers to overcome incompatibility issues by integrating existing mainframe business logic into .NET Framework applications without having to redevelop the code that already exists in CICS.

You have decided to implement the *Gateway* pattern by using Microsoft Host Integration Server 2004 and its Transaction Integrator (TI) feature to enable .NET Framework applications to invoke mainframe transactions, to pass the proper input parameters to the transactions, and to finally receive the output parameters that are returned from the executing transactions.

Background

The Global Bank infrastructure integrates applications that run on several platforms. The account management system runs on a mainframe. Account management operations such as Create Account, Check Balance and Debit, Credit Account, Delete Account, and Get Account Information are implemented as CICS transactions. The integration solution must be capable of executing these transactions from the Microsoft Windows operating system. Global Bank decided to use Microsoft Host Integration Server 2004 and its Transaction Integrator (TI) feature as a *Gateway* implementation to invoke the individual CICS transactions included in the mainframe account management system. Using TI to call mainframe programs from a .NET Framework application is known as *Windows-initiated processing*.

Figure 6.19 depicts a high-level view of this configuration.

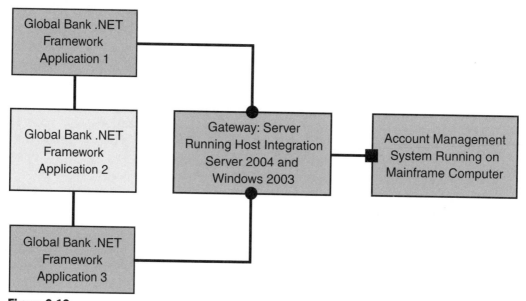

Figure 6.19
Global Bank implementation of Gateway

Although it does not apply in the case of Global Bank, a mainframe application developer can also use TI to access .NET Framework applications from a mainframe application. Using TI in this manner is known as *host-initiated processing*.

Note: The TI feature of Host Integration Server 2004 was named COM Transaction Integrator for CICS and IMS (COMTI) in previous releases of Microsoft Host Integration Server.

Implementation Strategy

Using Host Integration Server 2004 to implement *Gateway* typically requires the expertise of many different people, including a .NET Framework developer, a Microsoft network infrastructure engineer, a mainframe CICS developer, and a mainframe systems administrator, just to name a few. It is important for all personnel involved to clearly understand the Host Integration Server 2004 components and the implementation steps that are required to successfully deploy this *Gateway* implementation.

Host Integration Server 2004 includes the following components that are required to access mainframe CICS transactions:

- **TI Manager**. TI Manager is the administrative component that allows developers to configure TI options. In a Windows-initiated processing scenario, these options include configuring the mainframe transaction's operating environment. This operating environment is known as the *remote environment*. These options also include configuring Windows-initiated processing objects that are used to associate the metadata file with the remote environment. The metadata file is addressed later in this pattern.

- **TI Designer**. TI Designer is a Microsoft Visual Studio .NET plug-in that developers can use to build TI client objects. TI client objects are used to specify the methods to invoke on the mainframe transactions and to specify the input and output parameters to use with those methods.

- **TI run-time component**. The TI run-time component intercepts the method calls to and from the mainframe and uses the information in the TI metadata file to perform the actual conversion and formatting of the method parameters.

Because the implementation strategy relies primarily on the TI feature of Host Integration Server 2004, most of the strategy involves configuring TI. To properly configure TI, follow these steps:

1. **Select the TI programming model**. A TI programming model determines the method used to access and to integrate host transactions. You must determine which of the eleven available programming models you need to use to access the transactions.

2. **Configure the mainframe environment**. Ensure that the mainframe environment is properly configured to allow access by TI.

3. **Configure the TI metadata file**. The TI metadata file defines the methods, parameters, and data type mappings that are used when mainframe transactions are invoked.

4. **Configure network protocol connectivity**. You must implement the appropriate network protocol to provide network communications between TI and the mainframe. You can use Systems Network Architecture (SNA) Logical Unit 6.2 (LU 6.2) or Transmission Control Protocol/Internet Protocol (TCP/IP).

5. **Configure a TI remote environment**. A remote environment is a collection of properties that describes a region on the mainframe. You must configure a remote environment.

6. **Add a Microsoft Internet Information Services (IIS) virtual directory**. This virtual directory is the virtual directory where the TI request is processed. The virtual directory is used to store the Windows-initiated processing object that you configure in the next step.

7. **Configure a Windows-initiated processing object.** A Windows-initiated processing object establishes a relationship between the metadata file, the IIS virtual directory, and the remote environment. You must configure a Windows-initiated processing object.

8. **Implement a .NET Framework client application to invoke the TI client interfaces.** Finally, after all the TI-specific configuration is finished, you must implement the .NET Framework applications that use TI to invoke the mainframe transactions.

The following paragraphs describe these implementation steps in greater detail.

Step 1: Select the Programming Model

A TI programming model determines the method used to access host transactions and the TI configuration requirements. You must coordinate with the mainframe CICS developer and with the mainframe systems administrator to select the appropriate programming model.

The first decision to make when selecting a TI programming model is to determine which of the three supported transactions—CICS, Information Management System (IMS), or AS/400—is being accessed. TI supports eleven programming models. Six of these models are used to access the CICS mainframe transactions that are the subject of this implementation. The six programming models used to access CICS transactions are the following:

- LU 6.2 Link
- LU 6.2 User Data
- TCP/IP Enhanced Listener Mode (ELM) Link
- TCP/IP ELM User Data
- TCP/IP Transaction Request Message (TRM) Link
- TCP/IP TRM User Data

The other five models are used for accessing IMS transactions or OS/400 transactions. They are not discussed here.

The next critical decision in selecting the programming model is to choose the network protocol to use. TI can use either the TCP/IP network protocol or the LU 6.2 network protocol to communicate between the mainframe environment and the .NET Framework environment. LU 6.2 is the recommended protocol to use with TI for the following reasons:

- CICS transactions run more efficiently in an LU 6.2 environment than they do in a TCP/IP environment. CICS transactions run more efficiently because of the costly task-swapping techniques that CICS employs for executing transaction programs initiated by TCP/IP.

- It is easier to configure LU 6.2 on the mainframe than it is to configure TCP/IP.

- The LU 6.2 protocol supports two-phase commit transactions; the two-phase commit protocol is required to allow transactions to execute in a distributed environment across multiple systems. Two-phase commit transactions are only supported when the TI metadata file (addressed later in this pattern) is configured to use a Component Object Model (COM) type library.

- LU 6.2 supports the IBM Parallel Sysplex technology for network redundancy. Parallel Sysplex provides a mechanism that allows mainframe sessions to be reestablished automatically across a different route when an established route is interrupted.

- You can use LU 6.2 over an existing TCP/IP network as long as the Enterprise Extender is deployed on the mainframe. The Enterprise Extender is a feature of IBM mainframes that supports running LU 6.2 over the TCP/IP protocol. This configuration also supports two-phase commit transactions when using COM type libraries.

The two programming models that support the LU 6.2 protocol are LU 6.2 Link and LU 6.2 User Data. The key difference between these two programming models is how each handles data communications between TI and the CICS transactions. The LU 6.2 Link is the only one of the two models that uses the COMMAREA. The COMMAREA is a feature of CICS that allows COBOL transactions to pass data between them without requiring developers to incorporate the data communication logic into their code. Input and output parameters are easily passed in and out of the COMMAREA. When the COMMAREA is not in use, all data exchanged between transactions must be explicitly handled in the transaction code. Because many of the existing CICS transactions that are deployed in mainframe production environments are already coded to use the COMMAREA, using the COMMAREA is the simplest way for a TI developer to access CICS transactions. Therefore, LU 6.2 Link is the recommended programming model for using TI to access CICS transactions.

Note: If the existing CICS transactions are not coded to use the COMMAREA, or if they contain code that is used for something other than for processing business logic, the CICS developer must modify the transaction code to use the COMMAREA. The COMMAREA limits the amount of data that can be passed in and out of invoked transactions to 32 kilobytes (KB).

LU 6.2 Link Model: Components

The LU 6.2 Link model relies on a number of critical run-time components that support its functionality. Figure 6.20 depicts the TI run-time environment and components for the LU 6.2 Link programming model. Following the figure are descriptions of each of these components.

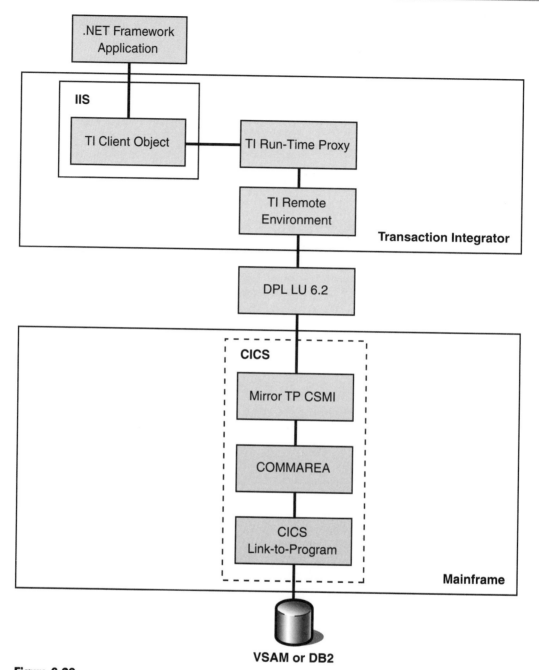

Figure 6.20

TI run-time environment for the LU 6.2 Link model

The LU 6.2 Link model uses the following components, as shown in Figure 20, to access mainframe transactions:

- **.NET Framework application**. The .NET Framework application invokes the TI client object for access to mainframe transactions.

- **TI client object**. The TI client object contains the necessary data and logic required to communicate with the CICS transactions.

- **TI run-time proxy**. The TI run-time component is used to establish the connection between the TI client object and the CICS mainframe transaction at run time.

- **TI remote environment**. The TI remote environment component is used to specify host connection parameters such as the network address, the security settings, and the communications model to use for accessing host transactions.

- **Distributed Program Link (DPL) LU 6.2**. DPL is the protocol that TI uses to communicate with CSMI.

- **Mirror TP CSMI**. The mirror CICS transaction is a special CICS transaction that acts as a gateway between transactions running in different CICS regions. The mirror transaction allows the transactions in the different regions to exchange data through the COMMAREA. TI takes advantage of this standard method of communication between CICS transactions to access mainframe transactions. The CICS transaction ID for the mirror transaction is CSMI. CSMI handles all LU 6.2 and transactional properties required on the communication.

- **COMMAREA**. The COMMAREA is an area of the mainframe transaction code that many CICS transactions that are written in COBOL use to exchange data. When using this model, TI appears to the mainframe transaction as a CICS transaction that exchanges data through the COMMAREA.

- **CICS link-to-program**. The CICS link-to-program is the CICS transaction that TI invokes on behalf of the client application. It contains the business logic being executed and is identified by its link-to-program name in the TI method call.

- **DB2/VSAM**. CICS usually uses the IBM SQL database that is named DB2 or the older Virtual Storage Access Method (VSAM) as the data storage mechanism for storing the data that is used by CICS transactions.

Using a Model Other Than LU 6.2 Link

If you cannot use the recommended LU 6.2 Link model because your existing environment does not allow you to use it, you can select one of the other five models to access CICS transactions:

- **LU 6.2 User Data**. Although this model uses the efficient LU 6.2 protocol, it does not use the COMMAREA. It therefore is more complex to implement. This model is best for situations where the mainframe transactions are not coded to use the COMMAREA and where the transaction code does contain communication handling data and business logic data. Because this model does not use the COMMAREA, it is not subject to the 32-KB COMMAREA limit. Instead, it supports an unlimited amount of data.

- **TCP/IP Enhanced Listener Mode Link**. This model is similar to the LU 6.2 Link model because it uses the COMMAREA. However, it uses TCP/IP instead of LU 6.2. The model also employs the mainframe's Enhanced Listener Mode (ELM). You would use this model when LU 6.2 is not configured for access to the mainframe and when CICS transactions are coded to use the COMMAREA.

- **TCP/IP Transaction Request Message Link**. This model is similar to the TCP/IP ELM Link model. The only difference is that it does not implement the ELM. ELM is preferred over Transaction Request Message (TRM); however, the newer ELM functionality may not be implemented in older versions of CICS.

- **TCP/IP ELM User Data**. This model is similar to the LU 6.2 User Data model because it does not use the COMMAREA. It therefore is more complex to implement. This model is best for situations where mainframe transactions are not coded to use the COBOL COMMAREA and where the mainframe only supports TCP/IP access.

- **TCP/IP TRM User Data**. This model is similar to the TCP/IP ELM User Data model. The difference is that it does not implement the Enhanced Listener Mode.

The remainder of this implementation focuses on the LU 6.2 Link model when programming models are mentioned. For more information about other programming models, see the Host Integration Server 2004 product documentation.

Step 2: Configure the Mainframe Environment

Mainframes are often already configured with everything that TI requires to gain access to the transactions, because most of what TI requires is used for internal integration between mainframe programs. The mainframe systems programmer and the CICS developer must make any changes that are required. .NET Framework developers are rarely capable of performing such configurations themselves. The following are the minimum CICS versions that must be installed on the mainframe to support TI in specific mainframe operating system environments:

- IBM CICS for MVS version 3 release 3, or later, to support an SNA LU 6.2 network connection

- IBM CICS Transaction Server for VSE/ESA version 2 release 1, or later, to support an SNA LU 6.2 network connection

- IBM CICS Transaction Server for OS/390 version 1, or later, to support an SNA LU 6.2 or TCP/IP network connection

- IBM CICS Transaction Server for z/OS version 2, or later, to support an SNA LU 6.2 or TCP/IP network connection

- IBM CICS Transaction Server for z/OS version 2 release 2, or later, to support Enhanced Listener Mode for a TCP/IP network connection

For more information about how to properly configure the mainframe for this or other programming models, see the Host Integration Server 2004 documentation.

Determine If Changes Are Required to the Existing Transactions

In some cases, CICS transactions may require some modification before you can use TI to access them. In the case of the LU 6.2 Link model, transactions that are not coded to use the COMMAREA must be modified by the CICS developer. Additionally, any embedded terminal-handling code must be removed before using TI with LU 6.2 Link.

Step 3: Configure the TI Metadata File

The TI metadata file is used to specify the methods, parameters, and data type mappings that are used when mainframe transactions are invoked. You must gather the pertinent information that is required to configure the file. This information is typically provided by the mainframe systems programmer, the mainframe CICS developer, and the .NET Framework developers who invoke the mainframe transactions.

The metadata file can be configured as a Component Object Model (COM) component library or as a .NET Framework client library by using the TI Designer plug-in for Visual Studio .NET.

▶ **To configure the TI metadata file**

1. **Create a Visual Studio .NET project**. When you create the Visual Studio .NET project, choose **HIS** as the project type and **TI Project** as the template.

2. **Add a .NET Framework client library or a COM client library**. You use either the Add .NET Client Library Wizard or the Add COM Client Library Wizard to add the client library. When using a wizard to add either a .NET Framework client library or a COM client library, you must specify the following properties for the remote environment that this library will be associated with:

   - **Vendor**. Specify the vendor for this remote environment. In the Global Bank scenario, the vendor is Microsoft.

   - **Protocol**. Specify the protocol used to access the remote environment. This could be either TCP/IP or LU 6.2. In this scenario, the protocol is LU 6.2.

- **Target Environment**. Specify whether the target environment is CICS, IMS, or AS/400. In this scenario, the target environment is CICS.
- **Programming Model**. Specify the programming model to use. In this scenario, the programming model is LU 6.2 Link.

3. **Develop the interface methods**. A method in the TI metadata file has a direct correlation to a CICS transaction program on the mainframe. You must define a number of method properties. One important method property is **Return Type**. The **Return Type** property enables you to specify whether the method has a return value and, if so, to specify the data type for the value. Whether a method has a return value or not depends on the existing COBOL program and on how you want to handle the output data. Another important method property is **Tran ID**. The **Tran ID** method property enables you to specify the link-to-program name of the mainframe transaction. The link-to-program name is how CICS identifies this transaction in its tables. CICS uses this name to invoke the transaction for execution.

4. **Configure method parameters**. You must configure the parameters for the method. The parameters are the input and output values that the method uses when communicating with the mainframe transaction. Before configuring the parameters, you must identify the input and output parameters in the existing COBOL source code. You must then determine the data type to use for each parameter.

Determining the Transaction's Link-to-Program Name

CICS transactions are usually invoked using their link-to-program name. You must consult with the mainframe developer to obtain the names of the transactions that you want to invoke.

Importing COBOL by Using the COBOL Import Wizard in TI Designer

You can use the COBOL Import Wizard in the TI Designer to import COBOL source code to configure a method. As you move through the pages of the wizard, you extract the data declarations specified in the COMMAREA. The data declarations describe the input that is sent to the mainframe transaction and the output that is received from the mainframe transaction. The wizard uses the parameters specified in the COMMAREA and ignores all other content in the source file. When the wizard finishes, a new method is added to your client library. The method uses the parameters specified in the source file's COMMAREA.

Step 4: Configure Network Protocol Connectivity

Assuming that the physical network that connects the server running Host Integration Server 2004 TI and the mainframe is in place, the first step to establish connectivity is to configure the protocol you are using to access the mainframe. You can use either LU 6.2 or TCP/IP.

Configuring LU 6.2 Access

The LU 6.2 protocol is based on IBM Systems Network Architecture (SNA) - Advanced Program-to-Program Communications (APPC) protocol for network communications. When using LU 6.2 to access the host applications, you must configure Host Integration Server 2004 for LU 6.2 access to the proper CICS region. Although a full description of how to configure Host Integration Server 2004 for LU 6.2 access to the CICS region is not part of this pattern, it is important to know the following when configuring LU 6.2 access:

- The name of the local APPC LU that is configured on Host Integration Server 2004 for access to the CICS region corresponds to the independent LU 6.2 configured on the Virtual Telecommunications Access Method (VTAM) PU definition for that Host Integration Server 2004 connection.

- The name of the remote APPC LU configured on the Host Integration Server 2004 connection to the mainframe corresponds to the APPLID as configured on the VTAM APPL definition for the CICS region.

- The APPC mode configured for the LU 6.2 communications must correspond to the mode configured on the VTAM LU definition for the local APPC LU and on the mode used by the APPL definition in VTAM. The APPC mode typically specifies parameters such as the number of parallel sessions supported and the communication partner that is the contention winner.

Note: For more information about the steps to configure Host Integration Server 2004 for LU 6.2 access to a mainframe computer, see the Host Integration Server 2004 product documentation.

Configuring TCP/IP Access to Mainframe Transactions

If you are using TCP/IP, you must determine the TCP/IP address and the port number to use to access the proper CICS region. You must specify the TCP/IP address of the mainframe you want to access and the port number of the CICS region you want to access. A TCP/IP port number is associated with a CICS region on the mainframe. The port statement is used to define this relationship. The IBM-supplied Concurrent Listener (program EZACIC02, transaction ID CSKL) binds a socket to the port specified for a given CICS region and then waits for a client request on that port. When a client makes a request on a port associated with that CICS region, TCP/IP forwards the connection request to the Concurrent Listener in that CICS region.

Step 5: Configure a Remote Environment

A *remote environment* is a collection of properties that describes a region on the mainframe. You must configure a remote environment to specify the programming model to use with a TI component, to specify the protocol used to access the mainframe, and to specify other connectivity properties. You use the Remote Environment Wizard in TI Manager to create a remote environment.

The wizard allows you to specify values for the following properties:

- **Remote environment name**. Specify a name for this remote environment.
- **Network protocol to use**. Specify LU 6.2 or TCP/IP. In this scenario, the protocol is LU 6.2.
- **Target host**. Specify whether this remote environment is used to access CICS, IMS, or OS/400 transactions. The target host is the name of the Global Bank mainframe.
- **Programming model**. Specify one of the eleven programming models to use with this remote environment. In this scenario, the programming model is LU 6.2 Link.
- **Local LU alias**. Specify the name of the local APPC LU that corresponds to the independent LU 6.2 configured on the VTAM PU definition for the Host Integration Server 2004 connection.
- **Remote APPC LU alias**. The remote APPC LU corresponds to the APPLID as configured on the VTAM APPL definition for the CICS region.
- **Mode name**. The APPC mode configured for LU 6.2 communications must correspond to the mode configured on the VTAM LU definition for the local APPC LU, and it must correspond to the mode used by the APPL definition in VTAM.

Note: For specific instructions on how to create a remote environment, see the Host Integration Server 2004 product documentation.

Step 6: Add an IIS Virtual Directory

The IIS virtual directory is used to store the Windows-initiated processing object configured in the following step. This IIS virtual directory is associated with Windows-initiated processing and with the remote environment. The IIS virtual directory is then made available to .NET Framework applications that use this TI configuration to access mainframe transactions.

Step 7: Configure a Windows-Initiated Processing Object

A Windows-initiated processing object is used to establish a relationship between the metadata file developed using the Visual Studio .NET TI designer plug-in, the IIS virtual directory, and the remote environment configured in the TI manager.

The New WIP Object Wizard allows you to specify values for the following properties:

- **Path**. Specify the path to the metadata file you created in step 3.
- **File**. Specify the name of the metadata file.
- **Virtual directory**. Specify the virtual directory where this object is stored.
- **Remote environment**. Specify the name of the remote environment.

Step 8: Implement a .NET Framework Client Application to Invoke the TI Client Interfaces

At this point, TI has been configured to provide access to the CICS mainframe transactions. All that is left is to develop the .NET Framework client application that invokes the mainframe transactions.

Example

The Global Bank scenario discussed in this pattern serves as a perfect example of how to deploy TI into production. The following example describes the specific functions and configurations that are required to meet Global Bank's needs. The steps in the example follow the same implementation strategy described earlier and explain the decisions you would make along the way if you were actually deploying TI into production.

Global Bank needs a solution that enables its .NET Framework applications to invoke business logic that resides on mainframe CICS transactions. The CICS transactions are used for handling typical banking operations, such as obtaining account balances and processing debits and credits. This example illustrates how the TI Windows-initiated processing features can be implemented to meet Global Bank's requirements.

Components

To deploy TI into production, the following components must be available:

- Host Integration Server 2004 with TI installed
- Visual Studio .NET with the TI Designer plug-in installed
- An ASP.NET Web application used by bank staff to manage accounts
- Mainframe CICS transactions that can be used to implement the required account management functions

Functions

The business logic implemented in the CICS transactions performs the following functions:

- It creates accounts.
- It obtains account details.
- It obtains lists of accounts.
- It deposits funds into existing accounts.
- It withdraws funds from existing accounts.

This example illustrates how the functionality currently implemented in mainframe CICS transactions can be invoked for execution from a .NET Framework application environment.

The following are the steps required for configuring TI for this example.

Step 1: Select the Programming Model

To access the mainframe applications for Global Bank, you must first select the appropriate programming model. The first thing to determine is whether the CICS transactions that you want to access use the COMMAREA. You then have to determine whether to use the LU 6.2 or the TCP/IP protocol for communications.

After conferring with the CICS developer, you learn that each of these transactions is coded to use the COMMAREA. You also learn from the mainframe systems programmer that LU 6.2 is configured for access to the CICS region on the mainframe. Based on this information, which you collected from the mainframe personnel, you determine that it is best to use the LU 6.2 Link programming model for access to the transactions.

Step 2: Configure the Mainframe Environment

Although this step is crucial to the successful deployment of a TI solution, it usually cannot be performed by the .NET Framework developer. You must rely on the mainframe personnel to properly configure the mainframe environment. Fortunately, the software required by TI is usually already installed in most mainframe environments. The mainframe systems programmer only needs to give you access to the transactions.

When contacting the mainframe personnel, you learn that they were able to review the Host Integration Server 2004 documentation and verify that all mainframe components are properly configured to allow access to the CICS transactions by using TI.

Step 3: Configure the TI Metadata File

You now have to develop the TI metadata file. In this case, you will implement the metadata file as a .NET Framework client library because the solution is being implemented in the .NET Framework, and you do not have a requirement to provide two-phase commit capabilities. To develop the TI metadata file, you must complete the following steps:

1. **Create a Visual Studio .NET project**. When you create the project, choose **HIS** as the project type and **TI Project** as the template. Name the project GlobalBank.

2. **Add a new .NET Framework client library**. Add a .NET Framework client library to the GlobalBank project and use the parameters specified in the following steps:

   a. On the Library page of the New .NET Client Library Wizard, type **GlobalBank** as the interface name, and then type a description for the interface.

   b. On the Remote Environment page of the wizard, select the following information regarding the host environment:

   - **Vendor**: Microsoft
   - **Protocol**: LU 6.2
   - **Target environment**: CICS
   - **Programming model**: Link

   c. On the next Remote Environment page, type **CSMI** in the **Transaction ID** box, and then type **MSTX** in the **Source** box.

   The new client library appears in the Visual Studio .NET main pane. The wizard uses the parameters you specified to create the default interface.

3. **Add the methods for the example**. After adding the .NET Framework client library, you can add the methods to the new library. The methods hold a one-to-one relationship with the CICS transactions being invoked. Table 1 lists all the transactions available to the client through Windows-initiated processing and the corresponding method name. You must configure one method for each of the transactions that appear in this table. All the transactions have an integer return value that is an error code.

   To add a method, follow these steps:

   a. In the Visual Studio .NET main pane, expand the **GlobalBank** component, and then select the **GlobalBank** interface.

   b. Right-click the **GlobalBank** interface, and then click **Add Method**.

   The Method1 method appears.

   c. Configure the method properties for this first method and for the other methods used in this example.

The following table lists the property values to use for each method. You can accept the default value for any of the properties not included in Table 6.5.

Table 6.5: Transactions Available to the Client Through Windows-Initiated Processing

Method name/ transaction name (Name Property)	CICS transaction link-to-program name (Link-to-Program Name Property)	Input parameters	Output parameters	Description
M**CreateAccount**	GBCREACC	AccountNumber AccountName	None	Creates an account with a zero balance.
GetAccountDetails	GBGETACC	AccountNumber	AccountName Balance	Retrieves details of a single account.
GetAccountList	GBACCLST	TotalCount Received	Array of Account Number, AccountName, and Balance	Gets list of accounts.
Deposit	GBDEP	AccountNumber Amount	NeGBalance	Deposits money in the account.
Withdraw	GBWDL	AccountNumber Amount	NeGBalance	Withdraws money from the account if the funds are available.

Figure 6.21 shows the way that the Global Bank client object should appear after you configure the interface and all its methods.

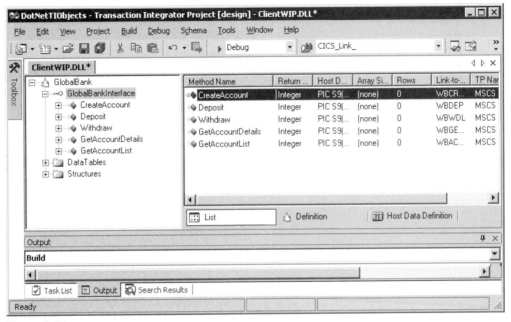

Figure 6.21
Global Bank client object with methods configured

4. **Add the method parameters**. The method parameters establish a mapping
   between the parameter types in the .NET Framework environment and the
   COBOL data types in the mainframe environment. Add the method parameters
   for each transaction according to the information in Table 6.6.

Table 6.6: Global Bank Method Parameters

Transaction	Input parameters	Input/output	.NET Framework data type	COBOL data type
CreateAccount	AccountNumber	Input	Decimal	PIC S9(n)V9(n) COMP-3
CreateAccount	AccountName	Input	String	PIC X(n)
GetAccountDetails	AccountNumber	Input	Decimal	PIC S9(n)V9(n) COMP-3
GetAccountDetails	AccountName	Output	String	PIC X(n)
GetAccountDetails	Balance	Output	Decimal	PIC S9(n)V9(n) COMP-3
GetAccountList	TotalCountReceived	Input	Integer	PIC S9(n) COMP
GetAccountList	Array of AccountNumber, AccountName, and Balance	Output	Decimal, String, Deciman	PIC S9(n)V9(n) COMP-3, PIC X(n), PIC S9(n)V9(n) COMP-3
Deposit	AccountNumber	Input	Decimal	PIC S9(n)V9(n) COMP-3
Deposit	Amount	Input	Decimal	PIC S9(n)V9(n) COMP-3
Deposit	NewBalance	Output	Decimal	PIC S9(n)V9(n) COMP-3
Withdraw Amount	AccountNumber	Input	Decimal	PIC S9(n)V9(n) COMP-3

Figure 6.22 shows the way that the Global Bank client object should appear after you configure the method parameters.

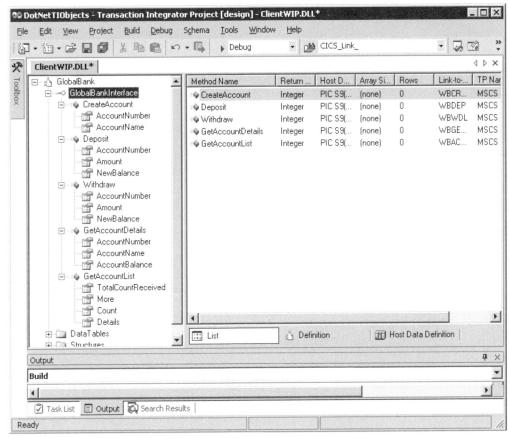

Figure 6.22
Global Bank client object with parameters configured

Step 4: Configure Network Protocol Connectivity

You have already learned that LU 6.2 communications to the Global Bank mainframe are available and that the mainframe systems programmer has configured the proper mainframe applications to allow access to CICS transactions. The mainframe systems programmer also informed you that you should set your local APPC LU name to Local and your remote APPC LU name to GBCICS1. The mode name is PA62TKNU. Using this information, you configure LU 6.2 communications by using Host Integration Server 2004. For more information about how to configure LU 6.2 communications, see the Host Integration Server 2004 documentation.

Step 5: Configure a TI Remote Environment

Use the TI Manager to implement the remote environment for Global Bank. In the Remote Environment Wizard, specify the values for the properties according to Table 6.7. Accept the default values for any properties that are not listed in the table.

Table 6.7: Global Bank Property Values

Property	Value
Name	Global Bank Host
Network type	LU 6.2
Target host	CICS
Programming model	Link
Local LU alias	Local
Remote LU alias	GBCICS1
Mode name	PA62TKNU

Step 6: Add an IIS Virtual Directory

The IIS virtual directory is used to store the Windows-initiated processing object that you configure in the next step. This IIS virtual directory is associated with the Windows-initiated processing object and with the remote environment. It is then made available to .NET Framework applications that use this TI configuration to access mainframe transactions. In this example, you create an IIS virtual directory named GlobalBank in the C:\Inetpub\Wwroot\GlobalBank physical directory.

Step 7: Configure a Windows-Initiated Processing Object

Complete the following steps to configure a Windows-initiated processing object. In the TI Manager, add a Windows-initiated processing object by using the parameters and values listed in Table 6.8.

Table 6.8: Windows-Initiated Processing Object Property Values

Property	Value
Path	C:\GlobalBankSource\GlobalBank\DotNetTIObjects
File	ServerWIP.dll
Virtual directory	DefaultWebSite/GlobalBankWIP
Remote environment	Global Bank Host

Step 8: Implement a .NET Framework Client Application

At this point, TI has been configured to provide access to the CICS mainframe transactions. All that is left is to develop the .NET Framework client application that invokes the mainframe transactions.

Resulting Context

The *Gateway* implementation described here results in the following benefits and liabilities:

Benefits

- **Reduced complexity**. The gateway encapsulates data and protocol translations required to use the account management system.
- **Reduced redevelopment efforts**. Business logic that already exists on the mainframe transactions does not have to be redeveloped in the .NET Framework environment.
- **Reduced need for retraining**. .NET Framework developers do not have to become familiar with CICS or COBOL to use the existing mainframe transactions.

Liabilities

- **Increased maintenance effort**. Host Integration Server 2004 is an additional system that must be maintained.
- **Lack of support for two-phase commit transactions when using .NET Framework client libraries.** The .NET Framework client library used in this scenario does not support two-phase commit transactions. Many organizations rely on two-phase commit transactions for day-to-day operations, so this configuration may not suit them. Instead, they would have to use a COM type library that does support two-phase commit transactions.

Tests

To fully test the deployment of TI in this scenario, you must have access to a mainframe computer that is running the proper CICS transactions. However, you can use the TI host-initiated processing capabilities to simulate this access. For instructions on how to configure this simulation, see the Host Integration Server 2004 online documentation at *http://www.microsoft.com/hiserver/techinfo/productdoc /default.asp.*

7

Project Notebook

"A business architecture is just an instruction set for extracting value. To extract value, a business must first create value for its customers; then extract some of the customer transaction value for itself." —Richard Sears, engineer and entrepreneur

While constructing the baseline architecture for Global Bank, the architecture team created numerous artifacts ranging in scope from business process models to executable bits. The team created these artifacts so that they could understand the business with sufficient clarity to create a technical architecture that would meet the needs of the business.

As they designed the technical architecture for Global Bank, they wanted to take advantage of reusable design elements (patterns) to mitigate technical risk and make the project more predictable. In addition, they knew that these patterns embodied design principles that would make it easier to evolve the architecture as the needs of the business changed over time. They wanted to take advantage of this extensibility after the system was delivered to lower the cost of new application development in the future.

This chapter presents some of the artifacts that the team produces while designing the baseline architecture. It starts with an overview of Global Bank's business environment, and then describes the viewpoints of five key business stakeholders. These viewpoints are captured in a set of models, which trace a path from business requirements to the technical solution. The chapter also presents some pattern-driven design models that capture the team's use of patterns during the process.

Interpreting the Artifacts

This chapter presents Global Bank team artifacts in a logical top-down progression, by starting with the high-level organizational processes and then disassembling these processes in progressive levels of detail. The order in which the chapter presents these artifacts does not, however, reflect the order in which the team produced them. The team produced the artifacts through an iterative process—building first cut approximations and then progressively refining them in subsequent iterations. They are presented here in logical order only to enhance readability.

The scenario presented in this book is intentionally incomplete. And although the artifacts presented here were used to build out an actual running system, it is important to remember that both Global Bank and the scenario portrayed are fictitious. They are intended only to demonstrate the application of patterns to the problems of integration within a representative enterprise scenario.

Let's examine the overall business context in more detail.

Global Bank Business Context

Global Bank is a midsize, traditional bank that has acquired a complete range of financial services capabilities through a series of acquisitions. The bank currently has a limited online presence that is fragmented across its various divisions. As part of its expansion strategy, Global Bank has decided to innovate in the online banking market by providing a host of value-added services on top of a fully integrated financial management capability. Some banks currently offer, or are developing the capability to offer, integrated online banking across all accounts (such as savings, checking, and credit cards). But no other bank offers a full range of value-added services such as financial advice, financial analysis and planning, and tax planning and filing. In addition, Global Bank has not seen the synergies it anticipated from offering a complete line of products. This lack of synergy is caused by its inability to effectively cross-sell based upon existing relationships and customer knowledge.

Convergence in the Banking Industry

In the late 1990s, the United States Congress began the process of deregulating the financial services industry. The Depression-era regulations restricted what services could be provided by specific types of financial services companies. Banking could only provide banking products and insurance companies could only provide insurance products. The deregulation of the industry had the effect of removing the legal barriers between various product types and between the companies that provided them. This triggered a mergers and acquisitions frenzy to broaden service offering portfolios.

Because he is familiar with the notion of profit patterns, the CEO of Global Bank quickly recognizes a particular pattern unfolding within his industry. He strongly believes that this *Convergence* pattern [Slywotsky99] will not only impact the global and national banks, but the whole industry.

The *Convergence* pattern describes the phenomenon in which businesses expand their offerings to related products and services along the value chain. Customers may forsake traditional suppliers in search of higher value, if not lower price (for example, the modern financial services industry). This complicates the market and presents a challenge because you must meet the new market by expanding your deliveries, which takes you outside your expertise. *Convergence* occurs when suppliers do one or more of the following:

- Expand up or down the value chain
- Substitute new products in place of existing ones
- Bundle products together

To apply the supplier *Convergence* pattern, you must do three things: first, successfully promote your product offerings; second, emphasize the portions of the chain which command the highest perceived value and; third, upgrade your delivery of the lower value products. *Convergence* requires gaining access to the other aspects of the bundled product. This usually involves mergers and acquisitions. It is wise to jump into mergers and acquisition activity early, when the choice of business combinations is best.

Bundling products together also increases efficiency due to economies of scope. That is, the cost of performing multiple business functions simultaneously should prove to be more efficient than performing each business function independently, and therefore drive down overall costs.

Applying the strategy of convergence, the CEO convinces the board of Global Bank to embark on a series of financial service acquisitions, which in effect creates a midsize, full-service financial company. To turn this strategy into concrete action, the CEO needs to charter several projects. For each one of these projects, there are key stakeholders, each with a unique viewpoint.

One of the key initiatives involves strengthening the bank's online presence. The online channel is an effective means of adding new services at relatively low cost. With many customers using online checking and savings today, it will be easy to move them to other value-added services if the bank can make the online services work better together. A key new service is the addition of an online bill payment feature. Let's take a closer look at the stakeholders in this initiative.

Stakeholder Viewpoints

There are five key stakeholders for the online bill payment initiative: the Board of Directors, the Chief Executive Officer (CEO), the General Manager of Banking Services, the Director of Electronic Bill Presentment and Payment (EBPP), and the Supervisor of EBPP.

Board of Directors Viewpoint

There are five members of the Board of Directors for Global Bank. One member is an experienced executive within the financial services industry and the others come from other industries. Members of the board are elected by shareholders to oversee management of the company. In this capacity, the board meets every six weeks with Global Bank's executive team to review operations and make critical decisions that affect the future direction of the firm.

The board is primarily concerned with the overall assets within the bank, and how these assets are used to create wealth. They want to understand what drives the return on capital invested and what the investment risks are.

The board is very interested in understanding how current and potential customers benefit by doing business with Global Bank. They know that satisfied customers are a key ingredient for any sustainable enterprise. For clarity and operational effectiveness, Global Bank's value to customers is clearly stated in a series of value propositions, one of which is for online services.

Value Proposition for Online Services

Global Bank's value proposition for online services is to provide an integrated, online financial portal for affluent clients that will enable them to view all of their financial assets at once. From this integrated view, clients will be able to seamlessly execute all of their financial transactions including those associated with savings and checking accounts, loans, stock trading, domestic and international bill payment and funds transfer. Clients will use this portal to save their most precious commodity: time. Through efficient operations, the bank will be able to offer this capability to clients without irritating service fees for each transaction.

In addition to serving affluent clients, the bank will also serve mass market customers with simplified services such as checking, savings, and mortgage origination. Customers will benefit from the intuitive user experience and integration with home mortgage loans and credit cards.

Providing this integrated service to customers will allow the bank to provide a higher rate of return on assets than other banks. Focusing on high-net-worth individuals means that the bank can manage more assets with fewer transactions. Fewer transactions result in lower total operations cost. Providing an integrated portal to customers enables effective cross selling from low margin service offerings (such as savings accounts) to high margin service offerings (such as loan and portfolio management services).

A compelling online user experience will drive adoption and attract new customers, including high-net-worth individuals and lower income, mass market accounts. Although the mass market accounts are less profitable, they will more than cover costs; the higher margins, however, will come from the wealthy individual segment. After the user experience is developed for high-end customers, it will be easy to offer a reduced-service version for the mass market.

Capital Expenditure

Delivering on this value proposition requires significant capital investment in new capabilities. In the past, technology investments have represented a high percentage of the bank's capital expenses. The Board also considers technology investments to be somewhat risky, due to the difficulty in predicting cost and schedule for both custom software development and system integration projects.

The Board wants better visibility into these projects at a high level. Recently, the Chief Technical Officer (CTO) briefed the board on a major project and visually presented a set of decision points related to the proposed technical architecture. The decisions points he presented (shown later in this chapter in Figure 16) reflected a set of choices containing *proven* design elements assembled together in a cohesive set. These elements were considered proven because they were harvested from other software engineering projects and had withstood scrutiny from the software design community. Creating a design based on these elements would mitigate some of the project's risk, making it more predictable. Of course, he explained, just using these design elements (patterns) was no guarantee of success—the real success would depend on the skill and experience of the team and how they implemented the actual system.

As the CTO presented, he talked through some of the design elements such as gateways to credit bureaus and message brokers. Although the board was not particularly technical, they got a sense of how the capabilities they were investing in were realized with technology at a high level. This understanding, and the vocabulary that went with it, allowed them to ask clarifying questions about the approach without getting bogged down with lower-level details. It also helped them to see the connection between the firm's value propositions and technical investments, and they expected this alignment to occur at various levels within the organization. The primary person they held accountable for driving this alignment throughout the organization is the CEO.

Chief Executive Officer

The CEO perspective focuses on defining the strategy and formulating a strategic portfolio of initiatives to take advantage of, or defend against, the opportunities and threats in the marketplace. The CEO of Global Bank defines a strategy and a set of initiatives that reflects his firm's approach in the financial services sector—a sector that is currently experiencing significant growth.

Evaluating the Current Situation

Driven by the explosive growth in home refinancing activity and the improved margins of full-service financial institutions, the banking industry is one of the few bright spots in this slow-growth economy. The CEO of Global Bank, however, has been frustrated by his company's lackluster profit margins and anemic growth in revenues. If the bank doesn't correct these trends quickly, its shareholders may miss out on the impressive returns of the rest of the industry.

Global Bank has been suffering from the growth in *customer churn*, which is defined as the loss of old customers and the acquisition of new customers where the net change in number of customers is close to zero. Customer churn has raised the bank's customer acquisition cost by 3 percent, which is a substantial increase. The loss in customers is believed to be caused by the lack of awareness and the inconvenient access to the firm's full suite of services offerings. Especially troubling is the loss of high-net-worth individuals. Many studies show that this particular market segment is the most likely to use fully integrated financial services; this segment also creates, on average, a 6 percent higher rate of profitability than other market segments.

Figure 7.1 correlates the bank's current portfolio allocation against average growth and profitability rates for the industry.

"As-Is" Portfolio vs Industry

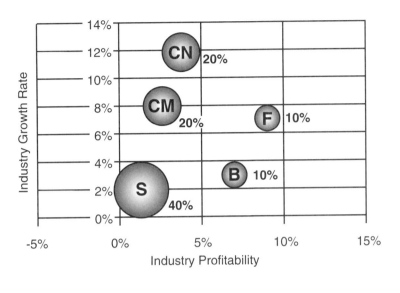

Figure 7.1
Initial allocation of Global Bank portfolio, according to service type

The bubbles in Figure 7.1 represent the share of the bank's portfolio. Current portfolio allocation shows that more than two-thirds of the bank's portfolio is invested into savings, the lowest-growth and lowest-profit of all service offerings based on current industry average growth and returns. Only 20 percent of the bank's portfolio is allocated to consumer lending, which is a high growth/high profit category. Table 7.1 shows the specific numbers associated with Figure 7.1.

Table 7.1: Global Bank Portfolio Compared to Average Profitability and Growth Rates for the Industry Segment

Services	Average profitability for the industry segment	Average growth rate for the industry	Share of Global Bank portfolio
Savings	1%	2%	40%
Commercial lending	3%	8%	20%
Consumer lending	4%	12%	20%
Brokerage	7%	3%	10%
Financial planning	9%	7%	10%

Formulating a Strategy

The CEO wants to change the bank's portfolio mix so that a higher percentage of the portfolio is in high growth and high profit categories. Specifically, the CEO believes that the bank could increase deposits, reduce churn, and dramatically increase loan origination by offering an integrated savings, checking, and mortgage solution.

There are four critical success factors for this initiative:

- Make the bank's complete suite of services easily accessible, both online and offline.
- Make the online services work better together to provide a richer, more integrated experience between offerings.
- Build awareness of the suite of services, both online and offline.
- Attract and retain high-net-worth individuals.

The CEO believes that the first two measures could reduce churn costs by 2 percent and increase loan origination to 40 percent of their business portfolio. The multiple entry points and the exposure of the bank's services to a wider array of customers will help drive the growth in these segments of the portfolio. Based on estimated customer value and acquisition costs, he projects that focusing on attracting and retaining high-net-worth individuals will affect profit margins by as much as 10 percent.

The overall strategy will be to bundle higher-profit services such as consumer lending (also known as mortgage) together with the basics (savings) to change the portfolio mix to things that are more profitable industry wide. By doing so, the CEO believes that he can increase customer loyalty and increase the cost the customer would incur to switch banks (switching costs). He also believes this integrated approach has the potential to increase the very profitable financial planning offering to 20 percent of the bank's portfolio. Figure 7.2 shows the CEO's projected portfolio allocation after the successful execution of these key initiatives.

"To Be" Portfolio vs Industry

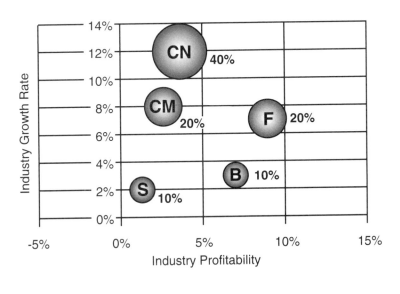

Figure 7.2
Projected allocation of Global Bank portfolio, after convergence

Table 7.2 compares Global Bank's projected portfolio to average industry segment growth rates and profitability after the successful execution of the consolidation initiative.

Table 7.2: Global Bank Projected Portfolio Compared to Average Profitability and Growth Rates for the Industry Segment

Services	Average profitability for the industry segment	Average growth rate for the industry	Share of Global Bank portfolio
Savings	1%	2%	10%
Commercial lending	3%	8%	20%
Consumer lending	4%	12%	40%
Brokerage	7%	3%	10%
Financial planning	9%	7%	20%

The CEO realizes that the firm needs to bundle together services that may never have been previously integrated. Given his convergence strategy, he also knows that the firm must aggressively and quickly acquire new capabilities. He expects to pursue partnering agreements, mergers, and acquisitions as soon as possible, but knows from past experience how challenging the integration issues could be. He is also aware of high-level service-oriented-architecture concepts that he's learned from his CTO and wonders if they might be applicable here. If so, they may have an impact on the execution of his strategy.

To move forward with this initiative, the CEO calls a two-day working session with bank executives who report directly to him. The session includes both general and administrative executive leadership. The CEO knows that this initiative requires significant capital investment and that the organization must focus on delivering as much customer value as possible for each dollar invested. To start, he will work with the General Manager of Banking to shape a more detailed customer value proposition.

General Manager of Banking

During the working session, the CEO briefs the service-line general managers, including the General Manager (GM) of Banking about his plan for dealing with convergence. To act on this plan, two teams are formed: banking services and financial planning services. The teams are organized as follows:

- **Banking services**. The GM of Banking will lead a team to create a service bundle that will integrate checking, savings, bill payment, and mortgage loan origination.
- **Financial planning services**. The GM of Financial Planning Services will lead a team to focus on creating a service bundle that will integrate financial planning, non-mortgage lending, investing, and insurance.

Other executives, including the CTO, and the Chief Financial Officer (CFO), are expected to support and report into each team. Each team is expected to find areas of synergy between service lines to enable cross-selling convenience and compatibility. The teams must also identify and support all real competitive differentiators.

The rest of the Global Bank scenario described here and earlier in Chapter 2, "Using Patterns to Design the Baseline Architecture," focuses on the effort to create the banking services bundle.

Banking Services Bundle

The GM for Banking Services is excited about the prospect of offering a more robust set of services to the general public. She believes the direct impact of the integrated service bundle will be a doubling of the consumer loan portfolio.

Zeroing in on the changes she wants to affect, the GM creates two visual models to communicate with her team. Figure 7.3 shows the current "as-is" situation with 40 percent of the firm's service offerings in savings, which is a low growth and low profit category.

"As-Is" Portfolio vs Industry

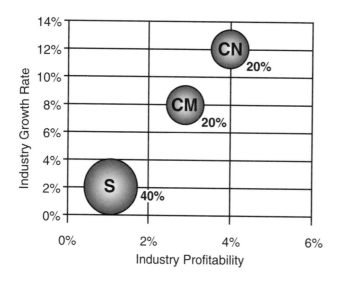

S Savings

CM Commercial Lending

CN Consumer Lending

Figure 7.3
Current portfolio allocation of services in the banking services bundle

Figure 7.4 shows the desired "to-be" situation after changes have been implemented. Notice that the portfolio has shifted, moving the majority of the service offerings to high growth and high profit categories.

"To Be" Portfolio vs Industry

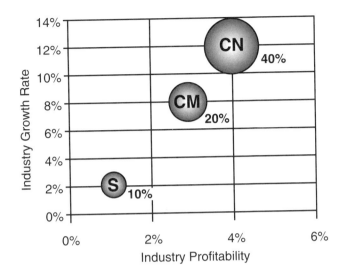

S   Savings

CM   Commercial Lending

CN   Consumer Lending

Figure 7.4
Projected portfolio allocation of services in the banking services bundle, after changes

The GM believes that the critical success factor to attracting and retaining new customers rests chiefly on the success of their bill payment service. Studies show that as customers successfully use online bill payment (which is the next logical service after online savings and checking services) they are much more likely to explore and use additional value-added services. From there, the GM believes that customers will naturally turn to Global Bank for loans.

The GM knows she must collaborate with two key members of the team. First, she must work with the CTO to smoothly integrate the value-added services with online bill payment. Next, she knows the online bill payment feature would require high level involvement of the electronic bill presentment and payment department. She would need to work closely with the director of that department.

Director of Electronic Bill Presentment and Payment

The Director of Electronic Bill Presentment and Payment (EBPP) is very excited about the prospect of the bank investing strongly in his area. Currently, only 3 percent of the bank's customers use online banking services. He believes that with a similar look and feel to the checking and savings offering, the online bill payment service will help increase the use of the online banking services to over 20 percent of the bank's customers.

To reach this 20 percent usage target, the director has identified the following requirements that are critical to the success of the system:

- **Similar user experience to the current checking and savings site**. More specifically, the number of key strokes required to complete a bill payment transaction must be less than or equal to the number required to complete a checking and savings transaction.

- **The time required to add a new payee to the system must be minimized**. The time needed to add payees (known as billers) to the system was expected to be a key barrier to adoption. Making this experience quick and painless would make the service very compelling for customers to use.

- **Bill payment must be prominent on the Global Bank portal page**. The bill payment service must be in an inviting and logical location on the portal main page (in relation to the checking and savings page).

To achieve these requirements, he would have to collaborate closely with the architects, designers, and analysts from the CTO's team. He would also have to work closely with the supervisor of electronic bill presentment and payment operations. Behind the user interface, it is the supervisor who has detailed knowledge of the processes and systems needed to make this system operational.

Electronic Bill Presentment and Payment Supervisor

The Supervisor of Electronic Bill Presentment and Payment Operations has just learned of the new strategic focus on EBPP as a key capability in the overall bank strategy and he is a bit concerned. The EBPP capability must be enhanced in several ways to meet the bank's growth objectives.

The focus of the Director of EBPP is primarily on the user experience and how the presentation and navigation of the EBPP functions should be similar to the existing checking and savings functionality. The main underlying issue for EBPP operations, however, is how to integrate the existing systems to provide a seamless experience without tightly coupling all of the systems together. In the past, the Supervisor of EBPP has been frustrated by systems that could not be replaced or changed because of tight interdependencies between systems. He wants to avoid that frustration in the future.

To meet its objective, the EBPP implementation must also streamline the addition of new billers and simplify the integration and processing for existing billers. This simplification will help control the operations costs of the EBPP system. One of the supervisor's goals is to automate the entire EBPP process, including the subscription management of EBPP users. The current manual subscription management process can take as long as 30 days to enroll a new EBPP participant. The manager considers this 30-day process to be a loss in revenue, as well as a barrier to adoption.

From Business Scenario to Technical Solution

The technical team at Global Bank now has enough business context to start their technical planning sessions. Now they need a way to organize their thinking about the overall enterprise. Although there are many valid models that they could use, the team started with an enterprise architecture stack as shown in Figure 7.5.

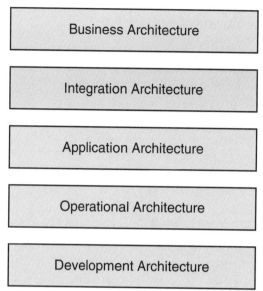

Figure 7.5
Enterprise architecture stack used by the Global Bank technical team

At the top of the stack is the business architecture, which captures the resources, processes, goals, and rules that the enterprise uses to generate revenue and profit. Underneath the business architecture are several levels of technical architecture that together enable the enterprise to realize its business architecture.

After business architecture, the next level on the stack is the integration architecture. This architecture describes an integrated portfolio of applications that support the business architecture. Underneath the integration architecture is the application architecture. For each application described in the integration architecture, there is a detailed description of the application in the application architecture. This includes (but is not limited to) platform infrastructure components such as application servers, Web servers, and databases.

After an instance of an application is built, it must be deployed into production, operated, and maintained. These concerns are described in the operational architecture. Finally, the development architecture describes how teams build instances of applications and integrations. This development level includes (but is not limited to) developer and lifecycle tools, build environments, and processes.

As teams make decisions within each level of architecture, they should verify whether they directly support the enterprise's value proposition. To make very detailed decisions about architecture, it is helpful to have a more granular perspective than architectural levels provide—such as a perspective based on viewpoints.

Viewpoints Within the Enterprise Architecture

Although the enterprise architecture stack in Figure 5 is useful to organize and classify initial architectural concerns, the team needed a more granular classification scheme. The team realized that the artifacts they produced to describe their systems would differ according to discrete viewpoints. A viewpoint is really just a lens into the enterprise, and from the perspective of these lenses, many snapshots, or pictures might be taken. They decided to organize these viewpoints from the perspective of various roles within the enterprise. Figure 7.6 shows three layers of the resulting model, which added some of the roles identified for the business, integration, and application architecture levels.

Business Architecture	
	Chief Executive Officer
	General Manager
	Process Owner
	Process Worker

Integration Architecture	
	Enterprise Architect
	Designer
	Developer

Application Architecture	
	Enterprise Architect
	Architect
	Designer
	Developer

Figure 7.6
Levels and viewpoints within the architecture stack

Figure 7.6 concentrates on the three layers of the architecture stack that are the focus of this guide. The business architecture includes the views of key stakeholders as well those involved with business processes. The focus on process is important, because processes are key interfaces between people and systems. Processes also enable the enterprise to complete the work from which it derives revenue.

In the areas of application and integration, viewpoints are organized according to traditional information technology roles. These viewpoints reflect the different concerns of various roles. For example, as a team builds an application an architect's concerns will be different from a developer's concerns.

Now that the team had a model with which to organize their approach, they built more detailed visual models that captured their stakeholder concerns.

Business Architecture Views

To model the business architecture views, they used the Erikkson/Penker Business Extensions to the Unified Modeling Language (UML) [Erikkson2000]. These extensions to the UML provide stereotypes for business concepts such as processes, events, resources (including people), goals, and rules.

To draw these models, they used the Microsoft Office Visio® Professional 2003 drawing and diagramming software as their tool of choice. They used a template created by Pavel Hruby (available at *http://www.phruby.com/stencildownload.html*) that contains more of the UML stereotypes than the standard Visio templates. Using these tools, the team created a series of views of enterprise processes.

CEO's View

The first model they created was the highest-level enterprise view, which reflected the CEO's viewpoint. Figure 7.7 shows this CEO view of the business architecture.

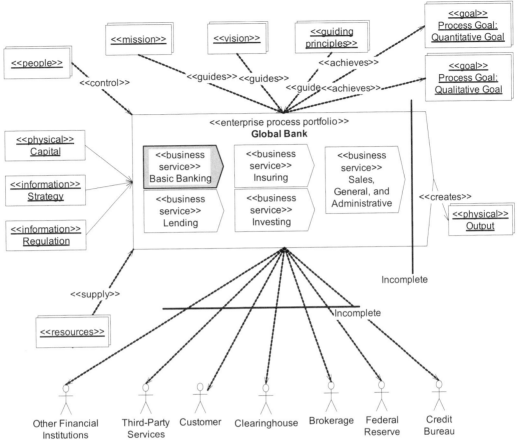

Figure 7.7
CEO's view of the high-level enterprise processes

In Figure 7.7, resources on the left are inputs into the bank. The elements on the top guide and constrain the activities of the bank, while the center contains groups of processes needed to run the bank. Beneath the Global Bank box are the entities with which the bank collaborates. The bank's output is modeled on the right.

Notice the core process groups within the bank include basic banking, insuring, lending, investing, and sales, general, and administrative (SGA). The processes of interest to the online bank initiative are in the basic banking group, headed by the General Manager of Banking. Let's now look into this group (shown in gray) in more detail.

General Manager's View

For the basic banking group of processes, the team created a model that describes the bank from the GM of Banking's view, as shown in Figure 7.8.

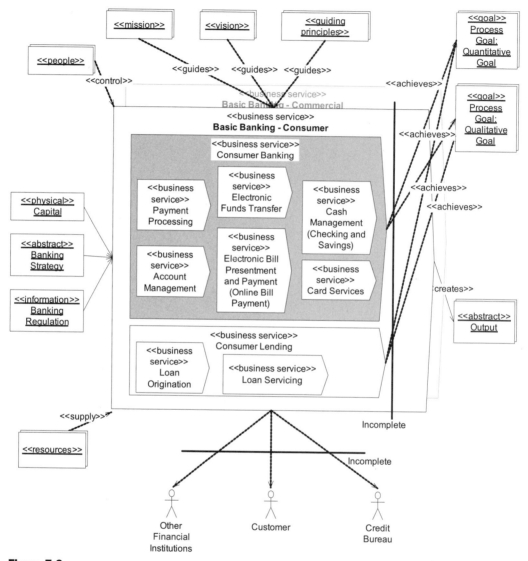

Figure 7.8

General Manager of Banking's high-level view of processes

Similar to the CEO's view, this view shows resource inputs on the left, guidelines and constraints on the top, outputs on the right, and entities (collaborators) on the bottom. Notice that basic banking includes both consumer (foreground) and commercial (background). Within consumer, there are processes related to consumer banking and consumer lending. Consumer Banking is highlighted in Figure 8 because the online application is oriented towards consumers. Figure 7.9 narrows the focus further to EBPP.

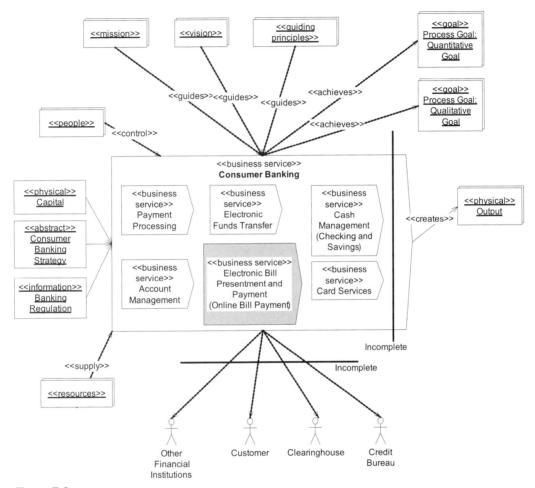

Figure 7.9
General Manager's view of Consumer Banking

Similar to the basic banking model, this view shows resource inputs on the left, guidelines and constraints on the top, outputs on the right, and entities (collaborators) on the bottom. Notice that there are six groups of processes within consumer banking: payment processing, account management, electronic funds transfer, electronic bill presentment and payment, cash management and card services. Because the online application involves electronic bill presentment and payment (shown in gray), this group of processes requires a closer examination. The individual responsible for this area is the Director of Electronic Bill Presentment and Payment.

Process Owner's View

The technical team is very interested in the business processes within the enterprise because they are key inputs into technical design. The team uses the role of process owner to indicate the individual directly responsible for the successful execution of a specific process within any given enterprise. With respect to electronic bill presentment and payment (EBPP) within Global Bank, this individual is the Director of Electronic Bill Presentment and Payment. The model representing this view is shown in Figure 7.10.

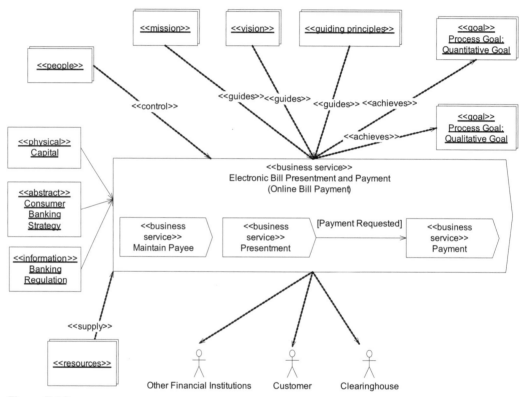

Figure 7.10
Director of EBPP's view of high-level processes

The Director of EBPP's view further refines the higher level process diagrams showing the subprocesses that the Director of Electronic Bill Presentment and Payment (EBPP) is responsible for. Like previous diagrams, this view shows resource inputs on the left, guidelines and constraints on the top, outputs on the right, and entities (collaborators) on the bottom.

This view provides a way to tie the specific unit's mission, vision, guiding principles, resources, and goals to the specific processes in the department. This linkage allows both the business owner and the technical architects to evaluate specific cost-benefit tradeoffs for the design and implementation based on the business value and goals while maintaining traceability to the organizational guidelines and goals.

This view is helpful because it breaks down processes to granular subprocesses, and approaches the level needed for detailed technical analysis. However, subprocesses are not granular enough. The team needs to identify the level at which a person or system (actor) interacts directly with another system. This actor/system boundary is the level which use cases describe, and the person who interacts directly with the system to perform part or all of a business process is called a *process worker*. One important process worker in Global Bank is the EBPP Supervisor.

Process Worker's View

The EBPP Supervisor works with his team to review the Director of EBPP's view (shown in Figure 7.10) and identify all of the related use cases as shown in Figure 7.11. For each use case, a description is created that includes preconditions, post-conditions and the steps involved in the use case. Steps are included for normal and exception scenarios.

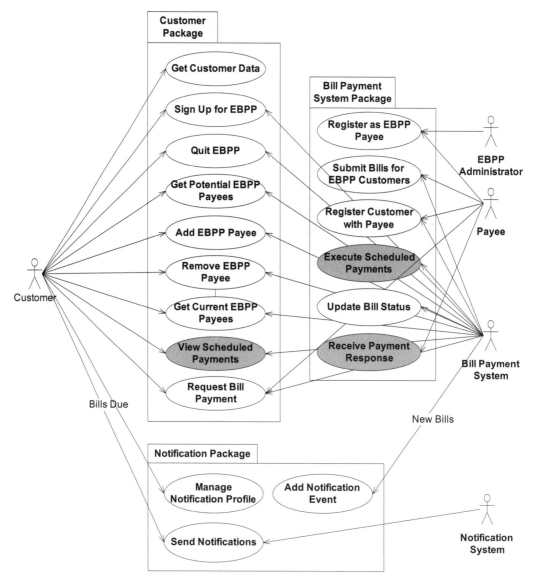

Figure 7.11
Significant EBPP use cases

The use cases outlined in gray are key parts of the online bill payment application. To further define these use cases, the team creates activity diagrams that show the details needed to realize the use case, such as conditional branching, transitions, forks, and joins.

Integration Architecture Views

Although architects were involved in understanding and modeling the previous views, more analysis is needed before the team can design a technical solution that meets the needs of the bank. Before the team spends time designing a technical solution, they want to make sure that the business processes that they want to automate will add as much value as possible to the enterprise. To determine this value, the architects work with business analysts to examine the business processes in more detail.

Process Value Analysis

Before rushing into defining requirements for the technical solution, the team wants to make sure that the processes they are automating are aligned with the enterprise's overall value proposition. To do so, they analyze each significant use case and business process according to the value it adds to the enterprise. To quantify value, they estimate the number of full-time employees and the cycle time needed for each step of the most important processes. They categorize each step as a value-add for the customer, a value-add for the business, or not a value-add.

The team tunes their processes to be as efficient as possible given the enterprise's value proposition. Working with the executive team where necessary, they are able to improve the firm's overall business process design and thereby avoid automating inefficient processes with technology. Also, during this analysis process they identify use cases that greatly enable the customer value proposition yet are inexpensive to implement. These items become high priority work items in early iterations. After they create a set of prioritized and well-designed processes expressed as use cases, they consider how to realize these use cases. A key step in the realization of these use cases is to identify the appropriate logical services.

Logical Services

The team reviews the EBPP process groups and identifies use cases for each process group. They step through each use case and design a collaboration of services that allows them to realize each use case. As they see multiple use cases using a particular service, they factor the service interface to make it as flat and stable as possible. They know that once they create these published interfaces, they will be much more difficult to change in the future. Therefore, time spent factoring these interfaces now will pay off with fewer versioning headaches later and allow them to support more use cases with each service. To communicate these relationships, they create the assembly line drawing in Figure 7.12.

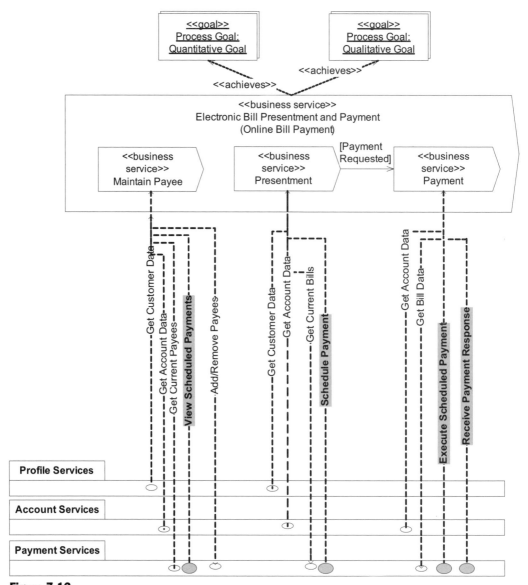

Figure 7.12

Assembly line drawing showing a candidate set of logical services for Global Bank

At the top of the assembly line diagram are the groups of processes within EBPP and their associated use cases. On the left side of the diagram are candidate logical services that will play a role in realizing the intersecting use cases. By identifying sets of use cases that must interact with a specific service, it is easier to design services that eliminate duplication and are more extensible.

With a set of prioritized use cases and an initial set of logical services needed to realize those use cases, the team then spends time deciding how to allocate these logical services to physical servers.

Technical Architecture

To allocate logical services to physical servers, the team starts by reviewing the enterprise's existing technical architecture. They want to use these existing investments as much as possible, and extend them to take advantage of commercial infrastructure platform components such as Web servers, databases, and integration servers.

Taking all of these factors and constraints into consideration, they arrive at a technical architecture as shown in Figure 7.13.

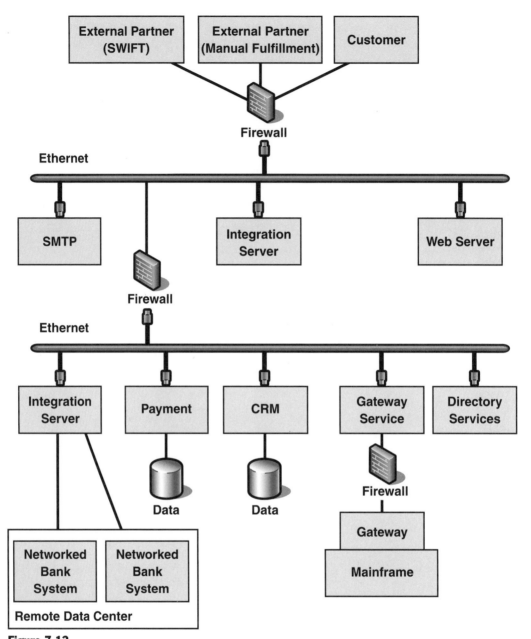

Figure 7.13

Global Bank's initial technical architecture

Given the system use cases and a first cut technical architecture, the team is able to identify some areas that represent high technical risks for the project. They want to make sure and tackle these areas first so they can "retire" these risks early in the project life cycle. To exercise these areas, they identify a set of architecturally significant use cases.

Architecturally Significant Use Cases

As described in Chapter 2, "Using Patterns to Design the Baseline Architecture," the architecturally significant use cases for Global Bank include the following:

- Schedule Payments
- View Scheduled Payments
- Execute Scheduled Payment
- Receive Payment Response
- Add Payee

For each one of these use cases, the team identifies how a set of server processes and nodes collaborate to realize each use case. They capture this high-level interaction with collaboration diagrams. In addition to collaboration diagrams, the team also creates a "port and wire" style model that shows service encapsulation and communication through ports, as shown in Chapter 2.

With high-level collaborations defined for server processes and nodes, the team needs to refine these collaborations down to more detailed design elements.

Integration Patterns

At this point, the team has a set of use cases that describe how users will interact with the system and how the system will respond. These use cases are prioritized so they represent the riskiest part of the technical implementation. Now the team has to consider various design alternatives and make a series of technical decisions and tradeoffs to design an integration architecture.

As the team considers the technical challenges and problems they must solve during the design process, their discussion naturally leads to patterns. Patterns contain concise, reusable elements of design knowledge and are organized as problem-solution pairs. The team uses patterns because they know reusable design elements can mitigate risk and make a project more predictable.

To think about their design alternatives for a given challenge, the team uses the visual model shown in Figure 7.14. This model shows a related set of patterns in the area of integration. These patterns are represented in the model as circles; the lines between circles indicate associations between the patterns.

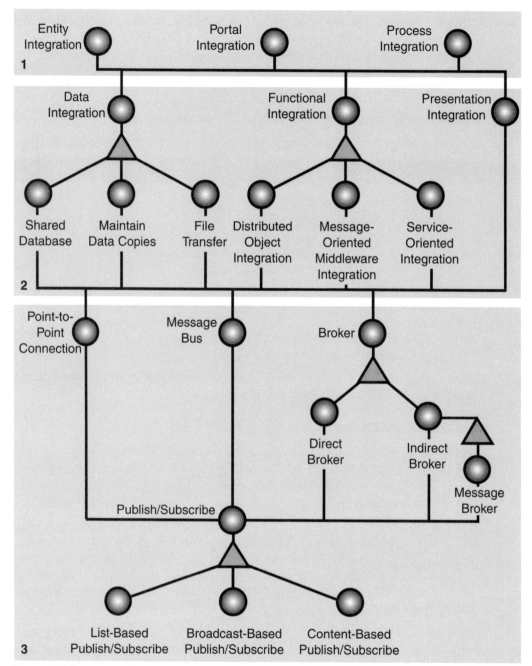

Figure 7.14
Integration patterns and their relationships

Row one (1) in the model shows patterns that represent three types of integrating layers: *Entity Aggregation*, *Portal Integration*, and *Process Integration* (for more information, see Chapter 3, "Integrating Layer"). As in many other areas of computer science, adding another level of indirection solves many problems in the integration space. These patterns describe specific integration problems and how the introduction of very specific new layers would solve these kinds of problems.

For each of these integrating layers to work, they must make one or more individual connections to target systems. Row two (2) in the model shows three logical levels at which these system connections could be made: data, functional (business logic), and presentation; each logical connection type represents a pattern. For *Data Integration* and *Functional Integration*, there are several pattern variations that further refine each pattern. These refinement relationships are shown as triangles.

Integrating at the logical data level, for example, has three variations: *Shared Database*, *Maintain Data Copies*, and *File Transfer*. Integrating at the functional (business logic) layer has three other distinct variations: *Distributed Object Integration, Message-Oriented-Middleware Integration* and *Service-Oriented Integration*. These patterns are discussed in more depth in Chapter 4, "System Connections."

As you decide about integrating layers and the various kinds of system connections you will need to make, you inherently must also determine a topology with which to connect these elements. Row three (3) in Figure 7.14 shows patterns (and their variations) that represent three different integration topologies: *Point-To-Point Connection*, *Broker*, and *Message Bus*. Any time two or more systems are connected, a topology decision must be made. The result may be a single topology or a combination of topologies depending upon requirements.

After systems are connected using a particular topology, it is possible to use a publish/subscribe mechanism to synchronize systems. The *Publish/Subscribe* pattern is shown at the bottom of Figure 7.14, along with three patterns that refine the basic *Publish/Subscribe* pattern: *List-Based Publish/Subscribe, Broadcast-Based Publish/Subscribe, and Content-Based Publish/Subscribe*. Chapter 5, "Integration Topologies," discusses these patterns in detail.

Pattern Types

Until now, this chapter has discussed patterns conversationally as is often done during typical whiteboard design sessions. To be a bit more precise about how the team uses patterns to explain their application, it is necessary to make a distinction between pattern types and pattern instances.

In object-oriented programming, the common example of type and instance is class and object. That is, a class defines a type of abstraction and an object is an instance of that abstraction. Because design patterns have been associated traditionally with objects, the distinction has not been important for patterns. For example, the *Singleton* [Gamma95] pattern contains advice that tells you how to create a singleton object.

In the integration space, patterns often provide advice that is much broader than classes and objects. To apply these patterns, it is helpful to clarify when you are talking about types and when you are talking about instances. Unlike typical design patterns, these pattern instances occur at several levels of abstraction, including objects, processes, and subsystems. Think of the pattern narrative as providing information about a *type* of compositional design element. When you choose to include some finite number of these compositional design elements in your specific design, think of these as *instances*.

Note: Because patterns contain a wide variety of design knowledge, not all patterns are about compositional elements of design. Thus the type/instance distinction will not apply to all patterns. Other authors have referred to similar categories of patterns as constructional design patterns [Yacoub04]. All patterns contained in this guide, however, are compositional elements of design.

Taken together, Figure 7.14 shows the patterns and their relationships as pattern *types* used in the integration space. These are types of patterns because they contain advice about a particular kind of integration problem. For this kind of problem, the patterns contain generative advice that tells you what to do, along with the pros and cons associated with following that advice.

For example, as the Global Bank team discusses their particular design problems, they know they need a portal integration layer that connects with multiple back-end systems. For each target system, they need an individual system connection. As they consider which type of connection they will use, they use the model in Figure 7.14 to narrow their choices down to three possibilities for where to make the connection: at the logical data layer, at the functional layer, or at the presentation layer. The team prefers to integrate directly to the functional layer whenever possible to present the most up-to-date information as directly as possible.

As they consider the types of *Functional Integration* they might use, they evaluate as alternatives *Distributed Object Integration*, proprietary *Message-Oriented Middleware Integration*, and *Service-Oriented Integration*. Because interoperability between platforms is important to them, they prefer to use *Service-Oriented Integration* whenever practical.

After deciding on the type of system connection to use for each system, they realize that they need a topology with which to connect these elements. A set of *Point-to-Point Connections* is the simplest to consider initially, but upon further reflection they realize they will have to connect with an unreliably connected data center and external trading partners. These different locations will use different systems and different data formats.

They could implement a *Message Bus*, but that would require defining a canonical data model and command messages between trading partners and acquired banks. This seems an unwieldy alternative when compared to a *Message Broker* approach.

In the end, they decide on a *Message Broker* topology and a *Publish/Subscribe* mechanism. The specific *Publish/Subscribe* mechanism they use is *Content-Based Publish/Subscribe*. All of these choices are shown in Figure 7.15.

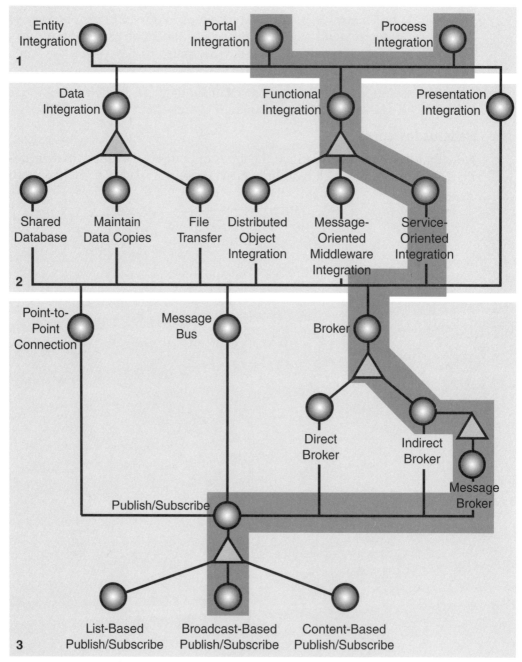

Figure 7.15
Types of patterns chosen by the Global Bank team

During the design sessions, the team uses the model in Figure 7.15 to help them think through the range of potential design alternatives that might apply to a particular design challenge that they are experiencing at the time. However, during the process of designing the architecture for Global Bank, they need more than design options. They need to make a set of specific design decisions that reflect *instances* of design elements.

Patterns Instances

Now that the team has identified the types of patterns that apply to their design, they need to decide which (and how many) specific *instances* of these patterns they will actually use. For example, the team decides that the *Message Broker* pattern (from Chapter 5) is a good choice for Global Bank because it solves the problems involved in integrating applications that do not have a common interface. The *Message Broker* pattern narrative describes how to solve this particular *type* of problem, but it does not specify if or where to place it in a specific design. These kinds of decisions are the responsibility of the Global Bank architecture team.

After careful consideration, the team decides to use two *instances* of *Message Broker* in their design; both instances are implemented with BizTalk Server 2004. One *Message Broker* instance integrates applications between their local and remote data centers for loan applications. The other *Message Broker* instance integrates applications between their payment system and external payment gateways.

These two *Message Broker* instances are shown in Figure 7.16 along with all of the other instances of design elements that the team identifies for their integration architecture. This pattern-based design model shows the architecture at a higher level of abstraction than conventional models. With each design element representing a named pattern, this model provides a rich set of abstractions and a vocabulary with which the team can reason about their system. It also allows them to have a high-level design dialog with other project stakeholders, without debating extraneous technical detail. Should these other stakeholders not understand a particular element, the team can point them to pattern catalogs that define these terms in more detail.

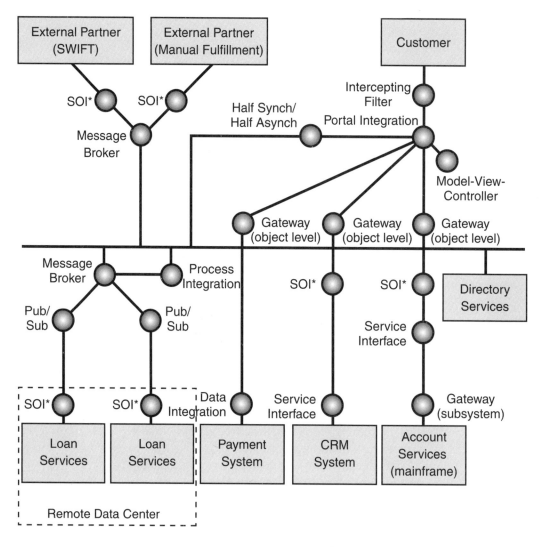

SOI* = Service-Oriented Integration

Figure 7.16

Pattern-based design model of the Global Bank bill payment system

With an initial set of high-level design decisions made, the team then needs to bind these decisions to specific implementation platforms. Although this binding may seem to be a top-down approach, it is actually an iterative process that requires full team involvement. For key design elements, platform infrastructure components are evaluated in terms of how well specific patterns can be implemented. Although this mapping from high-level design to technology often is quite straightforward, it is often not. Difficult cases require the team to either change their design to optimize a particular platform or choose an alternative platform that better fits their architecture. When the team is finished, they produce the diagram shown in Figure 7.17.

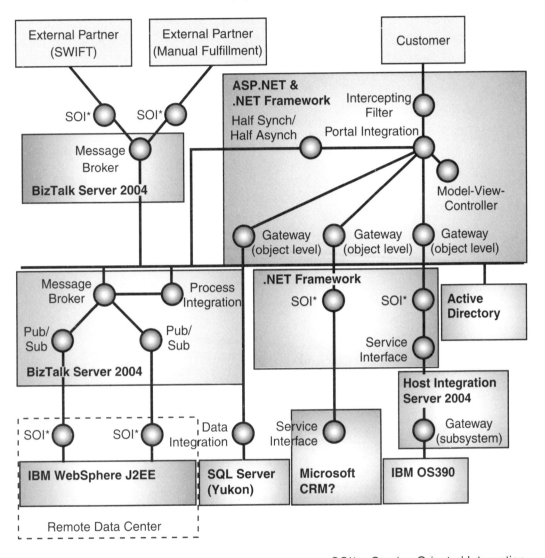

SOI* = Service-Oriented Integration

Figure 7.17
Mapping the patterns to implementation technologies

Figure 7.17 shows Global Bank's integration architecture to be composed of numerous pattern-based design elements implemented on the Microsoft platform. To trace the implementation of these elements down to running bits, refer to the appropriate implementation pattern in previous chapters. For example, to understand how to implement the gateway to the mainframe, refer to *Implementing Gateway with Host Integration Server 2004* in Chapter 5, "Integration Topologies." This pattern includes the details of connecting Global Bank's .NET Framework–based portal application with their existing COBOL-based CICS transactions.

Going Forward

The last few pages of this chapter focused on distinctions between pattern types and instances that may not be important for many design conversations. In conversations that require a precise distinction, it is helpful to clarify how you are using patterns. In these cases, using a pattern type model to enumerate design options and a pattern instance model to articulate specific design elements can be a very effective communication tool. Even if you are not interested in types and instances, however, patterns are a useful vehicle for communication among different levels of the enterprise.

This communication aspect of patterns is the main message of this chapter. The progression of pattern models discussed here will become increasingly important in the future as developers, architects, and business leaders increasingly use patterns to build technology that meets business requirements.

Appendix

List of Patterns and Pattlets

This appendix contains a table that lists patterns and *pattlets* that are referenced in this book. *Pattlets* are actual patterns that this book refers to; however, the book does not discuss them in detail. The table also provides a reference to the original work that identified the pattern or pattlet, if applicable.

Table A.1: List of Patterns and Pattlets

Pattern or pattlet	Problem	Solution	Source
Entity Aggregation	How can enterprise data that is redundantly distributed across multiple repositories be effectively maintained by applications?	Introduce an *Entity Aggregation* layer that provides a logical representation of the entities at an enterprise level with physical connections that support the access and that update to their respective instances in back-end repositories.	
Process Integration	How do you coordinate the execution of a long-running business function that spans multiple disparate applications?	Define a business process model that describes the individual steps that make up the complex business function. Create a separate process manager component that can interpret multiple concurrent instances of this model and that can interact with the existing applications to perform the individual steps of the process.	

(continued)

Pattern or pattlet	Problem	Solution	Source
Portal Integration	How can users efficiently perform tasks that require access to information that resides in multiple disparate systems?	Create a portal application that displays the information that is retrieved from multiple applications in a unified user interface. The user can then perform the required tasks based on the information that appears in this portal.	
Data Integration	How do you integrate information systems that were not designed to work together?	Integrate applications at the logical data layer. Use a *Shared Database*, a *File Transfer*, or a *Maintain Data Copies* implementation.	
Shared Database (a kind of data integration)	How can multiple applications work together to exchange information?	Have multiple applications store their data in a single database. Define a schema that handles the needs of all the relevant applications.	*Shared Database* pattern [Hohpe04].
Maintain Data Copies (a kind of data integration)	How can multiple applications work together to exchange information?	Have multiple applications access multiple copies of the same data. Maintain state integrity between copies.	*Maintain Data Copies* is the root pattern for twelve patterns (the data movement cluster) that are presented in "Data Patterns" [Teale03].
File Transfer (a kind of data integration)	How can multiple applications work together to exchange information?	At regular intervals, make each application produce files that contain the information that the other applications must consume. After a file is created, do not maintain the file.	*File Transfer* pattern [Hohpe04].

Pattern or pattlet	Problem	Solution	Source
Functional Integration	How do you integrate information systems that were not designed to work together?	Integrate applications at the logical business layer. Use *Distributed Object Integration*, (proprietary) *Message-Oriented Middleware Integration*, or *Service-Oriented Integration*.	
Presentation Integration	How do you integrate information systems that were not designed to work together?	Access the application's functionality through the user interface by simulating a user's input and by reading data from the screen.	
Message Broker	How do you integrate applications without enforcing a common interface and also allow each application to initiate interactions with several other applications?	Extend the integration solution by using *Message Broker*. A message broker is a physical component that handles the communication between applications. Instead of communicating with each other, applications communicate only with the message broker. An application sends a message to the message broker to give the message broker the logical name of the receivers. The message broker looks up applications that are registered under the logical name and then passes the message to them.	
Distributed Object Integration (a kind of functional integration)	How do you integrate applications at the logical business layer?	Develop systems that have object interfaces that can be consumed remotely by other systems.	*Remote Procedure Invocation* [Hohpe04].

(continued)

Pattern or pattlet	Problem	Solution	Source
Message-Oriented Middleware Integration (a kind of functional integration)	How do you integrate applications at the logical business layer?	Use proprietary message-oriented middleware to send messages asynchronously.	*Messaging* [Hohpe04].
Service-Oriented Integration (a kind of functional integration)	How do you integrate applications at the logical business layer?	Use Web services to expose interfaces that can be consumed remotely by other systems.	
Point-to-Point Connection	How do you ensure that exactly one receiver receives a message?	Use *Point-to-Point Connection* to integrate two systems. The sending system must translate the message into a format that the receiving system understands.	When you use point-to-point connections, each system determines the address of all the other nodes that it communicates with.
Broker	How can you structure a distributed system so that application developers do not have to concern themselves with the details of remote communication?	Introduce a broker whose tasks are to locate services, to forward requests, and to return responses to clients. Services register themselves with the broker. Clients access services by making a service request through the broker.	[Buschmann96].
Direct Broker	How do you integrate applications without enforcing a common interface, allow each application to initiate interactions with several other applications, and reduce hot spots (performance problems that occur under high loads in specific areas)?	Extend the integration solution by using a direct broker component that handles the communication between applications. Initially, the application asks the broker to locate the other registered applications based on the logical names of those applications. From this point forward, all communication is made directly between applications.	

Pattern or pattlet	Problem	Solution	Source
Indirect Broker	How do you integrate applications without enforcing a common interface, but allow each application to initiate interactions with several others?	Extend the integration solution by using an indirect broker component that handles the communication between applications. Instead of communicating directly, applications communicate only with the message broker. An application sends a message to the broker. This message provides the logical name of the receivers. The broker then looks up applications that are registered under the logical name and passes the message to that application.	
Publish/Subscribe	How can an application in an integration architecture only send messages to the applications that are interested in receiving the messages without knowing the identities of the receivers?	Extend the communication infrastructure by creating topics or by dynamically inspecting message content. Enable listening applications to subscribe to specific messages. Create a mechanism that sends messages to all interested subscribers. There are three variations of the *Publish/Subscribe* pattern that you can use to create a mechanism that sends messages to all interested subscribers. The three variations are *List-Based Publish/ Subscribe*, *Broadcast-Based Publish/ Subscribe*, and *Content-Based Publish/Subscribe*.	

(continued)

Pattern or pattlet	Problem	Solution	Source
Message Bus	As an integration solution grows, how can you lower the cost of adding or removing applications?	Connect all applications through a logical component known as a message bus. A message bus specializes in transporting messages between applications. A message bus contains three key elements: a set of agreed-upon message schemas; a set of common command messages [Hohpe04], and a shared infrastructure for sending bus messages to recipients.	
Pipes and Filters	How do you implement a sequence of transformations so that you can combine and reuse them independently?	Implement the transformations by using a sequence of filter components, where each filter component receives an input message, applies a simple transformation, and sends the transformed message to the next component. Conduct the messages through *pipes* [McIlroy64] that connect filter outputs and inputs, and that buffer the communication between the filters.	
Gateway	How can you make the applications of an integration solution access an external system without introducing many-to-one coupling between the applications and the external system?	Add a *Gateway* component that abstracts the access to the external resource. The gateway presents a single interface to the integrated applications while hiding the external resource interface. In addition, the gateway encapsulates any protocol translation that may be necessary to communicate with the external resource.	

Bibliography

[Alexander79] Alexander, Christopher. *The Timeless Way of Building*. Oxford University Press, 1979.

[Alur01] Alur, Deepak; John Crupi, and Dan Malks. *Core J2EE Patterns: Best Practices and Design Strategies*. Prentice Hall, 2001.

[Baldoni03] Baldoni, R.; M. Contenti, and A. Virgillito. *"The Evolution of Publish/Subscribe Communication Systems." Future Directions of Distributed Computing*. Springer Verlag LNCS Vol. 2584, 2003.

[Bertrand00] Meyer, Bertrand. *Object-Oriented Software Construction*. 2nd ed. Prentice-Hall, 2000.

[Box04] Box, Don. "Code Name Indigo: A Guide to Developing and Running Connected Systems with Indigo." *MSDN Magazine*. January 2004. Available from the MSDN Windows Code-Named "Longhorn" Developer's Center at: *http://msdn.microsoft.com/longhorn/understanding/pillars/indigo/default.aspx?pull=/msdnmag/issues/04/01/Indigo/default.aspx*.

[Britton01] Britton, Chris. *IT Architectures and Middleware — Strategies for Building Large, Integrated Systems*. Addison-Wesley, 2001.

[Buschmann96] Buschmann, Frank; Regine Meunier, Hans Rohnert, Peter Sommerlad, and Michael Stal. *Pattern-Oriented Software Architecture, Volume 1: A System of Patterns*. John Wiley & Sons Ltd, 1996.

[Chandra03] Chandra, David; Anna Liu, Ulrich Roxburgh, Andrew Mason, E. G. Nadhan, Paul Slater. *Guidelines for Application Integration*, Microsoft *Patterns & Practices*, December 2003. Available on MSDN at: *http://msdn.microsoft.com/library/default.asp?url=/library/en-us/dnpag/html/eappint.asp*.

[Chapell03] David Chappell, Chappell & Associates. "Understanding BizTalk Server 2004." Microsoft Corporation, 2003. Available at *http://go.microsoft.com/fwlink/?LinkId=21313*.

[Crocker02] Crocker, Angela; Andy Olsen, and Edward Jezierski. "Designing Data Tier Components and Passing Data Through Tiers." *MSDN Library*, August 2002. Available at: *http://msdn.microsoft.com/library/default.asp?url=/library/en-us/dnbda/html/boagag.asp*.

[Erikkson00] Eriksson, Hans-Erik, and Magnus Penker. *Business Modeling with UML: Business Patterns at Work*. John Wiley & Sons, Inc., 2000.

[Firesmith95] Firesmith, Donald G., and Edward M. Eykholt. *Dictionary of Object Technology*. Signature Sounds Recording, 1995.

[Fowler01] Fowler, Martin. "To Be Explicit." *IEEE Software*, November/December 2001.

[Fowler03] Fowler, Martin. *Patterns of Enterprise Application Architecture*. Addison-Wesley, 2003.

[Gamma95] Gamma, Erich; Richard Helm, Ralph Johnson, and John Vlissides. *Design Patterns: Elements of Reusable Object-Oriented Software*. Addison-Wesley, 1995.

[Garlan95] Garlan, David; Robert Allen, and John Ockerbloom. "Architectural Mismatch: Why Reuse Is So Hard," in *IEEE Software*, Volume 12, Issue 6, November 1995: 17-26.

[Hohpe04] Hohpe, Gregor, and Bobby Woolf. *Enterprise Integration Patterns: Designing, Building, and Deploying Messaging Solutions*. Addison-Wesley, 2004.

[Januszewski01] Januszewski, Karsten. "Using UDDI at Run Time, Part I." December, 2001. Available on MSDN at *http://msdn.microsoft.com/library/default.asp?url=/library/en-us/dnuddi/html/runtimeuddi1.asp*.

[Januszewski02] Januszewski, Karsten. "Using UDDI at Run Time, Part II." May, 2002. Available on MSDN at *http://msdn.microsoft.com/library/default.asp?url=/library/en-us/dnuddi/html/runtimeuddi2.asp*.

[Kent00] Kent, William. *Data and Reality*. 1stBooks Library, 2000.

[Larman02] Larman, Craig. *Applying UML and Patterns*. Prentice-Hall PTR, 2002.

[Levine03] Levine, Russell. "The Myth of the Disappearing Interfaces," in *Business Integration Journal*, November 2003.

[Linthicum04] Linthicum, David. *Next Generation Application Integration*. Addison-Wesley, 2004.

[Mackinnon00] Mackinnon, Tim, et al. "Endo-Testing: Unit Testing with Mock Objects." *eXtreme Programming and Flexible Processes in Software Engineering — XP2000* conference.

[Manolescu97] Manolescu, Dragos. "A Data Flow Pattern Language," in *Proceedings of the 4th Pattern Languages of Programming*, September 1997, Monticello, Illinois.

[Marcus00] Marcus, Evan, and Hal Stern. *Blueprints for High Availability: Designing Resilient Distributed Systems*. John Wiley & Sons, 2000.

[Martin02] Martin, Robert. *Agile Software Development: Principles, Patterns, and Practices*. Prentice-Hall, 2002.

[McIlroy64] The fluid-flow analogy dates from the days of the first UNIX systems and is attributed to Douglas McIlroy; see *http://cm.bell-labs.com/cm/cs/who/dmr/mdmpipe.html*.

[Microsoft02-1] Microsoft Corporation. "XML Web Services Overview." *.NET Framework Developer's Guide*. Available on MSDN at: *http://msdn.microsoft.com/library/default.asp?url=/library/en-us/cpguide/html/cpconwebservicesoverview.asp*.

[Microsoft02-2] Microsoft Corporation. "Application Architecture: Conceptual View." *.NET Architecture Center.* Available on MSDN at: *http://msdn.microsoft.com /architecture/default.aspx?pull=/library/en-us/dnea/html/eaappconland.asp.*

[Microsoft02-3] Microsoft Press. *Microsoft Computer Dictionary, Fifth Edition.* Microsoft Press, 2002.

[Microsoft04] Microsoft Corporation. "Certificate Stores." *Windows XP Professional Product Documentation.* Available from Microsoft.com at *http://www.microsoft.com /resources/documentation/windows/xp/all/proddocs/en-us/sag_cmuncertstor.mspx.*

[Mowbray97] Mowbray, Thomas J. *Corba Design Patterns.* John Wiley & Sons, 1997.

[Newcomer02]. Newcomer, Eric. *Understanding Web Services: XML, WSDL, SOAP, and UDDI.* Addison-Wesley, 2002.

[Noble98] Noble, J. "Classifying Relationships Between Object-Oriented Design Patterns." *Proceedings of the Australian Software Engineering Conference (ASWEC),* 1998.

[Oki93] Oki, B.; M. Pfluegel, A. Siegel, and D. Skeen. "The Information Bus - An Architecture for Extensive Distributed Systems." *Proceedings of the 1993 ACM Symposium on Operating Systems Principles,* December 1993.

[PnP02] *Patterns & Practices,* Microsoft Corporation. "Application Architecture for .NET: Designing Applications and Services." *MSDN Library,* December 2002. Available at: *http://msdn.microsoft.com/library/default.asp?url=/library/en-us/dnbda/html /distapp.asp.*

[Reilly02] Reilly, Douglas J. *Designing Microsoft ASP.NET Applications.* Microsoft Press, 2002.

[Ruh01] Ruh, William. *Enterprise Application Integration. A Wiley Tech Brief.* Wiley, 2001.

[Schmidt00] Schmidt, Douglas; Michael Stal, Hans Rohnert, Frank Buschmann. *Pattern-Oriented Software Architecture, Volume 2: Patterns for Concurrent and Networked Objects.* John Wiley & Sons, 2000.

[Shaw96] Shaw, Mary, and David Garlan, *Software Architecture: Perspectives on an Emerging Discipline.* Prentice Hall, 1996.

[Skonnard03] Skonnard, Aaron. "How ASP.NET Web Services Work." *MSDN Library,* May 2003. Available at: *http://msdn.microsoft.com/library/default.asp?url=/library/en-us /dnwebsrv/html/howwebmeth.asp.*

[Skonnard03-2] Skonnard, Aaron. "Understanding SOAP." *MSDN Web Services Developer Center,* March 2003. Available at: *http://msdn.microsoft.com/webservices /understanding/webservicebasics/default.aspx?pull=/library/en-us//dnsoap/html /understandsoap.asp.*

[Slywotsky99] Slywotsky, Adrian J. *Profit Patterns: 30 Ways to Anticipate and Profit from Strategic Forces Reshaping your Business.* John Wiley & Son Ltd, 1999.

[Tannebaum01] Tannebaum, Andrew. *Modern Operating Systems.* 2nd ed. Prentice-Hall, 2001.

[Teale03] Teale, Philip, Christopher Etz, Michael Kiel, and Carsten Zeitz. "Data Patterns." *.NET Architecture Center.* June 2003. Available at: *http://msdn.microsoft.com /architecture/patterns/default.aspx.*

[Trowbridge03] Trowbridge, David; Dave Mancini, Dave Quick, Gregor Hohpe, James Newkirk, and David Lavigne. *Enterprise Solution Patterns Using Microsoft .NET.* Microsoft Press, 2003. Also available on the *MSDN Architecture Center* at: *http:// msdn.microsoft.com/architecture/patterns/default.aspx?pull=/library/en-us/dnpatterns/html /Esp.asp.*

[W3C04] "Web Services Architecture W3C Working Draft 11 February 2004." Available on the W3C Web site at: *http://www.w3.org/TR/2004/NOTE-ws-arch-20040211/.*

[Wanagel03] Wanagel, Jonathan, et al. "Building Interoperable Web Services: WS-I Basic Profile 1.0." *MSDN Library*, August 2003. Available at: *http://msdn.microsoft.com /library/default.asp?url=/library/en-us/dnsvcinter/html/wsi-bp_msdn_landingpage.asp.*

[Yacoub04] Yacoub, M. Shreif and Hany H. Ammar. *Pattern-Oriented Analysis and Design: Composing Patterns to Design Software Systems.* Addison-Wesley, 2004.

Index

A

3270 terminal standard, 208
<types> element, 177
ABA routing numbers, 35
abstraction level, 56
account services
    accessing on the mainframe, 44–46
    tradeoffs, 46
ACID
    Data Integration pattern, 130
    Process Integration pattern, 81
ACORD XML, 290–292
Activator.GetObject() method call, 219
Active Directory directory service, 46–50
Adapter pattern, 142, 222
adapters
    Message Broker pattern, 247–248
    SQL Server, 90
American Bankers Association *See* ABA
Application vs. *Integration* patterns, 48, 213
applications
    adapters, 247–249
    communication with *Message Bus* pattern, 262
    dependencies, 260
    monitoring with BizTalk Server 2004, 306
    redefining concept of, 3
architecture
    approaches to *Entity Aggregation* pattern, 66–67
    enterprise architecture stack, 355–356
    integration architecture views, 365–378

technical architecture, 51, 367–369
    See also baseline architecture
artifacts
    interpreting, 342
    purpose of, 341
ASCII, 283
ASP.NET *See Service-Oriented Integration* pattern with ASP.NET
Assembly Key File name property, 101
associative tables, 224
asynchronous interaction
    with callback, 189–190
    with polling, 189–190
asynchronous Web services, 188–190
atomic transactions, 81
Atomicity, Consistency, Isolation, and Durability *See* ACID
audience for this book, xi–xii
authoritative source, 71
authors, xvi
    contributors, xv
automation level, 55–56

B

B2B integration, 310–311
BAM, 60
banking services bundle, 351–354
baseline architecture
    basic purpose of, 33
    mapping to technologies, 52–53
    SWIFT gateway, 35–43
    using patterns to design, 19–53
    See also architecture
bibliography, 385–388
    integration patterns and their relationships, 389

binding files, 101
BizTalk Server 2004, 86–105
    background, 86
    benefits and liabilities, 103–104
    and *Broker* pattern, 221
    context, 86
    correlating messages and process instances, 88
    diagram, 87
    Execute Scheduled Payments orchestration, 90–103
        example, 91–103
    handling exceptions and compensating transactions, 89–90
    implementation strategy, 86–90
    Indirect Broker pattern, 221
    Message Broker pattern, 221, 243, 245–259
    operational considerations, 105
    orchestration, 86–88
    Orchestration Designer, 87
    with port-level tracking monitoring, 306–307
    process managers, 104
    process modeling, 86–88
    Publish/Subscribe pattern example, 280
    related patterns, 105
    Scope shape, 89
    security considerations, 104–105
    Send shape, 88
    and subscriptions, 253–255, 280
    testing considerations, 104
    See also Message Broker pattern; *Pipes and Filters* pattern; *Service-Oriented Integration* pattern with BizTalk Server 2004

Blackboard pattern, 271
books, 48
BPEL, 82
BPML, 82
Broadcast-Based Publish/Subscribe
    pattern, 223–224, 232
    List-Based Publish/Subscribe
        pattern, 274
    Message Bus pattern, 263, 265
    Publish/Subscribe pattern, 274
    security considerations, 281
Broker pattern, 215–221, 231
    communication responsibilities
        of, 215–216
    diagram of related patterns, 216
    Distributed Object Integration
        pattern, 215
    and Ethernet, 231
    examples, 218–221
        BizTalk Server 2004, 221
        CORBA, 220
        DCOM, 219
        .NET Framework remoting,
            219–220
        UDDI, 220
    intent of brokers, 215
    logical topology, 231
    physical topology, 231
    Service-Oriented Integration
        pattern, 215
    UDP, 220, 231
    vs. *Point-to-Point Connection*
        pattern, 221
bus arbitration, 266
bus contention, 266
bus latency, 266
Business Activity Monitoring *See*
    BAM
business logic, 132
Business Process Execution
    Language *See* BPEL
Business Process Modeling
    Language *See* BPML
Business Rule Engine, 257–258

C

canonical schema, 68
capital expenditure, 345
Catch SOAP Exception, 96
CEO
    scenario context, 4
    viewpoints, 346–351
certificate thumbprints, 299
change management, 71–72
CheckBalanceAndDebit, 95–96
chief executive officer *See* CEO
chief technical officer *See* CTO
churn, 346, 348
CICS
    acronym defined, 5
    business logic, 332
    compatability with .NET
        Framework, 319
    mainframe connections, 25
    transactions, 322–327
        choices, 322
class-responsibility-collaboration
    See CRC
Client-Dispatcher-Server pattern, 243
client-side asynchrony, 188, 190
COBOL Import Wizard, 328
COMMAREA, 323, 325, 332
commercial off-the-shelf software
    See COTS
Common Object Request Broker
    Architecture *See* CORBA
communication in *Broker* pattern,
    215–216
community, xiv–xv
compensation in *Entity Aggregation*
    pattern, 70–71
composite applications, 78
configuration in *Entity Aggregation*
    pattern, 71
Content-Based Publish/Subscribe
    pattern, 223–225, 234–235
    Message Bus pattern, 263–265
    Publish/Subscribe pattern, 275
    routing, 264, 275
Content-Based Router pattern, 243,
    258

content-based systems, 224–225,
    275–276
context properties, 248
contributors, xv
conventions, xiv, 20
convergence, 342
Convergence pattern, 343
CORBA
    acronym defined, 38
    Broker pattern, 220
    Direct Broker pattern, 231
    Service-Oriented Integration
        pattern, 147
correlation set, 88
COTS, 11
coupling, 57
    Gateway pattern, 314
    Message Broker pattern, 240
    Pipes and Filters pattern, 292
    Service-Oriented Integration
        pattern, 146–147
CRC, 14
CreditAccount web method, 100
CRM
    Gateway object, 49–50
    in Global Bank scenario, 5
    overview of system connections,
        24–25
cross-pane interactivity, 108
CTO
    decision points, 345
    scenario context, 4–5, 11
    scenario requirements, 21
Cunningham, Ward, 19
custom pipelines, 298–299
customer churn, 346, 348
customer information, 69
Customer Information Control
    System *See* CICS
Customer Relationship
    Management *See* CRM

D

Data and Reality, 57
Data Consistency Integration pattern,
    134

Data Flow architecture *See Pipes and Filters* pattern
data governance in *Entity Aggregation* pattern, 67
data identification in *Entity Aggregation* pattern, 67
Data Integration pattern, 124–134
  benefits, 130–131
  choosing between alternatives, 129–130
  design tradeoffs, 126
  diagram, 115, 125
  example, 127
  File Transfer pattern, 129
  layered applications, 113
  liabilities, 131–132
  maintain data copies approach, 128–129
  Message Broker pattern, 38
  payment systems, 34
  problem, 124–125
  related patterns, 134
  resulting context, 127–130
  security considerations, 133
  shared database approach, 127–128
  solution, 125–126
  system connections, 23–26, 114–117, 124–134
  testing considerations, 133
  vs. *Functional Integration* pattern, 132
data layer integration, 114–117
  major patterns, 114–115
data model in *Entity Aggregation* pattern, 72
data operation in *Entity Aggregation* pattern, 67
Data Patterns, 48, 129
Data Replication pattern, 116
data representation in *Entity Aggregation* pattern, 67
data store diagrams, 116
Data Transfer Object pattern, 140
data values in *Entity Aggregation* pattern, 72

data warehouses, 66–67
DCOM in *Broker* pattern, 219
Decide shape, 96–97, 99
decision points, 345
diagrams
  alternative *Functional Integration* pattern, 120
  Application patterns vs. *Integration Patterns*, 48
  asynchronous Web services implementation choices, 188
  BizTalk Server 2004, 87
  customer information, 69
  Data Integration patterns, 115, 125
  data replication in *Data Integration* pattern, 128
  Data Replication pattern, 116
  data store, 116
  Direct Broker implementation, 217
  Entity Aggregation pattern, 59, 63–65
  Execute Scheduled Payment use case, 40–41
  family of *Broker* patterns, 216
  Functional Integration pattern, 25, 39, 136
  Gateway object, 50
  Global Bank's final pattern choice, 374, 376, 377
  Indirect Broker pattern, 218
  initial network diagram with server types, 12
  integrating layer patterns, 60
  of integration patterns, 370
  integration patterns and their relationships, 389
  Intercepting Filter pattern, 47
  Layered Application pattern, 112, 113
  Message Broker pattern, 27–29
  Message Bus pattern, 28, 265
  network diagram with server types, 51–53
  pattern diagram mapped to implementation technology, 16–17

pattern model, 15
Pipeline Designer, 294
Pipes and Filters pattern configurations, 288
Point-to-Point Connection pattern, 27, 230
port-and-wire model, 31–33
Portal Integration pattern, 22, 58–59, 108
Presentation Integration pattern, 117–118
process integration layer, 59–60
Process Integration pattern, 36–37, 77, 79, 80, 84–85
Publish/Subscribe pattern implementation with *Message Bus*, 222
related patterns, 85
schema reconciliation in *Entity Aggregation* pattern, 69
Service Interface pattern and *Gateway* pattern, 45
Service-Oriented Integration pattern, 148
  with ASP.NET, 157, 158, 160
shared database approach, 127–128
stubs to test the process manager, 85
of SWIFT message process, 152
system connection pattern relationships, 121
system connection patterns, 114
test driver, 84
Three-Layered Services Application pattern, 23, 112
View Scheduled Payments, 30–31
View Scheduled Payments collaboration, 13–14
Direct Broker pattern
  CORBA, 231
  diagram of implementation, 217
  diagram of relationships, 216
  UDDI, 220
director of EBPP, 355
display-only, 108

Distributed Common Object Model
See DCOM
Distributed Object Integration
pattern
Broker pattern, 215
CORBA, 220
DCOM, 219
Functional Integration pattern,
119–120, 138, 140, 143
Global Bank alternative, 372
programming models, 141, 143
vs. *Service-Oriented Integration*
pattern, 159
DMZ, 44
document/literal SOAP styles,
149–150
documentation conventions, xiv
domain knowledge, 34
duplicate messages, 141
dynamic configuration, 257
dynamic subscriptions *See*
subscriptions

E

EBCDIC, 283
EBPP, 354–355
EBPP Supervisor, 355, 363
Einstein, Albert, 1, 11
Electronic Bill Presentment and
Payment *See* EBPP
encapsulation, 24–25, 132, 143
endpoint registration, 216
Enterprise Application Architecture,
49
enterprise architecture stack,
355–356
Enterprise Information Integration,
75
enterprise integration, 310
*Enterprise Integration Patterns:
Designing, Building, and
Deploying Messaging Solutions*,
221
Enterprise Integration Patterns, 128,
191
Enterprise Resource Planing *See*
ERP

*Enterprise Solution Patterns Using
Microsoft .NET*, xi, xvi, 6, 44,
215
class-level *Gateways*, 49
other patterns in, 48
Entity Aggregation pattern, 59, 61–
75
architectural approaches, 66–67
benefits and liabilities of, 73
change management, 71–72
compensating, 70–71
configuration, 71
context, 61–62
data governance, 67
data identification, 67
data model, 72
data operation, 67
data representation, 67
data values, 72
design considerations, 67
diagrams, 63–65
entities, 61
entity representation, 67–68
inquiring vs. updating, 70
integration layer types, 59
known uses, 75
operational considerations, 74
ownership, 71
Phone Number entity example,
64–66
Portal Integration pattern, 62
process, 63–66
references, 70
related patterns, 75
schema reconciliation, 67–69
schema reconciliation diagram,
69
security considerations, 74
solution, 62–66
testing considerations, 74
entity references in *Entity
Aggregation* pattern, 70
entity representation in *Entity
Aggregation* pattern, 67–68
ERP, 104–105, 127
error handling, 92

Ethernet, 226–229
Broker pattern, 231
Execute Scheduled Payment use
case, 33–35
baseline architecture, 33
models, 40–43
Pipes and Filters pattern with
BizTalk Server 2004, 296–297
Execute Scheduled Payments
orchestration, 90–103
example, 91–103
process model, 92
SQL Server adapter, 90, 101–103
experience, 11
external gateway for B2B
integration, 310–311

F

far links, 26
fault tolerance, 257
feedback and support, xv
File Transfer pattern, 114–117
Data Integration pattern, 129
logical data layer, 126
filter reuse, 305
filters *See Pipes and Filters* pattern
financial planning services team,
351
fixed subscriptions *See*
subscriptions
Following Correlation Set, 88
Fowler, Martin, 44, 49, 128
Functional Integration pattern, 24–26
accessing account services on
the mainframe, 44
Data Integration pattern, 132
Data Transfer Object pattern, 140
diagram, 39
diagram of alternatives, 120
Distributed Object Integration
pattern, 119–120
for functionality sharing, 38
layered applications, 113
Message Broker pattern, 38
*Message-Oriented Middleware
Integration* pattern, 119–120,
140–141

privacy and encryption issues, 133
Process Integration pattern, 79
programming models, 143, 144
relation to *Data Integration* pattern, 134
Remote Facade pattern, 140
requirements, 137
Service-Oriented Integration pattern, 119–120, 138–139, 141–142
system connections, 118–120, 135–145
  benefits, 142–143
  choosing between alternatives, 139–140
  choosing Distributed Objects, 140
  credit scoring example, 119
  diagram, 136
  Distributed Object Integration pattern, 138, 140
  forces, 135–136
  integrating external applications, 137
  kinds of functional integration, 119–120
  liabilities, 143–144
  Message-Oriented Middleware Integration pattern, 138, 140
  problem, 135
  resulting context, 138
  security considerations, 144
  Service-Oriented Integration pattern, 139, 141–142
  solution, 136–137
  table, 137
  testing considerations, 144
functionality sharing, 38

G

gateway chaining, 311–312
Gateway object
  CRM, 49–50
  diagram, 50

Gateway pattern, 33–35, 308–318
account system testing, 46
benefits, 314–315
context, 308
described, 44–45
example, 312–314
gateway choices, 310–311
with Host Integration Server 2004, 319–339
  background, 319–320
  benefits, 339
  components, 331
  context, 319
  example, 331
  functions, 332
    selecting the programming model, 332
    configuring the mainframe environment, 332
    configuring the TI metadata file, 333–337
    configuring network protocol connectivity, 337
    configuring a TI remote environment, 338
    adding an IIS virtual directory, 338
    configuring a Windows-initiated processing object, 338
    implementing a .NET Framework client application, 339
  Global Bank property values table, 338
  implementation strategy, 320–331
    selecting the programming model, 322–326
    configuring the mainframe environment, 326–327
    configuring the TI Metadata File, 327–328
    configuring network protocol connectivity, 328–329

    configuring a remote environment, 330
    adding an IIS virtual directory, 330
    configuring a Windows-initiated processing object, 331
    implementing a .NET Framework client application, 331
    liabilities, 339
    processing object property values, 338
    tests, 339
liabilities, 315
operational considerations, 317
overview, 44–45, 284–285
problem, 308
related patterns, 317
responsibilities and collaborations, 310
security considerations, 316
Service Interface pattern, 44–45
solution, 309–312
testing considerations, 315–316
General Manager of banking *See* GM of banking
Global Bank scenario
asynchronous business practice, 151–152
baseline architecture role design, 21–50
  account services on the mainframe, 44–46
  Execute Scheduled Payment and Receive Payment Response, 35–43
  implementing the Global Bank scenario, 50–53
  message broker for the loan systems, 29–33
  portal Web application, 46–50
  scheduled payment use case, 33–35
  View Scheduled Payments use case, 21–33

Global Bank scenario *(continued)*
context, 4, 342–343
described, 4–6
enterprise architecture stack,
355–358
Execute Scheduled Payments
orchestration, 90–103
example, 91–103
final pattern choice, 374, 376, 377
method parameters, 336
network diagram with server
types, 51–53
next steps, 6
pattern instances, 376
patterns, 11–17
patterns to communicate design
decisions, 20
requirements, 4–5, 19–21
See also project notebook; View
Scheduled Payments use case
GM of banking, 351–354, 359
GotDotNet community, xiv–xv
granularity, 126

H

Half Synch/Half Asynch pattern, 49–
50
HAT tool, 203, 204, 255, 307
health, 273
HLLAPI, 208
host-initiated processing, 320
how this book is organized, xii–xiii
Hruby, Pavel, 358
hub-and-spoke architecture, 218, 237
See also Message Broker pattern

I

idempotent messages, 141
IDL, 147
IIS, 161, 321
virtual directory, 330
*Implementing Broker with .NET
Remoting Using Client-
Activated Objects*, 220
*Implementing Broker with .NET
Remoting Using Server-
Activated Objects*, 220

*Implementing Gateway with Host
Integration Server 2004* pattern,
317
*Implementing Pipes and Filters with
BizTalk Server 2004* pattern,
295
*Implementing Process Integration
with BizTalk Server 2004*
pattern, 85
*Implementing Service-Oriented
Integration with ASP.NET*
pattern, 155
*Implementing Service-Oriented
Integration with BizTalk Server
2004*, 155, 179, 243
IMS transactions, 322
In-band and Out-of-band Partitions
pattern, 295
Indirect Broker pattern
and BizTalk Server 2004, 221
diagram of relationships, 216
implementation diagram, 218
similarity to *Mediator* pattern,
217
initial network diagram with
server types, 12
initial subscriptions *See*
subscriptions
Initializing Correlation Set, 88
inquiring vs. updating in *Entity
Aggregation* pattern, 70
instance-based collaboration, 119
instance-based integration, 159
instances, 375–378
integrating layer, 55–110
choosing an integration layer
type, 57–60
coupling, 57
integrating layer patterns, 60
level of abstraction, 56
level of automation, 55–56
maintaining state, 56–57
semantic dissonance, 57
types, 370–371
See also BizTalk Server 2004;
Entity Aggregation pattern;
Portal Integration pattern;
Process Integration pattern

integration
applications, 3
patterns, 1–17
problem of, 1–3
integration layer types, 57–60
Entity Aggregation pattern, 59
Portal Integration pattern, 58–59
process integration layer, 59–60
integration layers patterns table,
285
Integration patterns, 369–378
types of patterns, 371
vs. *Application* patterns, 48, 213
integration topologies, 26–28, 213–
282
Broker pattern, 215–221, 231
examples, 218–221
integration topology level, 229
logical topology, 226–230
Message Broker implementation
with BizTalk Server 2004, 245–
259
Message Broker pattern, 237–244
Message Bus and *Publish/
Subscribe* patterns, 231–235
Message Bus pattern, 221–223,
260–271
physical topology, 226
Point-to-Point Connection pattern,
214–215, 229–230
Publish/Subscribe pattern, 223–
225, 272–282
subscription mechanisms, 277
table of integration patterns, 236
topology levels, 225–229
using topologies together, 229–
235
See also Broker pattern; *Message
Broker* pattern; *Message Bus*
pattern; *Publish/Subscribe*
pattern
integration topology, 226
Intercepting Filter pattern, 295
diagram, 47
further information on, 48, 295
portal Web application, 46–50

internal gateway for enterprise integration, 310
interprocess communication mechanisms, 317

J

Januszewski, Karsten, 220

K

Kent, William, 57

L

languages for defining process models, 82
latency tolerance, 126
Layered Application pattern
  Presentation Integration pattern, 206
  system connections, 111–112
layers
  Process Integration pattern, 36–37
  Three-Layered Services Application pattern, 23
  See also integrating layer
link-to-program name, 328
list of patterns and pattlets, 379–384
List-Based Publish/Subscribe pattern, 223, 232–233
  Broadcast-Based Publish/Subscribe pattern, 274
  Message Bus pattern, 263, 265
  Publish/Subscribe pattern, 273–274
load-balancing, 257
loan system
  connection, 26
  Message Broker pattern, 29–33
logical data layer, 126
logical services, 365–367
logical topology
  Broker pattern, 231
  CORBA, 220
  integration topologies, 226–230
loose coupling, 57

LU 6.2 protocol, 322–323
  alternatives, 326
  components, 324–325

M

mainframes
  accessing account services on the mainframe, 44–46
  connection overview, 25
Maintain Data Copies pattern, 114–117
  considerations, 130
  Data Replication pattern, 116
  list of other patterns, 129
  logical data layer, 126
master references in *Entity Aggregation* pattern, 70
master/subordinate relationships, 126
Mediator pattern, 217, 243
MEP, 150–151
mergers and acquisitions, 342–343
Message Broker pattern, 27–28, 237–243
  benefits, 240–241
  and BizTalk Server 2004, 221, 243, 245–259
  adapter types, 247–248
  benefits, 255
  business rule engine, 257–258
  context, 245
  context and background, 245–246
  diagram of internal publish-subscribe architecture, 247
  example, 249–255
    creating the receive port and defining message schemas, 250–252
    defining maps to convert between message formats, 252–253
    creating subscriptions to messages, 253–255
  implementation strategy, 246–249

liabilities, 255
  operational considerations, 257
  related patterns, 258–259
  security considerations, 256
  testing considerations, 256
  variants, 257
  business rule engine, 257–258
  characteristics of, 218
  context, 237
  and coupling, 240
  Data Integration, 38
  diagram of relationships, 216
  example, 239–240
  Functional Integration pattern, 38–39
  known uses, 243
  liabilities, 241
  for loan system, 29–33
  loan system, 29–33
  operational considerations, 243
  for payment channels, 37–38
  problem, 237–238
  routing, 255
  security considerations, 239, 242
  Service-Oriented Integration pattern, 38–39
  solution, 238–239
  subscriptions, 256, 258
  testing considerations, 242
  variants and related patterns, 243
Message Bus pattern, 28, 221–223, 260–271
  application communication, 262
  benefits, 269
  with *Broadcast-Based Publish/Subscribe*, 263
  with *Content-Based Publish/Subscribe*, 263–264
  context, 260
  difficulties of, 237
  example, 266–268
  liabilities, 269–270
  with *List-Based Publish/Subscribe*, 263

Message Bus pattern *(continued)*
   Message Router, 262
   operational considerations, 270
   physical topology, 232–233
   with *Publish/Subscribe*, 222–225,
      231–235, 262
   related patterns, 271
   responsibilities and
      collaborations, 266
   routing, 234
   security considerations, 270
   solution, 261–266
   subscriptions, 264
message buses, 214
message exchange patterns *See*
   MEP
Message Router pattern, 262
message switch, 264
*Message-Oriented Middleware
   Integration* pattern, 119–120,
   138, 143
   Functional Integration pattern,
      119–120, 140–141
   Global Bank alternatives, 372
Messaging Gateway pattern, 317
Microsoft books, 48
models for Execute Scheduled
   Payment use case, 40–43
MSMQT, 248, 250

N

near links, 26
.NET Framework, 159–161
   compatability with CICS, 319
   LU 6.2 protocol, 324–325
.NET Framework remoting, 219–
   220
network diagram with server
   types, 51–53
NUnit, 144, 178, 202, 204

O

object request broker *See* ORB
object-oriented design and
   abstraction, 56
Observer pattern, 223, 273–274

Open Systems Interconnection *See*
   OSI
ORB
   Broker pattern, 220
   Service-Oriented Integration
      pattern, 147
   See also CORBA
orchestration
   BizTalk Server 2004, 86–88
   Execute Scheduled Payments, 90
   Orchestration Debugger, 204
   Orchestration Designer, 87
organization of this book, xii–xiii
OS/400 transactions, 322
OSI stack, 225
ownership in *Entity Aggregation*
   pattern, 71

P

Party Resolution component, 248
pattern-based design, 10
*Pattern-Oriented Software
   Architecture, Volume 1: A
   System of Patterns*, 215
patterns
   applying, 11
   communication aspect of, 378
   data layer integration, 114–115
   derived from *Maintain Data
      Copies* pattern, 129
   diagrams
      implementation technology,
         16
      of integration patterns, 370
   Global Bank, 11–17, 374, 376, 377
   instances, 375–378
   instances in project notebook,
      375–378
   model diagram, 15
   in music, 9
   other Microsoft guides, 48
   overview, 7–11
   pattern-based design, 10
   in sports, 7–8
   structure of, 9–10
   system interactions, 11–13
   table of system connection
      patterns, 122–123

   types, 371–375
   types and instances, 372
patterns and pattlets list, 379–384
*Patterns of Enterprise Application
   Architecture*, 44
pattlets list, 379–384
payment channels, 33–34
payment system connection, 24
perimeter network, 44
Phone Number entity, 64–66
physical topology, 214
   Broker pattern, 231
   choices, 225
   integration topologies, 225–228
   Message Bus pattern, 232–233
Pipeline Designer, 294
Pipes and Filters pattern
   benefits, 292–293
   with BizTalk Server 2004, 296–
      307
      background, 296–297
      benefits, 305
      custom pipelines, 298–299
      example, 299–304
         creating a custom send
            pipeline, 299
         assigning and configuring
            the filters, 299–301
         building and deploying
            the pipeline, 301
         assigning certificates,
            301–303
         configuring the send port
            to use the custom
            pipeline, 304
      implementation strategy, 297–
         299
      liabilities, 305
      operational considerations,
         306–307
      Pipeline Designer, 294
      receive pipeline, 298
      security considerations, 306
      send pipelines, 300
      testing considerations, 305–
         306
      transformation components,
         298

context, 286
diagram of different
    configurations, 288
example, 290–292
forces, 286
liabilities, 293
overview, 283
problem, 286
related patterns, 295
responsibilities and
    collaborations, 290
SLA, 293
solution, 287–290
testing considerations, 293–295
Point-to-Point Connection pattern,
    26–27
diagrams, 27, 230
Global Bank alternatives, 372
integration topologies, 229–230
payment system, 34
strengths and weaknesses, 214–
    215
vs. *Broker* pattern, 221
port management, 258
port-and-wire model, 31–32, 40–43,
    369
port-level tracking, 306–307
Portal Integration pattern, 58–59,
    106–110
and ambiguity, 57
analogy to *Entity Aggregation*
    pattern, 62
benefits and liabilities, 109–110
context, 106
diagram, 22, 108
example, 109
flavors, 108
integration layer types, 58–59
and semantic dissonance, 57
solution, 107–109
table of solution components,
    109
vs. *Process Integration* pattern,
    107, 110
portal Web application
Global Bank, 46–50

Half Synch/Half Asynch pattern,
    49–50
Intercepting Filter pattern, 46–50
predictive routing, 258
preface, xi–xvi
Presentation Integration pattern,
    24–26
diagram, 117
HLLAPI, 208
Layered Application pattern, 206
layered applications, 113
system connections, 117–118,
    206–212
benefits, 210
brittleness of, 208
context, 206
example, 209
forces, 206–207
liabilities, 210–211
security considerations, 212
solution, 207–209
table of components, 209
testing considerations, 211
privacy and security issues, 133
Process Integration pattern, 76–85
ACID, 81
benefits and liabilities, 83
choosing, 59–60
collaboration table, 79
context, 76
correlating messages and
    process instances, 81
diagrams, 36–37, 77, 80, 84–85
Execute Scheduled Payment and
    Receive Payment Response,
    35–43
Functional Integration pattern, 79
handling exceptions and
    compensating transaction, 82
implementation details, 80–82
integration layer types, 59–60
pattern described, 36–37
problem, 76–77
process integration components
    table, 79
process managers, 79–80, 82–83,
    85

process model, 107–108
solution, 77–80
straight-through processing, 82
testing considerations, 84
transaction, 81
vs. *Portal Integration* pattern, 107,
    110
Process Manager pattern, 85, 105
process managers
BizTalk Server 2004, 104
pattern, 105
Process Integration pattern, 79–80,
    82–83, 85
process model
BizTalk Server 2004, 86–88
Execute Scheduled Payments
    orchestration, 92
Portal Integration pattern, 107–
    108
Process Integration pattern, 77–79
process value analysis, 365
programming models
to access CICS transactions, 322–
    327
and BizTalk Server 2004, 103
Distributed Object Integration
    pattern, 141
Functional Integration pattern,
    143, 144
and *Gateway* pattern, 49
.NET Framework remoting, 219–
    220
TI, 321–323
project notebook, 341–378
banking services bundle, 351–
    354
banking services team, 351
bundling services, 350
business architecture views,
    358–364
business context, 342–343
from business scenario to
    technical solution, 355–369
current portfolio vs. industry
    average, 346–348
current services bundle vs.
    industry average, 350–354

enterprise architecture stack,
355–356
Global Bank business context,
342–343
going forward, 378
integration architecture views,
365–378
architecturally significant use
cases, 369
integration patterns, 369–371
logical services, 365–367
process value analysis, 365
technical architecture, 367–369
integration patterns, 369–378
interpreting the artifacts, 342
pattern types, 371–375
patterns instances, 375–378
stakeholder viewpoints, 344–355
board of directors viewpoint,
344
CEO viewpoint, 346–351
director of EBPP, 354, 362–363
EBPP supervisor, 355
GM of banking, 351–354
strategy formulation, 348–350
value proposition for online
services, 344–345
viewpoints
of CEO, 358–359
described, 357
of GM, 360–361
integration architecture, 365
of process owner, 362–363
of process worker, 363–364
within the enterprise
architecture, 357–369
See also Global Bank scenario
promoted properties, 248
property schema, 248
Pub/Sub *See Publish/Subscribe*
pattern
Publish-Subscribe Channel pattern,
282
Publish/Subscribe pattern
applying, 275–278
benefits, 280
BizTalk Server 2004, 280

Broadcast-Based Publish/Subscribe
pattern, 274
Content-Based Publish/Subscribe
pattern, 275
context, 272
dynamic subscriptions, 277–278
example, 280
fixed subscriptions, 277
integration topologies, 272–282
liabilities, 281
List-Based Publish/Subscribe
pattern, 273–274
Message Bus pattern, 222–225,
231–235, 262
operational considerations, 281
problem, 272–273
refinements, 223
related decisions, 279
related patterns, 271, 282
responsibilities and
collaborations, 279
security considerations, 281
solution, 273–279
subscriptions, 225, 234, 275, 277–
278
testing considerations, 281
See also Broadcast-Based Publish/
Subscribe pattern; *Content-*
Based Publish/Subscribe
pattern; *List-Based Publish/*
Subscribe pattern
purpose of this book, 1–2
push vs. pull, 126

Q

QoS, 238, 239, 241
quality of service *See* QoS

R

Receive Payee Response shape, 98
Receive Payment Response use
case, 35–44
receive pipeline, 298
Receive shape, 92
ReceiveDebitResponse shape, 95
ReceivePaymentRequest
orchestration port, 92, 101

ReceivePaymentResponse, 98, 101
receiver adapters, 248–249
references in *Entity Aggregation*
pattern, 70
remote environment, 321, 330
Remote Facade pattern, 140
Remote Method Invocation *See*
RMI
Remote Procedure Call *See* RPC
Remote Proxy pattern, 317
replication approach, 66–67
RMI, 38
ROM, 4
rough-order-of magnitude *See*
ROM
routing
Content-Based Publish/Subscribe
pattern, 264, 275
Content-Based Router pattern, 243
described, 214–215
Message Broker pattern, 255
Message Bus pattern, 234
SWIFT, 35
RPC, 149–150

S

Saarinen, Eliel, 213
sales, general, and administrative
See SGA
scenarios *See* Global Bank scenario
schema reconciliation, 67–69
Scope shape, 89, 96, 100
screen scraping, 24, 113, 206, 207
screened subnet, 44
Sears, Richard, 341
security and *Message Broker*
pattern, 239, 242
security and privacy issues, 133
semantic dissonance, 57, 132
send pipelines, 300
Send shape, 88
SendDebitRequest shape, 95
SendPaymentRequest, 98, 101
server types network diagram,
51–53
service, definition of, 120, 139, 148

Service Gateway pattern
  further information on, 48
  Service-Oriented Integration
    pattern, 139
Service Interface pattern
  account system testing, 46
  further information on, 48
  Gateway pattern, 44–45, 317
  Global Bank portal application,
    49–50
  related patterns, 317
  Service-Oriented Integration
    pattern, 41, 139, 141–142
  Web services, 148
service level agreement *See* SLA
service stubs, 84–85
Service-Oriented Integration pattern
  acronym, 15
  alternate implementations, 53
  Broker pattern, 215
  Functional Integration pattern,
    119–120, 138–139, 141–142
  functional integration with
    Message Broker pattern, 38–39
  with *Gateway* pattern, 44
  Global Bank alternatives, 372
  system connections, 141–142,
    146–156
    benefits, 154
    context, 146
    diagram, 148
    document/literal SOAP styles
      and encoding, 149–150
    example, 153
    explicit boundaries, 153
    interoperability concerns,
      149–150
    liabilities, 155
    problem, 146–147
    related patterns, 155
    resulting context, 153–154
    security considerations, 155
    services, 153
    solution, 148
    temporal coupling, 150
    Web services, 149
  vs. *Distributed Object Integration*
    pattern, 159
  WSDL, 148

Service-Oriented Integration pattern
  with ASP.NET, 157–181
  system connections, 157–181
    accessing mainframe gateway
      example, 164–178
      binding element, 177–178
      build and run the Web
        service, 176–178
      connect the service
        interface, 169–175
        interface creation, 172
        service implementations
          creation, 173
        plug-in factory creation,
          174
        Web service method
          implementing, 175
      define operations that the
        service exposes, 168–169
      develop XSD documents,
        166–167
      generate data transfer
        classes, 167
      messages section, 177
      services section, 178
      test client creating, 178
      <types> element, 177
    ASP.NET Web services, 159–
      161
    background, 157–158
    benefits and liabilities, 179
    building ASP.NET Web
      services, 162–163
    developing code first, 162
    developing WSDL first, 163
    implementation strategy, 158–
      159
    security considerations, 181
    specifying XML Schemas first,
      163
    testing considerations,
      179–181
      service interface separation,
        179–180
      service stubs, 180–181

Service-Oriented Integration pattern
  with BizTalk Server 2004, 182–
    205
  system connections, 182–205
    asynchronous interaction,
      186–187
    asynchronous Web services
      choices, 188–190
      asynchronous interaction
        with polling, 189
      client-side asynchrony,
        188
      implementation, 187–190
    background, 182–183
    benefits, 203
    example, 186–203
      defining message schemas,
        190–192
      defining logical request-
        response ports, 192–193
      defining orchestration and
        connecting to logical
        port, 194–200
      building and deploying
        the orchestration, 200
      running BizTalk Web
        services publishing
        wizard, 200
      binding orchestration's
        logical port to the
        physical port, 200–201
      starting orchestration, 201
      creating a test client that
        invokes the Web service,
        201–203
    exposing as a Web service,
      184–186
    implementation choices,
      asynchronous interaction
      with callback, 189
    implementation strategy, 183
    liabilities, 204
    operational considerations,
      205
    security considerations, 204–
      205
    service-oriented integration,
      183
    testing considerations, 204

Set Error Status Expression shape, 96

SGA, 359

Shared Database pattern, 114–117
considerations, 130
logical data layer, 126

simple post-processing, 108

single application interaction, 108

single sign-on *See* SSO

Singleton pattern, 371–372

sink system, 283–284

SLA
in Global Bank scenario, 5
Pipes and Filters pattern, 293

Society for World-wide Interbank
Financial Telecommunication
See SWIFT

SOI *See Service-Oriented Integration*
pattern

source system, 283–284

SQL Server 2000, 257

SQL Server adapter, 90, 101–103

SSO, 105

state, 56–57

static or dynamic subscriptions, 279

status, 273

STP *See* straight-through
processing

straight-through processing, 66, 82

strategy formulation, 348–350

structure of patterns, 9

stubs, 84–85

style conventions table, xiv

subscriptions
and BizTalk Server 2004, 253–
255, 280
initial subscription, 279
integration topologies, 277
Message Broker pattern, 256, 258
Message Bus pattern, 264
Publish/Subscribe pattern, 225,
234, 275, 277–278
dynamic subscriptions in,
277–278
fixed subscriptions in, 277
static or dynamic subscriptions,
279
topic discovery, 279
wildcard subscriptions, 279

SWIFT
described, 33–34
diagram of message process, 152
Gateway pattern, 33–35
gateway use for baseline
architecture, 35–43
routing, 35

swivel chair integration, 106

synchronization logic vs. latency,
126

system connections, 111–212
connecting to layered
applications, 111–114
CRM, 24–25
designing baseline architecture,
23–26
Layered Application pattern, 111–
112
diagrams, 112, 113
loan system, 26
mainframes, 25
patterns, 120–123
diagram of patterns, 114
diagram of relationships, 121
table, 122–123
payment system, 24
See also Data Integration pattern;
Functional Integration pattern;
Presentation Integration
pattern; service-oriented
integration; *Service-Oriented
Integration* pattern with
ASP.NET; *Service-Oriented
Integration* pattern with
BizTalk Server 2004; *Three-
Layered Services Application*
pattern

system interactions, 11–13

T

tables
components of *Presentation
Integration* pattern, 209
Functional Integration pattern,
137
Gateway pattern, 310
Global Bank method

parameters, 336
Global Bank property values,
338
integration layers patterns, 285
integration topology patterns,
236
Message Bus pattern, 266
Process Integration pattern, 79
processing object property
values, 338
system connection patterns, 122–
123

target audience for this book, xi–xii

technical architecture, 367–369

Terminate shape, 97

terminological conventions, xiv

test stubs, 84–85

3270 terminal standard, 208

Three-Layered Services Application
pattern
diagram, 112
system connections, 23–24, 111–
112

thumbprints, 299

TI, 319
CICS link-to-program, 324–325
client object, 324–325
COMMAREA, 324–325
DB2/VSAM, 324–325
DPL, 324–325
metadata file configuring, 327–
328, 333–337
Mirror TP CSMI, 324–325
programming models, 321–323
remote environment, 324–325
run-time component, 321
run-time proxy, 324–325
table of Global Bank method
parameters, 336
table of transactions, 334
transaction choices, 322

TI Designer, 321

TI Manager, 321

topic discovery, 279

topic-based systems, 224–225, 275–
276

topology *See* integration topologies

Transaction Integrator *See* TI

Transform shape, 95

transformations
components, 298
described, 216
implementing, 286

TransformPayment2DebitRequest, 95

transport adapters, 247–249

<types> element, 177

U

UDDI, 155
Direct Broker pattern, 220

UDP, 220, 231

UML
asynchronous interaction, example, 187
Erikkson/Penker Business Extensions, 358

Unified Modeling Language *See* UML

unified view, 68

unit test cases, 179–180

Universal Description Discovery and Integration *See* UDDI

updating vs. inquiring, 70

User Datagram Packet *See* UDP

V

value proposition for online services, 344–345

View Scheduled Payments use case, 21–33
collaboration diagram, 13–14, 30
system connections, 23–26

viewpoints
of CEO, 358–359
enterprise architecture stack, 357
of GM, 360–361
of process owner, 362–363
of process worker, 363–364
within the enterprise architecture, 357–369

W

Web services
defining, 149
for printing, 290–292
Service Interface pattern, 148

Web Services Choreography Interface *See* WSCI

Web Services Description Language *See* WSDL

WebServiceHandler, 161

Wheeler, David, 55

who should read this book, xi–xii

wildcard subscriptions, 279

Windows-initiated processing, 319

WIP, 331

WMI interface, 185

WS-I, 148

WS-Security specification, 181, 205

WSCI, 82

WSDL
components, 176–178
Service-Oriented Integration pattern, 148, 162
style and serialization, 149

X

XML
Service-Oriented Integration pattern, 141–163
transformations, 286

patterns & practices

About Microsoft *patterns & practices*

Microsoft *patterns & practices* guides contain specific recommendations illustrating how to design, build, deploy, and operate architecturally sound solutions to challenging business and technical scenarios. They offer deep technical guidance based on real-world experience that goes far beyond white papers to help enterprise IT professionals, information workers, and developers quickly deliver sound solutions.

IT Professionals, information workers, and developers can choose from four types of *patterns & practices*:

- **Patterns**—Patterns are a consistent way of documenting solutions to commonly occurring problems. Patterns are available that address specific architecture, design, and implementation problems. Each pattern also has an associated GotDotNet Community.

- **Reference Architectures**—Reference Architectures are IT system-level architectures that address the business requirements, LifeCycle requirements, and technical constraints for commonly occurring scenarios. Reference Architectures focus on planning the architecture of IT systems.

- **Reference Building Blocks and IT Services**—References Building Blocks and IT Services are re-usable sub-system designs that address common technical challenges across a wide range of scenarios. Many include tested reference implementations to accelerate development. Reference Building Blocks and IT Services focus on the design and implementation of sub-systems.

- **Lifecycle Practices**—Lifecycle Practices provide guidance for tasks outside the scope of architecture and design such as deployment and operations in a production environment.

Patterns & practices guides are reviewed and approved by Microsoft engineering teams, consultants, Product Support Services, and by partners and customers. *Patterns & practices* guides are:

- **Proven**—They are based on field experience.

- **Authoritative**—They offer the best advice available.

- **Accurate**—They are technically validated and tested.

- **Actionable**—They provide the steps to success.

- **Relevant**—They address real-world problems based on customer scenarios.

To learn more about *patterns & practices* visit: **http://msdn.microsoft.com/practices**
To purchase *patterns & practices* guides visit: **http://shop.microsoft.com/practices**

Patterns & practices guides are designed to help IT professionals, information workers, and developers:

Reduce project cost

- Exploit the Microsoft engineering efforts to save time and money on your projects.
- Follow the Microsoft recommendations to lower your project risk and achieve predictable outcomes.

Increase confidence in solutions

- Build your solutions on proven Microsoft recommendations so you can have total confidence in your results.
- Rely on thoroughly tested and supported guidance, but production quality recommendations and code, not just samples.

Deliver strategic IT advantage

- Solve your problems today and take advantage of future Microsoft technologies with practical advice.

patterns & practices: Current Titles

October 2003

Title	Link to Online Version	Book
Patterns		
Enterprise Solution Patterns using Microsoft .NET	http://msdn.microsoft.com/practices/type/Patterns /Enterprise/default.asp	▣
Microsoft Data Patterns	http://msdn.microsoft.com/practices/type/Patterns /Data/default.asp	
Reference Architectures		
Application Architecture for .NET: Designing Applications and Services	http://msdn.microsoft.com/library/default.asp?url= /library/en-us/dnbda/html/distapp.asp	▣
Enterprise Notification Reference Architecture for Exchange 2000 Server	http://msdn.microsoft.com/library/default.asp?url= /library/en-us/dnentdevgen/html/enraelp.asp	
Improving Web Application Security: Threats and Countermeasures	http://msdn.microsoft.com/library/default.asp?url= /library/en-us/dnnetsec/html/ThreatCounter.asp	▣
Microsoft Accelerator for Six Sigma	http://www.microsoft.com/technet/treeview /default.asp?url=/technet/itsolutions/mso/sixsigma /default.asp	
Microsoft Active Directory Branch Office Guide: Volume 1: Planning	http://www.microsoft.com/technet/treeview /default.asp?url=/technet/prodtechnol/ad /windows2000/deploy/adguide/default.asp	▣
Microsoft Active Directory Branch Office Series Volume 2: Deployment and Operations	http://www.microsoft.com/technet/treeview /default.asp?url=/technet/prodtechnol/ad /windows2000/deploy/adguide/default.asp	▣
Microsoft Content Integration Pack for Content Management Server 2001 and SharePoint Portal Server 2001	http://msdn.microsoft.com/library/default.asp?url= /library/en-us/dncip/html/cip.asp	
Microsoft Exchange 2000 Server Hosting Series Volume 1: Planning	Online Version not available	▣
Microsoft Exchange 2000 Server Hosting Series Volume 2: Deployment	Online Version not available	▣

Title	Link to Online Version	Book
Microsoft Exchange 2000 Server Upgrade Series Volume 1: Planning	http://www.microsoft.com/technet/treeview /default.asp?url=/technet/itsolutions/guide /default.asp	
Microsoft Exchange 2000 Server Upgrade Series Volume 2: Deployment	http://www.microsoft.com/technet/treeview /default.asp?url=/technet/itsolutions/guide /default.asp	
Microsoft Solution for Intranets	http://www.microsoft.com/technet/treeview /default.asp?url=/technet/itsolutions/mso /msi/Default.asp	
Microsoft Solution for Securing Wireless LANs	http://www.microsoft.com/downloads /details.aspx?FamilyId=CDB639B3-010B-47E7-B23 4-A27CDA291DAD&displaylang=en	
Microsoft Systems Architecture— Enterprise Data Center	http://www.microsoft.com/technet/treeview /default.asp?url=/technet/itsolutions/edc /Default.asp	
Microsoft Systems Architecture— Internet Data Center	http://www.microsoft.com/technet/treeview/ default.asp?url=/technet/itsolutions/idc/default.asp	
The Enterprise Project Management Solution	http://www.microsoft.com/technet/treeview /default.asp?url=/technet/itsolutions/mso/epm /default.asp	
UNIX Application Migration Guide	http://msdn.microsoft.com/library/default.asp?url= /library/en-us/dnucmg/html/ucmglp.asp	
Reference Building Blocks and IT Services		
.NET Data Access Architecture Guide	http://msdn.microsoft.com/library/default.asp?url= /library/en-us/dnbda/html/daag.asp	
Application Updater Application Block	http://msdn.microsoft.com/library/default.asp?url= /library/en-us/dnbda/html/updater.asp	
Asynchronous Invocation Application Block	http://msdn.microsoft.com/library/default.asp?url= /library/en-us/dnpag/html/paiblock.asp	
Authentication in ASP.NET: .NET Security Guidance	http://msdn.microsoft.com/library/default.asp?url= /library/en-us/dnbda/html/authaspdotnet.asp	
Building Interoperable Web Services: WS-I Basic Profile 1.0	http://msdn.microsoft.com/library/default.asp?url= /library/en-us/dnsvcinter/html/wsi-bp_msdn_ landingpage.asp	
Building Secure ASP.NET Applications: Authentication, Authorization, and Secure Communication	http://msdn.microsoft.com/library/default.asp?url= /library/en-us/dnnetsec/html/secnetlpMSDN.asp	

To learn more about *patterns & practices* visit: **http://msdn.microsoft.com/practices**
To purchase *patterns & practices* guides visit: **http://shop.microsoft.com/practices**

Title	Link to Online Version	Book
Caching Application Block	*http://msdn.microsoft.com/library/default.asp?url= /library/en-us/dnpag/html/Cachingblock.asp*	
Caching Architecture Guide for .Net Framework Applications	*http://msdn.microsoft.com/library/default.asp?url= /library/en-us/dnbda/html/CachingArch.asp?frame= true*	
Configuration Management Application Block	*http://msdn.microsoft.com/library/default.asp?url= /library/en-us/dnbda/html/cmab.asp*	
Data Access Application Block for .NET	*http://msdn.microsoft.com/library/default.asp?url= /library/en-us/dnbda/html/daab-rm.asp*	
Designing Application-Managed Authorization	*http://msdn.microsoft.com/library/?url=/library /en-us/dnbda/html/damaz.asp*	
Designing Data Tier Components and Passing Data Through Tiers	*http://msdn.microsoft.com/library/default.asp?url= /library/en-us/dnbda/html/BOAGag.asp*	
Exception Management Application Block for .NET	*http://msdn.microsoft.com/library/default.asp?url= /library/en-us/dnbda/html/emab-rm.asp*	
Exception Management Architecture Guide	*http://msdn.microsoft.com/library/default.asp?url= /library/en-us/dnbda/html/exceptdotnet.asp*	
Microsoft .NET/COM Migration and Interoperability	*http://msdn.microsoft.com/library/default.asp?url= /library/en-us/dnbda/html/cominterop.asp*	
Microsoft Windows Server 2003 Security Guide	*http://www.microsoft.com/downloads/ details.aspx?FamilyId=8A2643C1-0685-4D89-B655- 521EA6C7B4DB&displaylang=en*	
Monitoring in .NET Distributed Application Design	*http://msdn.microsoft.com/library/default.asp?url= /library/en-us/dnbda/html/monitordotnet.asp*	
New Application Installation using Systems Management Server	*http://www.microsoft.com/business/reducecosts /efficiency/manageability/application.mspx*	
Patch Management using Microsoft Systems Management Server - Operations Guide	*http://www.microsoft.com/technet/treeview/ default.asp?url=/technet/itsolutions/msm/swdist/ pmsms/pmsmsog.asp*	
Patch Management Using Microsoft Software Update Services - Operations Guide	*http://www.microsoft.com/technet/treeview/ default.asp?url=/technet/itsolutions/msm/swdist/ pmsus/pmsusog.asp*	
Service Aggregation Application Block	*http://msdn.microsoft.com/library/default.asp?url= /library/en-us/dnpag/html/serviceagg.asp*	
Service Monitoring and Control using Microsoft Operations Manager	*http://www.microsoft.com/business/reducecosts /efficiency/manageability/monitoring.mspx*	

Title	Link to Online Version	Book
User Interface Process Application Block	http://msdn.microsoft.com/library/default.asp?url= /library/en-us/dnbda/html/uip.asp	
Web Service Façade for Legacy Applications	http://msdn.microsoft.com/library/default.asp?url= /library/en-us/dnpag/html/wsfacadelegacyapp.asp	
Lifecycle Practices		
Backup and Restore for Internet Data Center	http://www.microsoft.com/technet/treeview/default.asp ?url=/technet/ittasks/maintain/backuprest/Default.asp	
Deploying .NET Applications: Lifecycle Guide	http://msdn.microsoft.com/library/default.asp?url= /library/en-us/dnbda/html/DALGRoadmap.asp	
Microsoft Exchange 2000 Server Operations Guide	http://www.microsoft.com/technet/treeview/default. asp?url=/technet/prodtechnol/exchange/exchange 2000/maintain/operate/opsguide/default.asp	
Microsoft SQL Server 2000 High Availability Series: Volume 1: Planning	http://www.microsoft.com/technet/treeview /default.asp?url=/technet/prodtechnol/sql/deploy /confeat/sqlha/SQLHALP.asp	
Microsoft SQL Server 2000 High Availability Series: Volume 2: Deployment	http://www.microsoft.com/technet/treeview /default.asp?url=/technet/prodtechnol/sql/deploy /confeat/sqlha/SQLHALP.asp	
Microsoft SQL Server 2000 Operations Guide	http://www.microsoft.com/technet/treeview /default.asp?url=/technet/prodtechnol/sql/maintain /operate/opsguide/default.asp	
Operating .NET-Based Applications	http://www.microsoft.com/technet/treeview /default.asp?url=/technet/itsolutions/net/maintain /opnetapp/default.asp	
Production Debugging for .NET-Connected Applications	http://msdn.microsoft.com/library/default.asp?url= /library/en-us/dnbda/html/DBGrm.asp	
Security Operations for Microsoft Windows 2000 Server	http://www.microsoft.com/technet/treeview /default.asp?url=/technet/security/prodtech /win2000/secwin2k/default.asp	
Security Operations Guide for Exchange 2000 Server	http://www.microsoft.com/technet/treeview /default.asp?url=/technet/security/prodtech /mailexch/opsguide/default.asp	
Team Development with Visual Studio .NET and Visual SourceSafe	http://msdn.microsoft.com/library/default.asp?url= /library/en-us/dnbda/html/tdlg_rm.asp	

 This title is available as a Book